# A History of Gannett

1906-1993

J. Donald Brandt

Gannett Co., Inc.
Arlington, Virginia

*A History of Gannett, 1906-1993* copyright © 1993 by Gannett Co., Inc. All rights reserved. First printing August 1993. Printed in the United States of America. No part of this book may be used or reproduced in any manner whatsoever except in the case of reprints in the context of reviews. For information write Gannett Co., Inc., Public Affairs, 1100 Wilson Boulevard, Arlington, Virginia 22234.

Editor: Sheila J. Gibbons
Production coordinator: Ashley Weissenburger
Design/production: Mary Zyskowski and Jenifer Walczak

Library of Congress Catalog Card Number: 93-79333
ISBN 0-944347-01-0

# Contents

| | Acknowledgments | v |
|---|---|---|
| Chapter 1 | Confounding Father | 1 |
| Chapter 2 | Genesis | 15 |
| Chapter 3 | Seeds of Autonomy | 28 |
| Chapter 4 | Romance and Rivalries | 40 |
| Chapter 5 | Full Speed Ahead | 49 |
| Chapter 6 | Support Group | 58 |
| Chapter 7 | Publishing and Politicking | 68 |
| Chapter 8 | Securing the Future | 77 |
| Chapter 9 | Which Frank Gannett? | 86 |
| Chapter 10 | Siren Song | 95 |
| Chapter 11 | A Reach Too Far | 104 |
| Chapter 12 | On the Home Front | 113 |
| Chapter 13 | Over There | 121 |
| Chapter 14 | The War Years - I | 133 |
| Chapter 15 | The War Years - II | 144 |
| Chapter 16 | The War Years - III | 154 |
| Chapter 17 | Confronting Peace | 166 |
| Chapter 18 | A Look at the Future | 179 |
| Chapter 19 | That's the Spirit | 190 |
| Chapter 20 | Renovations | 197 |
| Chapter 21 | Clear Signals | 210 |

| Chapter 22 | Editorial Clinic | 225 |
| --- | --- | --- |
| Chapter 23 | 'Yielding Place to New' | 235 |
| Chapter 24 | Gannett à la Miller | 248 |
| Chapter 25 | The Prize and A Prize Catch | 259 |
| Chapter 26 | The Carl Lindstrom Matter | 269 |
| Chapter 27 | Line of Succession | 289 |
| Chapter 28 | Growth and Acclaim | 304 |
| Chapter 29 | The Next Step | 313 |
| Chapter 30 | Spreading the Word | 324 |
| Chapter 31 | Quickening Pace | 337 |
| Chapter 32 | Change is Progress | 346 |
| Chapter 33 | Mixed Emotions | 362 |
| Chapter 34 | Production Values | 371 |
| Chapter 35 | Big Deals | 382 |
| Chapter 36 | Years of Change | 392 |
| Chapter 37 | Innovation and Imitation | 409 |
| Chapter 38 | Who's in the Wings? | 427 |
| Chapter 39 | Certifiably Bigtime | 436 |
| Chapter 40 | A Stronger Lineup | 452 |
| Chapter 41 | It's Show Time | 462 |
| Chapter 42 | Change of Command | 474 |

| Footnotes | 497 |
| --- | --- |
| Index | 522 |
| Gannett Co., Inc. Operations | 546 |
| About the Author | 549 |

# Acknowledgments

This book owes its existence to a retirement party. The guest of honor was Jane Donnovan, a Gannett employee for 43 years who served both as secretary to the company and its board of directors and as a legal assistant to Doug McCorkindale.

Jane and her friends were happily recalling memorable colleagues and occasions in her four-plus decades with the company. Several guests lamented that many such engaging personal stories would die with the surviving contemporaries of Frank Gannett and his early associates.

A few days later, Brian Donnelly, the first Gannett publisher for whom I worked, and Doug McCorkindale asked whether I would be interested in documenting as oral history the tape-recorded reminiscences of Gannett oldtimers willing to share their memories.

Thus began an uncertain courting of Gannett veterans – including some in their 80s, a few in their 90s and one 100 – by a stranger with a tape recorder and a lot of personal questions. The enthusiasm with which all of them greeted the project quickly turned the hesitant courtship into a labor of love.

Almost all of them eagerly took part. Many said they hoped that finally someone was going to challenge misrepresentations and public misunderstandings of the Gannett Company's contributions and achievements. They were keenly interested in more than a modest anthology of taped recollections. They were proud of the company and their associations with it. That was true even of some who recalled unpleasant experiences. They urged an honest account of the company's history.

A bare-bones history of the Gannett Company would have been simple to catalog – Elmira in 1906, Ithaca in 1912, Rochester in 1918, and so on – but that would reveal little about the real Gannett. This book seeks to put flesh and blood on those bones. It recognizes established chronology but listens also for intimations of the company's evolving character and personality.

Support for this more comprehensive project grew slowly, and its realization owes most to the support of two people. Vincent S. Jones, former executive editor of The Gannett Newspapers, responded instantly with strong encouragement and generous cooperation. Vin's friendliness and hospitality were genuine motivators for the author, who hoped the result would justify those significant contributions. Unfortunately, Vin's death prevented his reading a copy of the manuscript that had been delivered to him only a few days earlier. As important as Vin Jones's enthusiasm was to this larger undertaking, even more vital to its completion were John Curley's continuing interest and support, for which the author is especially grateful.

This book's indebtedness begins, however, with those Gannett veterans who readily shared their memories, and whose contributions are hereby acknowledged. Thanks to Russell and Connie Davenport Chapman, Henry Clune, John Curley, Phil Currie, Tom Dolan, Brian Donnelly, Jane Donnovan, Gene Dorsey, Bob Eckert, Charlie Edwards, Mrs. Joseph Freudenberger, Wes Gallagher, Dixon Gannett, Jack Germond, Mary Golding, Jack Heselden, Moe Hickey, Vin Jones, Cal Mayne, Doug McCorkindale, Florence Messman, Warren McClure, Louise Miller, Al Neuharth, Gerry Papero, John Quinn, Nancy Tripp Rose, Ann Battley Rosenberg, John Seigenthaler, Vince Spezzano, Gary Watson and Ron White.

The archival versions of all these interviews owe their existence to the able and patient Karen Ammerman and Barbara Dutchak, who transcribed them.

Additional thanks are due to Jack Heselden, who helpfully suggested inclusion of events on the production side of Gannett that were not as readily accessible as the documented records on editorial activities.

At The News Journal in Wilmington, Del., where the author had spent many happy years, he especially appreciated the ready provision of equipment, desk space and moral support from Sal DeVivo, Henry Freeman, Sue Klimaszewski and John Taylor. Charlie Brewer's competent solving of computer woes that befuddled the author was indispensable.

Two contributors have been held out for special recognition because, aside from the author, they have been most challenged by this project. Sheila Gibbons participated in the discussions of the original proposal for a volume of oral history. She warmed quickly to the idea of a more complete history. Since that time she has distinguished herself as a patient editor, indomitable optimist, competent therapist and valued friend. Patience and forebearance are the qualities with which Alberta Brandt deepened the author's affection and respect for her. Thanks to those qualities, she endured nearly three years of travail without lasting damage to our domestic tranquillity.

All those who favored and successfully encouraged the broader approach of this book must answer only for that support. Whatever faults and shortcomings the reader finds in its execution are entirely mine to bear.

J. Donald Brandt
Mendenhall, Pa.

# Chapter 1

# Confounding Father

*"There is nothing more fascinating than the stories of success won by the youth of America through their thrift, industry, character, high ideals and ability."*

Frank E. Gannett
May 9, 1942

Pivotal events for nations or organizations are not always immediately seen as such. It is human to recall where one was when Pearl Harbor was bombed by the Japanese in 1941 or when Neil Armstrong first stepped onto the moon in 1969. Their deeper relevance, however, takes time to comprehend. History is the sorting out of yesterday's unrecognized relationships.

On Dec. 3, 1957, Paul Miller presided from his Rochester, N.Y., office over the Gannett Company's 22 newspapers, eight radio stations and two television stations. In Florida, Allen H. Neuharth confronted the day's concerns as an assistant managing editor of the *Miami Herald*. And in Carlisle, Pa., John Curley and his sophomore classmates at Dickinson College pursued their undergraduate interests.

These three men were on different compass headings to a common destination. On that cold Tuesday, Frank E. Gannett, the 81-year-old newspaper executive, died in Rochester. The newspaper empire he had built over 51 years from a tiny purse, dauntless will and enormous energy would be theirs to preserve and expand.

Although it would be 10 more years before Gannett Co., Inc. became publicly owned, without Frank Gannett it was already changing. To comprehend what the organization became in its second half century, one must understand something about the pioneer who navigated its first 50 years.

Gannett was as complicated as his times, and his life spanned years of stunning change.

He was born Sept. 15, 1876. The nation was still smarting over the deaths nearly three months earlier of Col. George A. Custer and 210 soldiers of the 7th Cavalry at the hands of the Sioux in the Battle of Little Big Horn. Transcontinental rail travel had been achieved only seven years earlier.

Three years before Gannett bought into his first newspaper partnership in Elmira, N.Y., in 1906, Wilbur and Orville Wright achieved the first powered flight of a heavier-than-air machine at Kitty Hawk, N.C.

Gannett saw warfare intensify from the Spanish-American War's mounted cavalry charges to World War II's atomic devastation.

Just a few weeks after he died in 1957, Explorer I was the first U.S. earth satellite to be launched into orbit at Cape Canaveral, Fla. And within a year, National Airlines began domestic jet airline service in the United States with a flight between New York City and Miami.

The contrasts in Gannett's own life were equally remarkable. At his death he had achieved wealth that amply qualified for the denigrating cliche "filthy rich." Yet he was born in upstate New York's hardscrabble country to struggling farmers who could accurately be described as dirt poor.

Despite having the means to indulge the trappings of leisure, he set a personal example of his belief in hard work.

He was accused by labor of being a pinch-penny, for which there is considerable evidence, yet condemned as a traitor by fellow businessmen for his early advocacy of profit-sharing and pension plans.

As a child of struggling parents, he wrote and spoke fervently against the railroads, the trusts and monopolies. As a successful businessman, he was distressed by envious condemnations of his newspapers as monopolistic predators on their communities.

His early newspapers staunchly supported the Democratic Party, yet he went on in his 60s to mount a quixotic and ill-fated campaign for the Republican nomination for president.

He was an acquaintance and early supporter of Franklin Delano Roosevelt, but founded and mobilized the National Committee to Uphold Constitutional Government, which was the primary deterrent to FDR's attempt to pack the U.S. Supreme Court.

He went from evangelical isolationism in the late 1930s to unstinting support of the Allied effort to win World War II.

His eloquent tributes to First Amendment freedoms were occasionally sullied by intemperate and unsubstantiated attacks on Roosevelt.

Stereotypical caricatures of him as a grasping profiteer contradicted his ready philanthropies, not the least of which was placing most of his fortune into a foundation to provide job security for Gannett employees and assist the communities they served.

His eight decades personified those motivational fictions written for boys by his older contemporary Horatio Alger. As a child, he was constantly reminded by his mother of the maxims commending industry, character and thrift as the keys to success. If his early life reflected any influence from Alger books such as *Ragged Dick* or *Tattered Tom*, there is no record of his testimonial.

Gannett was the fifth of six children, the first of whom, a girl, lived only eight months. When he was born, his parents, Charles and Maria Brooks Gannett, had been married 11 years. Their farm was one of four that Charles and three of his brothers had cleared for their families from woodland on a remote rise called Gannett Hill. It was two miles from the nearest store and 16 rugged miles from Canandaigua, N.Y.

The soil was marginal and the farm's productivity assured the growing family of hard-earned subsistence. It promised no prosperity, however, so Charles and Maria Gannett had talked of moving before the birth of their third son.

His mother's prolonged labor was nearly fatal. Samuel T. Williamson, the publisher's biographer, wrote that delivering the 12-pound infant had been Maria Gannett's most difficult childbirth and that Frank was her favorite child. In acknowledging that, Gannett told Williamson, "Some people are fondest of those they do the most for."[1]

The Gannetts remained on Gannett Hill through the winter after Frank's birth, but early the following year they sold the farm and moved a few miles to Blood's Depot, known today as Atlanta, in Steuben County. Charles Gannett leased some land near the tiny community and became a tenant farmer, pledged to share whatever his labors produced with the man who held his lease.

Here too the family's lot was subsistence but little income, and Frank Gannett had his first practical lessons in industry and thrift. As a 9-year-old he took on a newspaper route, soliciting subscribers and delivering to them the *Democrat and Chronicle* of Rochester, N.Y. He recalled later that this was the start of his financial self-sufficiency. The youngster's hard-pressed parents could provide food and shelter but he understood that whatever money he needed he would have to earn.

After nine years Charles and Maria Gannett despaired of sharecropping. They decided to invest his affability and her skill as a cook in the hotel business, so they moved a few miles south to the small community of Howard and leased the Bishop Hotel. The family's lot finally began slowly to improve.

# Young Entrepreneur

Successive moves to larger hotels, first in Wallace and then in Bolivar, improved the elder Gannetts' ability to pay their bills, even as they forced young Frank Gannett to scramble for new ways to make money. In Wallace, he expanded his delivery of Buffalo and Rochester newspapers. He harvested crops for pay and picked wild berries to ship to city markets.

He began helping immigrant Italian laborers unversed in English by addressing the envelopes of their letters home. Then he realized they could do it themselves with rubber stamps, one bearing the name and address of the family in Italy, the other the sender's return address in Wallace. He solicited orders among the laborers, had the stamps made and delivered them at a small profit.

In *Imprint of a Publisher,* his biographer described another venture that occurred to the enterprising 12-year-old:

"Noticing that the countryside about Wallace was rather untidy with the skeletons of dead animals, he addressed a short inquiry to the [fertilizer] firm of Laney and Barker in Rochester. Back came its reply addressed 'Frank E. Gannett, Esq.' It read:

" 'Will pay you for old bones 50¢ per hundred pounds delivered here. Advise and ship at once.' . . .

"The opportunity opened up a considerable commercial enterprise to which Frank was not equal all by himself. He organized a staff and he became – for the first time – an employer. . . . He met his payroll in nickels and sticks of candy. . . . A complete search for old bones in Wallace and on all adjacent farms was instituted and vigorously carried out. The discarded skeletons of departed horses, cows, dogs, cats and woodland varmints were accumulated and transported to the freight depot. Before long 'Frank E. Gannett, Esq.' had shipped two complete freight carloads of bones to Laney and Barker. . . . What detached him from a possibly brilliant future in the fertilizer business was his passion for handling newspapers and for reading them, especially the columns which dealt with public affairs." [2]

When Gannett was 14, his parents moved the family about 40 miles southwest, to the two-hotel town of Bolivar in Allegany County. Rochester newspapers were no longer available to him there, so he concentrated on selling both Buffalo newspapers and bought the town's first modern bicycle to speed his deliveries.

He got his high school education there, at Bolivar Union School and Academy. When he was a junior, his family decided there were greener pastures for hotel keepers in Oneonta, nearly 200 miles to the east. Gannett stayed behind to complete high school. He became a lodger in the house of A.J. Glennie, the high school principal, and paid for it by working as a waiter, odd jobs boy and part-time bartender in the hotel that had competed with his parents' tavern.

While a student he also earned his first money as a news correspondent, reporting events in Bolivar to *The Buffalo News* at $1 per published item. At high school graduation in 1893, all nine seniors made commencement addresses. Seventeen-year-old graduate Frank Gannett spoke on "The Press and Public Opinion."

Glennie counseled Gannett during and after high school. To qualify for graduation, a student had to pass the New York State Board of Regents examinations, and the principal advised diligence. When the 1893 results were announced, Gannett had passed the examinations in more subjects than any other high school student in the state.

He had the qualifications but not the means for college, so he stayed in Bolivar to earn and save more. Glennie urged him to forego his interest in newspapers in favor of engineering, given the likelihood of his winning a congressional appointment to West Point. Gannett rejected that advice and turned instead to a competitive state examination for college scholarships. His resolve was vindicated by the award of full tuition, $200 a year for four years, at Cornell University.

Culture shock, the phrase that defines the stress of being exposed to a strange social and cultural environment, had not been coined when the class of 400 Cornell freshmen arrived in Ithaca, N.Y., in 1894. Gannett might never have heard of the term but he surely encountered the phenomenon.

The 1,800 students at Cornell constituted a community far larger and generally more affluent than those in which Gannett had spent his first 18 years. What he lacked in resources, social rank and sophistication he made up in determination, energy and self-assurance. They were invaluable assets. A full-tuition scholarship may pay the price of scholastic admission but it doesn't put food in a student's stomach or a roof over his head.

## Busy Man on Campus

Gannett began his freshman year with a serviceable wardrobe and $80, all the money he had managed to save. His challenge was obvious and he met it with the ingenuity he had shown in his Bolivar bone business. By persuading four other students to take rooms in his boarding house, he got his room free. With lodging assured, he turned to meals. These he earned by waiting on student tables. For money, he undertook three more jobs. He picked up dirty clothes and linens and returned them after laundering. He collected rumpled trousers and returned them neatly pressed. And he went to work as an usher in the college chapel at $2 a week, until he became chief usher at $4 a week.

His financial prospects improved in his sophomore year, when he assumed a seat on the board of editors of the college daily paper, the *Cornell Daily Sun,* to which he had been elected late in his freshman year. The staff of the *Sun* shared in its profits, and Gannett's annual share would be $200. That was not his only significant gain. His reporting assignment included a daily stop at the office of the university president, Dr. Jacob Gould Schurman, who would guide and influence Gannett's future even more than had his high school principal in Bolivar.

Gannett was a conscientious student and carefully followed Schurman's advice on the electives to pursue to achieve the broadest background for newspaper work. While the president saw to the young student's curricular advancement, Gannett broadened his practical experience with extracurricular reporting of Cornell scholastic and athletic events for receptive newspapers.

This freelance activity was so rewarding that he quit the student paper in his junior year in order to devote his time to those newspaper clients and to accept assignment at $3 a week as campus reporter for *The Ithaca Journal.* Later that year, he set up his own news network, soliciting assignments and transmitting stories to major newspapers in New York City, Boston, Philadelphia and Chicago, and to smaller regional New York papers.

The business prospered and he hired other students to meet the increasing demand for news of Cornell. Back in Bolivar, the *Breeze* reported of the hometown boy making good:

"During the past year [Gannett] has more than paid his way through Cornell by special work for Buffalo and Chicago newspapers. He will adopt journalism as his profession – and he will score a success."

Many of today's collegians studying journalism gain valuable experience working as summer interns on recruiting newspapers. Gannett created a vacation internship of sorts for himself in the summer between his junior and senior years.

During his years at Cornell, his parents had continued in the hotel business, moving from Oneonta to Mohawk. Although the new venture prospered, Charles Gannett's health forced them to sell out. They moved to Syracuse, where Frank Gannett went to spend the summer of 1897.

He wanted to work for the summer on *The Syracuse Herald*. For six weeks he worked a variety of beats, without pay. At the end of six weeks, however, he had proved to the satisfaction of the editors that he was worth $10 a week for the balance of the summer.

Back at Cornell for his senior year, he returned to studying and reporting. His dispatches from campus had caught the eye of the managing editor of New York City's *Herald,* who invited him to drop in. Gannett did so. The editor offered a job at $25 a week to this college senior who had worked the previous summer for $10, then advised him to reject it and go back to upstate New York to learn the newspaper business.

Both flattered and startled, Gannett returned to complete his senior year and be graduated in late spring of 1898. He took home with him to Syracuse a bachelor of arts degree and $1,000 that he had saved from his campus enterprises. Editors at *The Syracuse Herald* raised his previous pay to $15 a week and he went back to work, but only for the summer.

At a time when college graduates who aspired to newspaper work were lampooned as overeducated, undertrained upstarts in many newsrooms, Gannett decided to return to Cornell to work on a master's degree. But he found in Ithaca a torrent of demands from his newspaper clients for sports and other news of Cornell. While he fulfilled their requests, the deadline for registration as a graduate student passed. He joined his parents in Syracuse for the year-end holidays with the intention of beginning advanced studies early in 1899.

Instead, he received a telegram from Schurman, not in his capacity as president of Cornell but as chairman of a commission appointed by

President William McKinley. The group was formed to determine how to govern the Philippines, ceded by Spain to the United States after the Spanish-American War.

An effusive headline on Jan. 2, 1899, in *The Syracuse Herald* provided the details:

### SYRACUSAN HONORED

### FRANK E. GANNETT, THE HERALD'S CORNELL MAN

#### Secretary to Schurman

#### Leaves On The Thirteenth For The Philippines

#### Will Receive Two Hundred and Fifty Dollars A Month And Enjoy Opportunities To Be Envied – He Is Only Twenty-Two Years Old

Schurman and his young secretary sailed for the Philippines, with stops in Japan and Hong Kong. They arrived in Manila at the height of the Philippine insurgency, which Schurman's straightforward concern for Filipino wishes helped to diminish. Gannett performed his assigned duties, sent reporter's letters to *The Herald,* and studied Spanish. He became fluent enough to translate a suppressed book written by José Rizal, a Filipino physician and patriot who had been martyred by the Spaniards three years before. Among readers of this English translation was Theodore Roosevelt, who wrote to congratulate Gannett on the work.

When the commission returned to the United States late in 1899, Gannett remained behind as office manager in Manila. Weeks later, Schurman directed him to return to the United States, which he did, but at a studied pace through India, North Africa, France and England. In London, a message from the chairman informed him that William Howard Taft was assigned to the Philippines as head of a second presidential commission. Gannett had been recommended to return as secretary and the future president had assented.

Upon his return to the United States, Gannett stopped at Cornell to seek Schurman's advice about the job. The man who had directed his choice of courses to provide the broadest background for newspaper work – the same man who had recommended him as secretary to William Howard Taft – counseled against acceptance, urging instead that he begin at once to establish himself in his chosen profession.

## Frank Gannett, City Editor

Gannett declined the appointment with thanks, turning his back on $3,000 a year. Still on campus, he met Prof. Duncan Campbell Lee, who had just bought the *Ithaca Daily News*. Lee offered Gannett $15 a week to be city editor, directing the one-man reporting staff of the *Daily News*. He accepted.

Within three years, the newspaper had prospered to the point where the city editor's pay was raised to $25 a week. With that financial security, he moved his parents and his two sisters to Ithaca in 1903 to live with him. That assured security would be theirs as long as it was needed, and for both his parents until their deaths.

Lee decided to travel to Europe and left Gannett in complete charge. The owner's absence coincided with an epidemic of typhoid fever, which doctors traced to unfiltered drinking water supplied by a private company from a polluted creek.

The newspaper reported the epidemic and doctors' advice that the public boil all drinking water. It editorialized in favor of unpolluted water supplied by a public company. The water company, merchants and other local influential citizens were outraged and threatened an advertising boycott unless references to typhoid disappeared from the paper.

Gannett refused to suppress news of the epidemic. At the same time, he learned an important lesson. The advertisers' threat of a boycott never materialized, because they needed the exposure to customers that the prospering newspaper provided them.

Soon after his return from Europe, an approving Lee promoted his city editor to business manager at a salary of $50 a week, and Gannett gained experience that helped lay the foundations of his later success. His biographer wrote:

"[Gannett] was shocked by his discovery of fuddy-duddy accounting methods which prevailed not only in the *Daily News* but quite generally. . . [T]here was no way of knowing quickly whether the publication was in the red or the black on any day. He devised a running balance sheet which broke down each day the many items of operating expenses. Forms for this balance sheet were struck off by a job printing house, which thought so well of Gannett's innovation that it did a lively little trade supplying other businesses and some newspapers with these sheets. Gannett had laid a foundation for modern newspaper accounting." [3]

Within two years, the business manager and the owner had come to an irreconcilable difference. *The Daily News*, whose owner and editorial policy were loyally Democratic, was offered a contract from the Democratic State Committee for printing campaign literature and posters worth a potential $200,000 a year. Gannett adamantly opposed the arrangement. He argued that a newspaper that depended on such large favors might later compromise its integrity rather than offend the party by publishing news it didn't like. It was time to leave.

Once again, just as his future looked uncertain, serendipity prevailed. The father of one of his fellow Cornellians was seeking recruits for *Frank Leslie's Illustrated Weekly*, a New York City periodical that he had just bought. The job was sub-editor at $50 a week. With no need to accept a cut in pay, Gannett accepted the offer and moved to New York City.

He was there only a few weeks when the publisher told him that a man in Pittsburgh, Pa., was planning a similar periodical, and would pay the editor $75 a week. Gannett's name had been submitted for consideration.

The details were supplied April 12, 1905, by his former colleagues on the *Ithaca Daily News*, who omitted mention of his brief interim at *Frank Leslie's Illustrated Weekly*. The Ithaca headlines suffice:

**FRANK E. GANNETT
LEAVES THE NEWS**

**In Charge of Pittsburgh Index
As Its Editor-in-Chief**

**Prosperous Literary Weekly**

**Will Endeavor to Give Periodical a
State and National Reputation –
Backed by Ample Capital –
Same Style as Collier's Weekly – Staff of
News Will Organize to Carry On Its Work**

Those confident assertions, "prosperous" and "ample capital," were typical headline hyperbole of the day. Gannett quickly recognized both that he was inexperienced in creating a new publication and that his publisher was rapidly losing his pioneering zest for an expensive undertaking.

So the *Pittsburgh Index's* "editor-in-chief" headed back to Ithaca for a visit. En route, he had to change trains in Elmira. He was seeking whatever opportunity might present itself.

Gannett learned in Elmira that a young man named Erwin R. Davenport, who had bought a share of the *Elmira Gazette* a year before, was looking for a new partner. His nominal partner was an elderly man to whom Gannett was referred. The "partner" told him that the real owner of his half of the loyally Democratic *Gazette* was a former mayor, governor and U.S. senator, David B. Hill.

Gannett was a guest of the influential politician for three days, after which he was told that he could have half interest in the *Gazette* for $20,000, the price that Davenport had paid for his half interest a year earlier. Gannett's biographer described the outcome:

"Gannett suggested that he pay part in cash and the rest in notes. Hill assented to the notes but wanted to know how much cash. 'Give me a little time to find out,' replied Gannett, and left. . . .

"He talked over the Elmira opportunity with two lawyer friends – Howard Cobb and his cousin Fordyce. The Cobbs were willing to endorse a note upon which he borrowed $2,000 from Ithaca's First National Bank. Next, Gannett visited Bolivar, whose weekly *Breeze* had so confidently predicted nine years before that he would be a success in journalism. He transferred his personal credit into bank credit; President William J. Hogan of the Bank of Bolivar let him sign a piece of paper which gave him a loan of $5,000.

"To the $7,000 borrowed on 'character loans,' Gannett added his $3,000 savings. He now had $10,000 in cash. Next he wrote out notes for an equal amount. Gannett took the $10,000 in cash and the notes for $10,000 to Hill, who accepted them. On June 6, 1906, Gannett became half-owner of a daily newspaper. He was 29 years old."[4]

# Chapter 2

# Genesis

*"Everyone digs in for me. I don't know why but they do. I am here as early as they are and stay later. I think that counts. And I am not idle a minute. I overheard the boys talking about what a worker I am."*

Frank E. Gannett
Undated letter

Today's Gannett Company traces its origins all the way back to Elmira in 1906. Nevertheless, it was not "founded" then. Gannett did not stride like a conquistador into Elmira, stick a standard into the sod in front of city hall and claim the territory in the name of The Gannett Newspapers.

He was undeniably ambitious, and he had certainly demonstrated his eagerness to grasp promising opportunities. But there is no evidence from those early days that Gannett or his early partners dreamed of a vast and booming media empire.

Indeed, for nearly 20 years, until his partners chose for personal reasons to withdraw from daily involvement in the operations of their group of newspapers, that enterprise never bore the name Gannett.

## Introduction to Elmira

During his three-day visit to Elmira, while he waited for his host David B. Hill to set the terms for acquiring co-ownership, Gannett had time to read the *Gazette*. It reported what Elmirans and Americans were talking about.

National news focused on the approaching Memorial Day. Theodore and Edith Kermit Carow Roosevelt and two of their children, Ethel and Quentin, would spend the holiday in Virginia. The president was to address the Army and Navy Union in Portsmouth, and then students and faculty only at Hampton Institute.

Social notes from the White House centered on the honeymoon abroad of the president's daughter Alice, who had recently married Sen. Nicholas Longworth.

And only eight years after the former Col. Roosevelt had led his Rough Riders against Spanish forces in Cuba, an ad in the *Gazette* classifieds was inviting young Elmirans "to see the world":

**"Wanted, for the U.S. Marine Corps, men between the ages of 21 and 35. . . . For full information, apply in person or by letter to U.S. Marine Corps recruiting office, third floor, Post Office Building, Elmira, N.Y."**

New Yorkers were pondering the political ambitions of William Randolph Hearst, and the *Gazette* reported that the Independence League planned to nominate the flamboyant publisher as its candidate for governor at a July convention. That worried the two traditional parties, the *Gazette* explained, because if they waited until September as usual for their state conventions, "Mr. Hearst and his associates would have the field to themselves for two months."

While Elmira was prospering economically, there were intimations of vice, irreverence and juvenile delinquency. The mayor challenged the Police Commission to be alert against "the vices that inhere in this as in other municipalities," namely, "dives," "sporting places" and "rooms, buildings and hotels rented for assignation purposes."

The same Police Commission responded testily to six clergymen who had complained about Sunday athletics in a city park. It wrote to the ministers:

"Differing as you evidently do as to the tenor of the Sunday law, you can rely upon it that when you are sufficiently moved to make a complaint, and supply evidence that the baseball exercise in Maple Avenue Park is a crime, the Police Department will promptly make the arrests, and not only that, but exercise due precaution that the complainants and witnesses shall be present in court to give their testimony."

The *Gazette* did not hesitate to name 11-year-old Sammy Butz and 9-year-old Morgan Clare when the lads "went bad," nor did it clutter headlines and stories about them with "reported" or "alleged."

**Little Boys Stole Two Stoves and Two Bikes**
Soon Tired of Their Load, They Sold
the Whole Outfit for Five Cents

After reporting that the two had been arrested and locked up until their parents came for them, the *Gazette* concluded:

"The recorder reprimanded the boys and released them, as they are too young to be punished, except by spanking. The parents were told to keep a watchful eye on their children in the future and keep them from running the streets."

If Sammy and Morgan's antisocial lapse was the result of a lack of positive youthful activities, the *Gazettes* that Frank Gannett read delivered no editorial reproach.

# Kindred Spirits

Having won Hill's confidence, Gannett enthusiastically assumed daunting personal debt in order to ally himself in Elmira with a 30-year-old fellow native New Yorker as ambitious and as tireless as he.

Erwin R. Davenport was born in Dryden, N.Y., about 15 miles east of Ithaca. Like Gannett's, his was a farm family, until the death of his father when the boy was 8 years old. His widowed mother moved her family to Nebraska, where he grew up. After he was graduated from the University of Nebraska, he went to work for the *Omaha Bee*.

While he worked for the *Bee*, Davenport was as innovative as Gannett had been working his way through Cornell. In Omaha, Davenport developed a system for reporting prices of grain, cattle and stock, and with three other young men set up a syndicate to do so. Memories differ on some of the details but agree that when managers at the *Omaha Bee* learned of its success, they blew the whistle.

Russell Chapman, one of Davenport's sons-in-law, said in a 1990 interview[1] that the owners of the *Bee* claimed the syndicate. Another chronicler said only that they disapproved. But both sources agree that Davenport and his partners sold the syndicate and he brought his proceeds east to New York. It was his $20,000 investment in a half-interest in the *Elmira Gazette* that Gannett had to match to become co-owner of a newspaper.

In that same 1990 interview, Connie Davenport Chapman lamented that most references to the beginnings of the Gannett Company fail to mention her father or to acknowledge the key role he played. It is a valid criticism and one that could never be made against Davenport's early partner. Whenever he recalled those first years of struggle, Gannett never failed to credit "Davvy's" friendship or the importance of his contribution. That respect was mutual. In the study in Gannett's home always was displayed a photograph of his first partner, signed, "To the best friend I ever had."

When Gannett was referred to his future partner on that stopover in Elmira, they were only acquaintances, having met at a newspaper function soon after Davenport's arrival in Elmira and while Gannett was still business manager of the *Ithaca Daily News*.

In June 1906 they were partners in a new relationship. As that *Gazette* announcement explained: "Mr. Gannett will at once assume the duties of editor while Mr. Davenport will become manager. Royal R. Soper, who has been manager of the *Gazette* since December 1876, retires from control and management of the paper."

A review of Elmira's economy in 1906 may help to put Gannett and Davenport's partnership into perspective. Gannett had come to this opportunity with $3,000 in personal savings. That and his borrowings enabled him to match his partner's $20,000 stake in the *Elmira Gazette*.

What did $20,000 represent? When the Gannett-Davenport partnership was formed, these monthly rentals were offered in the *Gazette's* classifieds: houses on Oak Street and Alexander Place for $7, one on Walnut Street for $14, houses on Main and Columbia streets for $18 and one on Market Street for $30.

On June 7, 1906, the *Gazette* reported that the Lackawanna Railroad had "increased the wages of the men employed at the local freight house as freight handlers to 15 cents an hour, an increase of 1 cent an hour. The men's regular day is 10 hours and for overtime they receive the regular rate. The company granted the increase unsolicited."

A Lackawanna Railroad freight handler was taking home $9 for his regular 60-hour week. Frank Tripp, who would go on to achieve both influence and affluence with Gannett, was earning $16 a week as a reporter on the *Gazette,* writing his news stories on a typewriter in which he owned shares.

So the average renter, freight handler or journeyman reporter would have looked on $20,000 as a considerable sum. To partners Gannett and Davenport their matching financial commitments were spurs to hard work, and they were industrious. Both maintained work schedules that a Lackawanna freight handler would have found oppressive. His biographer wrote that Gannett started "at seven in the morning and left at nine at night. Sundays he dropped around to 'pick up the pieces.'"

# The New Gazette

The new partners' names appeared together for the first time on the editorial page of the *Gazette* on June 6, 1906. Page 1 on the following day bore a three-column box headlined:

### Keep Your Eye on the Gazette

It pointed out that it would take a little time for the new operators to put their plans into effect but promised that "the people in this part of the state can find out what a treat is in store for them." It pledged to continue to be strongly Democratic but first of all to be a good newspaper. And it concluded:

"To repeat the motto of one of the first papers established in America, the *Gazette* will stand

"For the cause that needs assistance.

"For the wrong that needs resistance.

"For the good that we can do."

Gannett's description of the new partners' equipment was detailed in *Imprint of a Publisher:*

"The *Gazette's* equipment was about one lurch this side of the scrap heap. Its press was an ancient contraption which was held together with wire. . . . The newsroom's furnishings encouraged no one to linger there . . . any longer than one had to. Reporter Tripp's veteran typewriter (which he partially owned) rested on a crude shelf nailed to the wall. Other members of the staff were no better provided for. An unshaded electric light dangled from the ceiling and two peach baskets held editorial debris." [2]

Its physical limitations notwithstanding, the *Gazette* appeared every day, reporting the news of a city whose prosperity must have been tantalizing to the newspaper's struggling owners. Just three days into their partnership, the paper headlined new surges in "Elmira's great boom."

Fitch, Aldritch and Bush, a company that manufactured hardwood doors, moldings and sashes, was being reorganized "by New York capitalists" whose $100,000 investment would employ 150 more men.

Eight representatives of the Rochester and Elmira Railroad Co. had filed with the county clerk their plan to capitalize a project at $4 million to build and operate a 120-mile trolley line between Rochester and Elmira.

On the editorial pages, the new editor was not loath to indulge in self-promotion. The gang in Ithaca from which he had separated so recently had remarked his new venture and Gannett reported it in his own paper:

### More Kind Wishes From The Ithaca News

"Under Frank E. Gannett's energetic management the *Elmira*

*Gazette* should at once take its place as one of the leading newspapers of the state. Elmira has started upward and forward on the way to attract wide attention. If the *Gazette* merely keeps up with the new Elmira, its influence and position will be notable. Here's success to our former scribe and his hobby."

## Signs of the Times

Gannett could not have imagined the far-flung interests of the modern Gannett Company, which came to include the largest outdoor advertising company in North America, when the *Gazette* published:

### Elmira Ahead Again

"As Buffalo is raising a howl against the billboard menace, Elmira can sit back and rejoice that the city is comparatively free from such eyesores.

"True, here and there you see a glaring sign, but it is the exception rather than the rule. The residents' section is entirely free from the nuisance and only in the outlying districts are the ugly signs noticeable to any degree. The city needs only to see to it that we are not further inflicted with the nuisance and we shall have little cause to complain. Some may think that a few signs do no harm, but it is just such things that make the difference between the beautiful and the ugly and it is such things that unconsciously impress themselves on the visitor and cause him to decide in his mind whether he likes a city or not. The absence of billboards to no small degree increases the beauty of Elmira. It is to be hoped the signs will grow less rather than more numerous."

The *Gazette* also was not reluctant to goad the opposition. Even before Gannett had bought into the paper, its pages had chided the competing morning *Advertiser* for publicizing rumors of a pending strike at a local shoe factory. The *Gazette's* headlines and lead adequately demonstrate its censure:

## No Thought of Striking

### Everything Is Harmonious at Richardson's Shoe Factory Union Men Are Content

#### Story of Approaching Trouble Entirely Lacking In Foundation – National Union Officer Here Arranging Next Year's Pay Schedule

"The rumor of a strike of the employees of the J. Richardson & Company shoe factory in this city, which were heard about the streets this morning, and which were reported in the *Advertiser* this morning, without reference to the particular plant, are without foundation. A better feeling between the company and the union could not exist."

Gannett hadn't been editor of the *Gazette* two weeks when the paper fired this shot across the bow of its afternoon competitor, the *Star:*

## Several Months Behind The Gazette

### *Star* Just Finds Out About Reliance Motorcycle Company of Edison Coming Here – Same Old Story

"Last February the *Gazette* announced the details of plans of the Reliance Motorcycle Company of Edison to move to Elmira. Yesterday, 'the only star that twinkles on Nix Street,' heard about it and told the story to its readers for the first time.

"This proves once again that readers of the *Gazette* get all the news and get it fresh. . . .

"Concerning a site, however, the *Star* was up to date, for as yet no place has been settled upon."

# That Was Then

Today's journalists occasionally disdain their pioneering predecessors as ill-bred, materialistic and old-fashioned, if not unprofessional. It is not unlike criticizing Paul Revere's warning New Englanders that the British were coming because he could have done it more quickly on a motorcycle.

Despite their hard work, Gannett and Davenport frequently found it difficult to cover the payroll. The *Star* offered Tripp $18 a week. Davenport persuaded his partner that the *Gazette* could not afford the extra $2 a week, so Tripp joined the competition. He would rejoin Gannett and Davenport within a year.

Lack of cash was not the end of their concerns. As Gannett's biographer wrote:

"The capacity of the *Gazette's* rattle-trap press was eight pages at a time. When there was much news to report, Gannett did not hesitate to give space for its coverage; and as advertising increased, eight pages were not enough. . . . This created an emergency in the *Gazette* printing plant; reporters, printers, Gannett and Davenport rushed down to the cellar and inserted a second section printed in the forenoon into a first section which was fresh off the press. The entire staff of the *Gazette* . . . was mobilized for the crisis. There was one single exception; one boy remained upstairs, standing guard over the cash drawer."[3]

Although prosperity was still only a dream, the two owners decided they could not succeed without a better press. They ordered a used one, having no idea how they would pay for it, and they jolted their competitors by reporting the purchase in the *Gazette*.

At the *Star*, the steady gains of the *Gazette* had been worrisome, but news of the new press was startling. The *Star's* owners were brothers-in-law, Isaac Seymour Copeland and James F. Woodford. The paper was edited by Woodford J. Copeland, who had abandoned medical practice as an eye, ear, nose and throat specialist when the aging partners, his father and uncle, asked for help.

The cockiness of Davenport and Gannett and the wariness of the management at the *Star* led to some furtive late-night conversations between the competing Gannett and Woodford Copeland. They recognized that Elmira wasn't big enough for two afternoon newspapers and agreed to merge – on Gannett's terms.

Williamson explained the arrangement:

"The *Evening Star* was a much more valuable property than the *Gazette* – some estimated that it was worth three times as much – yet Gannett proposed, and the Copelands and Woodford agreed, to merge upon an equal-share basis. No money, no notes, no securities were put up. Davenport, Gannett and Woodford each had 25 percent of the merged publication. The remaining quarter interest was held by Dr. Copeland and his father." [4]

# And Now We Are One

Just five days short of a year after Gannett and Davenport pooled their energies as co-owners of the *Gazette*, Elmira subscribers found a new afternoon newspaper on the stoop. The *Star-Gazette* introduced itself in a manner similar to that used by editor Gannett a year earlier:

**Watch the Star-Gazette**

"Today the *Star-Gazette* makes its bow to the public.

"But in reality this is not a new paper. It is merely the result of consolidating in one set of printed pages all the good features and good qualities which have made the *Evening Star* and the *Elmira Gazette* what they were heretofore. By welding the two papers together it is intended to give all readers more news, better news and to put it all in better form than has been possible before.

"This issue of the *Star-Gazette* is published under trying conditions, with parts of the plant separated in two buildings. In the short time since the question of consolidating the two papers was first taken up it has been impossible to arrange for all the details which need attention to make the paper on the start anywhere near the ideal which the publishers hope to achieve. Gradually, however, many improvements will be brought about which should make the *Star-Gazette* the foremost newspaper in this part of the Empire State. . . .

"[T]he policy of the *Star-Gazette* will be Independent-Democratic. All political bias and prejudice will be excluded ABSOLUTELY from the news columns, which will be strictly non-partisan.

"Our own political opinions will appear on this page ONLY, and then it shall be the aim to present our views free from bitterness and with no trace of an intolerant spirit."

On the same page was a smarmy thank-you note to competitors for their kind words and good wishes. The era of good feeling had been declared in Elmira's newspaper community. It read in part:

"One of the finest things about newspaperdom in Elmira is the cordial relations that exist between the different publications. There is a feeling of fellowship and a fraternity spirit . . . which unfortunately does not exist in many other cities where there is rivalry. . . . Long ago Elmira newspapers recognized that they had tasks before them more important than fighting each other and as a result the days of bitterness and mud-slinging are over – we trust for all time to come."

Obviously, the new merger meant that the *Star* could no longer be "several months behind the *Gazette*" on any story and apparently there was a moratorium on reminders of the *Advertiser's* reporting of anything "without foundation."

The masthead of the new newspaper listed the partners and identified their responsibilities. Isaac Copeland was president; Davenport was business manager; Woodford was circulation manager, and Woodford Copeland and Gannett were editors.

Another asset that partners Davenport and Gannett regained in the merger was reporter Tripp, presumably at the $18 a week that they had decided a year earlier they couldn't afford.

The two editors, who had spent a year competing for Elmira's afternoon readers, divided their duties. While one directed news coverage, the other wrote editorials. Then they would exchange roles.

But the younger Copeland lacked his fellow editor's energy and zest for long hours. Gradually he conceded the upper editorial hand to Gannett.

Almost immediately, fortune smiled again on Gannett, and his enlarged partnership. As *Imprint of a Publisher* explains:

"The press which Gannett and Davenport had the temerity to order when they were running the *Gazette* was a sort of talisman. It had undoubtedly scared the *Star's* owners into a merger. It was a second-hand affair, and when the Goss press people took it apart to be shipped, they found that it failed to measure up either to sales promises or the old *Star* press. Whereupon, Goss replaced it with a new machine, with the result that Gannett and his partners got a new press for the price of an old one." [5]

The *Star-Gazette* was staffed and equipped to prosper.

# Chapter 3

# Seeds of Autonomy

*"I have repeatedly indicated that I do not wish to dictate editorial policies . . . . Each newspaper is an institution built up after years of effort. Each has a flavor and atmosphere of its own. Each has its traditions, and these traditions should be maintained."*

Frank Gannett
1935

The *Star-Gazette* was a marriage of economic convenience, so the loyally Democratic *Gazette* and the loyally Republican *Evening Star* were reborn as an Independent-Democratic newspaper.

Editorially, it retained the *Gazette's* faith in the Democratic Party. That loyalty was consistent with Gannett's earlier commitments. If former *Star* editor Copeland considered his earlier Republican sympathies compromised, any such protests were unavailing.

The *Star-Gazette's* national partisanship was total. It provided loyal but ill-fated support for presidential candidates Alton B. Parker in 1904 and William Jennings Bryan in 1908. Although its editorial enthusiasm for the Democratic Party's national agenda was undiminished, its zeal for local partisans was beginning to crumble.

Political power in Elmira was almost equally divided between Democrats and Republicans. Local political offices were hotly contested, and campaigns had grown costly. So the two parties formed the Elmira Compact, chose Zebulon R. Brockaway and installed him as mayor.

The Democratic Party withdrew its support almost immediately after his inauguration. At the next election, the Democratic boss ran for mayor and won. That campaign coincided with William Jennings Bryan's 1908 candidacy for the presidency, and the *Star-Gazette* loyally supported all Democratic candidates.

Soon after the mayor won a second term, a traveling evangelist chose Elmira as his next representation of Sodom and Gomorrah. He railed against the profusion of saloons and denounced the police force and elected officials for protecting the gambling and prostitution on which such establishments relied for their survival.

The outraged local authorities conspired to frame the evangelist. Policemen waited until his male music director and female pianist were in the same room, then arrested them and charged them with adultery. The *Star-Gazette* put out an extra to publicize this alleged moral lapse, but Elmirans soon figured out where the corruption really lay.

Citizens formed a Civic League and nominated a fusion slate of candidates to clean up the city. The formerly loyal *Star-Gazette's* editorials joined the campaign against Elmira's Democratic machine, although they remained faithful to the Democrats at state and national levels.

## The Morning After

The Democratic machine and the city's saloonkeepers retaliated by starting their own afternoon newspaper, the *Herald*, whose principal aims were to thwart the reform slate and punish the *Star-Gazette*.

Despite the appearance of the *Herald*, the cleanup ticket of the Civic League won the mayoral election. Whether the *Herald* would fare better in its effort to ruin the *Star-Gazette* was not clear. The combative Gannett persuaded his partners to adopt a policy that would become his hallmark. Since the *Herald* was the voice of the liquor interests, the *Star-Gazette* would refuse to accept any advertising for alcoholic beverages.

Attempting to dissociate itself from local Democratic politics while remaining loyal to state and national tickets created new complications for the *Star-Gazette*. Voters chose the Republican candidate for governor over the Democratic incumbent, whom the *Star-Gazette* had supported editorially.

Gannett's biographer lauded the editor's next move as a perceptive act of political independence. Whether it was a declaration of independence or an act of canny expediency, Gannett took the editorial podium of the *Star-Gazette* to proclaim the end of party-organ journalism. "[M]ost newspapers of influence and standing," he wrote, "[have] ceased to support organization candidates merely because they bear a party label, regardless of other considerations."[1]

Despite the uncertainties of the local scene, national Democratic prospects brightened in 1912 for the *Star-Gazette* in the presidential candidacy of Woodrow Wilson. Years before in Ithaca, Gannett had expressed his preference for public utilities over private interests. In Elmira he was championing domestic reforms such as women's suffrage, trust-busting and strict enforcement of New York's child labor laws. Wilson's strong condemnation of paternalistic government and his calls for tariff reform were a serenade to Gannett. Elmira's afternoon newspaper would eagerly champion the Wilson candidacy.

The year presented Gannett with a new opportunity as well.

## On the Road Again

Six years after they had helped Gannett buy a half interest in the *Elmira Gazette*, lawyers Irwin and Fordyce Cobb called from Ithaca inviting him to go even deeper into debt. *The Ithaca Journal* was being run by the executors of co-owning estates and they needed experienced help.

The Cobbs were settling one of the estates. They suggested that Gannett buy that interest and manage the newspaper. The Cobbs's own financial contribution and their willingness to endorse his notes enabled Gannett to become a partner in the newspaper for which he had worked for $3 a week when he was at Cornell. This time he was its publisher. (Neither his personal papers nor Williamson's *Imprint of a Publisher* reveal the size of this investment. We do know what it came to mean to him, though: In 1929 he sold his shares in *The Ithaca*

*Journal* to the Gannett Company for $255,000.)

His duties as editor in Elmira required Gannett's constant attention, but Ithaca was only 30 miles away, so he could make weekly trips to oversee its progress. Crows may have found that 30 miles relatively easy, but in the infancy of the motorcar, passage over the ridges separating Elmira and Ithaca was a racking trek – racking but not deterring.

Gannett made those regular trips, but only to assure himself that his accounting standards were being met and that he was not plunging further into debt. The editorial direction of *The Journal* remained the responsibility of those who had been producing the newspaper when he bought his share.

He made one exception. As its campus reporter at Cornell, he had been appalled when *The Journal* gave him a list of names. The list comprised all those Ithaca businesses that did not advertise in *The Journal*. Their names were never to appear in a *Journal* news story.

That black list was scrapped with Gannett's arrival as publisher. The editorial traditions of *The Journal*, however, were maintained. As a result, his newspaper in Ithaca editorialized on the virtues of Republican William Howard Taft and his newspaper in Elmira pleaded for the election of Woodrow Wilson.

At that early point in his career, Gannett established the unwavering company principle that later became known as local autonomy. He sincerely believed that every newspaper has editorial traditions and a sense of community that new managers or new owners should preserve.

Cynics have scoffed at the principle. Some have deliberately ridiculed it to bolster their scorn of Gannett newspapers as invariably mercenary and mediocre. Gannett's newspaper catechism made clear distinctions. He imposed the same precise, regimented accounting procedures on all his newspapers. Yet he genuinely respected each newspaper's news and editorial distinctiveness. He advocated improving newly acquired newspapers rather than making them over into something that might dismay or alienate their loyal readers.

# The Battle of Elmira

While the *Star-Gazette* and the *Herald* waged economic warfare for advertising revenue, Gannett fired an editorial cannonade with seven successive appeals for National Prohibition. It was a sensible strategy. The *Star-Gazette* had eschewed any advertising for alcoholic beverages, and the liquor industry had a major role in the special interests bankrolling the competing *Herald*.

This call for Prohibition was no battlefield conversion. It was an article of faith for Gannett and would remain a personal crusade long after the nation had repudiated the 18th Amendment as an ignoble experiment. He would frequently explain his position in terms of his work in that hotel back in Bolivar:

"It was my unpleasant duty to tend bar in the hotel while the regular bartender went to his meals. There, as a bartender, I saw what alcoholic beverages do to men. I saw liquor make good men bad, but I never saw it make bad men good." [2]

National and world events surely played a greater part in the prosperity of the *Star-Gazette* than did its endorsement of National Prohibition. Elmirans became more attentive as events grew more explosive. And their attention translated into greater circulation for newspapers.

That interest began to grow in 1914 with the assassination of an Austrian archduke. It intensified with the outbreak of war in Europe and President Wilson's declaration of U.S. neutrality.

In 1915, German submarines sank the *Lusitania*, with 128 Americans among the dead. Early the following year, Gen. John J. Pershing and U.S. troops pursued the forces of Pancho Villa into Mexico.

The *Star-Gazette* reported the news of these events and of President Wilson's 1916 campaign for re-election, a cause to which Gannett remained committed. The president wrote to acknowledge that support:

"Your letter gave me the keenest gratification. It means a great deal to be approved of by those who speak so nearly in the name of the great public itself."

By the time the United States had committed 1 million troops to the war in 1917, the Elmira portion of "the great public itself" had planted the seeds of confidence in the owners of the *Star-Gazette*. They set new rates so high that advertisers could afford to use only one afternoon newspaper. Most of the advertisers chose the *Star-Gazette* and the *Herald* faded away.

# The Seekers

Success, as the maxim says, may be its own reward, but the successful partners in the *Star-Gazette* found their rewards insufficient to satisfy the financial desires of five partners. To Gannett and Davenport, that meant shopping for an additional newspaper.

Gannett told Williamson, his biographer, that they had been eager to buy the *Beacon-Journal* in Akron, Ohio, when it was put up for sale. They certified their interest by giving a $10,000 deposit to its owner, Charles Langdon Knight. The Ohioan changed his mind, however, when he announced for Congress and decided that his candidacy needed the *Beacon-Journal*. He returned the deposit. The newspaper eventually passed on to his son, John S. Knight. Along with subsequent acquisitions, it formed the basis for merger into today's Knight-Ridder newspapers.

Back in Elmira, the dispirited partners explained their failure to J.P. McKinney, who was their newspaper's national advertising representative. He was a native of Rochester, N.Y., and suggested they look there. The men who had become partners in the *Elmira Gazette* were looking for a newspaper in a market of opportunity. McKinney had referred them to a city with five competing newspapers.

Early Rochester had earned the nickname "The Flour City" for its mills, which were powered by the cascading Genesee River and ground the wheat grown in that fertile region. By the time Gannett and

Davenport turned their eyes toward Rochester, it had become "The Flower City," thanks to a 20-acre city park celebrated for its lilacs.

Among Rochester's five newspapers, three served Republican interests, two the Democrats'. In the morning, Rochesterians could read the pro-Democratic *Herald* or the solidly Republican *Democrat and Chronicle*. Afternoon newspapers were the *Post Express* and the *Times*, both Republican and the latter the tool of party boss George W. Aldridge, and the Democratic *Union and Advertiser*.

Gannett and Davenport were interested only in the afternoon newspapers, since that was their background. They were not eager to own and operate only one among three afternoon newspapers in Rochester, so they decided they would have to try to buy two of the three and merge them.

Their choices were bipartisan, the *Union and Advertiser* and the *Times*. Obviously, their efforts to buy both could not be known to either owner if they were to avoid extortionate prices. Thus began a cat-and-mouse game in which Davenport and Gannett stealthily bargained with separate law firms representing the owners of the two papers.

Once again the problem was money, but this time they required sums far beyond the $20,000 shares with which the two acquired the *Elmira Gazette*. The success of the *Star-Gazette* was their collateral, and Woodford Copeland, Davenport and Gannett used it to persuade two banks to lend them $150,000 secured only by their signatures.

Davenport then imposed on his boyhood friendship with John N. Willys, maker of Willys-Overland automobiles, to raise another $100,000. The automaker pledged a large block of tire company stock as security for another bank loan in that amount.

The exact total price for the 1918 purchase of the two Rochester papers was a guarded secret. In *Imprint of a Publisher*, Williamson was allowed to reveal:

"The Elmira combination now had its $250,000 in cash. This, together with notes for large additional amounts, including $400,000 secured by assets of their newspapers, they conveyed to the owners of the *Times* and the *Union and Advertiser*." [3]

# Wartime Rochester

While the negotiations with lawyers for the two newspapers were going on, citizens of Rochester were preoccupied with the war abroad and its effects on them at home.

Shortages of food, materials and labor were raising prices and that information was part of the daily newspaper fare. A Page 1 box in the *Union and Advertiser* reported that the Federal Food Administration had advised citizens to stop eating eggs in order to overcome "an egg famine in New York."

"[W]ith the price at from 80 to 90 cents a dozen retail," the news story said, "the administration struck eggs from the list of necessities and listed them as luxuries."

Brighton Place Dairy Co. announced, "in view of the high cost of everything," that milk prices would be increased to 16 cents a quart for Grade A, and light grade, medium grade and extra heavy cream would sell respectively for 16, 18 and 30 cents a half-pint.

New York newspapers announced that the increased costs of materials and labor necessitated a daily price of 2 cents an issue.

The challenges of the "War to End All Wars" brought out the Pollyanna even in a New York jurist. Charles Evans Hughes, who would later become chief justice of the United States, told the New York State Bar Association meeting in Albany that the U.S. Army was the real American melting pot. He predicted "that the war might rid the United States of racial bigotry and class distinction."

These appeals to patriotic sacrifice and idealism were occasionally supplemented by brazenly mercenary flag-waving, such as this large advertisement obviously subsidized by Rochester auto dealers but bearing no identification of its source:

### The American Eagle Won't Sell His Wings

"Suggest to the American eagle, perching on the edge of his rock, that his wings are merely 'pleasure wings' and that he should sell his left wing and save the money, he'll laugh and sail across the valley to get away from a man who would make such a foolish suggestion.

"But it's no more foolish than the suggestion of the Business Bolsheviki of America who tell you to stop buying and selling, to stop manufacturing and trading. In other words, to 'drop a monkey wrench in the machinery of commerce' and thereby help Germany win the war.

"Automobiles are the 'wings' of 99 out of 100 men who own them.

"Automobiles add hours to their days, days to their years, years to their lives, and life to their years.

"The automobile is no longer a businessman's pleasure car. It's his necessity, his education, his family doctor, his business partner.

"If you haven't got an automobile, get one.

"*When you have decided to get one, do not delay.*

"This year's cars are here. Order now and be sure.

" *'They',* the enemy, *'We,'* Americans."

# Wedding Announcement

On March 9, 1918, the *Union and Advertiser* displayed a large advertisement across the bottom third of Page 7: Under a graphic representation of a nameplate reading

> *Rochester Times-Union*
> *and Advertiser*
> 2 cents    Tuesday evening, March 12, 1918

was this text:

"The oldest and the newest are now brought together, consolidated into one GREAT NEWSPAPER under new and progressive management and united for A GREATER AND BETTER ROCHESTER. [Signed] Frank E. Gannett, president and editor; Woodford J. Copeland, vice president; E.R. Davenport, secretary-treasurer and manager. First issue out Tuesday. Order early."

The first issue of the *Times-Union* would have been no surprise to Elmirans familiar with the editing of Frank Gannett. Page 1 carried a story from Albany about Monroe County's assemblymen, [Rochester is in Monroe County] who apparently were hoping to straddle the fence on Prohibition. The story said "all five ... have practically decided to vote in favor of a statewide referendum on the question of ratification of the Federal Prohibition Amendment. If that is defeated, a majority, if not all five, are likely to vote to ratify the federal amendment."

The only break with tradition in the new paper's editorial debut was the lack of a headline similar to Elmira's "Keep Your Eye on the *Gazette*" and "Watch the *Star-Gazette*." The *Times-Union* bowed to its readers with this announcement:

### Under Big Handicap

"The first issue of the *Times-Union* is produced under a great handicap due to the confusion incident to the combining of the two plants.

"This issue gives only a faint idea of the aim of the publishers in producing a great paper for Rochester. It will require several days to get all the departments reorganized and working smoothly. Then the *Times-Union* will develop rapidly into more nearly the ideal that its promoters are striving to attain.

"In the meantime, they feel certain that Rochesterians support their efforts and approve of changes which will follow as fast as they can be carried out."

Among immediate changes in that first *Times-Union* was a page containing new features that Gannett considered essential to increasing readership. They included the comics *Mutt and Jeff, Petey Dink, Bringing Up Father* and *Squirrel Food*, and *Today's Short Story*, the first being "Imogene the Impulsive," by Olive Roberts Spartan.

Gannett's influence on the editorial page was apparent. The editorial pages of the two papers that were merged to create the *Times-Union* had been gray masses of untitled, stodgy and wordy editorials about remote places and on topics of little relevance to Rochester readers. In its second issue, the *Times-Union's* editorial page was a lively package of short, headlined editorials discussing matters that Gannett considered relevant to readers.

His loyalty to Woodrow Wilson and the American Expeditionary Forces produced an endorsement of a new draft for the war and a pledge of "as many millions more as needed because the war must be won."

Another called for amendment of a bill that had been passed to control sheep-killing dogs in rural areas. It said the enactment had prevented the Humane Society from caring for strays in Rochester and decried similar prospects for other cities unless the bill were changed.

A third suggested that Rochester needed a subway system and that the bed of the old Erie Canal, which passed diagonally through the city, should be used as part of the route. That proposal, made on Gannett's second day as an editor in Rochester, would become an editorial drumbeat in the *Times-Union*.

Finally, a brief memorial editorial saluted Lena Guilbert Ford, author of the lyrics of the old song, "Keep the Home Fires Burning," who was one of the victims when a German airship bombed London.

So Rochester had one newspaper less and two new resident capitalists in the persons of Davenport and Gannett, who moved there from Elmira. Although Woodford Copeland was a partner and vice president of the *Times-Union*, he remained behind as editor of the *Star-Gazette*. To fill the business manager vacancy created by the departure of Davenport, he chose reporter Tripp, for whom that move would be transforming.

# Chapter 4

# Romance and Rivalries

*"At the age of 48, [Gannett] was the controlling owner of six newspapers. . . . [U]nless the papers yielded above operating expenses $300,000 for interest and retirement of notes, he would lose his shirt."*

Imprint of a Publisher,<br>Page 132

*Imprint of a Publisher* made much of the folk wisdom instilled in the young Frank Gannett by his mother. The diligence and hard work he demonstrated as a boy were reflected by his first 12 years in the newspaper business. Maria Gannett must have been pleased to see such loyalty to Ben Franklin's reminder that time is money.

One of her favorite maxims was the gospel according to *Poor Richard's Almanac,* "He that goes a-borrowing goes a-sorrowing." Here mother's boy seemed a bit of an apostate.

Gannett embraced a debt of $17,000 for the sake of a half interest in the *Elmira Gazette.* He borrowed an undetermined amount to become publisher of *The Ithaca Journal.* In Rochester, he and his partners pledged to repay well over a half-million dollars in order to create their new *Times-Union.*

Nevertheless, as World War I was winding down and Gannett and Davenport set to work in Rochester, the city remained conservative and insular, even though the U.S. commitment of troops and treasure had broadened the outlook of the American people, including many in The Flower City. Rochester was not so much narrow-minded as self-satisfied.

While they were not treated inhospitably, Gannett and Davenport encountered a coolness felt by all newcomers in Rochester at that time. A native son, Curt Gerling, in an irreverent but affectionate chronicle of the city, later dubbed it "Smugtown U.S.A."

The city was Republican politically and prosperous economically, thanks to a pair known as "the two Georges." One was George Eastman, the multimillionaire founder of the Eastman Kodak Company, whose bachelor reclusiveness made the city's unsociability warm by comparison.

Political power lay in the hands of George Washington Aldridge, whom long-time Rochester columnist Henry Clune described:

"He was the Republican boss, and Rochester was the [most] Republican city in the state. . . . He lived excellently, for the greater part of his career, without visible means of support, and his wife had a pleasant little token of $350,000, which her husband now and then had given her, she once said, 'for jewelry.'

"Aldridge was in the tradition of such political dictators as . . . Boss Tweed, and his downstate Republican rival, Tom Platt. He was a Protestant, but faith and race meant nothing to him when he was putting together political combinations. . . . He wheedled Democrats into the Republican fold, and they voted his way for the city and county ticket; after that they were on their own. These renegades were, of course, rewarded. They were known as 'Aldridge Democrats' . . . and sometimes were a vital force in keeping the city solidly Republican, and securing the seat of power for the boss." [1]

Even if Aldridge was familiar with the generally Democratic editorial positions of the *Elmira Gazette*, he had one reason to hope that Gannett and Davenport might become "Aldridge newspapermen." They were heavily in debt to him. According to Williamson, their annual interest payment to the man from whom they had bought the *Times* was $36,000.

*Imprint of a Publisher* tells of a move by Aldridge consistent with the political maneuverings described by Clune. As Republican boss, Aldridge saw to the publication of legal notices for Monroe County. This was worth about $50,000 a year to the newspaper to which the bone was thrown. An Aldridge minion informed Gannett and Davenport that his patron believed this bounty could be obtained for the *Times-Union*.

Davenport knew that Gannett had left *The Ithaca Daily News* rather than accept the publisher's heavy reliance on printing business from the Democratic Party. He understood that decision and approved. The partners politely declined the Aldridge proposal, and probably perplexed the boss of Rochester by doing so. The evidence suggests that Rochester's more conservative grandees were as startled as Aldridge with the posture of the *Times-Union.* Blake McKelvey, the city's historian, said they were "severely jolted by Gannett's aggressive liberalism on local civic issues [because] his editorial policy often seemed a bit radical in these years." [2]

In rapid succession the *Times-Union:*

• Accused Rochester police of violating the principle of free speech by breaking up a meeting of striking workers.

• Opposed a 1-cent fare increase to 6 cents by the city's trolley system and suggested the city buy and operate the trolleys.

• Objected to a rate increase granted to Rochester Gas & Electric and proposed that New York State, rather than the private utility, should build a new hydroelectric dam on the Genesee River.

• Protested a rate hike to Bell Telephone Company and its merger with Rochester Telephone Company, calling instead for public ownership of the telephone system.

• Successfully campaigned for pasteurization of milk sold in the city, over the protests of the health commissioner that raw milk was better.

# Keeping the Faith

Although both the *Star-Gazette* and the *Times-Union* were showing signs of vitality, the owners remained afloat on a sea of debt. They set course for Utica, N.Y., where two papers, the Democratic *Observer* and the Republican *Herald-Dispatch,* were dividing but failing to conquer the afternoon field.

Assuming enough additional debt, the partners bought control of the two papers and combined them to form the *Observer-Dispatch.* In

Ithaca, Gannett did the same thing, buying *The Daily News* and merging it with *The Journal*.

All that may have consolidated their strengths in Elmira, Ithaca and Utica, but in 1922 their increasingly comfortable position in Rochester was shaken by the gate-crashing William Randolph Hearst, publisher in search of the Democratic nomination for governor of New York.

Gannett and Davenport were first asked to lease their *Times-Union* presses each week to print a Hearst Sunday *American*. Although their presses were idle at the time needed for the new Hearst paper, the partners rejected any association with the project or its wealthy lessee. Their refusal delayed but did not prevent the debut of the new Sunday paper.

The *American* soon had a daily Hearst companion. With the debut of the Hearst *Journal*, Rochester once again had three afternoon newspapers. Two more newspapers in a new market turned out to be no help to the political ambitions of Hearst, who lost the Democratic nomination to Al Smith. That left plenty of time for business, so the man who had wanted to rent space from Gannett and Davenport turned instead to trying to displace them and the *Times-Union*.

Razzle-dazzle was the established Hearst approach to competition – puzzles, games, prizes, all designed to lure readers to the newspaper in their town that was a clone of Hearst newspapers in all others, and cost be damned. If he couldn't outperform competing newspapers, he could try to outspend them. And he frequently did.

The *Times-Union* even helped the Hearst cause briefly by raising its advertising rates. Offended merchants transferred their patronage to the less expensive pages of the *Journal*, until a lack of customers showed them the folly of their pique.

# Subdivided Loyalties

Soon after Gannett arrived in Rochester, he presented a letter of introduction from a mutual acquaintance in Elmira to Mrs. William E. Werner, the widow of a judge on the New York State Court of Appeals and the mother of three daughters.

After a casual introduction and several chance meetings, the youngest daughter, Caroline, and Gannett, then 42, began dating. Despite the difference in their ages – she was 17 years younger – they became engaged two months later. They were married on March 25, 1920, in a ceremony postponed two months by a severe influenza epidemic that confined members of both families, including the bridegroom and his mother, to their beds.

Gannett's commitment to newspapers remained total, but his personal affections now had to be shared by his new bride and his aged mother.

Emotional ties competed heavily for Gannett's attention at the start of 1923. Maria Gannett, who had been ailing since her severe influenza at the time of her son's wedding, was a patient in a convalescent home in Clifton, N.Y. She never recovered enough for her promised return to the home of her son and daughter-in-law in Rochester, and died before the year was out.

During that final illness, her son wrote to her nearly every day, and went to see her as often as possible. Those letters were nearly equivalent to a personal diary. A few are included here not only because they continue the chronicle of Gannett's activities but also because they provide glimpses of that relationship. Throughout his childhood and adolescence, Gannett was constantly reminded by his mother to work hard and "be somebody." That "somebody" is implicit in many of those letters.

At 46, the industrious newspaperman had just become the proud father of a daughter, Sally. He was struggling with his partners to establish some order among their newspapers and particularly on the troublesome Utica *Observer-Dispatch*. He was also taking outside financial risks in the hope of profits.

The demands of writing so frequently were easiest to meet by telling his mother of all that filled his busy days.

On Feb. 12, he wrote from Rochester, "I expected to run down yesterday to see you but . . . some matters came up about Utica that made it necessary for the Utica men to come up here. We are trying to raise the price to 3 cents in Utica, [which] will increase our profits about $100,000 a year. So it was important."

Gannett was careful not to mix business and personal finances. Juxtaposed with that forecast of profits in Utica was a letter he wrote on March 3. "We had a fine time showing you your granddaughter," he wrote. "She slept all the way home and never peeped till we got in the house. . . . Carolyn is crazy over the little coat you gave the baby and the little boots. She wanted just such a coat but did not think she could afford it. It cost a lot of money."

Three months later he would write jubilantly to his mother about an unidentified oil venture in which he was a partner:

"Good news! We got another well. . . . We are going to have three fine wells there and it is sure to make me a lot of money. . . . They expect the three wells will produce 1,500 barrels a day under pumps. That would mean about $400 a day for each of us. Of course we don't get the money for some time as we have $100,000 invested there but we got no dry holes and are sure of lots of oil. Probably will be several months before we get out of debt but then it will be all velvet."

The most important business development he reported to his mother was the creation of the Empire State Group, which the partners formed at the start of 1923 with their four newspapers. That March 7 letter to his mother was written on the new official stationery of "Frank E. Gannett, Editor in Chief" of the group, which dubbed itself "Heart of New York State." The letterhead had a half-page outline drawing of the state with a heart covering the region occupied by Rochester, Utica, Elmira and Ithaca. It listed all four newspapers with the boast, "Each the leader in its field."

Soon thereafter, the partners bought the *Telegram* and the *Advertiser* in Elmira without assuming significant debt. The *Advertiser* was Elmira's morning paper. The *Telegram* was a formerly successful Sunday paper whose profitable market by mail across the eastern United States had been eroded by new local Sunday papers.

Hints of his competitive cares at the *Times-Union* can be found in other letters to his mother. On March 3: "The boys are cutting Hearst but we got them not to strike for we don't want an open fight." And on May 15: "Had to go to a meeting with [George] Eastman last night and did not get home till late. We prevented a lot of advertising from going into the Hearst papers. . . . The fact that we got Eastman to stand up with us last night helped make me feel good, I guess."

## Alone at the Helm

Gannett's concerns with Hearst were mild compared to what came next. He was still mourning the death of his mother in October 1923 when Woodford Copeland told his Rochester partners that Hearst had offered him $1 million for his share of the Empire State Group. He was obligated by their partnership agreement to offer first to sell to them, but he was ill and wanted to retire.

Gannett and Davenport were no more eager to have their competitor as a partner than they had been originally to have him as a lessee. But Davenport, too, had health problems and he did not want to aggravate them. He knew that his remaining partner was not about to slow down as he wished to do.

Both partners agreed to give Gannett enough time to find a way to buy them out. The details of that arrangement were set in motion Dec. 27, 1923, by a call for the first meeting of directors of the Gannett Company Inc., on Jan. 3, 1924, with Gannett as temporary chairman, Frank Tripp as temporary secretary.

At that meeting, two of the three directors of the company elected officers. Gannett was elected president. Douglas C. Townson, Caroline Gannett's brother-in-law, was elected permanent secretary and treasurer. The absent director, J. Arnot Rathbone, husband of Gannett's sister Gracia, was elected vice president.

The directors then began the dissolution of the partnership. They agreed to pay $1 million each to Davenport and Copeland for their stock in the member newspapers. The payment was to be two successive annual payments of $100,000 to each withdrawing partner, followed by lower annual payments with interest through 1945.

They authorized the corporation to borrow up to $300,000 to carry out those agreements. That done, the directors estimated the reasonable worth of Frank Gannett's stock in all those newspapers at $1,015,240 and replaced that stock with 5,077 shares in the new corporation.

Not quite 18 years after borrowing $17,000 to become half-owner of a newspaper, Gannett was head of his own corporation with newspaper assets valued at more than $3 million in four New York cities.

If he had any reservations – and that would have been out of character – they were locked in his agreement with his former partners. In case the Gannett Company failed to meet an interest payment to them, Davenport and Copeland were free to take over the newspapers in Elmira, Rochester and Utica. In that unlikely event, Gannett would return to publishing *The Ithaca Journal-News*.

# Chapter 5

# Full Speed Ahead

*"Frank Gannett . . . took life's chance on me and I on him, with no regret, and fought it through in days of want, of hope, to days of joy and plenty, accepting each the mood, the faults and the word of the other as if it were a bond."*

*Frank Tripp*
*Unpublished Memoir*

Frank Gannett found himself in 1924 in familiar surroundings. He owned six newspapers and still was heavily in debt. There was one flagging difference. Erwin Davenport, his friend and partner of 18 years, was no longer there to share the burden.

That may have made him seem vulnerable. For whatever reason, the man who had sought to buy the Woodford Copeland share of the Empire State Group tried again. An agent of William Randolph Hearst asked whether Gannett would sell the *Times-Union* for $2 million. No. Then $3 million? No. According to Samuel Williamson, the final rebuffed bid for all Gannett's newspapers was $6 million.

About a year earlier, while Davenport was on vacation in the Caribbean, Gannett had written his convalescing mother:

"I expect Dav will land Monday. . . . I'll be glad to see him back. It is too much for one man. I am going to find a high-priced man to take some of the load off me anyway. I am doing too much detail."[1]

Laying aside the temptation to fantasize about what he would have considered "a high-priced man" in 1923, one can sense Gannett's fatigue. Within a year of assuming control of Gannett Company Inc., he cast an improbable actor in the role abandoned by Davenport. Frank Tripp, former reporter and business manager at Elmira and standby troubleshooter for problems in Utica, was named general manager of The Gannett Newspapers.

# Advance Man

Tripp wrote in an unpublished memoir:

"The day Frank Gannett walked through the *Gazette* news room for the first time I was working at a typewriter. . . . I hesitated in some important narrative to be introduced to the new editor.

" 'I've seen you before,' said Gannett.

" 'Yes, in Ithaca,' I replied and, thinking of my job, I added, 'I hope you'll see a lot more of me.' "

A year before Gannett's death, Tripp reminisced about those early days:

"How I wish that Frank Gannett had strength to re-enact with Davvy and me the scenes of his Elmira beginning. His work day began at 7. He changed into his old pants and shoes to save his clothes. He came back every night and Sundays.

"His cranky double keyboard typewriter was on a discarded sewing machine base. Mine rested on a triangular board nailed into a corner of the room. Downstairs, Davvy had a 'private' office, a windowless cubicle hardly 6 by 8. All hands had to squeeze through it to reach the single toilet.

"The roof leaked, the stairs creaked, the press groaned. The natural gas engine shook the building; its cough echoed for blocks. The sheriff kept himself ready." [2]

As noted earlier, Tripp left his $16-a-week job as a reporter with the *Gazette* for the lure of $18 a week on the *Star*. He soon found himself back in the employ of Gannett and Davenport with the merger that created the *Star-Gazette*.

There were other disruptions in their association. Williamson quoted Tripp in *Imprint of a Publisher:*

"At one time when I was a sports editor I let my yen for the show business and press agentry interfere with my newspaper work. I would leave whenever I felt like it, and knew that I could get back my job with Gannett whenever I wished. It was my first test of Frank's unending patience.

"Finally, I did this once too often. I went on the road with my own comic opera company. Gannett decided enough was enough and told me that I'd better stay in show business. At last I had succeeded in getting fired! And by a man who was not the firing kind and never has been. After my show troupe went bust I walked the [railroad] ties back to Elmira and dropped into the *Star-Gazette* office. I found Gannett's office door open and threw my hat in. When my hat wasn't kicked out, I followed it in through the door. Since then I guess I've been fire-proof."[3]

## Unlikely Alliance

Tripp's penchant for theatricals was not his only dissimilarity to the man for whom he would be a lifelong right hand. In a few things they were alike. Both rose from modest beginnings, Tripp as the son of a hard-working locomotive engineer. Each had been taught that of the deadly sins, sloth was among the most despicable. They shared given name and middle initial, which confused inattentive Gannett subordinates because the two Franks were frequently identified only as FEG and FET.

Gannett, inspired by his mother and two outstanding teachers, worked his way through Cornell University. Tripp, despite the hopes of his parents, walked away from high school weeks before his scheduled graduation rather than sing a solo in a school program. Soon after that, he began his informal training in newspapers as a $5-a-week reporter on the *Elmira Advertiser*.

The most astounding difference between them, given their close working relationship, was liquor. Gannett was a committed Prohibitionist and condemned the evils of booze at every opportunity. Tripp had no such constraints.

The publisher never spoke openly of his feelings about this deviation. Tripp alluded to it frequently, saying only half in jest that he did the drinking for both of them.

Gannett's reliance on Tripp began with his appointment as business manager. It would continue for a quarter of a century, until the Gannett Company outgrew the reach of this close relationship.

Elmira was to remain Tripp's base of operations, even as the company's second in command. Wherever duty or opportunity sent him he would go, and stay as long as the job required. When that work was done, it was back to the place he loved most.

Tripp's tasks were unpredictable and his responsibilities heavy. Nancy Tripp Rose recalled:

"There wouldn't have been a company without Dad, because Frank [Gannett] would commit them to something and then go off and do something else – well, run for president. Somebody had to run the business while he was flying his kite." [4]

## Here a Paper, There a Paper

Tripp was to be Gannett's alter ego. His dutiful performance would more than double the number of Gannett newspapers within five years.

This spurt of growth began in 1925 when the company bought the *Newburgh Evening News* and the *Beacon News*. In 1927, it illustrated the wisdom of abandoning the short-lived name Empire State Group by buying two newspapers outside New York state for the first time.

The closer of the two newspapers acquired was the *Courier-News* of Plainfield, N.J., now of Bridgewater. The other became one of those strokes of luck that occasionally blessed Gannett.

He sent Tripp all the way to Winston-Salem, N.C., to buy *The Sentinel* for $600,000. He was confident that Winston-Salem's remoteness from Rochester was no obstacle, but after six months Gannett decided to concentrate his attentions farther north. A buyer emerged and Tripp gave new meaning to the term capital gain by selling *The Sentinel* for $900,000.

Calvin Coolidge had declined to run for re-election as president in 1928, but his doctrinal "the business of America is business" was still an article of faith. During that year, Frank Gannett demonstrated what columnist Henry Clune described as "something of the plunging instincts of Nick the Greek, the celebrated dice shooter, or Pittsburgh Phil, who reputedly made $2 million betting on race horses. Dice and horses, however, were not Gannett's game. He gambled on newspapers." [5]

And gamble he did, borrowing heavily to buy in four cities, beginning with the morning *Democrat and Chronicle* in Rochester. He bought it for $3.5 million, covered by a cash down payment and the rest in bonds. In his third foray outside New York State, he paid $5.5 million for *The Hartford* (Conn.) *Times*. That was covered by $3 million in bonds, preferred stock worth $1.7 million and the balance in common stock.

He turned then to Albany. The owner of the morning *Knickerbocker Press* and the *Evening News* had died and the heirs chose to sell. Gannett paid $2 million for the papers, $450,000 in cash and the balance in bonds and notes.

Finally, there was the *Brooklyn Daily Eagle,* which Gannett hoped to move to Manhattan as the "dry" voice in that wilderness of "wet" newspapers. It was his most ambitious purchase to date, requiring a down payment of $2.2 million on a purchase price of $4.6 million, with the balance as a note.

On top of all this, the Cobb cousins, Howard and Fordyce, needed money for their own ventures. Gannett had to borrow still more to satisfy their needs and keep the *Ithaca Journal-News* afloat. [6]

In a year's time, Gannett had spent more than $13 million to buy five newspapers and refinance another. Commercial interest rates were intimidatingly high. Then in an apparent stroke of that Gannett luck, along came a businessman willing to lend money at attractive rates of interest in return for sales guarantees. Within a year, this presumably happy arrangement would bedevil Gannett into a scramble to preserve the integrity of his newspapers.

# Power is poison [7]

It is necessary here to emphasize Gannett's strongly held antitrust views and his repeated advocacy of municipal ownership of utilities supplying electricity, transportation and telephone service. He scurried publicly to reaffirm those beliefs in his defense when Hearst and other competitors misrepresented him in 1929 as a pawn of the Power Trust.

An alliance of utility companies, the Power Trust was waging a well-financed war against public ownership with deceitful methods that were under investigation by the Federal Trade Commission.

Gannett's apparent luck had entangled him. One source of the vast sums he had borrowed to cover his 1928 purchases was Archibald R. Graustein, president of the International Paper Company. He willingly lent Gannett a lot of money in the hope of selling a lot more newsprint.

International Paper had long been supplier to *The Hartford Times* and its president hoped to win all Gannett newspapers as customers. Gannett readily agreed to newsprint contracts from the newly acquired papers in Albany and Brooklyn, and from the refinanced *Ithaca Journal-News.* As for other Gannett newspapers, he promised only to encourage them to invite bids from International Paper but to continue to buy on the most attractive terms.

Gannett's indebtedness was to International Paper Company. That relationship became clouded when the paper company was reorganized and it became a subsidiary of International Paper and Power Company. Graustein testified as a witness before the Federal Trade Commission that International Paper and Power held $10 million in securities from 13 newspapers. Four of those were Gannett newspapers, whose securities totaled $2.75 million.

That loosed the Hearst-led pack of hounds on Gannett, baying that he had been bought by the insidious Power Trust. Even his newest newspaper, the *Brooklyn Daily Eagle,* was stirred to editorial dismay, the unimpeded publication of which was apparently lost on those most eager to discredit its new owner.

Associate editor H.V. Kaltenborn, later a nationally famous radio news commentator, wrote:

"The standing of these newspapers – and the *Brooklyn Eagle* is one of them – is bound to be injured by these revelations. The editors of this newspaper knew nothing about the facts. They have recently printed and will continue to print editorials and signed articles favoring the state development of water power and opposing newspaper influence by the Power Trust. This writer will continue to do so while he is a member of the staff of this paper. . . . This writer hopes for the sake of the high ideals in journalism which Frank E. Gannett represents that the International Paper and Power Company will be eliminated from *Eagle* ownership at the earliest possible moment."[8]

That was not a faint hope. Gannett promptly turned to the bank that had helped him buy *The Hartford Times*. He borrowed $2.5 million for 120 days, combined it with available cash, and paid off a sympathetic Graustein with $2.78 million. His business sense prompted him to acknowledge to the lender "appreciation of your willingness to part with a good investment by agreeing to sell to me securities not yet callable."[9]

He went to Washington and appeared before the Federal Trade Commission. His answers under questioning satisfied the commission that he had acted properly to eliminate any public misunderstanding of his indebtedness to International Paper and Power Company.

Public reaction was complimentary. Even the competitive press commended him. Nevertheless, he came away from the experience this much wiser:

"I've been in the newspaper business 33 years and I've seen yellow journalism in all its aspects; but not until I became a victim of attacks such as have been made upon me did I know what it means to be treated unfairly and unjustly, or how far it is possible to go in dishonest implications and misrepresentations. These attacks have only intensified my determination that the newspapers I control shall be fair and just to all."[10]

# Forgive Us Our Debts

Boom to bust in 10 months may be too glib as a summary of the national economy in 1929, but it was a year of sharp contrasts. That was true of the Gannett Company as well. Early in the year it bought 51-percent control of the Ogdensburg (N.Y.) Publishing Company for $12,750. Six months later, its 120-day debt of $2.5 million had been cut within 10 days by $375,000. That money had been garnered from available funds at all Gannett newspapers to startle bankers unaccustomed to hasty repayments. Nevertheless, the company still owed Chemical National Bank $2.12 million, due in September.

Gannett was typically unalarmed, although his underlings were not. They foresaw the worst even as he voiced confidence in the bank. He was vindicated when the bank accepted $1.02 million in reduction of the loan and willingly extended the note for another 120 days.

Those four months would prove no more intimidating, despite the collapse of the national economy with the stock market crash of Oct. 29. The directors of the Gannett Company authorized a special issue of preferred stock, which they offered to sell to employees on installment for a total of $85 a share. By the time the note came due in January 1930, the stock sale had raised $1.21 million dollars. That was more than enough to clear the books of the debt hurriedly incurred the year before in response to the canards about Gannett and the Power Trust.

# Chapter 6

# Support Group

*"By getting up early in the morning and staying up late at night, I managed to always stay one step ahead of the boss. It meant, of course, getting to the office very early in the morning, often staying very late at night; it meant working through lunch hours and on holidays and Sundays. . . . I didn't walk, I ran."*

Florence Messman
Secretary to Frank Gannett

Frank Gannett's early days as president of the Gannett Company were busy enough as he and Frank Tripp rapidly expanded the fledgling organization. But growth was not his sole concern. During those years, he also remained the committed publisher of Rochester's *Times-Union*, the one Gannett newspaper whose editorial positions spoke directly for Frank Gannett.

The *Times-Union* was his pulpit in the evangelical crusade for Prohibition. It was his crystal ball in which he saw a better Rochester. It was his soapbox for gradually shifting political loyalties. It was his thorn in the side of William Randolph Hearst.

In 1923, the bustling year in which the Empire State Group became the Gannett Company, the owner of the afternoon *Journal* found a nettle of his own with which to irritate his crosstown competitor on the *Times-Union*. It was Associated Press membership.

Neither newspaper had AP's wire services. Hearst's *Journal* naturally had his International News Service. The *Times-Union* was served by the United Press. But Hearst bought the third afternoon newspaper, the *Post Express*, and folded it, keeping its AP membership for the *Journal*.

Gannett applied to the AP for a *Times-Union* membership. At that time, publisher members of the Associated Press required a two-thirds majority vote in favor of newspaper applicants. The Hearst forces thwarted the application and Gannett had a new grudge against his determined adversary.

Three years later, in 1926, AP's board of directors, whose members had failed earlier to accept the *Times-Union,* unanimously agreed to invite it to join. Gannett had made no overtures to the AP since his earlier application had been rejected.

The fact that the bid had come from the AP board was of no consequence to Hearst. He was still against it and his forces at the annual AP convention once again denied, by 49 votes, the two-thirds majority needed by the *Times-Union.* Samuel Williamson described Gannett's reaction:

" 'The AP is the loser,' he said, 'not I.' What he meant was that all AP news originating in Rochester was at the mercy of the owner of a competing news service. The *Journal* could shut off the AP from its important local news and give it to Hearst's [International News Service]." [1]

Hearst's campaign for governor of New York in 1922 had been ended by the return of Alfred E. Smith from political retirement. While a number of Gannett editors were highly critical of this Hearst nemesis turned Democratic governor, Frank Gannett was personally friendly to him. *Times-Union* editorials supported him, particularly his advocacy of state development and ownership of hydroelectric power.

A handwritten, undated letter to the vacationing Caroline Gannett illustrated her husband's links to Smith and hinted at faint stirrings of personal political ambitions:

**Executive Mansion**
**Albany**

12:45 a.m.
Tuesday a.m.

"Sweetheart –

"Just a line to tell you I am thinking of you. Wish you were here. Some day we may be here together. Yes? It would be fun for Sally and you. Had a great evening. Al and I talked state politics up and down. Nothing else much. He wants my help on the executive budget, four-year term, consolidation, etc. He is right about it and sincere. I'll tell you all when I see you. . . .

"Must go to bed. Am tired. Lots of love and kisses. I'll be lonely till you get back. . . .

"Affectionately,
"Your lover" [2]

## So Much to Do

Gannett recognized the pressures he put on his associates. He told Samuel Williamson:

"I am always thinking of things I want to do and get done. . . . I know I must be hard to get along with sometimes. I do things fast. I do things that make a lot of trouble for the people with me. Yet they never fail to help me." [3]

One of those helpers-in-spite-of-trouble was his secretary, Florence Messman, who joined Gannett in 1926. As the 24-year-old secretary to a vice president of the *Rochester Herald,* she found herself in need of a job when the morning newspaper went into receivership.

She recalled her predicament:

"Word came over from the *Times-Union* that Mr. Gannett was in need of a secretary so I made an appointment with Leroy E. Snyder, Mr. Gannett's assistant, and when I saw him I was asked just two questions – 'What kind of a typewriter do you want?' and "Are you fast?'

"I said to Mr. Snyder, 'There must be someone here that should have [the job].'

"He said, 'Oh, no, nobody wants it.'

"After I got there I found out why." [4]

Despite their friendliness, and the editorial support of Gov. Smith by the *Times-Union,* the publisher was straining at the leash of his traditional pro-Democratic sentiments. The reason was Smith's strong support for repeal of Prohibition.

That quandary would be resolved in the 1928 rush of activity that marked the Gannett Company's greatest growth even as it retested Frank Gannett's commitment to the principle of local autonomy.

# The 'Drys' Have It

The man whose experience as a standby bartender in a Bolivar, N.Y., hotel had fueled his Prohibitionism could not bring himself to support Smith's militancy on repeal. In 1928, Gannett threw his personal support and the editorial support of the *Times-Union* to the Republicanism of Herbert Hoover. It was a permanent commitment of political loyalty and energies.

*The Times* of Hartford, Conn., acquired that same year, was a newspaper with a history of strong editorial support for the Democratic Party. Gannett's editorial turnabout in Rochester to the support of Hoover caused the cynics to smile whenever *The Hartford Times* was mentioned.

Such skepticism prompted Gannett to travel to Hartford to explain the differences between his personal feelings and his professional standards. Editorial policy on any Gannett newspaper, he explained to the Hartford Chamber of Commerce, was for local management to decide. That would remain the case in Hartford.

It was 1912 all over. Just as the Elmira *Star-Gazette's* editorials had supported Woodrow Wilson while *The Ithaca Journal* urged the election of William Howard Taft, Rochester's *Times-Union* was an editorial champion for Hoover while Hartford's *Times* maintained its Democratic loyalties by supporting Smith.

This busy year also offered Gannett the opportunity to overcome the blackballing campaigns of Hearst. The daily and Sunday morning *Democrat and Chronicle* became the second Gannett property in Rochester in 1928. Columnist Henry Clune was already a reporter on the paper when Gannett bought it. Clune wrote that the publishers had "made the *Democrat and Chronicle* the second-best paying enterprise, per dollar invested, in the entire city, and working for them was a joy if one was only mildly interested in wages and considered a 64-hour workweek a privilege. A reporter's job, however, did have the virtue of permanency if a man once was fully established in it, for only high crime was considered a reason for dismissal."[5]

If job security was an advantage offered by the *Democrat and Chronicle*, it was no great attraction to Frank Gannett. There was, however, one happy coincidence. The paper was a member of the Associated Press. Having been denied AP membership twice by Hearst, Gannett might have retaliated. That would have been out of character.

*Imprint of a Publisher* explained his strategy:

"Gannett took a train for New York City and made an appointment with Mr. Hearst. When face to face with his competitor, he said in effect: 'Your Sunday *American* in Rochester has no AP membership. The Sunday edition of my *Democrat and Chronicle* has. I won't make any objection if you apply for an AP membership for your *American*, provided you won't object to my *Times-Union* obtaining a membership.'

" 'Fair enough,' said Hearst."[6]

Biographer Williamson pointed out the disdainful reaction of Roy Howard of Scripps Howard, whose United Press had been the exclusive news service to the *Times-Union:* "Pretty soon you can swap an AP membership for a new hat."[7]

Before the year was over, Gannett outmatched Hearst again. He recruited as general auditor of Gannett Newspapers Herbert W. Cruickshank, who had both guarded the accounts of Hearst newspapers and spent money lavishly on the publisher's many bizarre promotional schemes.

Cruickshank's frugality was a heaven-sent match to Gannett's attentiveness to the balance sheet and standardized accounting procedures. It was he who combed Gannett Newspapers' reserves in 1929 to obtain the $375,000 with which Gannett slashed his debt 10 days after borrowing $2.5 million.

# Down in Albany

The *Times-Union's* editorial endorsement of Hoover and the Republicans in 1928 did not close the door to support of Democratic policies that seemed sensible to its publisher. The result was a lukewarm relationship with the man who succeeded Al Smith as governor of New York, Franklin Delano Roosevelt. Richard Polenberg, a history professor at Cornell, described it:

"Their correspondence while Roosevelt was in Albany suggests a genuine attempt by both to avoid misunderstandings and to keep lines of communication open. Gannett wanted Roosevelt to know that his editors set their own policies, and that their criticisms of Roosevelt's acts did not necessarily reflect his own views. He congratulated Roosevelt on his attempt to enforce anti-gambling ordinances, adding, however, the inevitable admonition: 'What I can't understand is why you don't take a similar position in regard to the enforcement of Prohibition.' Roosevelt thanked Gannett for supportive editorials, when they appeared, invited him to the governor's mansion to chat about current issues, and told him that he believed the Depression, not Prohibition, deserved priority." [8]

Gov. Roosevelt's concern over the Depression may have seemed excessive to Gannett because of the Gannett Company's ability to endure. He regularly encountered loyal employees who voluntarily had bought enough preferred stock to pay off the huge debt incurred in 1929. Thanks to the strict accounting practices applied by the trio of Gannett, Tripp and Cruickshank, every Gannett Newspaper remained in the black despite the Depression.

Gannett resources were severely pressed, however, by the *Brooklyn Daily Eagle*. Gannett's hopes to pair the newspaper with a Manhattan daily had been dashed. His efforts to extend its coverage to Long Island involved costly new presses and construction that cost much more than expected.

The man for all emergencies, Frank Tripp, was challenged as well. Gannett needed a surrogate on the scene if there was to be any hope for the *Brooklyn Daily Eagle* and the man from Elmira got the job.

Tripp's younger daughter Nancy has vivid memories of that assignment:

"The only bad time that I really remember was when FEG – we called them FET and FEG – had bought the *Brooklyn Eagle*. That was quite a stone around their necks. Dad had to be in Brooklyn most of the time. He would go down on the sleeper, the Phoebe Snow, on Sunday night and return on it Friday night, getting in Saturday morning. That went on for well over a year. And I didn't like it. I was just a kid then, but I missed him. He was fun to play with. And he played with me." [9]

# Release the Eagle

Tripp's commuting was a marathon against impossible financial odds. Gannett's gambles on the future of the *Brooklyn Daily Eagle* had been made when the state of the national economy was deceptively bright. The debt incurred to create a newer, stronger newspaper had been undertaken at pre-Depression interest rates. The economic outlook two year's after the stock market crash of 1929 remained bleak.

Preston Goodfellow, the *Eagle's* business manager, had told Gannett and Tripp that he would like an option to buy the paper if the Gannett Company ever decided to sell. After the unavailing efforts of Tripp, the Gannett Company was considering it.

The board of directors met on Dec. 31, 1931, to hear this bleak summary of the situation by Gannett and Cruickshank:

• Net profits, after taxes, of the *Brooklyn Daily Eagle* would be approximately $97,000. Since the Gannett Company owned 76 percent of the paper's outstanding stock, its share of the net would be $73,000.

• The original purchase price of $4.6 million had been reduced by $2.2 million, exclusive of interest. Payments totaling $273,000 would be due on Jan. 1, 1932, on $2,445,500 in notes outstanding.

- "By reason of the economic depression and . . . the tremendous decline in security values during the past 30 days," *Brooklyn Daily Eagle* stock was probably not worth 50 percent of the price originally paid. That being the case, the company's outstanding capital stock in the newspaper was of no value.
- The large mortgage and bank loans on the *Brooklyn Daily Eagle* ruled out any stock dividends for at least three years.

That dire litany concluded, the directors unanimously authorized the sale of "the entire 1,000 shares of common stock . . . for the sum of $1, or other nominal consideration." [10]

So Goodfellow got his wish. Gannett told him that if the employees of the *Brooklyn Daily Eagle* would assume the outstanding indebtedness, the newspaper was theirs. The Gannett Company had shed its second newspaper with unhappier results than the six-month, $300,000 profit on the Winston-Salem *Sentinel*. It had hung on to the *Daily Eagle* for four years, and was relieved of it only after the unaccustomed writeoff of a huge loss. Whatever the nominal considerations cited by the directors when they approved the sale, official corporate records place the price Gannett received for the *Daily Eagle* at $1 million.

It was an inauspicious year for Gannett politically, as well. He added the *Times-Union's* editorial voice to those calling for Hoover's re-election. He applauded Hoover's support of individualism. "Others in another school," he wrote, "believe that government should provide and take care of everything and everybody – a policy which beyond doubt would lead us to disaster and destruction ultimately."

So much for his sometime host at the Governor's Mansion in Albany. Auguring a breach to come, Gannett editorialized in Hoover's behalf: "Roosevelt as governor of New York State has been a failure. . . . We mustn't let this patent medicine vendor get away with the stuff he is peddling." [11]

However, Gannett's great hope against government paternalism, Herbert Hoover, lost to the exponent of vague promises called the New Deal.

The continuing economic storm signals put the brakes on any

immediate new surges in the Gannett Company's growth. That freed Gannett to concentrate on those newspapers he had and to brood over what he saw as an ideological threat to the American virtues of initiative, thrift and hard work.

Frank Gannett had repeatedly pointed out that Gannett editors spoke for their own newspapers. Now he was about to test whether the American people could listen to a crusading Frank Gannett without concluding that what he was saying was the mandated editorial position for all of his newspapers.

# Chapter 7

# Publishing and Politicking

*"On our newspapers we want men who are ambitious, men who have their eyes on positions of greater responsibility. Some are content merely to keep their eyes on these positions. Others prepare for them. To which do you belong?"*

*Frank Gannett*
*February 1934*

After October 1929, the din of the Roaring '20s had turned quickly into the dirge of the '30s. The former were symbolized in the 1931 opening of the Empire State Building, a marvel of engineering and a magnificent exclamation point for that era. The latter were punctuated by the mark of despair, embodied in the 12 million unemployed counted by the U.S. government.

The magnitude of those economic straits and growing public disquiet moved the national government to extreme measures. Among them were the Federal Emergency Relief Administration and the Civil Works Administration, through which $500 million was allotted to mayors and governors. That money to build schools, bridges, streets and roads meant work for many idle citizens. Borrowing it also increased the national debt.

Some of Roosevelt's programs defied traditional virtues of frugality and prudence and thus alarmed many Americans to whom those virtues were articles of faith. Frank Gannett and his associates shared that alarm. Perhaps they were skeptical of the need for drastic national measures because they turned faithfully to the tried and true to assure the survival of their company. Sacrifice, retrenchment and prudence were their watchwords.

Soon after the stock market crash, they had reduced salaries an unspecified amount for all non-union employees in the company. Gannett's salary also was reduced. Although his salary was not known, one can assume that it was significantly more than the $20,000 paid to general manager Frank Tripp, which exceeded the $9,000 to Herbert W. Cruickshank, general auditor, and $3,500 to Leroy E. Snyder, executive assistant.

Frank Gannett's financial sacrifices were addressed by the board of directors at its meeting on March 17, 1931:

In a resolution, the directors acknowledged that Frank Gannett had personally paid $87,722.08, representing all the dividends on the seven-year-old corporation's preferred stock since it was issued. It was decided at that meeting that the corporation should pay such dividends, so Gannett was repaid the $87,722.08.[1]

Retrenchment and prudence did not rule out investing in new properties if it seemed sensible. One such opportunity came in 1932, when one of the founding owners of radio station WHEC in Rochester was forced by illness to sell. Frank Gannett bought a 60-percent interest in WHEC for 600 shares of Gannett preferred stock valued at $60,000.

It was a purchase probably based more on speculation than enthusiasm. Gannett had had an apple from the radio barrel before, coincidentally with Lawrence Hickson, from whom he bought controlling interest in WHEC.

Hickson was a Rochester radio pioneer. *Imprint of a Publisher* described their association:

"[Gannett] backed Hickson's application for a Department of Commerce license. On March 1, 1922, Station WHQ of Rochester, on top of the old *Times-Union* building on Exchange Street, became the 26th broadcasting station in the United States."[2]

WHQ was a novelty to listeners fascinated by its experiments in broadcasting. Their fascination did not translate into profits, however, and after five years of losses, Gannett happily sold his share to Stromberg-Carlson (radio manufacturing and broadcasting firm) for $6,500.

Lack of enthusiasm for radio was not unusual in newspaper publishers of that day, many of whom saw it as a competitive nuisance if not a threat. As Gannett pointed out, the sale of his interest in WHQ "occurred before radio advertising possibilities had developed."[3]

## Stimulating the Troops

Gannett and Tripp had rubbed elbows with subordinates from their earliest days together. They created annual conferences at which department heads of Gannett newspapers compared problems and exchanged ideas. They developed various publications to motivate executives and keep all employees informed. They met the economic threat of the '30s by relying even more heavily on these tools.

*The Bulletin,* a weekly, was begun in 1926 by M.V. Atwood, then editor in Utica and later associate editor of The Gannett Newspapers and head of corporate's News and Editorial Office. It came from that office in Rochester and was, according to its nameplate, "For Executives of The Gannett Newspapers and to Be Kept Confidential Within the Organization."

The *Gannetteer* was launched in 1928 as an employee news organ. It was a monthly that encouraged a sense of family. Births, marriages, promotions, transfers, community service, individual and group achievements all were chronicled.

Frank Gannett also used the *Gannetteer* periodically to foster ambition among his subordinates with signed messages. One excerpted example:

### As to the Other Fellow's Shoes

"Can you fill the shoes of the man ahead of you?

"Measure them. Try them on when you get the chance.

"When moving up day comes, you can't join the procession if you have to wear your old shoes or go barefooted. . . .

"I am convinced that the man who gets ready while faithfully performing his present job will find the way of advancement opened to him sooner or later.

"Get ready to fill the shoes of the man ahead of you. And help the man below you prepare to fill yours.

"You won't lose by helping another man advance."[4]

As the national economic clouds darkened in the early '30s, the *Gannetteer* passed along Tripp's prediction that newspapers would cost 5 cents a copy within five years. It also reported candidly the bottom-line signs of hope for Gannett newspapers. For instance, the April 1933 issue told Gannett employees that corporate profits for 1932 were $684,609, down 22 percent from 1931's $879,400. The clear message was that *we are in this together, and that while we continue to profit we cannot afford to abandon the spirit of sacrifice.*

The same strategy of identifying common concern was pursued in the annual conferences. In July 1933, executives of the newspapers' mechanical departments gathered in their first such meeting. The *Gannetteer's* summary of that conference verified the deadline tug of war between production departments and newsrooms everywhere:

"It was found that late copy caused many worries."

Editors and advertising managers had been attending joint conferences for several years. Their October 1933 meeting focused on heightening the value of their newspapers to readers. It also reflected their leader's concern over the national economy, particularly the decline in consumer spending.

At the conference dinner, Tripp called for intensely local service by each Gannett newspaper. Editors, he said, should "put the high hat on the shelf, and paint the fences and marry off the beautiful daughters."

Gannett told the audience, "We should not forget that war and abuses of alcohol are two of the greatest evils in the world. Taxation is another problem demanding the attention of newspapers. Real estate can no longer stand the tax burden placed on it."

Describing his concern with the national economy, the *Gannetteer* reported: "Again he referred to his belief that the country must develop more purchasing power by distributing more of the profits to the consumer, to management, and to the worker, rather than to the capitalist."

At the first conference of circulation managers, in December 1933, Gannett demonstrated the distinction he expected between Gannett newspapers and those of his arch-rival Hearst:

"The taste of the readers is constantly changing. Watch it. People are not so concerned about a murder, but they are interested in government, finance, economics, business, science, discovery, achievements, and sports of all kinds, especially local."

## Spreading the Word

Both Franks took their messages of alarm and hope on the road. Despite their opposition to the election of Franklin Roosevelt, Tripp pledged support for the New Deal's national recovery plan. He pointed out, however, that it was wrong in failing to recognize the power of advertising "to create demand, restore buying, reopen factories and create jobs." He might have added, "sustain newspapers," but perhaps he considered that patently obvious.

Gannett took to commencement at Keuka College in Keuka Park, N.Y., the concerns about finding better ways to share the nation's wealth. He told the graduating seniors:

"Better distribution – that is what we need. Better distribution of the products of farm, field, forest and mines. Better distribution of the wealth produced, less reward for capital, more for labor, security for our savings, and security against unemployment. An equal opportunity for all to work and enjoy life." [5]

These are words of genuine concern, for the nation's unemployed millions, for the continued security of thousands of Gannett employees, but especially for acceptable alternatives to what he feared from the social experimenters in Washington.

In December, he was almost effusive in praising FDR's adoption of a theory on gold prices suggested by George F. Warren and Frank A. Pearson, two professors at Cornell. Richard Polenberg described the theory "as seductive as it was simplistic."

The president abandoned the theory after several months, but not before Gannett extolled him again in a November speech. It prompted such a heavy response that the publisher issued a pamphlet of the text.[6]

That was not the last note of approval Gannett would send to the man he had dismissed in 1932 as "a patent medicine vendor," but his forbearance was beginning to fade.

# New Horizons

It had been nearly five years since the Gannett Company had added a newspaper to the group. Despite the nation's economic inertia, the corporate bottom line was solidly black. Opportunities for expansion came in quick succession in 1934.

DePauw University of Greencastle, Ind., had been bequeathed the Commercial-News Company of Danville, Ill. The university invited the Gannett Company to consider purchasing the newspaper. In January, the *Commercial-News* became a Gannett newspaper for $1 million – $75,000 in cash, a $625,000 mortgage and Gannett preferred stock worth $300,000.[7]

Three months later, Gannett bought *The Saratogian* of Saratoga Springs, N.Y., for $155,000 – $55,000 in cash and Gannett preferred stock worth $100,000.[8]

These acquisitions were not the only things to strike Frank Gannett's fancy in 1934. He took his first ride in an airplane on a short flight over Lake George. He was thrilled but still skeptical of the safety of air travel. Then he met Lieutenant Commander Russell Holderman, an expert in soaring and powered flight.

Gannett recalled later:

"Commander Holderman invited me to the airport. He placed a newspaper on the field, fastening it down with four rocks. He then hitched his glider to a plane, went up to 2,000 ft. The glider was cut loose, and Holderman finally brought the glider down so its nose rested on the newspaper. I marveled at his accuracy and his ability to control the glider.

"As a result of this demonstration, I authorized Commander Holderman to buy an airplane that would be suitable for our purposes, and in a few weeks we were going places in a Stinson Reliant."[9]

The Gannetts' son, Dixon, whom they adopted as an infant in 1929, considered Holderman a childhood hero. He filled in details that his father had omitted:

"[Dad] liked Russ so well that he said, 'Russ, I want you to go to work for me.'

"And Russ said, 'I've got an air service, you know, and I have to make a living.'

"My dad said, 'Well, I still want you to go to work for me.'

"And Russ said, 'I'll do it on one condition, that I can run my Holderman Air Service.'

"My dad was so eager to get hold of Russ that he said, 'Sure, go ahead.' And Russ moved his whole operation up to Rochester [from Lake George] and ran his Holderman Air Service."[10]

Frank Gannett, reared on the idea that time is money, realized that air travel made his scattered newspapers accessible in much less time than train or automobile. He enjoyed flying, but this new fascination was practical, not recreational.

In a similar vein, only a year earlier, Gannett had persuaded the board of directors that his personal yacht, the *Widgeon*, moored on Lake Ontario, "was used practically entirely for entertaining advertisers of Gannett Newspapers and for the benefit of employees of those newspapers. . . . [O]wing to his salary being reduced, he thought the company should bear this expense, an expense which he has hitherto paid for personally."

The directors voted to buy the *Widgeon* for $5,556 and refund to him the undisclosed sum he had spent in fitting out the yacht for the season.[11]

It had been the most dynamic year for the Gannett Company since 1928's flurry of acquisitions. Fifty-six-year-old Frank Gannett had found a new way to save time and cover vast distances comfortably.

Aside from being diabetic, a condition which he controlled by diet, he was in good health. Nevertheless, he frequently pondered the future of The Gannett Newspapers and what might happen to them if he were gone.

That preoccupation would make the year 1935 pivotal in the history of the Gannett Company and earn Frank Gannett new renown for employee relations and philanthropy.

# Chapter 8

# Securing the Future

*"Even before . . . 1935, I had decided that I did not want our great group of papers to get into undesirable hands in case of my death — in hands interested only in making money. . . . Along with my desire to perpetuate the newspapers themselves, I [was] concerned over the future of the thousands of men and women connected with them."*

Frank Gannett
January 1950

It is difficult more than a half century later to disregard apparent contradictions in Frank Gannett's personal principles. Strong opposition to government paternalism was to be expected in one whose life exemplified American individualism – the self-made man. Yet his concern for and devotion to his employees surpassed the paternalism that was the measure of so-called good employers of the day.

The spirit at The Gannett Newspapers was emphatically family. If employees found their pay scales miserly, they did have secure jobs when millions of Americans had none, and they knew the story of their employer's rise from want to wealth. In any case, they believed he cared about them.

First, the *Gannetteer* reported his repeated speeches calling for better distribution of wealth, for giving "more of the profits to the consumer, to management, and to the worker, rather than to the capitalist."[1] Secondly, most of them had chatted briefly with him at company functions or during his rounds of their newspaper. They felt he was one of them.

A veteran employee explained, "He was just a very nice person and he treated everybody the same. It didn't matter if you were a high official or if you were one of the mailers or the printers. He was nice to everybody. He was just very gracious – and so was [Mrs. Gannett]. They were interested in everybody, it didn't matter who you were. You felt that they were really interested in you when you were talking to them."[2]

By any standards, Gannett in 1935 was a wealthy man. He acquired that wealth through hard work alone. He considered that a worthy example for others, even his family.

Florence Messman recalled:

"He wanted a successor . . . and after Mrs. Gannett lost four children in six years, he decided that he couldn't have an heir to the newspapers. So they adopted [Dixon]."[3]

Dixon was adopted as an infant when his father was 53 years old, and always busy. The occasions of father-son companionship were rare.

"I spent a great deal of my time away from home," Dixon remembered. "If it wasn't at camp, it was away at school. . . . I wasn't one of the fortunate youngsters that spent a great deal of time at home. . . . I came home for holidays."[4]

Even though he had a potential successor in his 6-year-old son, Gannett's intent was firm.

Messman restated that intent:

"Mr. Gannett said, 'I will never leave a wealthy son.' "[5]

He showed the strength of that determination in 1935. After setting up "a modest trust fund for his family, who it was agreed, [would] have nothing to do with the operations of his papers after his death," he established the Frank E. Gannett Newspaper Foundation Inc. with a large block of stock. Upon his death, "the foundation [would] own all the Class A Common stock of Gannett Co., Inc., and have complete control of all Gannett newspapers."[6]

# 'Independent and Useful Newspapers'[7]

Vincent S. Jones, who was executive editor of Gannett Newspapers for 15 years and then vice president and secretary of the foundation, explained its genesis:

"Twenty years before his death in 1957 [Gannett] . . . had anticipated the coming of the Grim Reaper. With the aid of expert (and expensive) legal advice, he had contrived to forestall most of the unpleasant consequences of losing control of a hard-earned fortune. . . .

"[W]hile the establishment of the Frank E. Gannett Newspaper Foundation, Incorporated, back in the poverty-stricken '30s, was scornfully dismissed by critics as a tax dodge (which it was, in one sense) few people saw the true significance of the founder's generous move.

"Later, while God-fearing newspapermen and women elsewhere were being delivered into the hands of people to whom newspapers were just another business because their employers had expected to live forever and their heirs had been caught short of cash, Gannett people were protected by the interposition of a special corporation."[8]

Jones said Gannett's "creation remained invisible for more than two decades, except to his family and a handful of business associates."[9]

Gannett acknowledged that in explaining the birth of the foundation. Referring to the $2.5 million in stock with which he created it, he said:

"This stock had all been owned by me. It would normally have passed, at my death, through my estate, to Mrs. Gannett. Through her unselfish cooperation, I was able to turn it over to the foundation."[10]

The publisher insisted that the foundation be dominated by newspapermen. Each of the 11 members of the board had to own at least 100 shares of Gannett stock. At least seven had to be experienced newspapermen. At least one had to be "an experienced attorney." In this way, Gannett hoped, the directors would "give first thought to maintaining vigorous and independent and useful newspapers."[11]

# The Essence of Frank Gannett

Gannett explained to his employees what he hoped to achieve through the Frank E. Gannett Newspaper Foundation, Inc. His explanation is included here in its entirety because it represents the clearest summary of his professional convictions.

He told his employees:

"First of all, I feel that newspapers are great public trusts and a mighty mechanism for good or evil.

"I have been distressed of late by the tendencies of some newspapers to play to the lower tastes and sensibilities, to exploit crime and sex affairs, and to arouse the baser instincts of readers. Our newspapers have not stooped to such practices. Nor can I conceive of any changes, even in this changing world, which should ever warrant departure from our ideal.

"Again, of great importance is it that our newspapers always shall be devoted to the best material as well as spiritual interests of our communities in which they are published. They should at all times vigorously support all movements to foster and promote the welfare of the communities.

"Our papers should always be sympathetic with the poor. They should oppose wrongs and defend the public against exploitation at the hands of powerful interests. They should always be on guard to protect the interests of the many rather than the few.

"In our editorial columns I expect and urge that the editors shall take definite positions on all questions in their honest efforts to inform the public and develop sound public opinion. Our editors should seek all the information possible on all issues and thus become so well versed on public questions that their opinions will carry weight. Only thus will our newspapers become leaders of public opinion.

"While maintaining strong and vigorous editorial policies, I hope the editors will always be tolerant. One who disagrees with the newspaper may be right, and the newspaper may be wrong. It is particularly important that readers have an opportunity to express themselves through our newspapers, with only such restrictions as space limitations, good taste and libel laws may impose.

"Our news columns must be free from bias in reporting news. Our headlines especially must be carefully watched lest they be inaccurate or biased. The news columns should reflect accurately the world as it is; we cannot be too careful in our efforts to prevent distortion of the true picture.

"As the directors well know, it has been my policy to leave the local management the fullest measure of autonomy. I like to have the editors express themselves freely. I have repeatedly indicated that I do not wish to dictate editorial policies for our group. Each newspaper is an institution built up after years of effort. Each has a flavor and atmosphere of its own. Each has its traditions, and these traditions should be maintained. I do not want our ownership to destroy the individuality of any newspaper.

"I hope, therefore, that the directors of the foundation and the directors of Gannett Co. Inc. will at no time impose drastic control over the policies or dictate to any newspaper what its editorial position shall be on any question.

"I have said I wish our newspapers to be fearless and independent. To be independent and of the greatest service to their communities, they must be operated at a profit, but profits should be made secondary to basic ideals. Our newspapers must be free from the influence of any interests that may have selfish motives.

"For this reason it is so obvious as hardly to require stating that none of our newspapers should ever accept any money or any valuable consideration, good offices or influence, from any sources, that may imply an obligation that any newspaper shall support any cause, issue, political party or faction.

"When public officials are compelled to publish in newspapers any public notice or advertisement, these should be accepted on a purely business basis with the explicit understanding that no 'political favors' may be expected in return. No advertising should be accepted which may infringe upon our freedom of editorial expression. I trust, also, that great care will be used in excluding any advertising which, in the judgment of the directors, will be injurious to the public. Our advertising should be honest in all its representations, that the public be not misled by it." [12]

Transformation of the Gannett Company into a publicly held corporation in 1967 and a series of changes in federal tax law over the years all affected the foundation's structure, its style of operation and its philanthropies. In 1991, the foundation was reconstituted as The Freedom Forum, focused primarily on First Amendment issues, after its Gannett stock was purchased by the company for $670 million.

Its existence as the foundation perceived by Frank Gannett, however, saw it evolve from the source of $2,250 in charitable donations in its first year to the beneficent provider in 1989 – the last year in which the foundation supported all programs then established – of $23.8 million in grants and programs.

# As Good As His Word

During that same part of late 1935, the company once again offered new convertible preferred stock to employees, this time valued at $110 a share rather than $100. Employees could buy stock through payroll deductions, for $95 a share at 50 cents a week for 190 weeks. Lincoln Alliance Bank & Trust of Rochester carried the loans for employees buying the stock. The 5 percent annual interest was deducted from the $6 per share annual dividend. [13]

At the end of 1935, three months after the foundation had become the new guardian of The Gannett Newspapers, Gannett Company, Inc., paid its creditors $2,173,123.33 to satisfy its only funded debt. [14]

With the foundation established and the company clear of funded debt, one goal remained. It was only a year later, in December 1936, that Gannett's directors delivered on Frank Gannett's call for greater distribution of profits.

They authorized the issuance of checks on these bases:

- Two weeks' pay to every person employed five years or more.
- One and a half weeks' pay to every person employed at least three years but less than five.
- One week's pay to every person employed at least six months but less than three years.

While this action affected only the Rochester properties, the directors urged the same profit-sharing by the subsidiary companies to the "extent justified by their 1936 earnings."

In a final acknowledgement that things were looking up for the company, the directors "decided that any employee, except those under a labor contract, who in 1929 received $4,000 a year or less, and whose wages were reduced by depression necessity, and have not yet been restored, shall, as of Jan. 1, 1937, be increased to his 1929 wages." [15]

The statement that accompanied each check made the intent clear. "It is not a gift, not a Christmas present. It is a share in the result of the year's efforts of you and your associates." [16]

# Making the Point

The *Gannetteer* description illustrated the paternalism personified by Frank Gannett:

"Part of a letter from an executive of the organization reflected the sentiment of employees toward FEG personally when he wrote: 'I wish you could have seen the faces of those to whom I passed out checks. . . . You say it was not a gift . . . but we all know it would not have been possible if you had not had a liberal heart.'" [17]

While profit-sharing was established, the 1936 method of payment was not. A year later, the directors outlined how profits would be shared beginning with 1937: The corporation would set aside 10 percent of net earnings, before crediting dividends from subsidiary properties and after taxes. "Said sum," the resolution said, "shall be divided among and paid to all such employees *pro rata* on the basis of the total earnings of each employee for the five-year period ending Dec. 31, 1937."

Again, the directors recommended the same course of action for all the corporation's subsidiaries "insofar as their respective earnings for the year 1937 may permit." [18]

Gannett was pleased that profit-sharing had begun. He told his employees:

"The most encouraging development of the past few months has been the realization, expressed in action, on the part of so many big industries, that sharing profits with workers is not altruistic, but essential if our economic system is to continue.

"Capitalism can only continue to function through a more equitable distribution of income. However economists and students of business may differ on other points, on this they seem agreed." [19]

Gannett had demonstrated the sincerity of his calls for a greater share for labor. The precepts with which he explained his intentions for his newspapers through the foundation were devoutly held until his death. Those qualities would be quickly forgotten or contemptuously dismissed by people who were to remember him only for activities in which he was just becoming involved, and for some political views as unreconstructed as his professional beliefs were progressive.

# Chapter 9

# Which Frank Gannett?

*"It would mean a great sacrifice for me to accept any public office, and I prefer to devote myself to my newspapers. . . . However, such a grave crisis confronts the nation that all who believe in our precious institutions must be ready to make many sacrifices."*

Frank Gannett
Time, *April 1936*

The confusing effect of Frank Gannett's non-newspaper activities, his public speaking and his increasing political visibility, can be inferred from Samuel Williamson's indirect approach in his approved biography:

"It is an unsettled question how far a newspaper editor or publisher should participate in public affairs. To some iconoclasts, the ideal publisher is without friends or relatives; he has no political ties or financial interests; he is churchless and belongs to no clubs or other organizations. . . . The crux of the matter is not so much whether a publisher engages in public affairs as whether and how he keeps one set of interests separate from the other."[1]

Such a balancing act for Gannett began soon after the advent of the New Deal. Gannett and Frank Tripp both appeared at the conference for circulation managers in 1934. The general manager called for more and better promotion to increase circulation. Their president reassured them, "The newspaper is about the last thing a family wants to give up in times of adversity. People are going to have their newspapers."[2]

At the same time, Gannett was both deploring and praising the New Deal. He decried farm policies that destroyed crops and curbed production while the world needed food and clothing, but he was pleased with Franklin Roosevelt's adoption of the Cornell professors' theory about commodities and the price of gold. He praised the president and declared "[that] we are no longer outsmarted by European financiers, that we shall have something to say about the price of gold, the purchasing power of our dollar and control of our destinies."[3]

He even advised the New York Republican Party, of which he was becoming a more active member, to stop "opposing every good that some other party proposes. People are more important than profits, the welfare of folks more important than business."[4]

## Broadening His Beat

As a man of means, Gannett strove to satisfy his innate curiosity. In 1934, he made two trips abroad. The first was a trip by air to Brazil and Argentina, where he studied both countries' methods of maintaining satisfactory income to farmers for goods sold abroad. The second was a tour of Europe during which he interviewed British Prime Minister Stanley Baldwin, Pope Pius XI, Italy's Benito Mussolini and French Foreign Minister Pierre Laval. Adolf Hitler was unavailable for their scheduled meeting and the publisher met instead with Rudolph Hess.

Gannett wrote news reports about these experiences and his newspapers took editorial positions on relevant issues. He also discussed them in public appearances. As these grew more frequent, he began to speak more openly of his distrust of the Roosevelt administration and of his fears that war loomed in Europe.

In mid-summer, Sen. William Borah of Idaho read a Gannett speech on monetary problems into the *Congressional Record*. It was a strong signal of mutual admiration developing between the two Republicans. The publisher suggested that the party needed Borah as its 1936 presidential candidate. The senator was thinking about it.

Gannett's active schedule as a speaker pressed him heavily for time. In addition to overseeing his newspaper company, he was also busy as a member of the AP board. He was elected in 1935 to fill the vacancy created by the death of Adolph S. Ochs of *The New York Times*.

He was traveling more than ever, most of the time by air. He wrote of the first year after purchasing the Stinson Reliant:

"I flew to places in two hours which would have taken me eight hours on the train. I found it possible to visit cities remote from my office and be able to sleep in my own bed instead of a Pullman. My working hours were thus multiplied, and by using the airplane it was possible to accomplish much more than before." [5]

## Gannett of the GOP

One of Gannett's flights early in 1936 took him to Washington, for a visit to the office of the senator from Idaho. Borah was willing to seek the Republican presidential nomination on one condition – that Gannett be his running mate.

According to Williamson, the publisher was dumbfounded:

" 'I don't want recognition,' he protested, 'and I don't want public office. I have always rejected such suggestions, and the last office I'd ever think of holding would be that of vice president. The thought of sitting in the Senate and listening to you fellows all day appalls me. . . . I have been used to a life of action. I couldn't bear just sitting still.'

" 'I need you,' Borah countered. 'You are a New York man. You're a businessman and a sound executive, and also you are a newspaperman. I need you on the ticket with me, and if you don't consent, then I'll refuse to run.' " [6]

Gannett consented, on the condition that no one be told, to which Borah agreed. Soon thereafter the publisher officially endorsed the man from Idaho:

"The Republican Party, if it is not to disappear, must select a leader who will bring it back to the people. There must be no suspicion that the nominee is susceptible to dictation or influence by anyone, any group or special interest. The times call for an independent, fearless statesman. His humanitarian instincts must be no less than his devotion to good government."[7]

The secrecy of their being running mates was quickly dashed by the Ohio primary, which required would-be delegates to indicate two choices for president. When the Borah people listed Gannett as their alternate, the intent was clear.

The *Gannetteer* reflects some of the conflicting pressures employees of The Gannett Newspapers felt at the time. One of the company's two newest newspapers, the *Commercial-News* of Danville, Ill., had thrown vigorous support to the Borah campaign for the Republican presidential nomination. The *Gannetteer* story reported that 365,000 copies of a special April 8 edition supporting the Borah candidacy were distributed in Ohio for the primary. It made no mention of the fact that Frank Gannett was the senator's running mate on the Ohio ballot.[8]

The same issue reported other ways in which Gannett was supporting the Borah effort, including his remarks in Rochester to the Monroe County Republican Committee: "We must do all in our power to drive the Roosevelt administration from power. We must win, or lose our liberties."[9]

Tripp, meanwhile, was echoing the message in Elmira, where he told the Rotary Club about a recent tour of Japan and Manchukuo. He punctuated his message, however, by attacking the president as a man fostering class hatred and intolerance.

Publishers and advertising managers gathered in Hartford, Conn., in May for the annual Gannett summer meeting. There, in his role as company president, Gannett was both sober and reassuring:

"As a group we are ready to go forward. We have the personnel, the experience and the financial resources needed for growth. We are on the lookout for good properties which we can take over without imperiling those we have."

General manager Tripp warned the publishers at the meeting that if Gannett newspapers were to maintain their standards, they needed increased revenues, either through higher advertising rates or subscription prices.[10]

# The Sunflower Candidate

At their national convention, Republicans nominated a publisher as their vice presidential candidate. To head the ticket, they ignored the Idaho maverick to anoint Alfred E. Landon, "the Kansas liberal." His running mate was Frank Knox, publisher of the *Chicago Daily News*.

Unlike the disappointed Borah, Gannett resignedly accepted the nomination of Landon and energetically supported the lost cause. That support was a test of Gannett's consistency.

Republicans in Hartford, Conn., concerned that the notoriously Democratic *Times* might undercut the Landon campaign in favor of "*that man* in the White House," appealed to Gannett to intervene.

Now more than a dabbler in politics himself, Gannett refused to intervene but went to Hartford and reassured the editor of his autonomy. He then shocked some fellow partisans in Hartford with this published statement:

"When I purchased *The Hartford Times* I said that I would try to preserve its tradition and its independence, and gave my word that I would not at any time use the paper for personal motives.

"The staff of *The Times* knows that I have never dictated its editorial policy. I have said that if I wanted to make a statement I would do so in the news columns over my signature. Frequently the editorial policy of *The Times* has been directly contrary to my own personal views.

"I believe that this is a wholesome situation. It would be a sad day for America if all our newspapers expressed only one view, or if they were owned by one person who insisted on expressing only his opinions or used the papers to promote his personal advantage.

"I regard *The Times* not as a personal possession to use as I may see fit; I regard it as a great institution whose first object is to serve its community. By our efforts to give it good management, to develop it and promote it as a great newspaper, we have accomplished much in making its position more secure." [11]

*The Times* was not alone in supporting "*that man* in the White

House." Landon met the most crushing defeat any presidential candidate had ever suffered, winning only eight electoral votes. Gannett feared more deeply for the republic.

## 'Reorganization of the Judiciary'

The strongest reason for Gannett's support of the Landon candidacy was that he wished Landon rather than Roosevelt to select the replacements for aging justices of the U.S. Supreme Court.

The president had been openly contemptuous of the nine robed incumbents since 1935 when the court had declared his National Recovery Act unconstitutional. Richard Polenberg of Cornell University described Gannett's concern:

"As early as the spring of 1936, [he] wrote that if Roosevelt were re-elected 'he will appoint during his term four or five justices of the Supreme Court to fill vacancies, which will naturally occur. If these judges are advocates of a planned economy and the New Deal, then the America that you and I love will be a thing of the past.' " [12]

Those vacancies failed to occur naturally as Gannett expected. Adding to his alarm were references by Roosevelt to the Constitution as a horse-and-buggy document not equal to the complications of the '30s. Early in 1937, the president confidently unveiled a plan that would allow expansion of the court to no more than 15 justices.

The announcement of this closely guarded strategy galvanized Gannett. He was transformed instantly from a determined opponent to a committed combatant. The bill that Roosevelt labeled the "Reorganization of the Judiciary" quickly became "the bill to pack the Supreme Court" to assure decisions favorable to the president's New Deal programs.

Williamson explained the situation facing the disconsolate Gannett:

"When Mr. Roosevelt read his court message in the Cabinet room on that February morning, no president of the United States had ever had a larger electoral vote than his in the 1936 election. No president ever had a greater majority of his own party in both houses of Congress. Mr. Roosevelt seemed irresistible. He stood at the height of his power – and he sought more." [13]

Gannett turned once again to Borah, and was even more dejected to learn that Borah didn't think anyone in Congress could block the bill's passage. Gannett's former running mate challenged him:

"With your newspaper training and your background you can inform the people back home of the dangers of this bill. Show them how it would destroy our constitutional form of government. You are especially fitted for the job, and you must undertake it." [14]

## To the Barricades

Gannett immediately set to work. He enlisted the help of Dr. Edward A. Rumely, an expert in mass mailings, and Amos Pinchot, a former supporter who had also become a vocal opponent of the New Deal. Just nine days after the president unveiled "Reorganization of the Judiciary," they had mustered Republicans, disaffected Democrats, independents, the famous and the unknown into a potent force christened the National Committee to Uphold Constitutional Government.

Polenberg summarized its activities:

"In the space of six months, the committee raised $200,000 from more than 10,000 contributors. It distributed 15 million pieces of literature opposing the court-packing measure. . . . The court bill went down to defeat in July 1937." [15]

Efforts to save the president's plan with a compromise measure were also thwarted. A special congressional committee vindictively tried to seize all the files and records of the National Committee to Uphold Constitutional Government. But it caved in to the open defiance of Gannett and Rumely and never carried out its threat to punish them for contempt of Congress.

# The Horse Trader

While Gannett and his associates sought to prevent loss of the Supreme Court's independence, the publisher was gravely concerned about losses closer to home. Newspapers, he insisted, could only maintain their independence if they were financially secure.

Albany had two Gannett newspapers, and the company could look on the capital city as a profitable market, although of the two, the *Evening News* was profitable, the *Knickerbocker Press* was not.

The man who had outmaneuvered William Randolph Hearst into supporting AP membership for Rochester's *Times-Union* knew that his long-time rival's afternoon newspapers were losing money both in Rochester and Albany.

Agents for Hearst had sounded out Gannett executives about buying him out in Rochester. Gannett was not interested. But Frank Gannett had another idea that Hearst might find as appealing as reversing himself on the AP membership had been.

He proposed that the Hearst afternoon *Times-Union* in Albany be issued as a morning newspaper. In return, the Gannett Company would merge its unprofitable morning paper into its money-making evening paper renamed the *Knickerbocker News*.

Hearst's only condition before accepting this offer was that the Gannett Company buy the Hearst equipment in Rochester. Hearst would close his Rochester paper. The deal was made, leaving each publisher with no Albany competitor in his time cycle and The Gannett Newspapers with Rochester all to themselves.

# Chapter 10

# Siren Song

*"Within the past year [Gannett] has emerged as a figure of national importance. Today there are few questions which arise involving national policies, especially as they affect fundamental concepts of our government, on which his opinion is not sought."*

M.V. Atwood
January 1940 [1]

Frank Gannett's preoccupation with the National Committee to Uphold Constitutional Government – and thwart the New Deal – is apparent in issues of the *Gannetteer* from late 1937 through 1938. Their references to the boss, however, were less related to his newspapers than to his migratory missions on behalf of the committee and the American ideals on which he had been reared.

At the 50th anniversary convocation of Keuka College he called for a "new appreciation by the American people" of the rights and privileges bestowed on them by the Constitution. At the state convention of the Women's Christian Temperance Union in Hornell, N.Y., he warned that despite the successes of the NCUCG, the Supreme Court was still not safe from domination by Franklin Roosevelt.

He appeared before the Union League Club in Chicago and a Lincoln Day Republican rally in Fort Lauderdale. In both, he warned that the president's effort to reorganize the executive branch of the federal government was "quite as dangerous as was the bill for packing the Supreme Court bench." After the Florida speech, the *Gannetteer* reported without attribution that Gannett was touted as the Republican Party's hope for the presidency in 1940. [2]

In Rochester, he was the unanimous choice among 10 candidates for the Rotary Club's Civic Achievement Award for greatest service to the community. In his acceptance speech, he told the Rotarians he had faith that "there are still enough courageous, patriotic Americans to see that any trend toward one-man government is checked once and for all."[3]

One of the reasons Gannett could devote so much time to his non-newspaper activities was that he had a Central Office staff capable of carrying on in his absence. He and Frank Tripp no longer bore the burdens alone.

Leroy Snyder remained Gannett's executive assistant. The two Rochester newspapers could be left in the capable hands of Erwin Davenport. He had come out of retirement two years earlier to become their general manager when his friend Roy Kates succumbed to illness.

Editorial decisions could be entrusted to his managing editors in Rochester, Lafayette R. Blanchard of the *Times-Union* or Joseph T. Adams of the *Democrat and Chronicle*.

Publishers or editors could turn to the Central Office's Matthew G. Sullivan for advice on circulation, J. Frank Duffy for help in advertising, or J.A. Burke for tips on production.

They all knew M.V. Atwood, associate editor of The Gannett Newspapers and head of the News and Editorial Office. Atwood and his colleague, Charles A.S. Freeman, stayed in constant touch with their colleagues through *The Bulletin*, the confidential weekly publication circulated to all Gannett executives. Freeman also edited the *Gannetteer*.

Gannett frequently counseled his executives to train understudies to fill in for them or succeed them if that became necessary. He was at last able to prove that by example and leave the helm whenever the mood struck him or "duty" called.

Summer issues of the *Gannetteer* told of the unsolicited endorsement of Gannett for governor in a front-page editorial by the *Watkins Glen* (N.Y.) *Express*. Some southern New York Republicans began touting him for the Senate, and, again according to the *Gannetteer*, he had been mentioned at a Republican State Executive Committee meeting as a "desirable candidate for governor."[4]

He flew to Moscow, Idaho, to address the American Cooperative Institute. Sounding like a candidate, he said, "If we are to save

America, we must save agriculture." Yet he was not a candidate in the fall of 1938. In fact, he publicly called for a halt by all those promoting him as a senatorial or gubernatorial nominee.

## Opening Skirmishes

If Gannett's early editorial and oratorical attacks on the New Deal were dismissed as pains in the ascendancy of the Roosevelt administration, its legislative defeats at the hands of the National Committee to Uphold Constitutional Government were not. President Roosevelt was angry and Harold Ickes, his secretary of the interior, was apoplectic.

The president denounced criticisms by newspapers "edited from the counting room." Gannett replied, "Of course, a newspaper, to be independent, fearless and in position to render maximum public service to its readers and its community, must be strong financially. . . . But that cannot mean, by any stretch of the imagination, that the editorial policy shall be dictated by the business office."[5]

Roosevelt needed only to recall the strong editorial support he received from a Gannett newspaper, *The Times* of Hartford, Conn., to concede the point of Gannett's rebuttal.

Ickes set an ambush for Gannett in a joint appearance on the radio broadcast, "America's Town Meeting of the Air." The Ickes-Gannett confrontation was both more calculated and more sensational than the publisher's exchange with the president. The topic for their January 1939 radio appearance was "Have We a Free Press in America?" Ickes's position, of course, was the negative.

"Mr. Gannett," he said, "ranks above the average among American publishers. Therefore, if it can be shown that freedom of the press does not exist for the Gannett newspapers, any conclusions drawn from that fact may fairly be applied to the American press generally." The champion of the New Deal then launched a generalized and undocumented attack both on Gannett and newspapers in general.

Gannett demolished one canard immediately. That was Ickes's reference to the loan from the International Paper and Power Company. "Did he tell his readers," Ickes asked, "when he wrote editorials against government ownership of power, that he was in hock to the power interests?"[6]

Whoever did Ickes's research for his frontal assault on Gannett had done the secretary of the interior wrong. Gannett could declare honestly and document it with ample editorial evidence that he had never written "editorials against government ownership of power."

He won considerable sympathy from the studio audience when he responded:

"I was warned not to engage my opponent in any debate. I was warned that he would resort to bitter, unfounded personal attack. That is just what he has done, and I resent it as entirely unfair and unwarranted."

Turning to Ickes's proposition, he said:

"Of course, a free press has flaws. Every freedom produces incidental, inevitable evils. . . . Every freedom is an act of faith. Its outcome cannot be planned. Part of the outcome will be bad. But in a democracy we are confident the good will far outweigh the bad. So it is with all our freedoms.

"Let us be candid regarding freedom of the press. It produces some publishers and editors who put too much of their own bias into the news; some who minimize one side of a news event, emphasize another; some who paint their enemies too black, their friends too white. Press freedom produces evils – at times, perhaps, *great* evils. Every freedom has to be operated by persons who, by original and inherent human nature, are imperfect. Publishers are human beings who have their ideals but also frailties.

"What we must look at is not errors of individual publishers, but the total performance of the entire press. Looking at that performance the country over, no one can truly say our press is not both free and fair. . . .

"What, in reality, does Mr. Ickes' proposition mean? Simply this. That, after a period of agitation by government spokesmen, we may expect bills to be drafted and passed of such a nature that any newspaper that opposes the administration will be in danger of prosecution of some kind, or of censorship. And this will bring about a situation where the one great essential of democracy, namely a free press, will no longer fearlessly inform the public about the public's business."[7]

Soon after the debate, Ickes denounced as unfair Gannett newspapers' treatment of his role in the debate. The Gannett Company's Plainfield, N.J., *Courier-News* challenged him and sent him press clippings of its coverage of the debate. In a letter to the editor, Ickes conceded that the space given to him by the *Courier-News* matched that given to Gannett and that its coverage was fair.

All this, according to Williamson, had an unintended result:

"Instead of blasting Gannett from the scene, it made him more of a public figure than ever. Gannett continued to oppose what he regarded as further attempts to consolidate presidential power."[8]

# Dinner with the Boss

Gannett returned occasionally from his ideological duels to renew his ties with his managers. In the News and Editorial conference in Rochester in June 1939 he presided, as usual, at the closing dinner. It was in this forum that he regularly reassured and recharged his editors.

The issue was kowtowing to advertisers, sources of revenue whom Gannett both courted and resisted. He told the editors:

"I am glad to see that you are not in favor of scattering comics throughout newspapers because advertisers think it might spread interest through the paper.

"Past experience shows that to spread comics gives the reader the impression that we are carrying fewer comics. . . . Furthermore, it is an inconvenience to the reader. . . .

"There are a lot of things that advertisers would like to have done to newspapers to help them, but they lose sight of the fact that they are helped best when the readers of newspapers are served and given first consideration, both in makeup . . . and in the handling of news."[9]

Back on the ideological trail later that month, Gannett sent a wire to every member of Congress denouncing Roosevelt's $4-billion "lend-spend bill." It was, he said, "a most flagrant approach to the purchase of an election with taxpayers' money and [an indication] that the president has thrown his hat in the ring for a third term."[10]

In a letter to his wife in November 1939, Gannett wrote, "Everyone thinks I am the man they want for president – at least they tell my men so."[11]

Well, not quite "everyone."

Florence Messman, Gannett's secretary for more than 31 years, said John Broderick, Republican Party chairman for Monroe County, was not enthusiastic. Then there was "this man at Bausch & Lomb, very high in the Republican Party," she remembered. "[He] called me and asked me if I could dissuade [Gannett] from running. And I said, 'Listen, why don't you call Mrs. Gannett?' Who was I to dissuade him from running?"[12]

Richard Polenberg points to a letter from Amos Pinchot to Edward A. Rumely, both close friends of Gannett and co-founders of the National Committee to Uphold Constitutional Government. Pinchot wrote that he had tried to dampen Gannett's enthusiasm with some political realities.

"I don't think I impressed him much," he said, "for no one has tried to modify Frank's extravagant ideas of his strength. . . . Frank is so inexperienced and naive in politics that he has no natural self-protection. The whole thing is new to him. He doesn't catch on or understand it. He is wandering around like a child in a glorious dream."[13]

Henry Clune, who worked full-time for the *Democrat and Chronicle* in Rochester until 1971, when he was 79, explained:

"They talked him into that presidential thing. The last person that told Mr. Gannett he was a great man, he believed. And that man kind of fell into favor."[14]

# The Glorious Dream

By December, after a Gannett speaking tour of the Pacific Coast, the *Gannetteer* was reporting about "demands he had received from every state to present himself as a candidate for the Republican nomination for the presidency."

The publisher responded:

"It is true that great pressure is being put on me. . . . I have never been ambitious for political office and have several times refused to be a candidate. . . . It is difficult to understand why anyone should seek the office merely for the power and position it affords. No American, however, would decline the nomination if it were offered him. I am, of course, giving my possible candidacy careful consideration." [15]

Gannett editors gathered in Rochester in January 1940 for the semi-annual "fall" News and Editorial Meeting. Busy as he was, Gannett sought to attend these sessions to provide an inspirational benediction to men he valued as friends and respected as professional associates.

At the closing dinner, Atwood introduced the boss:

"It is no news to any of you that he may soon be called upon to assume greater public responsibilities even than he has yet shouldered. FEG, we are looking forward eagerly and sympathetically to the important message which I know you have for us tonight." [16]

Gannett first assured his audience that the group was doing well. He may have startled skeptics among them by announcing that a recent survey had shown printing and publishing to be paying top wages and that "our company was tops in the list. Years ago I concerned myself with the difference in pay between men in the newsroom and men in the composing room. I determined to correct that."[17]

He predicted that the Democrats would nominate Roosevelt to run for an unprecedented third term. He generalized about newspaper production, even acknowledged that there was greater optimism that the Allies would win in Europe. Then he turned to what Atwood had hinted:

"I am still wearing the same size hat as I wore before I started my trip West. I was impressed by the demand that I take leadership of the Republican Party. I shall announce my decision soon. If I am a candidate for the presidency, I hope you men will keep your heads. Continue to be newspapermen. Print the news fairly, but give me at least an even break. . . . I know I'll have your sympathy. Treat me as you would any other candidate. But don't treat me any worse." [18]

Less than a week later, on Jan. 16, 1940, 1,400 Rochesterians gathered at the Powers Hotel for what was billed as a testimonial dinner for Gannett. According to reports, every nook and cranny of the hotel that would accommodate a dining table was pressed into service.

The "testimonials" surprised few of the guests. A procession of dignitaries urged Gannett to do what he wanted them to urge him to do. The president of the Gannett Company bowed to "everyone's" wishes and declared that he hoped to be the Republicans' standard bearer.

He resigned his chairmanship of the National Committee to Uphold Constitutional Government and from the board of the AP to protect both, he said, from the taint of partisanship. With that, he set his sights on the White House, expecting that the Republican Party would be unable to choose between Sen. Robert A. Taft of Ohio and Gov. Thomas E. Dewey of New York and turn to him as its nominee. [19]

# Chapter 11

# A Reach Too Far

*"Politics has got so expensive that it takes lots of money to even get beat with."*
*Will Rogers* [1]

Frank Gannett, who never did anything by half, launched a free-spending, physically demanding six-month campaign. He and his staff traveled 55,000 miles for 150 speeches in 38 states. Florence Messman recalled that "he took off in his plane and did not really return to Rochester until after the Philadelphia convention." [2]

The biggest trip she made with him was to California. "When I left," she said, "I told my husband I'd be away three days." It was more than a week. Storms forced the plane south from its intended destination of Fargo, N.D. The party landed in St. Louis, then went north through Wyoming, into Washington, then south to California.

The physical demands were not on Gannett alone.

"One time he rapped on my door at night," Messman said. "'Florence, you're keeping me awake with your typewriter.'

"And I said, 'How the hell do you think you're going to get a speech in your hand tomorrow noon' – he'd dictate after he came in in the evening, for the next day's noon – 'if I don't work all night?'" [3]

The *Gannetteer* recounted Gannett's flying tours to all parts of the land. It remarked on the success of a trip to Nebraska and Kansas, which won him pledges of support from Democrats opposed to a third term for a U.S. president. It described the travels of Caroline Gannett, who was stumping New York State for her husband.

# Campaign Literature

Frank Gannett had no publication to keep his name before the voters, but his candidacy was promoted by two professionally produced vehicles. The first was a subsidized biography of the candidate written by an employee of *The New York Times,* Samuel T. Williamson.

It was a typical campaign document portraying the rags-to-riches aspects of Gannett's life. It emphasized his humble origins, described his indoctrination in "true" American values and documented his success in creating a newspaper empire.

*Imprint of a Publisher* was its name. Eight years later it was expanded into a complete, authorized biography. In a preface to the 1948 volume, Williamson described the 1940 campaign version:

"My first was shorter and as inclusive as I could make it in the time at my disposal; but it was turned out in considerable haste so as to be in the hands of delegates and alternates to the Republican National Convention of 1940." [4]

The second piece of campaign artillery billed itself as a "documentary motion picture." On today's television it would be a 15-minute infomercial.

The introductory crawl, in its entirety, read:

"The American Institute of Motion Pictures is privileged to present to the American public the first of a series of documentary motion pictures on outstanding personalities qualified for the presidency of the United States. These presentations are accurate portrayals of the candidate, his aims, policies and principles."

In the affected newsreel style of the day, a stentorian narrator defied heavy background music to describe the perils facing the nation and Frank Gannett's unique qualifications to deal with them.

The film opened with terrifying scenes of warfare in Europe, food lines, urban rubble, crying babies, air raids and naval bombardments.

"Amidst this world-wide madness," said the voiceover, "the people of the United States demand a leader who believes we can best fulfill our destinies at home. Such a leader is Frank Gannett, outstanding newspaper publisher of Rochester, N.Y. . . . The wars of the world must not blind us to the great failures of the New Deal these past seven years."

The soundtrack reminded viewers of unemployment at 10 million, mounting national debt, distressed agriculture and depressed industry. As the camera panned front pages of every newspaper in the Gannett Group, the narrator described Gannett's business acumen, his phenomenal success and the continued employment of a workforce of 4,000 through the Depression.

"Government is a vast business, running in the red," the narrator said, "and requires a sound, successful businessman to put it on a sound basis."

The film echoed the Williamson biography in relating the "simple and humble surroundings [in which] he was schooled in the principles of true Americanism." It recounted his childhood, his education and his early newspaper career.

Its most misleading exaggeration was its home-and-hearth stage setting for this always-busy publisher, his socially active wife and the two children who spent much of their time in schools away from home.

To the proselytizing filmmaker, the Gannetts had "those qualities of wholesomeness and stability which go to make up a real American family." To wit:

- Action shots of the entire family playing Ping-Pong doubles, from which "Mrs. Gannett derives as much pleasure . . . as the others."
- Sally discussing plans for her college education while her mother smiles and knits.
- Ten-year-old "Dickie" [Dixon] Gannett sitting on the lap of his 63-year-old father, who is reading the comics aloud, while the narrator assures the readers that "the two are great pals."
- The elder Gannetts playing Chinese checkers, "with the children retired for the evening."

The final three minutes of the film featured Gannett himself giving a speech for the camera before an imaginary audience. He was an experienced speaker but his voice was weak and tremulous.

After restating the film's stirring promises that he would restore industrial growth, agricultural prosperity, amity between capital and labor, and full employment, the publisher closed with an uncertainty to match the quality of his voice:

"If I am chosen to lead, I'll lead to the best of my ability. If it is mine to follow, to fight in the ranks as I have fought, there you'll find me, fighting."

## The Gannett Message

Gannett frequently warned his editors against excesses in their editorials:
- "Vigor doesn't mean viciousness."
- "Attack erroneous measures and conditions – not the men who may be blind agents of such forces."
- "Try to be constructive. Dynamite the slums but be sure you have a plan for rebuilding."
- "Give your readers something hopeful. They can get fed up on denunciation." [5]

Editors and listeners aware of his admonitions were hard-pressed to identify those ideals in his campaign oratory. Richard Polenberg of Cornell says the publisher explained his strategy to a friend:

"The majority of Republican leaders are dead set against every bit of the New Deal, and it weakens my position to pay tribute to any part of it." [6]

He was so busy on the campaign that he could not speak to the closing dinner of the semi-annual meeting of editors in late May. Instead, he assembled them in his Rochester office for a special morning session.

There was little talk of newspapers, much of politics. "I am pleased with the result of the tour I am making, and find much enthusiasm," he said.

The president/publisher/candidate told the editors, "If nothing came out of my campaigning, our papers will be better known." Then he said, "If I don't get the nomination, I'll have a happy place to go – back into the newspapers." [7]

# Changing Times

As the Republican convention approached, Gannett reacted swiftly to current events in hopes of bolstering his chances of nomination. He hastily appeared on Gannett radio station WHEC in Rochester on June 11, 1940, to reply to President Roosevelt. The day before, the president had told the graduating class at the University of Virginia of Italy's announced state of war against France.

"On this tenth day of June 1940," Roosevelt said, "the hand that held the dagger has struck it into the back of its neighbor."

True to his determination that the United States should not get involved in Europe, Gannett told his radio audience:

"On the whole it was a belligerent and skillfully inflammatory speech in which Mr. Roosevelt made commitments he had no right to make without congressional action. It sounded more like the utterances of a dictator than those of a chief executive elected by the people of a republic."

He warned the audience that the United States was woefully unprepared for war and urged them to "write, wire or telephone your representative and senator not to permit Congress to be adjourned until this critical moment has passed." [8]

*The Bulletin* kept Gannett editors informed on the activities of their boss and the reactions of group newspapers:

"There was divergent Group editorial opinion on the president's speech at Charlottesville, in which he lambasted the dictators again and pledged support to the Allies. These ranged from close to 100 percent approval in *The Hartford Times* to expression of grave fears by the *Times-Union* [FEG's pulpit] that the president came close to a declaration of war without authorization by Congress." [9]

Other observations in the same *Bulletin* are worth noting:

"So far there appears to have been little witch-hunting in Group cities.

"One editor, unfortunately, does report that the head of a leading fraternal order said he had the names of 300 'traitors.' When asked what proof he had, [the 'patriot'] replied: "Oh, from things they've said.' Three of the suspects, [the editor] said, were fellow lodge members who, as loyal Irish, had spoken their minds about England.

"Utica has a population which is [one] quarter Italian. Both Group papers did a wise thing in printing, in English and Italian, 'A Statement to Italians of Utica.' It was signed by prominent Italian citizens. Writes Joe Torbett [editor at Utica]:

" 'This resulted from fear that innocent Italians would be persecuted by over-zealous persons the minute war was declared by Italy. The subject was discussed with some prominent Italians, who thought the papers themselves should run statements urging Italians to keep level heads. I thought the statement would be more effective if signed by Italian leaders. The only adverse criticism heard came to one of the men who signed the statement. It was from an Italian who said he was a good American and no one had a right to suspect him.' " [10]

## The Zealous Campaigner

Gannett quickly turned the Nazi occupation of France into a primer on the perils besetting the United States. On the backs of the pages of a speech he had planned to deliver in Springfield, Ill., on June 13, Gannett dashed off a handwritten substitute. He mourned the fate of France and praised the history of sacrifice that characterized that nation.

"It is no wonder," he wrote, "that we in our intense sympathy for this latest victim of the aggressor should be utterly sick at heart over the defeat of another democracy.

"What a lesson for America!

"In a few days the Republican Party will hold its convention in Philadelphia. Upon the delegates that will assemble there rests a tremendous responsibility, the greatest since the party was born. . . .

"[France's] downfall began under the administration of Leon Blum, who put in force a New Deal much like that we have had here for seven and a half years.

"Under such policies a great nation became soft, lost interest in its rich heritage, began to depend on government for everything, expecting the abundant life without work or effort. . . .

"Hitler, when rising to power, said:

" 'It gives us National Socialists special secret pleasure to see how the people around us are unaware of what is really happening to them.'

"Isn't that just our situation? We don't know what is happening to us. In the name of social reform, social gains and social security, the abundant life and other similar fine-sounding phrases we have been following disastrous theories, worshipping false gods.

"It is a critical time in our history, the most critical since the founding of the Republic. The times call for a rebirth of patriotism, a revival of the spirit of our forefathers, a readiness to sacrifice for others, and most of all a rebirth of rightness and religion, a new vital interest in the teachings of Our Savior." [11]

# At the Convention

*The Bulletin,* in the words of author M.V. Atwood, expressed "the sentiments of all Group editors" to Gannett on "the last lap of [his] vigorous campaign":

"It is a grand fighting campaign you have put on, one that has seldom been equalled in a pre-convention canvass. But that, of course, is the only kind you would be interested in. When you go after things – you go after 'em!" [12]

The Gannett forces lumbered into Philadelphia in June for the Republican National Convention with three elephant mascots, the usual noisy marching bands and fluttering banners. Their hospitality suite was remarkable for the intoxicants available at its bar, which was a source of quiet ridicule among some veteran Gannett employees but made it quite popular with the press. That was verified by *The*

*Bulletin,* which boasted:

"Newspapermen in Philadelphia paid him high tribute when one columnist gave him top ranking for amiability and knowing how to meet the press. FEG is considered 'one of the boys' among working correspondents."[13]

Polenberg described Gannett's "abrupt awakening. He had counted on a deadlock between Ohio Sen. Robert M. Taft and New York Gov. Thomas E. Dewey, in which event, he thought, he would emerge as the logical compromise. Instead, the convention chose Wendell Willkie, who, like Gannett, was a businessman with no previous political experience, but who was a much more charismatic figure."[14]

The former candidate supported Willkie's campaign against Franklin Roosevelt, but it hurt. He wrote to his wife, "I am a little bit sore that he should reap the benefits of the fights that I waged."[15]

Gannett was wiser but poorer. Estimates by associates on what he spent range as high as $650,000. His overreaching political effort surely cost him half a million 1940 dollars, almost all of which was his own money.

Would-be presidential candidate Gannett ran into a political stonewall that he simply could not see, even though powerful friends who knew much more about politics told him it was there. His oratorical assaults on the New Deal, and by implication on Roosevelt, would reverberate in public suspicion of his newspapers long after he had lost his appetite for the presidency.

# Chapter 12

# On the Home Front

*"The institution that means more than any other to the preservation of the American way of life is the newspaper. It is the bulwark of all our liberties."*
Frank Tripp<br>November 1941 [1]

While as a presidential hopeful Frank Gannett intermittently touched base with his newspapers, the managers of those properties constantly debated their professional responsibilities.

Successive issues of *The Bulletin* reflected both their parochial concerns and broader common issues, such as how prominently to display the war news from abroad. The newsletter's approach illustrated Gannett's emphasis on the editorial autonomy of his newspapers and the need for publishers and editors to understand the individuality of their communities.

*The Bulletin's* practice was to describe a situation and how one Gannett paper dealt with it. For instance, Franklin R. Little, general manager and publisher, sought to dramatize to his employees and the community the economic importance of the *Ogdensburg Journal* and the *Massena Observer*.

He met the January payroll (which included the apportioned shares of 1939's profits) in silver dollars. The order was beyond the capacity of the Ogdensburg bank, so a sack containing 95 pounds of silver dollars had to be shipped from New York City.

More frequently, *The Bulletin* posed editorial dilemmas and then asked other editors and publishers what they would have done:

"*The Newburgh News* published on Page 1 a three-column photo of a wrecked automobile, showing plainly the faces of two persons killed in the accident. . . . We'll be glad to hear from other Group editors as to whether they would have used a picture of this kind."

John Bowen of the Albany *Knickerbocker News* replied:

113

"It is against policy here to run such death pictures and also any morbid scenes like a coffin, even in a funeral procession. The same prohibition is applied to gangster pictures, etc."

But Fred Keefe of Newburgh explained why his paper published the photo: "Because of the large local circulation of the New York papers, we have become accustomed to gruesome pictures and things of that sort and the publication of the one referred to created no comment whatever." [2]

Free publicity was a pestilence demanding constant vigilance:

"Em Evans, managing editor of the *Utica Press,* calls attention to some publicity put out by the Bureau of Motor Vehicles. It is a two-column mat of a 'drive safely' calendar carrying at the bottom the script trademark signature of Pepsi-Cola. The sheet accompanying the mat from the bureau frankly states that the calendar 'is made available by the Pepsi-Cola Company.' Group editors all have a handy place to consign such material." [3]

M.V. Atwood wrote angrily in *The Bulletin* about what he considered unjust criticisms of the press in any guise. Early in 1940, he identified a villain at Columbia University whose name would become synonymous in *The Bulletin* with treachery:

"The *Olean Times-Herald* devoted more than five columns the other day to a report on textbooks charged with being unsympathetic with American ideas and democracy. The material was presented at a meeting of the Olean Chapter of the DAR. Textbooks were those written by Prof. Harold B. Rugg of Columbia University. It was a book by Rugg which has been criticized recently by advertising organizations as being hostile to advertising and belittling its function in modern distribution." [4]

At the semi-annual editors' meeting in Rochester in May, the associate editor stoked the fires:

"Atwood presented in more detail the danger to newspapers of unintelligent criticism of them on the part of some professional groups, especially teachers. He gave a report on the inaccurate and unfriendly treatment in 'Citizenship and Civic Affairs' by Harold Rugg, whose textbooks have been subject to much criticism of late.

Atwood said he thought editors should inquire of their own children and others if an unfriendliness toward newspapers and newspaper workers is expressed in school classrooms. . . . He was requested to make available to the Group copies of a talk, 'The Public Responsibility of the Newspaper,' which he had found effective for use before groups known in advance to be critical and unfriendly to newspapers. This will be done."[5]

## Don't Hype the War

The editors were quite aware of Frank Gannett's strong opposition to any U.S. involvement in the war in Europe. They were personally concerned that the war news coverage in their papers be fair and unsensational. This was a major topic at their May 1940 meeting.

Joseph Torbett, managing editor at Utica, spoke of "the importance of keeping war news objective, and despite general sympathy for the Allies, to avoid emotion-creating words, especially in heads.

"In Utica, he said 'We qualify headlines and do not print as accomplished facts the claims of either side. We delete from war stories glittering generalities and any colorful adjectives that show bias.'

The editors debated the use of bold headlines, the wisdom of compiling war news from a variety of sources, how to distinguish rumor from fact, and the impact of war coverage on their budgets. In that last regard, *The Bulletin* reported:

"A letter from Kent Cooper of the AP . . . [referred] to announced increases in charges to newspapers and contemplated increases of competing press associations. He asked if Gannett editors wished an expansion of the war service if it entailed extra assessments. [Atwood] was instructed to notify Mr. Cooper there was no feeling that the service should be amplified, and certainly no desire for increased assessments. Rather the desire was for a more compact, usable report, one giving a broader, general picture and fewer minute details."[6]

The same issue cited examples "of emotional heads in an old newspaper of great prestige, and not published in hectic New York City." It referred to a May 11 headline,

**Poilus, Tommies Stop Hun Hordes**

and added:

"Those who recall World War I will notice the similarity in technique. This week also [Newspaper Enterprise Association] came through with a strip of war-horror pictures in which captions and cutlines were extremely emotional. Pictures were of civilian casualties, both buildings and persons. Top line was ' "Military Objectives" in the War for "Living Space."' Caption over cut of tanks, 'Mechanized Death: "Made in Germany." ' "[7]

Ray McKinney, national advertising representative for Gannett newspapers, joined the chorus of concern:

"I suggest the press of this country . . . eliminate the name Hitler in every news story and picture. Nothing hurts a narcissus complex like being ignored. In every reference to Germany, say Germany, not Hitler or Nazi. . . . Each day the newspapers scream: Hitler Attacks! Hitler's Army Takes Paris!! Hitler Bombs England!!! In the first place it isn't true. It isn't accurate. German Army Attacks! Germans Occupy Paris!! German Planes Bomb England!!! is correct. I say this in all seriousness and I believe it will produce results."

*The Bulletin* replied:

"With the principle we agree. But a newspaper must print news. If Hitler makes a speech it is news. An editor can't say a German made it. But editors must accept the responsibility of deciding how big news it is, how big the play. With the suggestion that it's better not to personify the Germans in Hitler, we agree. Ray's right in saying his suggested heads are more accurate. But we prefer Nazi to German as fairer to the German people, not all of whom by a jugful approve [of] Nazi ruthlessness."[8]

# Changing Policies

By mid-summer of 1940, the Democrats had nominated Franklin Roosevelt to seek a third term and National Guard units were mobilizing for encampments and military maneuvers to test their readiness for war. Both realities affected Gannett editors and managers.

*The Times* in Hartford, for instance, had been soul-searching its past since suggesting, just before the Democratic convention, that the party consider nominating Wendell Willkie, the Republican standard bearer, for president.

In July, it announced that for the first time in nearly half a century, it would not support a Democratic presidential candidate. The National Guard maneuvers and the prospect of the nation's first peacetime draft were not lost on Gannett management. General manager Frank Tripp wrote to all publishers that labor laws and union regulations permitting, the company would "hold for any man called to military service the position which he leaves to enter the service until such time as he is released by the government."

He reminded publishers that in hiring replacements they had to make "plain at the time of employment of any person to fill a vacancy thus caused that the duration of his employment is for the period of absence of the drafted employee and he should be caused to sign an understanding to that effect." [9]

Also that month, the number of Gannett newspapers grew to 20 with a Sunday newspaper in Ogdensburg. The *Advance-News*, published daily and Sunday, had been a competitor of Gannett's Ogdensburg *Journal*. It folded as a daily publication but was bought and continued as a Sunday paper by the Gannett subsidiary, the Northern New York Publishing Company, of which Franklin R. Little was general manager and publisher.

*The Bulletin* explained that the Sunday paper would be put out by *The Journal* staff, along with a few former *Advance-News* workers, that days off during the week would be given to those who worked on the Sunday paper, and that the paper's editorial position "was and will remain Democratic."

In the Good News/Bad News category, the economic outlook was bright for Rochester's *Democrat and Chronicle,* which boasted a 64-page paper on Aug. 15. The outlook for the general economy was less bright. Thirty-nine of those 64 pages listed Monroe County sales of property for unpaid taxes.

# 'Fair' or 'Foul'?

As the presidential campaign intensified, Gannett editors were especially concerned about evenhanded treatment of the candidates. *The Bulletin* reported on the use of two special features, "Presidential Battle Page" and "Both Sides." The first was offered to newspapers free by the Chicago Tribune-New York News Syndicate. It comprised parallel columns describing the Republican and Democratic campaigns and used material furnished by each party's national committee.

"Both Sides" was produced by The Associated Press and discussed campaign issues from Republican and Democratic viewpoints. The feature was intended to present both sides in parallel columns in a single publication. *The Bulletin* pointed out that some papers were publishing the two sides separately, in successive editions. "It seems to us," *The Bulletin* said, "this is not nearly as effective as the parallel column presentation."

Roosevelt easily won a third term. The presses printing that news had hardly stopped rolling before the curmudgeonly Harold Ickes was again denouncing newspapers. He may have been rankled by the once-loyal *Times* in Hartford, which threw its editorial support in the election to Willkie. The only Gannett newspaper that did not support the Republican challenger was its newest, Ogdensburg's Sunday *Advance-News.* That curiosity was addressed by *The Bulletin* of Dec. 5, 1940, which explained:

"The *Advance-News* has been a Democratic paper for years, and its political policy was continued when purchased by the Northern New York Publishing Company."

In any event, Ickes was still indignantly insisting that the press was not free. Newspapermen proud of their profession and their organization were not about to tolerate such slanders from the man who had tried to ambush their boss in that long-ago radio debate.

Tripp responded in remarks to Gannett advertising executives at their fall meeting in Rochester in November. He warned that attacks on the press were subtle propaganda by enemies of democracy and freedom. "Whenever you hear a jibe," he said, "don't laugh it off."

At the editors' semi-annual meeting two weeks later, the question of defending newspapers from such attacks was dominant.

*The Bulletin* summarized the issue: "It is already clear that hostility to the press, which has so characterized President Roosevelt's previous administrations, is not going to be lessened in his third term."

Atwood challenged the editors:

"When we speak up for the newspaper, we are not only speaking up for our bread and butter, but for just about everything Americans hold dear. It is not merely fine language or special pleading when we say that freedom of the press is a basic freedom – yes, **the** basic freedom. Without it no other freedom can long exist.

"No one has any cause to apologize for the newspaper of today, despite its admitted imperfections. The least every editor can do, therefore, is to speak up for it forthrightly and instantly whenever it is attacked, either by those enemies on whose toes it has trod or by honest critics whose opposition is based both on lack of knowledge of the history and nature of the newspaper and [of] the functions which it should and must perform if it is to endure." [10]

# Chapter 13

# Over There

*"I yield to no one in my real sympathy for the British and in my intense desire to help them in every possible way, but not to the point of involving us in actual warfare."*

Frank Gannett<br>May 1941

The day-to-day distractions of editing and publishing gradually grew less significant as the menacing effects of the war in Europe spread to the United States.

Gannett executives remained attentive to *The Bulletin's* catalog of group ideas, innovations and concerns. They continued to participate in its round-robin approach to problem-solving. They were torn, however, between Frank Gannett's unwavering opposition to U.S. involvement in the spreading war and the growing evidence that such involvement was inevitable.

They hoped to continue to serve their communities, improve their newspapers, and increase the prosperity of the company. Stability was necessary for them to do that but their situations rapidly grew more unstable. Military mobilization was beginning to reduce their staffs. Prices were rising, particularly for newsprint and metals, and even for buyers undeterred by cost, those necessary materials were becoming scarcer.

Even the freedom that newspapermen knew as a constitutional birthright was at risk, on the official grounds of national security. They expressed the hope for a system of voluntary restraint by responsible editors even as they feared an unspecific censorship code administered by improvising, overzealous military officers.

# Stressing the Basics

Editors and publishers bemused by the clouds of war were frequently reminded by *The Bulletin* not to take the routine for granted. The Jan. 16, 1941, issue, for instance, suggested a New Year's resolution to meet press deadlines.

"Editors become careless about this," it said, "and soon find their papers late in getting to press. Then they must spend several days trying to break a habit of delays which should not have been permitted in the first place."

"[W]ars, threats of wars, and defense plans dominate Page 1 these days," the Jan. 23 issue said. "Of course these things have to be reported and covered as fully as possible by newspapers. But wouldn't it be a good idea to deliberately plan that no day shall pass without Page 1 containing a human-interest story or a story with some humor?"

The Feb. 6 *Bulletin* observed that a number of Gannett newspapers seldom printed letters to the editor. While it did not order a lockstep approach on letters, *The Bulletin* did mention that a number of group papers ran letters to the editor daily, and in the same place. "Not only do letters have great reader interest," it said, "but it also shows the paper is ready to give space to all reasonable and temperately expressed opinions, whether or not they agree with those of the editorial policy of the newspaper."

The variations in size and resources among Gannett newspapers were vividly illustrated by publication of the woes of a small newspaper whose staff was beset by illness. The author was Harry Stutz, managing editor of *The Ithaca Journal*, who wrote in haste:

"We have emerged from the devastation caused by the spread of flu throughout the plant. Two weeks ago Monday I came in the office to discover that Waters and Cochran were off the news desk and two of four city reporters were in bed; one went to bed that afternoon and the business manager, the circulation manager, two advertising solicitors and two men in the circulation department also were down and out and within 24 hours six men of the mechanical staff also were hit. That, incidentally, was the week we produced one of the largest Winter Dollar Day numbers in our history. I discovered that week what a really loyal organization we have and how much can be done by honest to goodness devotion and willingness to do more than one's share.

"Our proofreader, a union printer, helped us out materially on the copy desk. My secretary, Miss McNally, helped in the proof room all week. Louis Pickering, our advertising manager, delivered in his own car a considerable part of our city papers to our newsboys. Everybody helped and some of the union printers worked six days and some day men were willing to come back and do night work too. It was really a most gratifying and thrilling experience." [1]

Stutz's good news about "one of the largest Winter Dollar Day numbers" was par for the Gannett course. Matt Sullivan was reporting "substantial increases" in circulation for all Gannett newspapers, morning, evening and Sunday.

|  | 1938 | 1939 | + | % | 1940 | + | % |
|---|---|---|---|---|---|---|---|
| A.M. | 104,063 | 106,443 | 2,380 | +2.2 | 109,287 | 2,844 | +2.7 |
| P.M. | 371,255 | 373,980 | 2,725 | +0.7 | 386,906 | 12,926 | +3.5 |
| Sun. | 178,816 | 185,616 | 6,800 | +3.8 | 194,210 | 8,594 | +4.6 |
| TOTAL | 654,134 | 666,039 | 11,905 | +1.8 | 690,403 | 24,364 | +3.7 |

He also reported revenue per thousand copies, with Newburgh leading the pack. That was because Newburgh had raised its prices to 5 cents per copy and 25 cents per week. "Although it still shows an expected drop in circulation," he reported, "the publisher feels that the situation is satisfactory to advertisers." That was confirmed by Newburgh's leading the group in revenue per thousand copies, at $31.29. The next highest was $21.84 in Plainfield, N.J.; the lowest, $15.05 in Elmira.

Sullivan reminded editors and publishers of the drain of unpaid printed copies. "An average of one unpaid copy of a daily newspaper," he reminded those slow in arithmetic, "piles up to over 300 copies in a year."[2]

# Those Blue Pencils

Hopes for voluntary rather than imposed censorship remained strong among Gannett editors when M.V. Atwood gently illustrated the importance of editorial responsibility. *The Bulletin* of March 27 reported that the managing editor of the *Elmira Telegram* had submitted to parents a feature that quoted their daughter about "blind dating" at Cornell. The grateful father confirmed the editor's guess that the parents would not like to see the story in print. It was not published.

True to the restraints of autonomy, *The Bulletin* observed:

"On feature stories, such a checkup with interested persons is well worthwhile for building good will for the paper. But in the case of an important spot story, the approach should be to verify facts, rather than to have the persons concerned determine whether the story shall run. That's a decision for the editor."

A week later, *The Bulletin* was able to report progress on Atwood's efforts to alter, if not censor, the works of the enemy at Columbia University.

"[L]ast year we presented in some detail some inaccuracies in the treatment of newspapers in 'Citizenship and Public Affairs,' by Dr. Harold Rugg. We sent copies to Dr. Rugg and to the publishers. Dr. Rugg never replied but the publishers did. We have now received a copy of the latest edition of the book in which practically all the inaccurate and misleading passages have been revised. The picture of newspapers the book as a whole now presents is not at all bad."

The question of genuine military censorship arose in New York harbor, where a damaged British battleship docked in full view. The wire services had reported the ship's arrival, but marked the item "not for publication" at the request of Frank Knox, secretary of the Navy and a newspaper publisher from Chicago.

Joe Torbett, whose Utica *Observer-Dispatch* was one of two Gannett papers to run the story – the Plainfield *Courier-News* was the other – precipitated corporate soul-searching with this explanation:

"A battleship anchored in New York harbor in view of millions is not exactly secret, but I doubt the wisdom of Knox in asserting we should censor such news because the British do it.

"The city edition of *The New York Times* did not have the story, but *The Tribune* carried it on Page 1 with a picture. My edition of *The Mirror* did not have the story, but *The News* used the full back page for a picture, with an arrow pointing to a hole in the ship's hull.

"AP carried several notes to editors explaining why it was not sending the news for publication. Finally, at 11:30 Monday morning the AP came through with a statement from Knox commending that part of the press which did not report 'the recent arrival of a British man-of-war in this country.' . . .

"We used a short story on the arrival, rewritten from *The Tribune*. All of us agreed that was the thing to do in this particular instance."[3]

Torbett's detailed explanation of his editorial judgment prompted a polite but detailed rebuke. *The Bulletin* commended as "on sounder ground" those papers that did not print the news of the British warship's arrival in New York harbor. It gave these reasons:

"1. Under voluntary censorship, Secretary Knox had asked specifically that such items not be printed.

"2. It was the first instance to come up of an item on a subject specified in advance as desirable not to publicize.

"3. Even though printing may seem harmless, the fact that Colonel Knox is himself a newspaperman would suggest there are reasons for the request which do not appear on the surface.

"4. Attitude of press on it was bound to be watched closely as an indication of how voluntary censorship would work.

"5. Not abiding by the request might be considered to indicate a belief that under press freedom there is no type of item whatsoever, if it can be obtained, that should not be printed.

"6. Or it might imply that statements made – not officially or binding we admit – by newspaper groups that newspapers recognize some kinds of news should not be printed, either did not express the feelings of all newspapers, or that the statement had been insincere.

"7. Merely printing news of arrival – probably harmless enough as it could not be kept secret – is almost sure to be elaborated into information about condition of vessel and disposal to be made of it. Such information might not be so easy for spies to obtain without newspaper aid."

Syndicated columnist Raymond Clapper was cited in support of *The Bulletin's* dismay. "[A] prolonged exhibition of lack of restraint and cooperation . . . will certainly lead to demand for imposed censorship. . . . This is a case where democracy can save its free press only by practicing self-restraint."

In a "yes, but" response, *The Bulletin* agreed with Harold Sanford, managing editor of Rochester's *Democrat and Chronicle*, that "Knox should not have objected to printing mere news of ship's arrival and even picture, but that details such as name of ship, geographical place damaged, etc., not obvious to persons along waterfront should not have been used."

Then it added, "[A]nd yet since Knox had asked in advance omission and no general newspaper protest had been made, we think newspapers' position would have been better if they had lived up literally to the request in this first incident."[4]

Censorship, voluntary or imposed, was not going to be easy.

# Mixed Emotions

When Gannett editors gathered in Rochester for their semi-annual conference in May, domestic and foreign issues competed for their attention. Their professional agenda centered on advertisements designed to look like news stories, what women like in newspapers and the gloomy effect of war news on their newspapers.

At the dinner, Frank Gannett's main topic was the war, but he touched, as usual, on the newspapers. "Our job," he told the editors, "is to make newspapers more indispensable." He praised their circulation gains, said they would have to fight harder for advertising dollars, and acknowledged the likelihood that many newspapers would follow Newburgh's lead and charge five cents per copy.

To the editors, he conceded, "I expect that we shall get into this war but we should fight against it until the last." Again he expressed deep feelings for Great Britain, but warned, "If we get into the war, our form of government will perish, and we'll pay in lives and money.

"After this war Great Britain is going to be ruined in every way, and if we get into it, we'll go down with her." And, he predicted, "There'll be a depression which will make the last one look like a picnic.

"I don't take the position any more of criticizing the president," he said. "I want to help him. But when this question of peace or war is before us, we have a right to free discussion." [5]

## State of the Fourth Estate

Dr. Virgil D. Reed, acting director of the Bureau of the Census, had spoken at the 1941 meeting of the American Society of Newspaper Editors. That prompted *The Bulletin* to recall some encouraging statistics from the 1940 census. For the calendar year 1939 there were:

- 2,040 daily newspapers, with circulation of 42,966,000.
- 6,209 weeklies (5,000 copies or more), with circulation of 19,296,000.

Daily and weekly circulation, 62,262,000, was the greatest ever reported by the census, and the average family was spending nearly $10 a year for newspapers.

Total revenues for 1939 were $845,687,000, of which $539,495,000 was advertising, $306,192,000 subscription and sales. *The Bulletin* hastened to point out that those revenues did not equal 1929's all-time total of more than $1 billion, but the 1939 circulation receipts were a record. Advertising, on the other hand, was more than $250 million below 1929's $797 million.

In 40 years, average circulation of the U.S. daily newspapers had trebled, from 7,000 in 1899 to 21,000 in 1939.[6] Gannett had no similar breakdown on average circulation for its newspapers, but its reach had grown in 33 years from its modest beginnings in Elmira to total circulation for 1939 of more than 690,000.

*The Bulletin's* interest in the proceedings of the American Society of Newspaper Editors in October 1941 extended to misrepresentations of Gannett's policy of editorial autonomy. It reported that Harold Sanford, managing editor of the *Democrat and Chronicle* in Rochester, had rebutted a speaker at ASNE, Dr. Peter H. Odegard of Amherst College, who had criticized newspapers in general and implied that Frank Gannett controlled the editorial policies of both the Rochester papers. Sanford told his ASNE colleagues:

"Since a Rochester situation was specifically referred to, I should like to put in two sentences for the record to correct the erroneous assumption about Mr. Gannett's relations to his newspapers.

"Mr. Gannett does not direct the editorial policy of the *Democrat and Chronicle,* nor of any other of his newspapers, except the Rochester *Times-Union.* We are freer to interpret our attitude toward the Republican Party under the ownership of the company which Mr. Gannett heads now than we were when the paper was independently owned."[7]

*The Bulletin* report on Sanford's remarks was followed by this item in the Oct. 23 issue:

"[Frank Tripp] in a bulletin to publishers – the subject of which also is of interest to editors – calls attention to a pamphlet titled, 'Undermining Our Republic,' which has just been published by Guardians of American Education, Inc. . . .

"Said FET: 'This is the first thing I have seen which does an independent job of analyzing and emphasizing subversive material contained in textbooks in use in America, very particularly the books of Prof. Rugg of Teachers College, Columbia University. It quotes and analyzes by chapter and page.'

"All Gannett publishers are ordering the pamphlet, and after having read it, will analyze their local situation, both as to public schools and higher educational institutions and determine to what extent they can effectively make distribution of the pamphlet.

"Group editors might take the GM's advice and borrow a copy of the pamphlet from their publisher and study it too, then confer with their publisher on how they can help him place it into the right hands."

## A Death in the Family

The 24th semi-annual meeting of Gannett editors in Rochester on Nov. 10, 1941, had an agenda packed with topics they had suggested to the News and Editorial Office, including sessions on copy editing, pages devoted to servicemen and their relatives, worsening relations with the Associated Press, the value of columns, and how to give an old newspaper a new dress.

Frank Gannett paid tribute to M.V. Atwood, who had succumbed to cancer just a week earlier. "Few men were so close to me. His life was devoted to truth and honesty. He was always preaching the truth. We heard the meaning of truth at noon today when Mr. [Richard] Hottelet spoke to us about Germany. He said Germany is the victim of propaganda. If they knew the truth things might be different."

Gannett repeated his opposition to the war. Then he said:

"If this war comes, and I am sorry to say I think it will come, fighting will be done back home, too. But until war comes I am going to resist it, but once we get into it, I'm going to get behind the government and do my share, take off my coat and not falter or fail."[8]

Gannett turned to the managing editor of his *Times-Union,* Lafayette (Fay) R. Blanchard, to replace Atwood as director of the News and Editorial Office. *The Bulletin* of Nov. 19 reported, "No changes of policy are involved. . . . LRB hopes to develop the same close friendships M.V. enjoyed with editors and other executives of the Group. He believes thoroughly in the policy of local autonomy and thinks within that framework there is plenty of room for the passing around of ideas tending to constantly better the newspapers."

# Tripp Speaking

Autumn 1941 was busy for general manager Tripp. He went to Chicago to speak to a meeting of newspaper advertising executives. His message was a rebuke of Leon Henderson, head of the Office of Price Administration, James L. Fly, chairman of the Federal Communications Commission, and Harold Ickes, secretary of the interior. All were outspoken critics of the press.

Tripp said:

"Speaking for that portion of the American press whose intestinal fortitude has not been spewed into the wash bowl, I want to say to Mr. Henderson that the real honest-to-God American press, about which he and many others in Washington seem to know nothing, recognizes no connection between its advertising rates and its freedom under the Bill of Rights to tell the American people what is happening in the world – very particularly what is happening in Washington." [9]

Back in Elmira, Tripp was surprised in November with a party celebrating his 40 years as a newspaperman. He told his friends, "The institution that means more than any other to the preservation of the American way of life is the newspaper. It is the bulwark of all our liberties." [10]

On Dec. 7, Tripp was serving as master of ceremonies on a radio program sponsored by the Arctic League, an Elmira group that helped the poor each Christmas. He put aside his script to tell the audience that the Japanese had attacked Pearl Harbor. He later recalled his earlier visit to the Far East and wrote:

"Japan's militarists could have made no greater mistake. They who have played with 'incidents' since 1932 and gotten away with them unleashed an 'incident' . . . which will destroy their nation. There is only one hope and that is impossible – a revolution by which the Japanese people could wrest their government from the war lords who today rule it."[11]

And Frank Gannett, true to his word, immediately wired President Roosevelt offering his service in any useful capacity to prosecute and win the war.

In *The Bulletin* of Dec. 18, 1941, he said, "Nothing matters now except to win the war. The quicker that war is over, the quicker we can get back into the old routine with all our old freedoms."

The Gannett Newspapers were gearing up for the war effort when their employees got one last item of good news from 1941. Frank Gannett announced the usual annual employees' share of 10 percent of the profits. But this year, they were awarded an additional 5 percent in recognition of the increased cost of living.[12]

# Chapter 14

# The War Years - I
## 1942

*"I am a little concerned about cutting into the editorial page in your efforts to save paper. The editorial page, after all, is the backbone of the paper, and it should not be destroyed. . . . I would rather restrict the amount of advertising than to pare the paper down so far that we will lose reader acceptance."*

Frank Gannett
September 1943[1]

Frank Gannett's prompt declaration to Franklin Roosevelt of his willingness to serve the war effort was not the offer of one aging body to the struggle. It was the enlistment of a small civilian army of men and women on 20 newspapers and seven radio stations.

Even while he was opposing U.S. engagement in warfare, Gannett had pledged to roll up his sleeves immediately and do his part when war inevitably came. Those who had worked for him longest knew that they too would be rolling up their sleeves.

Editors and managers had learned during Gannett's civic and political campaigns how to keep several balls in the air at the same time. Their support of the war effort would be forged and sustained with the same collegial give-and-take that shaped their newspapers.

It was not that they had a new job to do. Their task was to bring greater judgment and wit to the jobs they had always done.

Gannett quickly rallied his subordinates to the mission of boosting morale. His concern for the power of phraseology led him to urge the use of English equivalents for the Nazis' "fearsome jaw-breaking" military terms. *The Bulletin* conveyed his message:

"The Nazi is the more readily accepted as unbeatable when we describe him with such terror-evoking words as *panzer, Luftwaffe, blitz* and *blitzkrieg, flammenwerfer* and *unterseebooten*. In English we would say armored division, air force, lightning war, flame thrower and submarines."[2]

Gannett's understanding of the emotional power of words was matched by the Nazis' dedication to propaganda. In that regard, they had a dossier on Frank Gannett, which would be discovered in Nazi archives by Allied occupation forces after the war.

It was an almost totally misinformed document titled "Jude Gannett," and appeared later in this translation in the *Gannetteer:*

"Name: Gannett, Frank.

"Country: USA.

"Nationality: Jew.

"Occupation: Publisher.

"Owner of a small concern of 5-6 newspapers in several small cities in the state of New York. These papers are of no political meaning. After reporting on Palestine's Jewish newspapers, he became a member of the Zionist Party. The statement that he entered the U.S. in 1923 is untrue. It deals with a long-settled well-to-do Jewish family from New York.

"Spoke in London while on a visit in November 1943 that the world could not figure on support by the USA after the end of the war, because the economic situation, especially pertaining to the foodstuffs market, is already in bad condition."[3]

# Rely on Facts, Not Rumors

*The Bulletin* distributed immediately following Pearl Harbor reminded executives that Gannett had always predicted a long war. It stressed his contempt for rumors and guesses in war coverage. "Perhaps most important, in his mind," *The Bulletin* said, "is the necessity for retaining our grips on local news. War news can't possibly be ignored. Indeed, it is very apt to overwhelm us, causing us to neglect our own fields. His advice is to keep after local news, keep it as cheerful as possible, seeking new ways to keep the paper bright despite restrictions which are sure to come."[4]

Chief among those restrictions was the anticipated censorship. Both Army and Navy quickly restricted all information following Pearl Harbor. President Roosevelt announced that a few high-ranking officials would decide what could be reported about the war. They would put such news to two tests, he said – (1) is it true? (2) does it give aid and comfort to the enemy?

The president soon named Byron Price, an Associated Press executive, to be director of censorship. Gannett editors and managers remained uncertain of what was to come but were fearful of draconian controls. "It should be self-evident," *The Bulletin* told them, "that too strict a censorship can defeat its purpose. Meanwhile, every editor should become familiar with the rules – and play the game straight. Let your readers know about censorship but don't try to evade it."[5]

A week later, *The Bulletin* reported:

" 'Everyone here is just as much at sea as you are,' writes a veteran Washington correspondent. . . . 'Tentative rules have been drafted in connection with the War and Navy departments. . . .

" 'These rules will apply to advertising as well as reading matter. For example, I understand, ads such as Ford ran, saying his factories are turning to defense production, and all that sort of thing, will be banned.

" 'It appears now that every story one takes up with Price is killed. Hence many of the fellows are taking no chances but sending the stuff out first, knowing just where to draw the lines.' "[6]

Even as they fretted about how much news they would be allowed to publish, editors learned that available space for news was likely to be cut. Newsprint manufacturers had forecast a 5-percent increase in the cost of paper. Gannett editors and managers were reminded of their own "simple equation" – "If white paper goes up 5 percent, space goes down 5 percent."

They were reassured that Gannett and Tripp would think "last of all about reduced manpower as a means of meeting rising costs throughout the plant. . . . In any event," they were told, "our entry in the war gives every editor a chance to go through his paper once more with a view to seeing what can be pruned in safety."[7]

By February, the publisher's life was not a happy one. General manager Tripp sent to all a memo warning them not to hurry to fill vacancies when employees left for military service. He said they might welcome the opportunity to offset the rising expenses that faced them.

Editors, meanwhile, learned that southern newspaper publishers had officially agreed to voluntary reductions in the size of their newspapers to meet the expected newsprint shortage. *The Bulletin* asked:

"If overnight the order came for you to reduce the size of your paper 20 percent, what would you throw out?

"Obviously, the last to be jettisoned will be news, and if it ever comes to a choice between foreign and local news, foreign will be dropped overboard before the local." [8]

A practice blackout came within a week.

"Editors are to assume that they have been ordered to reduce their space 20 percent, effective Tuesday, Feb. 24.

"Please send to this office your paper of that date, marked to indicate material which would have to be discarded or revamped if you were to carry out the order literally."

At the same time, they were warned that Tripp considered it dangerous "to make the reductions in such way that the appearance of the paper would be altered noticeably." He conceded the vulnerability of the editorial page to change, but opposed putting ads on the page because it "would change its character and make the tightening process too obvious."

With a bow to autonomy, the editors were assured, "The views above are entirely informal and not to be construed as directions." [9]

Tripp's wish to guard against making space tightening too obvious was reflected in remarks by corporate circulation director Matt Sullivan. His concerns were handouts of unpaid newspapers and the likelihood of higher prices for readers and subscribers.

"Circulation men are doing everything possible," he said, "to conserve newsprint so that editors may have the necessary space to produce the best possible newspaper. Then when the time comes for increased price (a major operation) present readers will continue to buy the paper." [10]

# Pitching In

Age exempted most Gannett corporate executives from the military draft but not from war-related civilian service. Erwin Davenport, Gannett's original partner and now general manager of the Rochester newspapers, was first. For more than a year, he had been chief of the Rochester Ordnance District, an advisory post in peacetime. But with the United States in the war, he became responsible for contracts for munitions and other supplies worth hundreds of millions of dollars.

Frank Gannett's first wartime assignment came in January 1942. As chairman of the New York State Civilian Committee of the Naval Relief Society, he oversaw fund-raising to benefit dependents and survivors of naval personnel.

Gannett and Davenport imposed no public service standards on their associates. They merely set an example that any Gannett executive who wished to volunteer for wartime public service could follow without hesitation.

Free time, always at a premium for Gannett editors and managers, was trimmed further by the constraints of war. That practice blackout on news space, for instance, required editors to submit examples of proposed trims on pages already produced. That was equivalent to doing the same job twice – the second time even more precisely.

In Rochester, Gannett personally presided over the *Times-Union*, but his presence was notable even to staffers on the *Democrat and Chronicle*. Those papers, working independently, according to *The Bulletin*, reduced their news space in March about 15 percent. The *Democrat and Chronicle* published 992 pages, with 4,337 news columns, as compared with 1,136 and 5,080 respectively the year before. Figures for the *Times-Union* were 802 pages and 3,357 news columns for March 1942, compared with 908 and 3,932 respectively the year before.

"So skillfully has the work been accomplished," *The Bulletin* assured its executive readers, "that, barring the use of a slide rule, no reader could tell that something had been snipped away."[11]

## Static on Radio

Gannett continued to own radio stations, probably because of the financial potential he saw in them. When it came to his professional loyalty, however, newspapers invariably carried the day.

The rapidity with which war news changed gave radio a new competitive edge. Managers of Gannett radio properties could not have been delighted *Bulletin* readers. Its radio references were rarely complimentary, often disdainful.

Inmmediately after Pearl Harbor, its Dec. 11 issue reported that Gannett was against "crediting radio too freely with news from abroad. He feels it should be enough to credit radio in general with such rumors and reports, but that it is hardly necessary to mention constantly such reports from Mutual, CBS, or NBC."

In March it reported that *Time* magazine said radio did a better job than newspapers in putting greater emphasis on a talk by President Roosevelt than on a Japanese submarine attack on the West Coast. "We don't have to agree with *Time's* flat statement that radio does a better job. That's hooey."

At the semi-annual editors meeting in May, Gannett said at dinner:

"I have always looked upon radio as a competitor but I don't think we need to worry about it. People still must have a newspaper to get all the news. I was to make a radio speech recently and before I could make it had to submit my manuscript. I was told that a statement about the war not going so well for us so far must be deleted. Due to this and other deletions, I said to myself, 'The day we feared is here.' We won't be able to tell the truth over the radio. We must look to our newspapers for it now." [12]

Vin Jones, who succeeded Fay Blanchard as head of the News and Editorial Office, recalled, "One of the odd things about Frank Gannett was he hated radio and television. God, he couldn't stand them, although he owned several radio stations. He never wrote anything that he didn't just absolutely castigate radio and television." [13]

# Appeal from the Top

Rising material costs and the scarcity of newsprint prompted Gannett to send executives a mixed but urgent message in mid-1942: "It's time to economize – really economize."

He urged them to talk to their employees about the drain of what appeared to be trifling waste. "People resent stinginess," he said. "They won't resent economy. . . . I suggest the posting of some such notice as this:

### It Isn't Penny-Pinching

"Legend says the head of a certain chain of stores demanded each of the 1,500 managers send him $1 daily. If a store couldn't show that profit, it was abandoned.

"No individual store would continue to operate on a $1 profit. To a big chain, that dollar was important.

"Big organizations find their profits in fractions of a cent. Likewise they find trifling leakages quickly become torrents. Our organization is so big that pencils are important, unused lighting is important.

"One pencil quickly becomes a gross throughout the Group. One hour of unused lighting soon becomes enough to run a small factory. One stamp fills a mail pouch.

"Careful saving is not penny-pinching. It is sound sense and the good it does is computable.

"In these times, we must economize. We need not be ashamed to nurse pencils and lighting and to save paper. Every saving you make, no matter how minute, contributes to the security of the Group and to your own.

"Frank Gannett"

On the question of newsprint, however, the boss warned editors and managers not to cut too close to the bone. "We have cut out some of the frills," he said, "we have found ourselves addicted to careless practices and these are cured.

"We must not forget, however, that until driven to it by direct necessity, we should not drop below a certain safety line.

"Be sure you are giving the reader a full meal."[14]

Editors and managers, meanwhile, were bemoaning to corporate bosses their own war-induced poverty. Photographers particularly were hobbled by tight restrictions on gasoline and their inability to replace worn-out tires. One editor described as his luckiest employee a man who could get all the obsolete tires he wanted for his 1930 Ford.

A War Production Board order caused a brief scare over the availability of zinc for photoengraving. Those fears were quickly eased when the American Newspaper Publishers Association persuaded the WPB that newspapers reused zinc and needed only small amounts to replace the little lost in reprocessing.

## The Demand for Junk

Newspapers got their first real opportunity to enlist in the war effort with the government's call for scrap metal. Tripp returned from a meeting of publishers in Washington with the zeal of a true believer. As a member of a new national newspaper salvage committee, he told Gannett newspapers:

"This is the first job the government has put directly up to newspapers. By no means can we fall down in any respect. Not only is it our patriotic duty to do this job well, but failure to do so will make that newspaper which neglects its obligation conspicuous in the record which will be tabulated. I expect you to go to town."[15]

As editors and advertising directors prepared for a joint semiannual fall 1942 session in Rochester, the scrap drive was a top priority. Tripp told all publishers to keep accurate records of text, pictures and advertising in connection with the campaign. They were to be submitted to the general manager's office at the end of the campaign. *The Bulletin* took the opportunity for a reminder of self-interest:

"[T]he campaign is not to be commercialized with solicited advertising. This is a job that was put up to newspapers. They will deliver. We hope they will deliver so impressively that unfriendly folk in Washington will be silenced."

Interdependence was the theme for editors and advertising directors at their joint meeting. They were encouraged to put aside their differences in support of their mutual interest in the success of Gannett newspapers.

Editors fretted over the inconsistencies of a new censorship for newspapers and ridiculed President Roosevelt's news blackout of his tour of major industrial plants. One editor grumbled that the public seemed to go right along with the censorship but would have been up in arms if the result of a World Series game had been held up for two weeks.

Gannett repeated his warning that a free press is impossible without financially sound newspapers. He did not let his commitment to the war effort dim his political observations. He echoed the ridicule of the president's plant tour. He praised the Congress as "a fine lot of men, hard-working and interested in the welfare of their country." To no one's surprise, he voiced his hope for a Republican House of Representatives after the coming elections.

He urged editors again to make their newspapers more interesting and more informative, to lace them with a bit of humor to cheer their readers, and to keep up such public efforts as the scrap drive.

Tripp was not disappointed with Gannett newspapers' achievements in that campaign. *The Bulletin* of Nov. 25, 1942, reported that scrap collections in the 15 communities with Gannett newspapers totaled 105,477 tons, a *per capita* average of 107.08 pounds. Money earned for charities through gift scrap sales totaled $116,319. Time contributed outside the office to the campaign was 9,867 man-hours, equivalent to "1,233 eight-hour days, 246.5 40-hour weeks, one man's time for 4 years, 9 months, 18 days."

The general manager was involved in one of the most notable incidents of the drive. Elmira's *Star-Gazette* removed its large electric sign from the building and gave it to the scrap drive. Tripp's reason was reported on Page 1 by many newspapers:

"If we win we'll get another. If we don't win, we won't need one." [16]

## After a Year of War

As 1942 wound down, 309 of Gannett's more than 4,000 pre-war employees were in military service. Included among those was the last of the *Newburgh News'* three photographers. In a Page 1 box it told its readers:

"In the future, [engravings] will be made out of town, compelling a delay of at least two days. The number of pictures published must be reduced because spot pictures will lose their timeliness."

In Olean, the *Times-Herald* was frank with its readers about impending shortages of newsprint and chemicals. At worst, the paper reported:

"It would mean elimination of all frills, all special pages and articles. It would mean the bare summarization of sports; women's pages would be likely to disappear altogether; and comics would be reduced to a minimum or eliminated entirely. News stories that ordinarily would be given half a column would be reduced to a few essential paragraphs." [17]

A corporate sacrifice was circulation director Matt Sullivan, who was called to full-time service as a $1-a-year consultant in the Printing and Publishing Division of the War Production Board. Frank Gannett said the company was proud that he had been chosen and glad to make the contribution.

Editors and managers got a mixed year-end holiday greeting from *The Bulletin*. It's good news was, "The year 1942 turned out to be better than most of us prophesied." The bad news? "Despite this all indications for 1943 are that it will require every ounce of energy we can assemble." [18]

# Chapter 15

# The War Years - II
## 1943

*"Information from a personal telegram is that William G. [Bill] Warnock, naval lieutenant, has been lost in action. If the bad news proves true, and it apparently is, Bill becomes the first Rochester Grouper to lose his life."*

The Bulletin
March 25, 1943

Wartime life in Gannett remained a confusion of competing pressures in the new year. Frank Gannett was still infatuated with politics, and still not successful. He and Frank Tripp were pressing themselves and their family of executives into greater service to war causes. Those demands, of course, were in addition to their daily newspaper regimen.

*The Bulletin* resolutely sought to relieve the chaos of their busy lives with its confidential weekly hodgepodge of the momentous and the mundane. The *Gannetteer,* meanwhile, put on a happy face in the interests of employee morale and dedication.

Interested Gannett employees knew that the boss had recently sought the chairmanship of the Republican National Committee, and lost. They learned from the January issue of the *Gannetteer,* however, that Gannett welcomed this outcome. It described him as "happy a satisfactory compromise had been achieved, the goal toward which he was working when he permitted his name to be used in the race for chairman."

That chairmanship eluded him, but he was busy with two fund drives. He was chairman of the annual Red Cross drive in Rochester, which had a goal of $900,000. The New York State Committee of the Naval Relief Society, to which he had been named chairman the year before, was seeking to raise $265,000.

# Let the Seller Beware

Gannett still found time to pay attention to his newspapers and the things he approved and disapproved. High on the disapproved list was promotion or publicity that he deplored as free advertising. It is unlikely that he knew or cared for stripteaser Gypsy Rose Lee, but he certainly would have identified with her professional dictum, "What you give away you can't sell."

Even the war effort was not immune:

**FREE ADVERTISING GROUNDED**
"For all his airmindedness and for all his boosting of air traffic, FEG thinks it's about time to end the free advertising of airplane manufacturers. The easiest and quickest way to meet this suggestion is TO DROP THE NAME OF THE MANUFACTURER WHEN REFERRING TO HIS PLANE. The newly announced scheme of giving pet names to all war planes will facilitate your handling of copy.

"It is pointed out that manufacturers have had a lot of field days since this war began. They have advertised their products in every newspaper in the country – for free. Meanwhile it is a shabby magazine indeed which doesn't carry at least one color page at a fat fee.

"Hereafter it should be the Wildcat – not Grumman Wildcat. Commando, not Curtiss Commando. Lightning, not Lockheed Lightning, etc. etc.

"Certainly occasions will arise when the manufacturer's name is a valuable part of a story. Such occasions can be recognized readily. If the name is not essential, give it the blue-pencil treatment."[1]

Editors were reminded by frequent examples in *The Bulletin* of the pitfalls of promotion and press agentry. The suspicion was deeply rooted in Gannett and his original partner, Erwin Davenport. Henry Clune, long-time columnist on Rochester's *Democrat and Chronicle,* described Davenport as "not much of a newspaperman," meaning he concentrated on business rather than news. He remembered:

"I ran a column for years called 'Seen and Heard.' Somebody sent me a perfume, very elaborate perfume, one time and I wrote a kidding story about it. And [Mr. Davenport] said, 'Henry, you were giving them free advertising, but it was a corking story.' He didn't know [the difference]." [2]

Even the inadvertent plug did not escape *The Bulletin's* scorn:

"Fillers are those little blossoms of wisdom which the lazy editor uses in place of brains to fill his columns. . . . At least two Group papers used one filler which told an absorbed world that Botany is a fine-grade wool, so called because it originated in Botany Bay. This was spotted by the Botany Worsted Mills of Passaic, N.J., which claims the name 'Botany' is copyrighted. It demanded the offending newspapers immediately print a correction. . . .

"In the end it seemed easier to give the Botany Company a line or two of free advertising than to bother with bales of insistent letters.

"It's worth all the annoyance of those piffling, peevish letters if the incident results in the killing of all fillers." [3]

# Victory Hoedown

*The Times* of Hartford was first of the Gannett papers to marry patriotism to self-sufficiency in a campaign for home vegetable gardening. It was a project after Gannett's heart and he endorsed it enthusiastically. "From the start," *The Bulletin* said, "[Frank Gannett] has been anxious about the country's food and worried about the possibility that without real encouragement the farmer would not be able to do the great job assigned him. [He] believes thoroughly in home gardening, means to rip up a large section of his own lawn for vegetables. He hopes all the papers will get into this activity with persistent campaigns and with the most complete detailed information on gardening that is available. . . . It is a good cause and with FEG's blessing each paper will want to do a job." [4]

Gannett editors and managers had barely had time to muster the gardening troops before they were mobilized to raise money to help pay for the war. Gannett had just completed the Red Cross and Naval Relief fund drives. Each had exceeded its goal by more than $100,000. Henry J. Morgenthau, secretary of the Treasury, asked Frank Gannett to join the Allied Newspaper Council and support the government's second Victory Drive. The goal was to sell $13 billion worth of war bonds.

Gannett joined, pledged the total support of Gannett newspapers and contributed Tripp to head the Allied Newspaper Council's effort. Morgenthau was relying totally on newspapers for the drive's success. They were responsible for everything but the actual bond sales. Those would be made by bankers and security salesmen.

The boss told his editors and managers: "We know you will give this drive the same responsive, cooperative and generous help that has proved so successful in the scrap campaign, and that as leaders of public thought you will accept the challenge that has been placed before you by your government."

Successive issues of *The Bulletin* pressed the point. "Time to sell bonds. . . . Continual hammering will do the trick."[5]

"Frank Tripp's appeal to all papers naturally got especially thoughtful consideration by the Group. The GM's prominence in the campaign makes it imperative that our papers do better than a good job."[6]

"No doubt exists now that the campaign will succeed. . . . Frank Tripp can be proud of the newspaper record. There never has been a better example of full cooperation in a patriotic effort. Not even the scrap metal drive got more enthusiastic backing."[7]

# Now We Are 21

Despite the Depression and the drain of war, Gannett newspapers continued to profit and grow. But the company that was both envied and derided for its venturesome growth seemed to have lost its momentum.

Although it had added the Sunday *Ogdensburg Advance-News* in the summer of 1941, the Gannett Company had not made a major purchase in nine years. The summer of 1943 changed all that with a new spurt of vitality. The company bought its 21st newspaper, launched a Washington bureau and its own national news service, and introduced an editorial digest that would quickly be in demand outside the family.

Late in 1941, treasurer Herbert W. Cruickshank had proposed the purchase of the *Binghamton* (N.Y.) *Press* from the estate of Willis Sharpe Kilmer for $1.5 million. Talks to that end did not succeed immediately. On May 27, 1943, however, the board of directors of Gannett Co., Inc., approved a complicated purchase.

The parties initially had failed to strike a deal because the Kilmer estate insisted that Gannett buy both the stock of Binghamton Press Company for $1.1 million and its real estate for $400,000, both payable in cash. That snag was smoothed when Cornell University agreed to buy the real estate for $400,000 on the condition that the Gannett Company would lease the buildings for 20 years, meet repairs, taxes and insurance, and pay an annual rental of $32,000.

The company agreed, paid $1.1 million to create a new Binghamton Press Company, and added a new masthead to its roster.[8]

The *Gannetteer* reported Mrs. Willis Kilmer to be pleased that "the *Press* goes into the hands of a company with an outstanding reputation in producing high grade newspapers under sound business management."[9]

Gannett executives were advised by *The Bulletin* that "acquisition of this newspaper rounds out the organization in Central New York. It means further opportunity for improving service to all readers in the area."

# Gannett National Service

The July 1 announcement that Gannett would open its own Washington bureau a month later was enthusiastically supported as a declaration of less dependence on the established wire services. As *The Bulletin* of that date reported, Gannett looked "forward to the day when news services and other papers will begin to quote what our [Gannett National] Service has to say."

Successive issues introduced Cecil B. Dickson, GNS chief, who described his plans for operation, and emphasized and re-emphasized the need to promote the service constantly before its launch Aug. 1.

Dickson had worked in Washington for The Associated Press, the International News Service and the *Chicago Sun*. "[He] is a Texan, a conservative Democrat and temperamentally opposed to much of the New Deal," *The Bulletin* explained. "He is too much [a] newspaper man, however, to let feeling interfere with his news judgment."

The bureau would have "a staff of three with a girl to handle mail, telephone and office duties." Frank Gannett hoped "that, without slanting the news, the service can build prestige with interpretive, analytical stories. . . . [T]he central idea will be to show readers how the news affects all and each of them." [10]

GNS copy would be transmitted daily from 9 p.m. to midnight. It would be received by wire in Hartford, Albany, Utica, Rochester, Elmira and Binghamton. Other Gannett papers were to be served by mail.

Editors were urged to display Dickson's columns prominently, "preferably Page 1." It was suggested that "[t]he slug Gannett National Service will become increasingly valuable. Be sure you use it. FEG hasn't formulated a rule but certainly at the start the full name after a dateline will be better than the initials 'GNS.' Let the reader become fully acquainted with the name before adopting the abbreviation." [11]

Less than a week into its operation, GNS was being acclaimed and Dickson's column declared an immediate hit. "Editors were quick to voice their appreciation of the quality of the service," *The Bulletin* of Aug. 5 said. "FEG is nursing a neat stack of congratulatory letters and among them is one from a [non-Gannett] newspaper editor who wants to know if he can't hook up with the circuit."

(GNS news, graphics and photographs became available to other newspapers through the Los Angeles Times Syndicate in April 1992.)

## Shop Talk on Record

Gannett editors had been conferring twice a year in Rochester to talk about mutual problems and study general professional issues. *The Bulletin* summarized each of those meetings for all Gannett executives who read its confidential pages.

Their exchanges were shared for the first time with other interested professionals with the introductory publication of *Editorially Speaking*. This 17-page booklet was a compilation by the News and Editorial Office of discussions at the May conference. Its contents included the text of the guest speaker, Rudoph W. Chamberlain, chief editorial writer of *The Citizen-Advertiser* in Auburn, N.Y., and professional papers by Vin Jones, senior managing editor in Utica, Ward E. Duffy, managing editor in Hartford, Paul B. Williams, editorial writer for the *Utica Press*, and William J. Woods, editorial writer for the Utica *Observer-Dispatch*. Its last page reproduced Eldridge A. Spear's editorial that was chosen the Group's best.

Gannett's foreword concluded, "It is my hope that this booklet will contribute something to every reader of it, more particularly to those tireless newspaper men who believe with us in the dignity and future of the American press."

*The Bulletin* of Aug. 5 reported requests for extra copies from newspaper staffers and schools of journalism across the country. It presented as typical the favorable remarks of *Editor & Publisher*, which commended its "uncommonly fine shop talk" and added:

"No one who read[s] it could fail to perceive the breadth and caliber of men who are thinking every day about The Gannett Newspapers. Nor could anyone fail to catch the affectionate concern with which all true newspapermen consider the opportunities to improve their techniques. Read this booklet if you can get a copy."

# Back to Newsprint

The era of good feeling about GNS and *Editorially Speaking* was cut short by another War Production Board order that reduced available newsprint by 5 percent. That reality would preoccupy Gannett editors and managers for the rest of 1943.

Matt Sullivan and Tripp did not relieve the gloom when they predicted a 30-percent cut in newsprint in 1944. The general manager distributed a plan he had produced for 1918, with space cuts of up to 50 percent for the larger papers. The end of World War I made the plan unnecessary.

Even before the conference, concerns voiced confidentially by Frank Gannett caused a flurry of misunderstanding. As he had done before, the boss said, "I am a little concerned about cutting into the editorial page in your efforts to save paper. The editorial page, after all, is the backbone of the paper and it should not be destroyed."

However that word got abroad, through eavesdropping or broken confidences, it came back to the News and Editorial Office from a magazine called *Tide*. Its editors had heard that Gannett newspapers had talked of dropping their editorial pages and asked for details. It received this reply:

"We'd no more cut out our editorial pages than you would amputate your tongue. Someone got the wrong idea.

"Both Frank Gannett and Frank Tripp were editorial men long before business forced them to turn their attention to the operation of newspapers. They have retained in full their appreciation of the importance of the news and editorial side. Mr. Gannett insists that the editorial page is the backbone of the newspaper.

"We've had a conference on newsprint in which we faced the probable necessity of curtailed space. Out of it came full agreement that once absolute minimum editorial space of a paper is determined, it is to be maintained. Circulation and advertising will have to make way.

"Mr. Gannett's idea is that newspapers must come out of this war unimpaired in the eyes of their readers and his crew agrees with him." [12]

Despite the frustrations of war-time shortages, Gannett executives could look back on a special year. The family was one newspaper larger, their professional exchanges were being read with approval by other journalists and their own wire service was a genuine asset.

# Chapter 16

# The War Years - III
## 1944-45

*"Groupers felt pretty good when Thomas E. Broderick, GOP leader in Rochester, announced that he had been unable to convince FEG he should run for the U.S. Senate. . . . Unfortunately, FEG coupled his declination with a statement that he intended to work actively for the election of Dewey and Bricker. That task, however, should be concluded by November. Then, perhaps, we can chain him to his desk."*

The Bulletin
Aug. 20, 1944

Years divisible by four quadrennially reminded Frank Gannett of his thwarted presidential ambitions, of his staunch support for Republican candidates and of the need to renew his opposition to that old acquaintance from Albany by way of Hyde Park.

Despite that, Gannett editors were less distracted by presidential politics in 1944 for several reasons. Since only one Gannett newspaper had supported the third-term candidacy of Franklin Roosevelt, the question of editorial autonomy on an expected fourth-term campaign was moot. More immediately pressing, however, was the war.

The shrinking supplies of newsprint were an unending frustration and Fay Blanchard acted to let Gannett editors and publishers know that others shared their misery. *The Bulletin* recalled the time when the accepted split between news and advertising was 60 percent news, 40 percent advertising. In 1944, it lamented, "it is much more likely to be 40-60." Then it reprinted a report from *Media Records* showing the average percentages of news content in 32 U.S. newspapers.

Only five reported news content of 50 percent or more: *Chicago Daily News, Toledo Blade,* Rochester *Times-Union, New York Sun* and *Detroit Times.*

Papers with news content between 45 and 50 percent were: *Pittsburgh Press, Indianapolis News, Providence Bulletin, Baltimore News-*

Post, Minneapolis Star-Journal, Cincinnati Times-Star and Atlanta Journal.

Between 40 and 45 percent news content were: *Newark News, Philadelphia Bulletin, The Buffalo News,* Akron *Beacon-Journal, The Hartford Times, Cleveland Press, Washington Times-Herald, St. Louis Post-Dispatch, Oakland Tribune, Seattle Times, San Diego Tribune-Sun,* and *The Columbus Dispatch.*

Below 40 percent news content were: *Washington Star, The Milwaukee Journal, The Detroit News,* Baltimore *Evening Sun, Boston Traveler, Dallas Times-Herald, Dayton News* and *Houston Chronicle.*

None of the newspapers listed reported news content below 35 percent.[1]

# A Gannett Christening

The *Gannetteer* of May reported that Frank and Caroline Gannett had watched their daughter, Sally, christen the Liberty Ship, *Deborah Sampson Gannett,* in Baltimore in April. The vessel was named for an indirect ancestor of Gannett's who distinguished herself during the Revolutionary War.

According to Gannett's biographer, Deborah Sampson Gannett was the only woman who served as a soldier in that war. Gov. John Hancock of Massachusetts signed a resolution of the General Court of Massachusetts honoring her. It said she "discharged the duties of a faithful, gallant soldier" and "preserved the virtue and chastity of her sex, unsuspected and unblemished."

She was wounded in a Tory ambush near Tarrytown, N.Y., for which she earned a disability pension. Samuel Williamson wrote:

"Deborah Sampson Gannett drew a pension until she died. Ten years later, in 1837, her husband Benjamin petitioned Congress for relief. He was then 83, and alone in the world. Declaring that he was a 'very upright and hard-laboring man' and that the 'whole history of the Revolution records no case like this,' the House Committee on

Revolutionary Pensions recommended payment of $80 a year; and thus Benjamin Gannett became the first widower of a war veteran to be enrolled on the pension rolls of the United States Government. He was Frank Gannett's great-great uncle." [2]

## The War Will End

The certainty that the Allies would eventually win the war was evident in the spring conference of editors and advertising directors. The message to all was, "Get ready for post-war progress." The blueprints, however, were consistent with most of the ideas for improvement they had heard before – vitalized editorial pages, greater use of pictures and maps, good local columns, and more promotion.

A week later, Blanchard published a list called, "I hereby resolve," based on the meeting. Among the resolutions:

• "That I shall seize every opportunity of telling my readers the sort of job I am doing."

• "That I shall study the possibilities of printing more and more local news tending to honor the little, forgotten man."

• "That I shall endeavor to avoid prodigality in space when and if paper restrictions end; I shall have learned that it isn't the space, it's what's in it."

• "That I shall cooperate with the advertising department by passing along all tips that I hear which may lead to new accounts."

• "That I shall at all times 'defend the unfortunate.' "

• "That I shall cooperate with the circulation department by producing the sort of editorial content that 'sells the newspaper.' " [3]

On June 6, 1944, two and a half years into the war, 5,000 Allied ships and 4,000 landing craft hit the beaches of France on a 50-mile front in the long-awaited D-Day invasion. They opened a stream of 3 million men and 16 million tons of arms onto the continent of Europe bent on driving the Nazis back to Berlin and defeat. Those constant Gannett reminders to be ready for the invasion of Europe paid off.

The next *Bulletin* applauded:
"Certain to be treasured by many a collector, certain to become historic curios, are the invasion extras turned out everywhere this week. Group newspapers have reported many an event in their comparatively short lives but probably never in such variety. Most striking will be those papers – like Rochester's – which met the demand for extra sales by cutting out all display advertising. Their action is a record in itself."[4]

*The Bulletin* took the opportunity to fault radio for "tiresome reiteration and lack of organization in the big story." It also pointed out that not all readers approved of the sacrifice of display advertising.

As prospects for the end of the war in Europe brightened, Byron Price asked newspapers to continue to observe the censorship code. For Gannett editors, wartime censorship had taken a back seat to efforts by the New York State Health Department to restrict publication of birth notices. New York law prohibited the reporting of illegitimate births and the bureaucrats sought to prohibit news of any births without the express consent of the parents. It was a battle eagerly joined by all Gannett editors, and their insistence that public records remain public records eventually prevailed.

# Prehistoric Sexism

One of the irresistible effects of the war's drain on civilian manpower was the need to recruit women as substitutes. Rosie the Riveter was a World War II folk stereotype, a heroine embodying the effectiveness of women who filled the jobs of men called to war. Her labors were acclaimed. Women in the newsroom did not enjoy the same cachet.

Before the war, most newsrooms consigned their few women employees to the ghetto known as the women's pages or to the switchboard. Military conscription and enlistments changed that.

Gannett had occasionally advised his editors and managers to hire "girls," even for such responsible jobs as copy editing and photography. This enlightened suggestion may have been an echo of mixed emotions he had expressed earlier to his biographer.

Gracia Gannett Rathbone and Frank Gannett were devoted sister and brother. She was active in Elmira in support of many charitable causes. Biographer Samuel Williamson recalled that Gannett had said of his sister, with what the biographer called "mixed admiration and regret":

"If she'd been a man, she would have been a great business executive." [5]

Employment of women had reached such magnitude by 1944 that *The Bulletin* polled Gannett editors with the question, "What's the value of girls on the staff?"

Remember that these responses represent the mores of the country a half-century ago:

- "It has been my experience that 99 percent of the girls are poorly equipped, think that life is moonlight and roses and want a tea party every afternoon. They are a nuisance around the office. The sooner we can get rid of them, the more efficiently our office will operate.
- "Girls are all right in their place – but they do not belong on my editorial staff.
- "Super. Read these stories. Could any man handle them better? Our experience has been generally good.
- "Girls have proved their worth in local newsrooms. . . . Three gals 'man' the proof desk, another runs a camera and brings back better pix, many times, than does her male contemporary."
- "We love 'em, especially the young and luscious numbers. We try to hire girls who are both handsome and intelligent, and with some degree of success. . . . Main problem seems to be a female contingent which lacks a minx or a born stirrer-upper."
- "On the whole, girls are working out well on our staff. As errand girls, morgue attendants and freshman reporters, they are leaving little to be desired. As a matter of fact, one of the important jobs on a newspaper, whether we all realize it or not, is that of the person who has first contact with the public – the telephone switchboard operator – and that person invariably and probably to the benefit of the paper

is NOT a man."
- "We have seven on a total staff of 18. Two of the seven are doing outstanding jobs, and I use the word 'outstanding' advisedly. One is holding down the city desk and outclasses two men who had trials there. Of the remaining five, their work ranges from mediocre to average. They'll do until the war is over."[6]

A week later, without explanation, *The Bulletin* ran an item warning Gannett executives, "Don't joke about pay for women." It reminded them that according to New York State law, "No employer may discriminate in rates of pay where men and women are employed in any specific job classifications, solely because of sex."

*The Bulletin* suggested: "Casual remarks comparing pay of men and women should be avoided. A statement that women are worth less pay than men, or vice versa, might cause trouble. In the course of scale negotiations don't allow yourself to be led into any careless statement which could be construed as a violation of the equal pay principle."[7]

# 'The Renewed Deal'[8]

On Oct. 21, in a campaign speech, Franklin Roosevelt denounced "the isolationist press – and I mean specifically the McCormick-Patterson-Hearst-Gannett press."

Gannett wired an indignant reply which said, in part, "(I)n calling The Gannett Newspapers isolationist you are guilty of a gross misrepresentation. The editors of The Gannett Newspapers are given full autonomy. Not one of these papers could by any stretch of the imagination be correctly characterized as isolationist."[9]

On Nov. 7, Roosevelt was elected to his fourth term as president. Gannett papers' editorials resignedly remarked the election results and acknowledged their "duty" to work together.

Gannett's *Times-Union* said: "The re-election of Mr. Roosevelt continues the government in the hands of one who has delighted in smashing precedents for 12 years. . . . The president, by reiterating his 'economic bill of rights,' indicated that his faith in a self-reliant people is still less than his belief in a super-state." [10]

Soon after the election, Gannett wrote in an undated letter to Caroline Gannett:

"I sent Roosevelt a telegram after his re-election, saying I'd support him, wishing him good health and success. I am enclosing his reply. It is very nice and is his own letter. I got a letter from Jim Hagerty acknowledging my wire to Dewey. If I don't hear from Tom himself, I am going to be a bit sore. O, well!" [11]

Just before Christmas, *The Bulletin* reflected a diminished editorial animosity on the part of Gannett and the *Times-Union* to the Roosevelt administration. The item did not mention either campaign criticism of Gannett and his papers, or an unaccustomed union confrontation that shut down the Rochester papers for five days.

It said that Gannett "recognizes the fact that the election is over . . . the people have spoken and for four years we have a government which all must respect."

"Now that the battle is over," Gannett declared, "we should extend every possible help to an administration faced with the gravest problems. If we have suggestions and criticisms, we'll present them. But it's time to forget the minor matters which can be interpreted as mere nagging. . . .

"Proper handling of the labor issue is of extreme delicacy, much more difficult than disposing of political matters. It is doubtful that any newspaper ever can satisfy labor but an honest effort to report stories factually and to avoid useless criticism will, at least, keep the record clear." [12]

## The Beginning of the End

As the war in Europe obviously wore down, editors had learned the ropes of editing and displaying war news. That left *The Bulletin* to delivering pats and slaps for a newspaper's efforts and occasionally nit-picking at radio. Confidential though it was, it contained no word of the note sent Feb. 1 by Gannett to all his newspapers. He had learned from confidential sources that President Roosevelt's health was precarious. He urged all editors to be prepared for the worst.

That came on April 12 in Warm Springs, Ga., and a week later *The Bulletin* commended them for their preparedness and the extras with which they announced the president's death:

"The Roosevelt tragedy couldn't have occurred at a more awkward time for newspapers of the East. It came when most of the mechanical departments had washed up, circulators were far out on their runs and news staffs had melted away. Tall scrambling was the order in some cities but the various organizations clicked into their places and produced a series of splendid editions. FEG asks that his congratulations be expressed here."

Circulation numbers showed *The Times* in Hartford had sold 12,000 copies of a replated edition and 13,000 of a supplemental four-pager. With help from *Democrat and Chronicle* staff, the *Times-Union* was delayed in order to produce an early extra that sold 18,000 copies. A *Democrat and Chronicle* extra sold 24,000 copies.[13]

Most startling to many readers was the editorial tribute to Roosevelt written by the man who had sought unsuccessfully to oppose him in 1940 and who had tirelessly flayed the New Deal ever since.

In an editorial for all Gannett papers entitled, "In Service to His Country, He Paid with His Life," Gannett lamented the loss of "a great leader, a great person, a friend of mankind whose name will be written large in the annals of history. Even his bitterest political opponents are saddened by the passing of Franklin Delano Roosevelt, for he never made a personal enemy, even among those with whom he differed on government policies. . . . He had a kind, friendly charm, which won for him millions of faithful, loyal supporters, a following such as few leaders in public life ever have had."[14]

Even with news of such moment, *The Bulletin* justifiably picked some nits:

"Some newspapers turned the rules for the president's death. Unfortunately, the modern machine-cast rule wasn't meant for such use and the well-meant mourning sign turned out botchy. If we revive a custom largely abandoned, it might be a good idea to revive, also, the old brass rules." [15]

(In earlier newspaper practice, the metal rules that created the thin lines separating columns were sometimes inverted to create wide black lines. Such use was traditional in cases of major disaster or the death of an important person. When stock column rules of brass were used, the resulting lines were sharply defined. Machine typecasting produced column rules that were inferior to brass. "Turning the rule" was generally abandoned because of the poor results.)

# Beyond the War

When the editors gathered for their spring conference in Rochester, they were still trading compliments about coverage of Germany's surrender. They were also meeting alone. Advertising directors had decided to forego the meeting. As *The Bulletin* commented, "Why should they worry about selling space?" when newsprint supplies made so little available.

Editors carried home from that meeting Frank Gannett's challenges for the future.

First, he assured them that new technologies were at hand to produce "the greatest revolution ever in printing." He urged them to stand up on their hind legs against advertisers, because "no advertiser is ever going to tell one of our papers what it shall print or shall not print."

Looking toward the end of the war, he said circulation would have to "go up and up and up." He said each of them must be interested in increasing the company's profits, promising that those would make it possible "to do a grand job of extending benefits to employees and [to] have the best of relations with labor." [16]

One example of such relations with labor was reflected in a letter to the company. Profit sharing for 1944 had been the same 15 percent paid since that higher rate was set for the year 1941. Cpl. Jimmy Wall wrote from Burma:

"Three years away from the place and I'm still pulling down a bonus check on my 6 1/2 years of labor back there. Quite an institution – America – what?" [17]

Improving prospects for the end of the war found Frank Tripp warning publishers to use any additional supplies of newsprint wisely. He dismissed the likelihood of significant increases in supply but proposed this order of use:

"First, any additional print should be used to recoup any extraordinary and conspicuous curtailing in the regularly served newspaper.

"Second choice is circulation service to people now on the waiting list in the newspaper's own parish. This does not mean promotional use.

"In third place is added service for permanent advertisers who are on a waiting list for space and whose rationing may have caused a hardship." [18]

By July, confidence in the war's end in the Pacific theater was high enough that Rochester's two papers proposed the erection of a $2.5-million war memorial to be financed by public subscription. Soon after V-J Day, the Gannett board of directors approved a $25,000 donation to that memorial in the names of the *Democrat and Chronicle* and the *Times-Union*. [19]

Early August found Gannett editors smiling over the fallout of a strike against newspapers in New York City. New Yorkers were questioned about the adequacy of radio in the absence of their newspapers. The first week, 76.6 percent of those asked replied that radio was not a satisfactory substitute. The second week, 89.2 percent faulted radio. [20]

*The Bulletin* reminded editors to remain aware of the censorship code because hard fighting was still possible in the Pacific. It repeated a general's assurances that "the War Department is fully aware of the desirability of reducing censorship as rapidly as may be consistent with military security." Fay Blanchard added, "That's a brush-off, but gentle." [21]

He was happy to report progress in Frank Gannett's determination to keep good men in the company. Editors and publishers knew, he said, that men with costly training were occasionally attracted to jobs elsewhere, "generally with better pay."

"Within the past six months," he wrote in *The Bulletin*, "three key editorial men left the Group to work under other editors. All three have sought to return. The pay was better, as promised, but living conditions were worse and the men missed the Group atmosphere." [22]

Two weeks later, the war was over. The nation was euphoric. Gannett sent "a heartfelt 'Well Done'" to all his newspapers for their coverage of the Japanese surrender. Blanchard warned editors and managers to keep things in perspective:

"It's early yet to talk about the future. . . . But it is not too early to start planning. The public is geared to a high pressure flow of news and will not be content with a meager and routine service. . . . [W]e shall have better mechanical equipment shortly. Improvements are coming in all printing and photographic lines. . . . Required will be aggressive leadership. Anyone who feels that war's end means an opportunity to relax is fooling himself – only himself." [23]

# Chapter 17

# Confronting Peace

*"I'm no genius in any way. I have no greater ability than many of you. I've worked hard. I've been lucky. I've had fortitude. And my parents blessed me with the gift of good health. . . . It's been you with me who've made it possible for us to have the best group of newspapers in the country."*

Frank Gannett
June 3, 1946

Horns, bells and whistles were still ringing in the ears of peace celebrants when *The Bulletin* threw a wet blanket on any Gannett editors and managers breathing sighs of relief. Summarizing what it called "The Problem of 1945," *The Bulletin* said the war's end "started a great raid on unemployment insurance funds, ended a great manufacturing era and, incidentally, tossed a weighty problem into the laps of newspaper operators.

"Here they were rolling along with record circulations, turning down advertising, saving white print. All of a sudden the war news was out. The all-absorbing story which had held attention for three years and more had reached its conclusion. . . .

"Some cities with swollen population[s] and swollen factory payrolls felt the slump immediately. The departing hosts represented many a newspaper buyer. . . .

"Peace hit the editorial side hard. Telegraph editors began to hunt for promising nuggets of domestic news. They felt again the necessity of making the most out of a little. Their problem is to help make the newspaper so enticing that all the new readers will feel compelled to keep on buying it."

As the fall conference of news and business executives neared, participants were urged to come prepared to offer ideas on how to make their newspapers more appealing, how to handle returning servicemen, what to do if more newsprint should become available.

Once again, Frank Gannett was urging greater efforts to improve editorial pages and their readership. He remained determined to instill in editors and business executives his own belief that editorial pages were the hearts of their newspapers.

He repeatedly emphasized comment on local issues, brighter writing, experimentation in layouts, generous use of photographs and maps, regular doses of humor, anything to avoid the predictability that he believed meant boredom for readers.

Details are scarce but it was about this time that the Gannett Company suddenly expanded into farming. It was not a planned diversification.

People who remember the company under Frank Gannett recall him with respect and sometimes disbelief. They praise his success in building The Gannett Newspapers. They marvel when they remember his naive trust in employees.

Samuel Williamson told of the time Gannett took an employee aside to berate him for continuously heavy drinking:

"By the time the session was over, the culprit had been given a bigger job at a bigger salary. 'To encourage him,' explained Gannett to his indignant associates; then he added serenely: 'Why, I've his word that he won't ever take another drink.' "[1]

Vin Jones, former executive editor of The Gannett Newspapers, told of another case in which a man caught stealing was given a raise by Gannett so he could repay the money.

It was a betrayal of that sort of trust that bought Gannett a 265-acre farm. According to Jones, the trusted employee in this case was fired for embezzlement but never prosecuted:

"Every Saturday [the employee's] secretary delivered five $100 bills to his desk . . . all of which he invested not on slow horses or fast women but a model farm on the outskirts of Rochester.

"Well, when they caught him and fired him, they took over the farm."[2]

Gannett's *Democrat and Chronicle* had had a farm editor for years, L. B. Skeffington. The publisher decided to turn adversity to advantage. He installed L.B. and Janette Skeffington as resident operators and turned the new property into an experimental farm.

Late in 1945, Gannett's directors bought the farm from Frank Gannett for $92,044.50. In its resolution, the board praised Skeffington. It added:

"[H]e has arranged for and is now receiving the active cooperation of Cornell University's farm experts in the conducting of experiments and the general operation of the farm; . . . the company intends to operate this farm experimentally so as to provide its farm editors with firsthand practical knowledge of the problems to be discussed by them in their columns."[3]

Gannett Farms, as it was called, would be operated in that manner for nearly 14 years, and then sold to two investors for $293,500.[4]

## New Horizons

When the conference finally convened at the end of October 1945, two topics got major attention. One was Gannett News Service, renamed from Gannett National Service as the war ended. Gannett praised GNS for the volume and quality of its output and urged all papers in the group to use more of its stories.

Many of the editors and managers were looking forward to invitations from Washington Bureau Chief Cecil Dickson to attend a GNS party Dec. 4 at the Mayflower Hotel "to meet Washington big shots."

A second source of excitement at the conference was word that editors would be in Albany Dec. 11 to watch wire transmission of photographs by The Associated Press, International News Service and Acme Photo. The editors were to decide for The Gannett Newspapers, "first, if a group installation is feasible and desirable; next, if desirable, which service offers the best return – and for how much money."[5]

Only a week after the conference, *The Bulletin* illustrated why Frank Gannett had made the case for GNS. Cecil Dickson had filed a story from Washington about labor unions – "the great revenues, the

unions' freedom from tax and some other features."
No Gannett paper played it as news "on Page 1 or elsewhere. Next day, Nov. 1, *The New York Times* played [its version of] the same story on Page 1.
"In the case of GNS," *The Bulletin* concluded, "it is to everyone's interest to make important use of what it offers."[6]

GNS's guests were not quite as indifferent to its party and the entree it gave them to prominent figures, including President Harry Truman at the White House. When they got home, some of them wrote columns about it.

C.C. Hemenway, editor of *The Hartford Times,* told his readers, "Dickson's guest list . . . included plenty who don't have to go to parties unless they want to, a long, long list of personal friends. And what a list of friends for a man to have! The grand event was a high compliment to the standing of the man who heads the bureau that furnishes Gannett newspapers with Washington news."

Frank Little, general manager and editor of Ogdensburg's *Journal,* wrote:

"The number of celebrities and world famed figures who attended demonstrated the esteem and regard in which Cecil Dickson is held in the national capital. . . . Paul Miller, chief of the Washington bureau of The Associated Press and slated to be the next executive director of AP on the retirement of Kent Cooper, told me he doubted if the mighty AP itself could give a party and get such a turnout of celebrities and notables as Cecil Dickson had done."[7]

Early in the new year, Fay Blanchard, now president of the New York State Society of Newspaper Editors as well as Gannett's associate editor, returned from a meeting of AP managing editors in Miami. He spoke highly of Paul Miller:

"Miller, by all odds, was the most impressive member of the battery sent in by AP. He is direct in his statements, forthright in his answers, even when he risks irritating his questioners. When one apparent New Dealer took Paul to task for calling one of Harry Truman's pet measures 'the so-called full employment bill,' he talked right back.

"His bureau, Miller said, makes it a practice to avoid identifying measures by the names of sponsors or by their announced intent. Full employment, he asserted, is just a name, because full employment can't be attained."[8]

If readers of *The Bulletin* heard an echo, it was because those very thoughts had come out of Gannett's mouth on many occasions.

## Acme's the One

Acme Telephoto won the transmission derby. April 1, 1946 was the scheduled start for linking its national network with the papers in Albany, Binghamton, Elmira, Hartford, Rochester and Utica. *The Bulletin* called it "an important landmark in the record and growth of the Group." Editors and managers of other Gannett newspapers, whose photo needs would continue to be supplied by parcel delivery, may have been less enthusiastic.

Telephoto was chosen because it offered two outstanding advantages: Gannett papers would be on a national network, which meant prints would be first run – clearer than any second or third run could be. And the assurance of a specialized service was most appealing to the Group.

Blanchard announced to *Bulletin* readers that he was off with nine other newsmen for a working tour of France, and would cable stories to GNS. He hoped for a chance to see some of the war crimes trial at Nuremberg, adding that "FEG thinks regulars over there have gone stale on the long drawn-out proceedings."

Before embarking, he took a shot at the New York Newspaper Publishers Association for favoring U.S. State Department interests over those of The Associated Press and United Press. The government was seeking free wire service from both to support Voice of America and other propaganda programs in Europe. Blanchard wrote:

"The publishers adopted what amounted to a censure of AP and UP for refusing to supply their services free to the propaganda agency. *Editor & Publisher*, which had urged compromise and delay, found that editors all over the country heartily endorsed the action of the two wire services. The publishers' resolution never could have cleared an editorial meeting." [9]

His parting advice to readers of the confidential newsletter came "from a newspaper executive who knows his stuff" – read that Frank Gannett or Frank Tripp. It read:

"Newspapers are suckers to print pictures of pickets and their placards. They give undue and unfair prominence to some crackpot who devises a smart or startling slogan. You will note that picket leaders are quick to emphasize the occasional veteran and his uniform, usually tied in with the placarded claim that all ex-soldiers are back of the strike. When we give Page 1 prominence to such guff we are encouraging strikers everywhere. Newspapers are much too eager to see peace restored industrially to give aid and comfort to the comparatively few radicals who live on the turmoil and enmity between workers and management." [10]

In June 1946 the company marked the 40th anniversary of Gannett and Davenport's partnership. Another cause for celebration was this salute from the U.S. Treasury Department to Frank Tripp for his wartime service as chairman of the Allied Newspaper Council:

"No single individual contributed more to the successful conclusion of the Treasury's war effort than did Frank Tripp. His record stood out above all others of six million volunteers."

Tripp responded:

"This is unquestionably the most flagrant miscarriage of justice that ever occurred in the age of free men. . . . I can only accept this undeserved citation with the understanding it is given to the newspapers and the newspapermen of the country. I'm only a symbol. They did the job." [11]

At the anniversary dinner provided by Hartford's *Times*, guests grew mellow on pit-baked clams, lobster, chicken and potatoes and the reminiscences of the original trio.

"We were like a group of travelers," Davenport said, "who, having met, agreed to travel on together. I came from the west; Frank Gannett from the east. And in Elmira we met Frank Tripp. . . . We've been picking up travelers ever since, all of you.

"We have watched the signposts along the road. And now, after 40 years, we see another sign: 'You are entering the atomic age; proceed at your own risk.' We see clouds and turmoil ahead. But there's no reason to be unduly afraid."

Master of ceremonies Tripp turned to Gannett. "I've never looked on you as an employer or as a co-worker," he said. "Instead, I've thought of us as two guys trying to do the same thing in vastly different ways."

Gannett briefly was unable to speak. Among the things he said when he regained his composure:

"Ordinarily I prefer to look ahead. . . . But probably the happiest days I'll ever have were those I spent climbing the *Elmira Gazette's* rickety stairs. For what's been done I give credit to Dav and Frank. . . .

"Our group of newspapers is just beginning. We're just beginning to go forward in a magnificent way. . . .

"I wish I had the sense of humor that Frank Tripp has. I wish I had his personality that captivates everyone. As with Dav, so with him, I've never had a harsh word.

"I want to pay tribute to them for what has **not** happened. Their spirit has gone on to others and to our whole organization. Everyone is pushing up, trying to do a better job instead of trying to get into the job of someone else."[12]

Innovation was encouraged, routine scorned when it came to creating better newspapers. The most notable example came in Utica. Vin Jones, then executive editor of both papers, bought from *The New Yorker* the text of John Hersey's *Hiroshima* for serialization in *The Observer-Dispatch*.

It was available but could be displayed only as *The New Yorker* required. Thus limited on typographical brightening, Jones sought photographs of the six persons whose personal experiences were recounted in Hersey's text. He was rebuffed repeatedly but persisted until the pictures were made available.

They not only were prominently displayed on Page 1 of *The O-D* but also became available to newspapers generally. In its salute to

Jones, *The Bulletin* of Oct. 3, 1946, said, "You and I gained from *The O-D's* alert and tireless efforts. The group's prestige is increased everywhere."

## Competitive Edginess

Although editors and advertising directors had been meeting jointly for several years, an undercurrent of mutual suspicion occasionally rose to flood stage. That was probably inevitable given the shortage of newsprint and the futility of an ad salesman's even seeking new business.

Several such incidents strained the amity in 1946. One began in the summer, when an editor innocently wrote *The Bulletin* that he was having trouble "getting printers enough to handle the advertising that rolls through our front door."

Group ad director Don Bridge huffed in response:

"It is safe to say that advertising 'rolls through the front door' about like all the news that is worthwhile 'rolls' through the door without being rolled in."

The not-so-remorseful editor replied:

"I most certainly was not unmindful of the efforts and responsibilities of our brethren in the advertising departments. After all, how could an editor forget when he is repeatedly reminded by the advertising men that they, and they alone, make it possible for the editor's wife and children to eat three meals a day and to be warmly dressed when wintry blasts blow. I am ever grateful that God blessed some of His children with sufficient brains and backbone to sell newspaper advertising. Praise be to Great Allah Bridge. . . .

"I stand by my guns and contend that we still are publishing little more than the advertising that rolls in the front door. Due to the shortage of paper in the past and now the scarcity of printers, we haven't sold a special edition of any type since the war. Our ad manager is getting grayer by the minute as he ponders how to keep advertisers happy while turning down their business."[13]

In October, an advertising man hotly protested a single-panel cartoon called Side Glances in which a housewife exclaims, "Our new neighbors have some new, expensive things – I can't wait to tell her how smart we have been not to buy at the high prices!"

The angered ad man denounced the cartoon as "the rankest kind of scare copy. I don't think it sound to preach buyers' strike," he said.

Harold Sanford, editor of Rochester's *Democrat and Chronicle*, wasn't having any of that "advertising yelp.

"We have remarked against buying real estate at too-high prices," he pointed out, and "that in the long run such sales benefitted neither the buyer nor the real estate man. . . .

"Mark Sullivan has been constantly warning GIs against buying farms at inflated values. . . .

"And we must be constantly vigilant on too-high prices on certain food items, cars, etc. . . .

"A buyers' strike on certain over-priced items is one way by which demand controls supply."

He conceded, however, "This situation should be handled with care, of course. Left-wing general buyers' strikes should be condemned."[14]

From Hartford, managing editor Carl Lindstrom asked, "Why is it that if an advertiser cuts his prices it's OK? But if a news story says prices are down it is scare copy?"

# Broken Ranks

By mid-autumn, Blanchard was deploring the call by Great Britain's National Union of Journalists for an investigation of the British press. "By naming specific 'evils' to be investigated," he said in *The Bulletin*, "the union puts the stamp of truth upon the claims of all critics of the press. The casual reader is sure to believe that if persons within the profession believe such evils exist, the general charges are true."

(Parliament approved in October 1946 a Royal Commission of Inquiry to investigate the British press "regarding ownership, control and monopoly." Prime Minister Clement Attlee announced to the House of Commons on March 26, 1947, the appointment of that 17-member commission. The commission's report to the House of Commons on June 29, 1949, cleared the British press of "charges of corrupt and monopolistic practices. It urged the press to create a general council to raise its standards and guard against monopoly.") [15]

Blanchard considered similar complaints from newspaper unions probable in the United States. "We have seen in the past few years a change in attitude of newspapermen," he wrote. "Their old loyalties to the paper they serve are being swept aside." [16]

His doubts about those old loyalties soon were confirmed. Two hundred six members of Local 15 of the International Typographical Union struck the Rochester papers on Nov. 8 without notice. Members of all but one other union either refused to cross ITU picket lines or to process typewritten copy prepared to produce an emergency newspaper. Publication was blocked for three months.

Members of the Newspaper Guild reported to work every day and handled the news reports as if each paper were being published. They prepared news bulletins for window displays and wrote radio newscasts for Gannett's Rochester station.

The *Gannetteer* summarized the impasse:

"The strike is the result of a wage dispute following expiration on July 31, 1946, of the former printers' contract. While the men had submitted demands for wages of $110 [night work] and $100 [day], a series of meetings between representatives of the company and of the union resulted in a final demand by the printers for $88 and $80 for a 37 1/2-hour week. Meanwhile the management had increased offers to $75 and $70, an increase of $12 a week over the 1945-46 contract. It also offered an alternative proposal to give the printers an option of taking a guaranteed $4 weekly increase in pay, thus reaching a top of $79 and $74 in lieu of the regular annual profit-sharing of the company, which all regular employees of the company now receive." [17]

Despite repeated offers of help from the New York State Mediation

Board, an ITU representative declined, arguing that direct negotiations would resolve the dispute more quickly.

The storied Gannett sense of a company family was severely strained as the strike grew longer. Dixon Gannett, who was then 17, said, "I knew a lot of people down at the office. I'd been running in and out of that building. I had free rein on that building. . . . I could go into the press room, the editorial room, I could go wherever I wanted.

"When this strike hit, my mom and dad told me, 'Don't go to the office. Stay away from there.' You know, like 'they'll kidnap you, and hold you for ransom,' and all this.

"I went. I went down to the office. . . . I think they had picket lines out front. I don't remember. I walked into the office. People said 'hello' to me; nobody bothered me; I went home. Nobody said, 'Boo.' Just like any other day.

"Man, my old man found out about it the next day and I'll tell you, it hit the fan. They were mad. 'We told you not to.' I said, 'Dad, nothing happened. Nothing happened. I said 'hello' to them. They said 'hello' to me." [18]

As the strike dragged on, the ITU representative sought to negotiate a master contract for all Gannett newspapers. When that was rebuffed he went to Washington on other union business and did not return for 22 days.

Early in January, management and the union agreed on the once-rejected package of $79 for night men and $74 for day workers. It took another month for the company to settle with other mechanical unions. Wage increases ranged from $12 to $16 a week over the 1945-46 scale. Members of the Newspaper Guild, which remained at work throughout the three-month strike, signed a contract giving them a $16-a-week raise.

# Shakeout

The strike was costly. Treasurer Herbert W. Cruickshank told the directors that the company lost more than $180,000 in January alone.[19]

Whatever the total cost – it was not made public – the price paid by all other employees of The Gannett Newspapers was cancellation of profit-sharing for the first time since it was instituted in 1936.

Gannett, feeling more bewildered than betrayed, told his executives:

"The strike hurt me, not so much financially as personally. I've given stock worth millions to the [Gannett] Foundation, and I couldn't understand why our men would hurt themselves by striking. The strike hurt all business. The innocent public was hard hit. There's only one explanation:

"The men who went out couldn't have understood what the foundation means to them. Our job, on all our papers, is to explain the foundation and to avoid further strikes." [20]

If there was a bright spot for Frank Gannett in those 90 days of frustration, it was summarized by his biographer:

"Paradoxically enough, Gannett's Rochester newspapers never attained so much local good will as after the community had to try to get along without them for a while. 'From this experience,' says Gannett, 'we learned how essential newspapers are.' " [21]

# Chapter 18

# A Look at the Future

*"I learned [simplicity of writing] from a hard-boiled old bird who was allotted 12 columns daily. He'd bellow, 'What the hell you writin', a book?'"*

Frank Tripp
1947

Labor relations was much on the minds of Gannett executives after the Rochester strike. Frank Gannett was stung by the rebelliousness of workers whose jobs he had always sought to make secure. Characteristically, he concluded that the workers, rather than he, did not understand what was in their best interest.

Immediately after the strike, *The Bulletin* sent this confidential advice to Gannett executives:

"At the moment any proposed labor legislation is referred to as 'anti-labor.'

"Actually most of the labor legislation under discussion [which came to be known as the Taft-Hartley Act] is as much pro-labor as it is pro-public. Some congressmen doubtless have a hope of punishing unions but their views will not prevail. Congress is seeking legislation which will curb labor evils, not labor itself. Some of the suggested measures are based on the idea that most laboring people will be helped under a fairer system.

"As a little test, suppose you go through a few wire stories and see for yourself how often 'anti-labor' can be removed without in any way changing the sense.

"We used to worry about becoming editorial in our copy. The phrase discussed here is pretty close to being editorial."[1]

And this:

"I feel we who are opposed to the closed shop are using the wrong phraseology. We should be talking about 'the right to work.' That is a fundamental American right and it should not be abridged or destroyed. The closed shop does destroy that right. Thousands of men in this country cannot get work without joining a union and agreeing to obey the orders that come from the top. This is in effect a form of slavery.

"If we say 'the right to work' we are speaking as friends of labor. The labor racketeers are always trying to make it appear that anyone who suggests bettering working conditions is anti-labor. It is the men who make a racket out of organizing and herding labor who are the real foes of the working man."[2]

That may have seemed the voice of sweet reason to *Bulletin* readers. Two issues later, however, in a notice headlined, "KEEP A CONFIDENCE," *The Bulletin* warned:

"*The Bulletin* is confidential. While its files do not reveal any items that couldn't be circulated freely, it prefers to remain an intimate medium for executives. . . .

"Recently Mr. Gannett was quoted in advising use of the phrase 'the right to work' instead of 'anti closed shop.' It was a reasonable and legitimate comment on the use of words. Rochester's labor paper picked it up, trying hard to make it a smear. Actually what it did was place before a labor audience the idea that it is being misled and abused by men whose use of the closed shop keeps it in servitude.

"We do not resent the labor paper's use of the statement. What we do resent is the fact that a confidential document should be quoted so exactly.

"The man who was careless enough to let it out of his hands is too careless to be a good executive. Any person guilty of betraying a trust by giving out such documents is no more than a rat."[3]

That was soon followed by this brief notice:

"With this issue *The Bulletin* mailing list is cut sharply. The action marks a return to the practice of circulating it as an intimate medium of exchange between executives. Editors and other executives on the list will know when portions of it should be passed on to other readers."[4]

Concern about *The Bulletin's* confidentiality was advisable. Its references to organized labor invariably were contemptuous and Fay Blanchard occasionally engaged in red-baiting by insinuation.

Democrat-turned-Progressive Henry Wallace was a favorite political whipping boy, scorned for having abandoned "hybrid corn for hybrid Americanism."

Anti-communism was a just cause for both Gannett and Tripp. *The Bulletin*, not they, however, sounded the alarms. As early as the preceding fall, syndicated columnist Constantine Brown had been guest speaker at the conference of editors and advertising directors. At that meeting, he flatly asserted, to no reported challenge, that Communists controlled the "sensitive American unions" of the CIO, "ready for the Moscow signal to strike and tie up this nation, come Pearl Harbor II."[5]

Vigilance was advised on letters to the editor:

"In these days when the country is being 'wallaced' [a reference to Henry Wallace] from within and without, it's well to keep an eye on the letter forum. . . . Some editors have decided to bar all Communist letters. They reason that to do so is no more suppression of freedom than is the application of the libel law or our more or less stringent rules against murder. . . .

"Letters constitute a valuable asset. They also afford a great danger. Names and addresses always should be checked. Above all they should be checked when they contain communistic, anti-American and anti-newspaper propaganda."

## Get Behind the Barn

Editors and advertising directors spent part of their spring session in brand new surroundings. They had lunch at The Barn, the new Gannett Youth Club built to provide a liquor-free Friday- and Saturday-night club for Rochester young people.

The Barn was created by Frank Gannett in response to concerns expressed by parents at a conference. It was designed to be run by the young people themselves. And it was presented to them in the names of the *Democrat and Chronicle* and the *Times-Union*.

Gannett told the executives the youth club cost a bit more than $30,000 and urged them to consider similar projects for their own communities.

The editors heard from Paul Miller, chief of the AP Washington bureau, during a round-table discussion on better writing. He suggested that each newspaper assign one staffer to study the entire newsroom operation and recommend ways to simplify staff writing. It isn't necessary to pay readability experts for advice, he told them, if reporters and editors realize that the simple approach is the best approach.

Gannett also offered a range of ideas to the audience. "Above all," he told them, "we must create more influential newspapers. Upon what they do and say may depend the future of civilization."

He re-emphasized the importance of a free press: "We must tell our readers again and again that our Constitution and our Bill of Rights have given this country the highest standard of living in the world, plus liberty and freedom. Our task is to ward off foes, be they called Communists, Fascists, or whatever."

On group operations, he suggested that Gannett News Service might benefit from a bureau in New York City. That would allow easy contact with people going to or returning from Europe, he said. Such a bureau also could supply more quickly digests of exclusives published by the metropolitan newspapers.

(The company set up a one-man GNS bureau in New York City in 1959, manned by Jack Germond.)

# Have a Pleasant Tripp

Tripp had been known for years outside Gannett as all business, the newspaperman who had steered the nation's successive war bond drives. His colleagues in The Gannett Newspapers knew another Frank Tripp, whose regular newspaper columns in Elmira had won him devoted readers and envy among his peers for his writing skill.

In the spring of 1947, General Features began syndicating a weekly Tripp column. Almost immediately it was appearing in 60 newspapers with an audience of 3 million readers. Eventually, 125 newspapers would subscribe.

More than one Gannett editor must have marveled at the ease with which Tripp captivated readers with simplicity and style. When Tripp talked about writing, he did not strut. He was disarming. "I use simple words because I can't spell the big ones," he said. "The only punctuation mark I know for sure is the period. So when I know I should make a mark of some sort I make it a period and start a new sentence."

He once suggested that would-be columnists try writing with a lead pencil on an ordinary tablet. "It is hard to write that way," he said. "That makes for brevity." He urged newspapers to be more intimate, closer to the people, to talk more to ordinary people. "We idolize officialdom too much," he said.[6]

Charles Barber, editor of the Elmira *Advertiser*, was an associate and friend of Tripp for most of his professional life. He once wrote to Blanchard an appreciation of Tripp's writing and its popularity. The nostalgia and memories about which Tripp wrote, said Barber, were "stuff that people like enough to save and read again and keep in their Bibles and paste in their scrap books and send to people far away. The affection they show for such things goes beyond the clippings; it sheds something on the man whose work it is and more than that, and more important, too, it binds people to their newspapers."[7]

While Tripp's popularity as a columnist grew, Gannett was off creating his own opportunities to write. He joined a group of publishers and other executives on a 13-day trip around the world. It was a preliminary one in Pan-American World Airways' effort to establish a round-the-world route.

With only 120 hours spent in the air, the party had ample time to see Manila, Tokyo, Shanghai, Istanbul and London. Gannett returned six pounds lighter but "reinvigorated." He spoke fondly of returning to Manila 47 years after working there as secretary to a presidential commission.

*The Bulletin* of July 3, 1947, reported that his "enthusiasm for General [Douglas] MacArthur appears at a new high. . . . The 'boss' shares MacArthur's optimism for Japan's future. He was encouraged by what he saw and heard in the Philippines. He appears somewhat less optimistic over China's future."

Gannett was writing a series on the flight for publication in the *Times-Union* and other interested Gannett newspapers. As with reports on his trip to England the year before, the series was published in booklet form. Both booklets, "The Fuse Sputters" and "Winging 'Round the World," were widely distributed.

## The AP Spills the Beans

Only weeks after Frank Gannett returned from his globe-circling trip, The Associated Press scooped him in August 1947 on a story involving his own newspapers. Kent Cooper, AP executive director and general manager, announced a series of personnel changes. They were made necessary, the wire story said, by the loss of assistant general manager Paul Miller, who had resigned to become executive assistant to Frank Gannett.

The publisher quickly confirmed the report, telling Gannett employees:

"For a long time I have been watching him very carefully and I was so favorably impressed by him that I urged him to come with us.

"Ever since the death of Leroy E. Snyder [in 1945], I have been searching for a man who could ably fill that place and add strength to our organization. This move does not in any way affect anyone in our organization. Mr. Miller will have special work of great importance and will relieve me of many of my burdens.

"Although Mr. Miller has gone far in the newspaper business he is only 40 years old. He has made friends throughout the country and few newspapermen are better known than he."[8]

Gannett may have been watching Miller for a long time, but as in other matters of special interest to him, Tripp was the matchmaker.

In 1990, Louise Miller recalled those days (a stroke had left Paul Miller unable to speak). Miller had met Frank and Caroline Gannett during the 1940 Republican National Convention in Philadelphia, she said. "He told me what nice people they were."

Although her husband was not warm to the idea when the two Franks first approached him about joining Gannett, his eventual decision to accept, she said, "was absolutely due to Frank [Tripp] being so persistent."

Miller discussed his indecision with Kent Cooper, a man many people expected him to succeed as head of AP.

"Kent Cooper treated my husband almost as a son," Louise Miller said. In that father-son exchange, she said, Cooper recalled offers he'd had to become a publisher or an assistant publisher and said he sometimes regretted not accepting one of them. "It's a different life," she quoted the AP chief, "but I don't see why you don't take a chance."

"I think PM took that advice after having told KC about Frank Tripp being on our doorstep," she said.[9]

Tripp's daughter Nancy Tripp Rose acknowledged her father's persistence in recruiting Miller. He would show up at the Miller household at 9 or 10 at night, she said, to try to persuade him to join Gannett.

Or, "He'd show up maybe at dinner time, or Paul would bring him home unannounced, and [Louise] was there with all the babies. . . . [T]hey'd . . . sit down and have a wonderful, warm time.

"I remember when Paul had finally decided to come. Dad was telling us about him, and he said, 'You'll like him. He's just like an old shoe.'"[10]

Gannett executives now had reason to think back to their spring conference, when Miller took part in that roundtable discussion on better writing. Louise Miller says she believes that by late 1946, Miller already was seriously considering the move. So he may have been taking the measure of future subordinates without their knowing it.

As for Gannett's assurance that the appointment would not in any way affect anyone in the organization, Miller's arrival was a fairly clear signal. Frank Little, editor and publisher at Ogdensburg, had described him after the GNS party in Washington as the man everyone expected to succeed Kent Cooper at The Associated Press. Surely "anyone in the organization" might have concluded that a man doesn't leave a job with such a promising future without some assurance of advancement.

When asked whether it was assumed at the time Miller was appointed executive assistant that he would succeed Gannett, Louise Miller replied, "As far as Mr. Tripp and Mr. Gannett were concerned, he was it. He was chosen."[11]

Soon after Miller's appointment, two veteran members of the corporate inner circle were given new titles. Herbert W. Cruickshank, former assistant general manager, was named general business manager, and Fay Blanchard, former associate editor, was named general executive editor of The Gannett Newspapers.

## Debating Reporters' Virtues

Rochester's Sheraton Hotel housed a pep rally of sorts when editors and advertising executives assembled for their 1947 fall conference. Vin Jones, who was tireless in trying to improve the readability of the Utica papers, urged his fellow editors at the conference to be daring. He particularly stressed making their papers appealing to women. Ask them "what they want to read tomorrow," he said, "not just what they didn't read yesterday."

Blanchard responded that The Gannett Newspapers had to find women who could write interestingly for other women. He asked how one could find out what women's interests really are.

Jones suggested that editors use women's panels, questionnaires, trial and error, shopping surveys, store interviews and, "if we can find any, women who are more interested in other women than they are in men."[12]

Carl Lindstrom, Hartford's managing editor, shared his reactions to a seminar he had attended for managing editors:

"I'll never be ashamed to be called 'provincial.' I'll battle all newspaper critics if I'm permitted to fight from a citadel of accurate local news. I'll trade a specialist for a good reporter any day." [13]

From Elmira, meanwhile, came word of Tripp's disdain for a newspapering tradition. George McCann, managing editor of *The Star-Gazette,* gave his judgment of comments he had heard in after-hours bull sessions there:

"Frank Tripp doesn't think much of the widespread practice of 'promoting' good reporters by making them into 'editors.' The plea that this is the only way of advancing a fellow, and thus justifying a fatter pay envelope for him, gets dim response from FET. He thinks, and has always thought, that the good reporter is the backbone of the news business — and that if the reporter IS good, he's worth his salt. And that salt, if I understand Brother Tripp correctly, could conceivably come in larger quantity than that received by the city editor who makes the reporter's assignments." [14]

## Back to Profit-Sharing

A year earlier, Rochester had been in the grips of its three-month newspaper strike. Once that was over, however, the Gannett Company returned to its accustomed profitability. At their meeting on Dec. 10, 1947, the directors of the company restored profit-sharing, but with a difference.

Members of the International Typographical Union had settled for the company offer of $79 a week for night work, $74 for day work. Other unions that supported the ITU received similar wage adjustments. Those weekly scales included a guaranteed $4, which the strikers accepted with the understanding that it was "in lieu of regular annual profit-sharing of the company," which all regular employees of the company then received. On the last year for which profits had been shared, 1945, employees got the standard 10 percent plus 5 percent to adjust for inflation.

Profit-sharing for 1947 came in two parts. Full-time employees of the mechanical department, including the mailroom – those covered by the recent contract – were awarded 4 percent of the profits. All other employees would share in 11 percent of the profits. Shares continued to be paid to all full-time employees with more than a year's service and prorated on length of service.

Bonuses of 20 percent, "to compensate them for the increased cost of living," were granted to all executives in the corporate offices, including the newly arrived Paul Miller, the managing editors of the *Democrat and Chronicle* and the *Times-Union,* and the chiefs of GNS bureaus in Washington and Albany.[15]

# Chapter 19

# That's the Spirit

*"Freedom of the press is well on its way out the window if newspapermen can't pursue their normal occupations without fear of being jailed for accepting information in confidence."*

Charles A.S. Freeman
Newburgh, N.Y., 1948

New Year's resolutions to work harder were not required of Gannett executives but instructive examples could serve as well. Fresh into 1948, editors and managers read of a Gannett fireball whose self-imposed schedule could intimidate the most dedicated among them. He was "that gamecock of a 'Bo' Gill from Newburgh," according to *The Bulletin:*

"Monday night he covered the fights in Newburgh, besides officiating as announcer and photographer. All he had to do was type out the judges' score cards, climb into the ring between bouts, collect cards, perform the introductions, then scramble down to tap out a few words about each of the preliminaries and occasionally poke a lens between the ropes to capture the knockout which he guessed was about due.

"When the fights ended, his story was complete, and, laden with camera, bulbs, typewriter and copy, he dashed to the parking lot to get his car out among the first. After that he drove a few miles to pick up basketball scores which had to be edited before 7 a.m. There was no fire in Newburgh that night but had there been one, he'd have been on the job. The truth is he's a vamp and would sooner miss breakfast than a fire." [1]

Fay Blanchard considered Gill's performance exemplary enough to be shared with other executives.

One person who could match Gill's diligence was Florence Messman, Gannett's personal secretary.

At 7:30 in the morning, her boss's chauffeur would deliver to her house the dictation records Gannett had made during the night. She would begin working on that when she arrived at the office soon after 8 a.m. Gannett's standing rule was that no matter how much dictation there was in the morning, it had to be typed and distributed that day.

If Gannett needed her at night, she would meet her husband for dinner and then return to the office. She frequently worked until 10 p.m. Her services were on call for both Frank and Caroline Gannett.

On Aug. 26, Messman was taking a letter that Gannett was dictating to his son, Dixon. "All of a sudden," she said, "I couldn't understand him. He never lost consciousness, but I thought, 'What's going on?' I didn't know what a stroke was. So I got up out of my chair and rapped on Mr. Cruickshank's door. 'Mr. Cruickshank,' I said, 'Mr. Gannett is ill.'

"So he came in. He didn't know what was the matter either, I suppose. So I said, we'll have to get the doctor. I rushed out and had one of the girls in the reception office call the doctor. That doctor was down there in 10 minutes. Mrs. Gannett always credited me with saving [Gannett's] life." [2]

The publisher, nearing his 72nd birthday, had suffered what would later be described as a slight stroke. However it was characterized, it was severe enough that he had to learn to walk again.

Gannett executives who were kept informed by *The Bulletin* were told in the Sept. 2 issue only that "when FEG fell ill during the recent heatwave, his doctors clamped down on him. They demanded that he take the rest they have been urging on him to restore some of the energy he has expended so prodigally through the years. Resentful of his idleness and counting days until he can return to his desk – and some golf – FEG is reported to be a good patient. For once he is obeying the MDs who have cut him off from telephonic or other contact with business for the time being. He is at home."

He was at home because his doctor, Dr. John R. Williams, thought he had not recovered enough to travel to his vacation home in Miami Beach. Gannett occasionally had told employees and the public that heavy travel, particularly political campaigning, had affected his health.

It was about this time that Caroline Gannett and Dr. Williams issued an ultimatum to Gannett. It resulted in a handwritten statement on official *The Gannett Newspapers* letterhead, Frank E. Gannett, President, Executive Offices, Rochester, N.Y. It was dated only 1948:

"I, Frank Gannett, do hereby solemnly declare that I will **never,** from now on – enter into politics – I swear this in the presence of my beloved wife – Caroline Gannett [–] and my loyal doctor – John Williams."

It was signed by Frank E. Gannett and co-signed by John R. Williams Jr. and Caroline Werner Gannett.[3]

Company publications contained few references to the convalescing publisher, since the editors knew that Gannett was reading them at home. The editors were as eager as his doctors to avoid any pressures that might disrupt his complete rest.

He could read the good news, of course. Part of that was the growing popularity of *Editorially Speaking,* the annual compilation of selected material from the editors' conferences. The sixth issue had been published in 1948, and its reception was warm. One thank-you note came from a reader identified only as the director of a school of journalism:

"Much matter of this type comes to my desk. When I began reading your booklet, I merely expected to browse a bit. Nevertheless, I soon found myself absorbed in the practical discussions and read everything to the end. I regard this sort of publication as having great value for not only the students but the teachers in a school of journalism.

"In our school we are realists with ideals. No matter what our dreams may be, we aim to keep our feet constantly on the ground. Those who participated in the discussions found in your booklet are also realists – a type that I especially like because of the great fund of common sense displayed in what is said. I shall take great pleasure in asking my staff to read these comments and shall be glad to see future publications."[4]

When Gannett read *The Bulletin* of Sept. 16, he found a definite change from its earlier coolness toward radio.

"Plans are being worked out," the newsletter said, "for real cooperation between Gannett station WHEC and the two [Rochester] newspapers. It's the first time the relationship between station and paper has been emphasized.

"It is planned now to make WHEC the NEWS station for the Rochester area. Full resources of the newspapers will be thrown into the effort. As part of the program a WHEC newsman will work in the newsroom itself, taking advantage of its gleanings. Probably he will pick up some of the local room's sense of urgency, too."

While that subtle change from veiled contempt to grudging coexistence was not explained, it may have been one of the first signs of Paul Miller's growing influence. Kind words for radio had not been in Gannett executives' lexicon before Miller arrived. Serious suggestions about cooperating with radio would have risked the scorn of colleagues.

Miller was a passionate newspaperman. His experience with The Associated Press, however, not only had required him to serve radio stations as well as newspapers but also had exposed him to radio's value as a news medium.

The inference that Miller influenced the changing attitude toward radio was strengthened in late 1948 with the creation of the Gannett Radio Group. It comprised the six Gannett radio stations and was Miller's latest responsibility. His immediate subordinates would be Gunnar Wiig and Bernard O'Brien, general manager and chief engineer, respectively, of Rochester's WHEC.

Post-election coverage found *The Bulletin* of Nov. 4 applauding group newspapers for their efforts. In an unprecedented observation, it added:

"Did you listen to radio? It really did itself proud with round-the-clock returns."

## Mrs. Gannett's Biggest Job

Frank and Caroline Gannett and Dr. John R. Williams boarded the Gannett Company airplane Nov. 12 for Miami Beach. There the publisher would continue his convalescence until his doctor approved his return to work.

Williams said Gannett had made remarkable progress in his recovery. The publisher was walking about a mile a day. The slight muscular impairment on his left side had practically disappeared.

The *Gannetteer* reassured company employees that "[his] blood pressure, almost perfect, has been important in bringing about his recovery. It also makes recurrence of this trouble most unlikely – if he obeys orders and avoids strain and heavy pressure. . . .

"Mrs. Gannett says FEG already has become too restive and her biggest job is 'holding him back, preventing him from doing what he feels he can do and wants to do – that is, almost anything that's to be done.' "[5]

Gannett remained in Florida throughout the winter, missing the January 1949 meeting of the Gannett board. At that session, the board was enlarged by two seats and Raymond H. McKinney, national ad representative, and Miller were elected directors.

Herbert Cruickshank reported to the board that he and Tripp had tried but failed to buy the Albany *Times-Union* from Hearst.[6]

Miller became more clearly first among equals in the corporate hierarchy in March 1949. He was named a vice president of the corporation. More significant to newsroom denizens, he was appointed editor of the *Times-Union*, a position held by Gannett since the paper's creation by merger in 1918. Gannett remained its publisher.

It was an added role for Miller, who remained the publisher's executive assistant and head of the Gannett Radio Group.[7]

# Back in Harness

Not quite 10 months after he had suffered the stroke in his office, Gannett was back. He called it "without doubt the happiest day of my life."

He said he had had plenty of time to think about his illness and the future.

"As a newspaperman," he said, "I'd been fighting the clock for more than 50 years, trying to crowd into every day everything possible. Such hurry is bad for anyone, and I've learned at great cost that I must never again force myself to hurry so. But I do hope to be able to do much of the work that I had done before."

He thanked employees for cards, letters and good wishes, particularly an oversized "Happy Birthday" postcard signed by hundreds of them.

"I hope that our Group can continue to grow," he said. We have in mind some other things we hope to do which would benefit all employees. I should like nothing so much as to be able to add to the happiness of all those who were concerned about my welfare."

Gannett had first acknowledged his mortality in 1935 when he created the Frank E. Gannett Foundation. He had been constantly reminded of it for the past 10 months. During the time he was gone, he told his family of employees, "Our papers came out without me and I was both proud and pleased." [8]

# Chapter 20

# Renovations

*"A newspaper isn't worth the ink used to print it if it doesn't stand for something. Yet, it doesn't merit a nickel of anybody's money if it doesn't go out of its way, if necessary, to provide a forum, to give a hearing, to all who want to get a word in on whatever side."*

*Paul Miller*
*1950*

Local autonomy was a privilege for which Frank Gannett's editors and publishers were grateful. Even in Rochester, editors of the *Democrat and Chronicle* could call their own shots. Gannett charted the editorial course for only one newspaper – the *Times-Union*.

Now, at 72 and just back from a long convalescence, he had supplanted himself with someone barely more than half his age. He remained publisher of the *Times-Union*, of course, but why would he turn his editorial pulpit over to a relative newcomer?

According to Louise Miller, Paul Miller was not dogmatic about public policy or politics. He had not voted or taken doctrinaire positions on any issues when he was with the AP. Miller told Gannett at the beginning, "I don't really have strong political views. I have known both Democratic presidents and Republican presidents, and I like something in all of them."

"Paul was not what you'd call a real political person," his wife said. "He thought there were two points of view." If the publisher and his new editor did not think alike, there were no signs of serious ideological conflict.

Louise Miller remembered telling her husband how highly opinionated some *Times-Union* readers considered Gannett. His reply, she said, was, "That's perfectly all right. If I owned a newspaper I'd want to express myself, too."[1]

Did Gannett see in Miller qualities he had hoped for in a male heir? That is unlikely. He had vowed never to leave a wealthy heir, his secretary, Florence Messman, had recalled. After adopting a son, the father did not try to bring him up as a future newspaper man. Quite the contrary.

Dixon Gannett, whose school years were spent away from home in one academy or another, said he was never an outstanding student. After earning a bachelor of arts degree from Bradley University, he told his father he wanted to work for one of the Rochester newspapers.

"But [my dad] said, 'No, you go to work for another newspaper and make a name for yourself. Then you come to work for me.'

"Well, he had his viewpoint on that and I had mine.

"I was very firm in my belief that if you're going to learn something, learn it from the best there is. And in my opinion, my dad was the best there was. If I was going to learn the newspaper business at all, I wanted to learn from him and from nobody else. So I never went into the newspaper business." [2]

Instead, Dixon Gannett worked for Ford Research in Dearborn, Mich., until a major staff reduction in the late '50s. He later went into the motel business. Today he lives with his family in Jupiter, Fla., where he oversees his personal investments.

# Ready and Waiting

Frank Gannett had always championed editorial pages in his *Times-Union* that took firm stands, stressed bright writing, used creative layouts and welcomed the widest range of viewpoints on issues. He had found in Miller an editor who shared those standards.

For his successor Gannett sought someone of stature who would continue the growth and enhance the prestige of The Gannett Newspapers. The man he had chosen was a tireless traveler, a comfortable speaker and a willing hand for worthy causes. Miller combined national and international news experience with the respect of professional friends who outnumbered even Gannett's industry acquaintances.

The man who still headed The Gannett Newspapers after 43 years also wanted a protege with patience. The Gannett Company had no rule requiring its founder to step down. True to the maxims of his youth, the infirm Gannett was determined to wear out, not rust out.

Miller had enough jobs, between the Gannett Radio Group and the *Times-Union*, to keep him busy and discourage impatience. Professional memberships also claimed his time. In June 1949, the Millers left Rochester on a three-week tour of Europe. He was representing the American Society of Newspaper Editors at an international newspaper conference in Holland.

Miller's office was separated from Gannett's by a reception area, including a secretary, and Herbert W. Cruickshank's office. The office beside Gannett's belonged to Messman, and she said Miller wanted it.

"We fought about my office," she said. "He had to have my office. And I said, 'You're not going to have my office. I came over here and walked on the beams on the floor when the building was being made. I'm outside of Mr. Gannett's door."

"Mr. Gannett would go home to lunch and come back, and he'd say, 'Florence, Mr. Miller wants your office.' And I'd say, 'He's not going to have my office. I'm not going to run up and down that hall all day long. You tell me half the time, if I don't answer the minute you buzz, "Florence, Florence, I've forgotten what I've wanted" – I've got somebody with me, I'm on the phone, I'm not there that minute. If you think I'm going to run up and down that hall, you're crazy. I'm not going to do it.'

"So I never gave Mr. Miller my office." [3]

# Times Do Change

Spring and summer of 1950 were unusually busy times for the company's board of directors. A June meeting considered a contract the directors had approved two years earlier with the Rochester Institute of Technology, giving RIT $25,000 a year for 10 years to do graphic arts research. The school had to get similar contracts assuring annual payments of at least $1 million. If RIT failed to reach that goal, the Gannett contract would be void and RIT would refund all payments made by Gannett.

Herbert Cruickshank, general business manager and board treasurer, reported that RIT had failed to satisfy the stipulation, making it liable for repayment of $50,000. The directors, however, decided to waive payment, instead reducing Gannett's annual contribution to $10,000. They agreed to continue to support the research.[4]

In September the directors re-emphasized the *Democrat and Chronicle* and the *Times-Union's* status as flagship papers. They authorized general manager Erwin Davenport to spend $1.2 million to expand and equip the *Times-Union* building.[5]

The company president, meanwhile, was being saluted by representatives of the Truman administration. Echoes of editorial assaults on the New Deal and the Fair Deal were muted in August when the U.S. Navy came to town. It gave its highest civilian honor, the Distinguished Public Service Award, to Frank Gannett. "He was among the first newspapermen in the country," the citation said, "to grasp the full significance of World War II and to warn the public that the war in the Pacific would be largely a naval war."[6]

At a Nov. 7 meeting, the Gannett board approved the first pension and life insurance plan for all employees with more than five years' service before Dec. 31, 1949. Other employees would become eligible on the Dec. 31 following their fifth anniversary with the company.

Staff contributions, by payroll deduction, would be 2 percent of yearly pay, plus 2 percent of normal earnings over $3,600.

Retirement annuities would be based on 3/4 of 1 percent of the basic pay an employee received before Dec. 31, 1949, and 1 percent of subsequent wages, multiplied by years of service, until retirement age of 65 was reached.

Coverage of past service for all employees was secured by Gannett with the payment of $5.5 million to the plan. In addition, it would pay about $5 for every $1 contributed by employees toward future annuities and life insurance. First-year cost to the company, including a portion of the past service payment, was estimated at $1.37 million.

The contributory plan was unprecedented in New York State and had specific approval of the New York State Insurance Board. For Frank Gannett, it fulfilled at last a tentative promise he had repeated since profits were first shared with employees in 1936. All employees received a *Retirement Plan* booklet in which Gannett wrote:

"Our motive is twofold – to provide a safe future for our employees and, selfishly, to bind them more tightly to us in a joint effort to advance the company.

"We have here what I believe to be the finest retirement program yet devised."

The speed with which employees enrolled testified to their enthusiasm. Jan. 31, 1950, was the deadline for eligible employees to sign up. More than 99 percent were enrolled soon after New Year's Day. Frank MacDonald, a compositor in Newburgh, said:

"Because I am one of the younger employees and already have 11 years of service, I'll be able to retire at quite a high rate of pay – about $40 a week."

Alvin S. Van Voorst, a pressman with 23 years of service in Albany and Saratoga Springs, was very happy:

"It means a lot to have back years of service on the paper taken care of, especially when the years go back farther than [our] membership in the Gannett Group."

The first benefits were paid even before the enrollment period had expired. Life insurance went into effect as soon as membership cards had been returned. Mrs. George Miles, wife of a veteran *Times-Union* engraver, was paid full life insurance benefits after her husband died in Rochester on Jan. 7.[7]

Soon after the pension plan was presented to employees, the board of directors met to approve profit-sharing for 1949. The rate was set again at 10 percent for all employees. Executives in the corporate offices, the Rochester editors and the GNS bureau chiefs all got bonuses equal to 20 percent of their pay. This year, however, the 20 percent was added in the form of a raise.[8]

# Changes of Scene

Miller and Gannett shared the spotlight at the 1950 spring conference of editors and executives. The boss's presence was especially welcome because it was his first such appearance before a company meeting since his stroke nearly two years before.

Now in his 74th year, he assured his associates, "This is too good a world to get out of at present." He urged them to work to keep people interested in their newspapers because television would soon be a factor in everyone's life. As important as newspapers were, he told them, the people who produce them are more important. For that reason, he said, "Our retirement plan has given me as much joy as any beneficiary."

Miller was beaming, having just been elected a director of the AP. This AP directorship attracted notice, especially in Gannett, because Miller was the first former AP staffer to be elected to the board of directors.

Now publisher as well as editor of the *Times-Union*, Miller was beginning to test his wings as vice president and executive assistant to Gannett. The death of Harold W. Sanford, editor of the *Democrat and Chronicle*, created a vacuum that had to be filled. Miller turned it into an opportunity to begin building his own team.

Fay Blanchard became editor of the *Democrat and Chronicle* but also retained his title as general executive editor of The Gannett Newspapers. Miller brought to Rochester Vincent S. Jones, executive editor of the Utica papers. Jones became director of the News and Editorial Office, working directly for Blanchard. His initials would supplant Blanchard's as the signature on *The Bulletin*.

The general executive editor had both encouraged and exploited the innovator from Utica. Jones was known as a missionary, both inside and outside Gannett, for editorial use of the Continuing Study of Newspaper Readership, conducted by the Advertising Research Foundation to evaluate selected newspapers. Its material had been used to advantage for years by newspaper advertising staffs to demonstrate to customers the effectiveness of white space, good illustrations, interesting copy and clear writing. Jones was one of the first editors to apply its findings to the improvement of the news pages of his newspapers.

He was an ardent campaigner for editorial use of readability studies, the work of Rudolph Flesch and others, and a zealot for improving the quality and display of news photography.

(Flesch was an author and educator who created formulas for determining the clarity and readability of written texts. They computed the numbers of words in sentences, the number of syllables in words and similar criteria to assign a readability index to the material. His most famous work, "Why Johnny Can't Read," was denounced as traitorous by many public schoolteachers when it was published in 1955.)

*Editorially Speaking* regularly carried texts of Jones's presentations on these subjects at the semi-annual editors' conferences. Members of the American Society of Newspaper Editors and the Associated Press Managing Editors respected him and his work.

Miller told Jones that he had not been called to Rochester just to be Blanchard's assistant, but eventually to head the news department.

Jones resisted the move at first. He had been working in Utica since leaving graduate school in 1930, when he started full-time on the *Daily Press,* the same newspaper on which his father had begun his career before the turn of the century. The elder Jones had been a reporter, managing editor, business manager and finally general manager.

Jones's reluctance to leave Utica was strong:

"I didn't want to come because I didn't think the job was going to be as interesting or as much fun. It certainly was a hell of a lot easier, because I was working about an 80-hour week then. . . .

"They were very annoyed with me. They said, 'You can't resist a promotion.' And Frank Tripp said to me, 'Vin, you won't accomplish much right away but you have a chance to accomplish more in the long run.'

"I'm not sure that was true. Gannett autonomy worked well for me in Utica, where I had a wonderful free hand — nobody knew what I was doing until it was done. When I got to Rochester, I had to give the same autonomy to other people, who were not as cooperative with me as I had been with Blanchard.

"So I was in that job in Rochester. I didn't like this because I was devoted to Fay Blanchard, who had been my mentor, and I knew that they were easing him out."[9]

## Spreading the Word

Jones's art of persuasion soon became evident in the weekly newsletter. A typical example was a comparison of news coverage of fires on two passenger ships. The first was the cruise ship *Noronic*, which burned in Toronto in August 1950 with a loss of 139 lives. The captain was charged with negligence, and the story was prominently displayed.

The other ship fire, on the *Quebec*, was handled skillfully by captain and crew, who docked the ship on the St. Lawrence River in time for most passengers to escape. "Most papers brushed off the story," Jones wrote, "apparently on the theory that success isn't nearly as interesting as a good old disaster."

Then he suggested:

"Wouldn't this have been a good chance to dig out a picture of the *S.S. Noronic*, twin it with the ruins of the *S.S. Quebec* and ask what miracle of luck or skill made such a vast difference in the tales of two ships?

"When we follow conventional patterns of news coverage we have the accumulated judgment of generations behind us. It takes courage, imagination – and work – to break out and to discover whether the conventional method really is a groove – or just another rut."[10]

Meanwhile, Miller was going public with his powers of persuasion. He began by explaining Gannett newspaper policies to the Rochester Rotary Club. "We regard it as equally a duty," he said, "to first, get and print all the news factually and without bias; and second, to comment on the news vigorously and honestly."

"There is no overall editorial policy of The Gannett Newspapers as such," he explained. "It is assumed that they will be clean and community-minded and patriotic and fair. From there on, the local management is on its own as to specific problems and issues."

He declared, as he would in many public appearances, his belief in providing a forum in newspapers for all points of view, "the more, the merrier."

"That," he concluded, "is in the spirit of a free press – the spirit in which the vast majority of America's daily newspapers are produced. Certainly, I hope and sincerely believe, it is the spirit of those serving you here at home." [11]

# Outreach

Gannett corporate executives were encouraged to exchange viewpoints and swap services with their professional counterparts outside the group. Miller played host to a group of foreign editors in the United States for an international seminar. Blanchard was asked to select the Ohio Newspaper Woman of the Year. Jones judged the New Jersey Better Newspaper Contest.

All of these efforts were mined for tips on good and bad that were passed on to Gannett editors. *The Bulletin* reported, for instance, that foreign editors had warned about U.S. anti-Communist campaigns. Their advice:

"It's a mistake to try to sell Europeans and Asiatics on the idea that communism is bad. It offers too much to too many people. We can, however, attack Stalin and the way his Kremlin crowd runs the Russian brand of communism."

Entrants in the New Jersey contest included the "very big and famous newspaper, the Newark *Evening News,* several fair-sized dailies and Sundays, and three smaller dailies." Gannett's *Courier-*

*News* of Plainfield was excluded because the judge came from the Gannett organization.

Jones gave the nod for general excellence to Newark's *Evening News*, the contest's result almost every year. He applauded all of the entrants for generous news content, particularly local, and for their editorial pages, and sports and society sections. "Beyond that," he told his colleagues, "their interest seems to have flagged. . . . Their inside pages ranged from plain dull to fancy chaos, with little effort to departmentalize or to dress pages likely to attract and hold readers. All of them jumped stories by the dozen; few of them used pictures effectively.

"A strictly personal and private by-product of this study was an increased pride in our own Group, whose papers uniformly are good to look at, easy to read, and fully abreast of the best thought and practice in typography and technique." [12]

Blanchard asked Jones and Hartford's Carl Lindstrom to help him judge the Ohio contest. He described their dilemma:

"We were bothered for a while because none of us ever had heard a definition of the term 'newspaper woman.' . . . Should we give first consideration to a woman who writes and edits primarily for other women? Or should we look for one who writes and edits for all readers? We finally settled on the latter definition. . . .

"The winner was selected because she writes well and with evident enjoyment. . . . We also felt that she brought to those assignments a sort of feminine understanding. It is a rather intangible quality, but it is something that many of the entries lacked. It strikes us that newspaper women feel complimented when told they write like men. Actually they should be proud of the ability to *work* like men but to *write* like women." [13]

Jones was one of five judges for the University of Missouri-Encyclopaedia Britannica competition for News Pictures of the Year. He subtly instructed his Gannett colleagues while describing the experience of judging 3,000 entries:

"There were fewer grab shots of mothers weeping over drowned children, gory corpses tumbling out of mangled motor cars, and only one rear view of Miss Gertrude Moran. [Miss Moran was a professional tennis player whose scanty and lace-trimmed court attire caused a public sensation and steady employment for news photographers.]

"There were enough pictures of monkeys to suggest that photographers be recalled from the zoo and put to work covering the later chapters of Darwin. . . .

"[The judges] gave first prize to the aerial picture of the resourceful farmer who beat the flood by using his tractor to run up a dike around his house and barn.

"Read a few thousand captions in a couple of days and you will be convinced that this branch of writing represents rock bottom. They reek with cliches. . . . On the other hand, even the finest picture can be enhanced by a good title."

Then, not so subtly, he added:

"To the best of our knowledge, no Gannett newspapers had entries in this contest – which is one way to make sure of not winning a prize." [14]

# Thank You Notes

Events at the end of 1950 made clear to Gannett employees that age and ill health were imposing some curbs on Frank Gannett.

His sister, Gracia Gannett Rathbone, died in Elmira in October. Many Gannett employees sent personal condolences to the president, who was too frail to attend the funeral in Elmira. He responded in the *Gannetteer* with a note of thanks:

"Some traveled long distances to be present at the services in Elmira. I could not be there because the doctors forbade me to go to Elmira, but I heard all about the different ones who were there." [15]

*Times-Union* staff members got the usual year-end rallying memo, but this time over Miller's signature. "Our aim," he wrote of their editorial page, "continues to be a lively, fair, informed page that will be recognized as a Rochester forum.

"*To be lively,* we need appealing dress, challenging and provocative headline treatment, down-to-earth writing, pin-pointing the catchy and unusual. Not necessarily in that order.

"*To be fair,* we must know where we are shooting before we fire – whether in praise or in criticism; and we must use care in word and expression with the end in view of remembering always that the page belongs to everyone in the community as surely as it belongs to any one of us. Our responsibility is great.

"*To be informed,* we must find out for ourselves insofar as it is humanly and practically possible. The recent trip of Gannett editors to Washington is an example of finding out for ourselves.

"But even more important is 'getting around' locally, because: Our whole setup is pitched at giving maximum attention to matters of city and area and related state concern. This goes for editorials and cartoons and special articles as well and a field we still have not begun to tap with full effectiveness – letters." [16]

The signature was different but Miller's marching orders were consistent with Frank Gannett's goals. The leadership was changing, but the vision remained.

A History of Gannett

THE ELMIRA DAILY ADVERTISER, MONDAY, JULY 1, 1907

## DEAL CLOSED BY WHICH GAZETTE AND THE STAR CONSOLIDATED

### Evening Papers Join Forces and Will Publish Star-Gazette the First Issue of Which Will Appear To-Day—Officers of Company

*The Gannett Company traces its origins to Elmira, N.Y., where company founder Frank Gannett purchased his first newspaper in 1906. What became the Star-Gazette remains in the company to this day.*

A History of Gannett

*Gannett's 1918 move to Rochester, N.Y., after the acquisition of two more dailies, presaged the company's growth as a large regional, and later national, newspaper publisher. The Gannett Rochester Newspapers still occupy this building, which was constructed in 1927.*

*Frank Gannett's interest in technological advancement was keen. He was one of the earliest champions of the teletypesetter, believing – correctly – that it would dramatically change the way newspapers gathered and reported news.*

*During the 1920s and 1930s, Frank Gannett's political ambitions intensified. In 1940, he made a bid for the Republican nomination for president.*

A History of Gannett

*Frank Gannett's reliance on Frank Tripp began with Tripp's appointment as the company's business manager in 1924 and continued for a quarter of a century.*

*For his successor, Gannett sought someone of stature who would continue the growth and enhance the prestige of The Gannett Newspapers. That man was Paul Miller.*

*In 1950, Vincent S. Jones was brought to Rochester from the Utica newspapers to head the corporate News and Editorial Office. In that role, Jones balanced Gannett's philosophy of local autonomy for editors with advice on standards, ethics and fairness.*

A History of Gannett

By the end of 1971, Gannett owned 51 daily newspapers. The last one acquired that year was the News-Press in Fort Myers, Fla. At Miller's side for that acquisition, as he had been since he joined the company in 1963, was Allen H. Neuharth. Neuharth succeeded Miller as CEO in 1973.

In 1980, under General Manager John J. Curley, Gannett News Service won the Pulitzer gold medal for public service, the first ever awarded to a news service. Sixteen years earlier, Gannett had become the first newspaper group ever to win the award. From left: Robert A. Dubill, Curley, Carlton Sherwood, Neuharth, John Hanchette, Bill Schmick and Roger Hedges.

A History of Gannett

*By 1981, Gannett's senior newspaper executives were consumed with the development of a national daily newspaper, USA TODAY. From left: Neuharth, Curley (the paper's first editor) and John C. Quinn, senior vice president/news.*

*USA TODAY sold out on its Sept. 15, 1982 debut in the Baltimore-Washington market. By 1985 it was being printed abroad. Neuharth, the paper's founder, could be found at market launches, inspecting the paper as it rolled off the presses, as he did in Switzerland in 1986 with Gannett International President David Mazzarella.*

*In 1985, Gannett acquired The Detroit News. In 1986, The Des Moines Register and The Courier-Journal at Louisville, Ky., also joined Gannett. Of these acquisitions, Neuharth said, "It feels like winning the Triple Crown."*

A History of Gannett

*In May 1986, Neuharth told shareholders at Gannett's annual meeting that he would step down as chief executive officer and would recommend to the board that John J. Curley, then Gannett's president and chief operating officer, become CEO. Afterwards, his successor took questions from the press.*

*Of Curley, Neuharth said: "He helped pull it all together – the people, the products, the profits. And his skillfull operational guidance of our newspapers, broadcasting and outdoor helped keep Gannett's record overall the envy of our industry."*

*Doug McCorkindale's zest for deal-making brought him from a New York law firm to Gannett, where he became deeply involved in making acquisitions.*

A History of Gannett

*Today, Gannett consists of the nation's largest newspaper group, with a circulation representing about 10 percent of total U.S. daily circulation. Gannett also operates television stations in major markets . . .*

A History of Gannett

... *along with radio stations, and owns the largest outdoor advertising company in North America. Gannett also actively explores new ventures in news and information.*

# Chapter 21

# Clear Signals

*"[Frank Gannett] is the American spirit incarnate. He is the small boy on the backwoods farm, who, by sheer application, a business head, a photographic memory, a nose for opportunities and a frightening alacrity in seizing them, made good. And like our own esteemed Chancellor, Lord Beaverbrook, whose friend he is, he made good in newspapers."*
University of New Brunswick<br>LL.D. Citation, 1951

Whereas World War II had been a persistent thorn for Gannett editors, with its constant grim news, censorship, worries about national security and material shortages, the Korean "police action" that began in 1950 rarely figured in their internal exchanges. Their newspapers carried reports from the battlefronts, but the conflict had caused them no great professional concerns since its start the previous summer.

Distance and the limited U.S. war effort made it less worrisome, except for those with sons or daughters in the conflict. Nevertheless, some news organizations reacted as they might in the event of all-out war. Acme Photo invoked a "war clause" in its contract and increased the cost of its telephoto service 15 percent. United Press did the same and raised its rates 10 percent. Vin Jones pointed out to his colleagues that the UP clients among them were still "paying the healthy 'war clause' boost invoked during World War II [and never rescinded] plus a string of increases attributed to unsuccessful wage negotiations with the telegraphers."[1]

King Features was asking clients to "cooperate" with some significant increases. While Jones conceded that the wire services faced cost-of-living problems too, he said they had done little to offset price increases with sensible economies.

He informed all readers of *The Bulletin,* in strictest confidence, that notices of cancellation had been sent to Acme and all commercial wire services except The Associated Press. Most service contracts renew automatically unless the client files before a specified date a notice of intent to cancel. Many an inattentive wire service or syndicate executive has been jolted into sweet reasonableness by such timely warnings.

Prices weren't the only syndicate sore spot with Gannett editors in the early 1950s. They fretted constantly about the content of comics, particularly violence and death in "Dick Tracy," or semi-nudity in "Steve Canyon" and "Terry and the Pirates." A special nettle was any strip that bit the hand by ridiculing newspapers.

One editor, Harry Stutz of *The Ithaca Journal*, fought back. A sequence of the comic strip "Nancy" showed a porch roof onto which a newspaper boy had pitched a dozen carefully rolled copies of his paper. In place of the daily title, "Nancy," on that day's strip, *The Journal* inserted, "This Does Not Happen to *The Ithaca Journal*."[2]

## Breaking the Ice

More than four years had passed since Rochester's newspapers had been shut down for three months. Early in 1951, relations between management and labor still were not easy but the parties were talking more.

Improved communication extended beyond the newspapers themselves. Editors from the *Democrat and Chronicle* and the *Times-Union* met for three hours with union leaders from the area. The guests acknowledged times when the newspapers had been helpful. They did not ask for the newspapers' support but they did ask that the papers present labor positions fairly, completely and regularly.

The willingness of the editors to talk to them for that length of time apparently startled – and encouraged – them. Jones summarized the outcome:

"Biggest problem was to explain that a newspaper is a medium of communication and not an end in itself; that a newspaper of general circulation cannot be the 'voice' of any one group.

"Both groups left the meeting with a feeling that much had been learned and that a way had been opened to bridge a gulf between the newspapers and a large and important segment of readers." [3]

The head of the News and Editorial Office was less encouraged with Gannett papers' handling of Gen. Douglas MacArthur's testimony at congressional hearings. A month-long national controversy had erupted on April 11, 1951, when President Harry Truman fired the commander of United Nations forces in Korea. Interest in MacArthur's testimony was high, but the hearings were neither televised nor broadcast.

Jones could not believe that most newspapers covered MacArthur's testimony with short wrapup stories. "For years," he said, "we have boasted that we are the only medium that can handle a detailed story. Yet when one comes along we dust it off, radio style."

He concluded:

"[M]ost newspapers showed a lamentable lack of flexibility in both thinking and mechanics.

"It takes courage to toss in a couple of open pages of scarce newsprint. But isn't this a public service which we cannot afford to neglect?

"Another type of enterprise would be to eliminate, ruthlessly, all secondary material, even some of our standing features, to make room for the news, which is our main reason for existence." [4]

That was as much as local editorial autonomy allowed Jones to do. It was one of the frustrations he had anticipated when Miller recruited him from Utica. Like Fay Blanchard before him, Jones could second-guess, he could ask, "what if?" but he could not direct.

Blanchard, meanwhile, was marking his first anniversary as editor of the *Democrat and Chronicle* by flexing restored editorial muscle. The U.S. State Department wanted two or three *D&C* editorials a week for the Voice of America. It asked Blanchard to send them promptly by wire, collect.

He declined:

"An editorial of any quality seldom depends upon immediacy. Opinion does not deteriorate, as news does, with the passage of time. You are welcome to clippings, which we will mail gladly. . . .

"The *Democrat and Chronicle* has supported the Voice. I should be sorry to see it adopt the prodigal spending habits of some other government agencies." [5]

Local elections were to be held in both Rochester and Monroe County. Blanchard offered all candidates for city and county offices a podium on his editorial pages:

"You have a cordial invitation to write, within the next three weeks, a letter to the *Democrat and Chronicle* expressing your views on municipal and county affairs, your criticisms of what you think may be going wrong now, the reforms for which you will work. Your letter will be printed – without immediate comment – as a service to you and to the public.

"This newspaper already has expressed a preference for the Republican ticket, for two main reasons. These are the record of present officeholders, and the underlying philosophy of the national Republican Party. That preference does not mean hidebound adherence to any one candidate; the newspaper is first and always for the best possible Rochester and Monroe County." [6]

# The Miller Style

Frank Gannett, at 75, was as active as his wife and doctor would allow. He was not as frequently at the center of important events as he used to be. His executive assistant, however, was increasingly prominent.

At the August 1951 meeting of the Gannett directors, Miller proposed a six-page statement of principles and practices for company radio stations. There were five at that time, four as sole ownerships: WDAN, Danville, Ill.; WENY, Elmira, N.Y.; WHEC, Rochester, N.Y., and WTHT, Hartford, Conn. The fifth was WHDL, Olean, N.Y., in which the company had a minority interest.

The board set standards on program content; controversial issues; religious, political and news broadcasts; editorializing; commercial programs; unacceptable content in programs and commercials; sales and business practices, and public interest programs.

Miller intended for the practices to maintain high moral standards, defined as respect for law, humaneness and good taste. Advertising for alcoholic beverages, of course, continued to be prohibited. Irreverence and blasphemy, social irresponsibility, glorified crime, graphic violence and sexual license were unacceptable in program content. Stations required all programming to be screened 48 hours in advance.

Such standards may appear puritanical this late in the 20th century, but those who set the ethical standards for "family entertainment" in that era drew a much finer distinction between prudery and prudence.

During the same meeting, the board approved Miller's recommendation that Station WDAN in Danville apply to the Federal Communications Commission for a television license.[7] Earlier in 1951, the directors had approved the spending of $785,000 by Station WHEC to build and equip a television station in Rochester.

As editor and publisher of the *Times-Union*, Miller expanded Frank Gannett's reach for opposing views on the editorial page. In September, he traded pulpits on Labor Day weekend with a Presbyterian minister. The cleric wrote the lead editorial for that Sunday's *Times-Union*, while the son of an Oklahoma Presbyterian minister preached to his counterpart's congregation.

That exchange created two opportunities for the *Times-Union:*

• The newspaper set up a seminar designed to teach churches and other organizations how to use newspapers to their advantage.

• Miller and Olin Archer, his chief editorial writer, were able to answer some misconceptions about editorials and news coverage exposed by the minister's editorial.

When the Empire Typographical Conference came to Rochester in November 1951, Miller eagerly walked to its podium. The conference was made up of International Typographical Union locals in upstate

New York, most of whose members worked for Gannett newspapers. It was a Rochester local that had shut down both Gannett papers for three months late in 1946.

Miller looked them straight in the eye and said he wanted to talk about common problems. "The biggest problem in the newspaper business today," he said, "is that of skyrocketing costs of operation – costs and taxes."

He reviewed the Gannett package of benefits, from profit-sharing through hospitalization insurance and the pension plan to paid vacations. No one, he said, wants to take any of that away.

"So what is the answer," he asked, "if we are going to (1) keep improving our product to give better service and meet competition and (2) earn enough to pay better and better wages, provide better and better benefits?"

His answer was, "Even better production records than we are setting today, plus new and cheaper ways of getting the job done."

He alluded to the teletypesetter, a tape-fed typecasting machine opposed by the unions. Rochester's newspapers had no immediate plans for the new machine, he said, but realism required that they would eventually.

"Why should I be telling you all this here and now?" he asked.

"There are 1,000 ITU employees in the Gannett Group. That is nearly one-third of the entire personnel. Therefore the responsibility these fine men and women discharge, the work they do, their equipment, naturally become of major concern when costs are discussed."

Then he proposed what few in his audience probably expected – a common approach to solve their common problems:

"Agreement by you to sit down with representatives of the management and discuss ways and means of applying joint efforts to some of the production problems I have outlined, would receive a cordial reception. If such a meeting were held, I would imagine that you should desire to have a large representation; that is, you would assign special representatives as well as your regular representatives for the broadest possible exchange of views. The other unions concerned with mechanical and production problems should, of course, be in on it, too. And all of us on the management end would be eager to join if we possibly could.

"Think it over. Talk it over. Do it soon."[8]

That performance was not the work of someone who saw himself simply as editor and publisher of Rochester's *Times-Union*. Nor were proposals of such importance the sort that could be made without the knowledge and assent of Gannett and Frank Tripp. It was the type of role at which Miller would come to excel. He would willingly appear before groups known or presumed to be unfriendly. If he didn't always disarm their hostility, he usually persuaded them that he was a reasonable man.

## The Golden Years

Gannett and Miller had both deferred to the guest at a 50th-anniversary party in September 1951. It was staged by Tripp's Elmira colleagues. The 19-year-old high school dropout who had begun as a "gofer" on the old *Advertiser* was now the 69-year-old general manager of the Gannett Company and gray eminence of Elmira journalism.

His youthful enthusiasm for the business was undiminished. He recalled for his guests an era when he would have starved without free passes and three banquet assignments a week. The real magic, he said, was seeing what he wrote in print.

"I'm not ashamed," he said, "to admit that to this day I still get a kick out of it. All who write conscientiously and all who read about themselves and their neighbors experience something of the same thrill. That is why people always will read newspapers. The printed word has magic indestructibility. It lives to check man's faulty memory and elevate his ego. . . .

"Yet humble, crude and unimportant as it may have been, all that I have written will survive me. It is not true that newspapers live but a day. In almost every mail, friends I've never seen tell me, 'I put it in my scrapbook.' "[9]

The board formally addressed Frank Gannett's mortality with a significant reorganization on Dec. 11, 1951. It created new corporate positions to protect the continuity of experienced leadership – chairman and executive vice president.

Tripp, formerly a vice president of the company, was named chairman. He would remain operating head of the organization.

Miller, formerly a vice president, was named executive vice president.

Herbert W. Cruickshank, formerly general business manager, succeeded Tripp as general manager. He continued as corporation treasurer.

Lynn N. Bitner, formerly general manager of Elmira newspapers and radio, succeeded Cruickshank as general business manager.

Cyril Williams, who had been corporation comptroller since 1945, was named secretary as well, replacing Cruickshank in that role.

Miller's election as executive vice president was the clearest signal yet that a successor to "the boss" had been chosen. If that was not enough, Gannett's comments clinched it:

"I am especially happy over the arrangement by which, as chairman, Mr. Tripp will continue as the operating head of our company. He will act for the president in my absence or disability. Mr. Miller, as executive vice president, will have full authority to act in the absence or disability of both of us." [10]

Tripp's private comments about his promotion were characteristically more droll. He said he felt like the dog that was so nice they made him chairman of the board, "and now all he does is sit on his ass and bark." [11]

# Picking Up the Tab

Employees got good news of their own from the company early in 1952. At the Feb. 25 meeting, the directors considered two main items of business. They agreed to buy for $450,000 the Binghamton Press building that they had been leasing from Cornell University. They also voted to have the company assume the complete cost of the retirement and supplemental life insurance plans for all eligible Gannett employees. On March 20 the board voted to repay employees all the money they had contributed toward pension and life insurance coverage since Dec. 31, 1949.

Editors, meanwhile, were discussing cooperation with competitors, conflicts of interest, freebies and how the public viewed their profession. *The Bulletin* reported to Gannett executives that one of their colleagues had turned down a regular role in a TV forum for three reasons:

"1. A newspaper editor has no business working [the pay is generous] for a grocery company on a TV program. Occasional participation in civic or sustaining programs is different.

"2. If the editor has something to say he has the best place in the world to say it – the newspaper.

"3. Is it wise to associate with your competitors on terms of equality?"

"This reasoning is sound," *The Bulletin* said. "It is in line with the thinking behind most unwritten policy and the few contractual agreements prohibiting staffers from exploiting their connection with the newspaper." [12]

Participants in the convention of the Associated Press Managing Editors fretted over the embarrassing results of an AP Continuing Study Committee poll. Newspapers in New Hampshire had badly missed the mark in a grassroots survey of support for presidential candidates. That prompted the observation that "AP now faces the fact that in many sections of the country the newspapers are controlled by men who are in politics up to their ears and who say what they hope will happen rather than what is likely."

Fred Stein, editor and publisher at Binghamton, got little support at the convention when he raised the question of freebies. He led off a panel discussion with the question, "How Much Can a Free Press Get for Free and Still Be Free?"

Editors were not comfortable with the question. Several replied that they had to be reasonable about gifts, passes and government junkets to their employees and themselves. Stein responded that newspapers could not convincingly call for clean government when their own practices deserved investigating.

*The Bulletin* concurred: "If reporters and sports writers go astray it may be because the big bosses set a bad example for them and it is not surprising that some discerning readers bracket us with the politicians." [13]

Just a few weeks later, *The Bulletin* was urging editors to prepare lists of desirable aerial photographs that might be taken on a single flight. "A good man operating a Speed Graphic can knock off a long list of assignments on a clear day," it said, "and the cost of chartering a plane is low." Then it added parenthetically, "Sometimes you can get the airplane service in return for a credit line." [14]

## Get Out the Vote

Gannett was typically confident about the future of his newspapers and predictably unflattering to the federal government at the 1952 spring editors' conference. "In the current political campaign," he said, "we should tell all the facts on every issue, then take a stand. I don't tell you what to say, but I do ask you to take a stand and fight for it."

That bow to autonomy was echoed by Miller, who described a voter information campaign launched by the *Times-Union*. Dubbed "Read-Think-Vote," its intent was to turn readers into informed voters and produce the greatest possible increase in the percentage of eligible voters who would go to the polls.

"I think I must be [attempting] one of the toughest projects ever undertaken," Miller said, "in trying to sell the Group something developed in Rochester." [15]

The News and Editorial Office promoted Read-Think-Vote by furnishing material to interested group newspapers.

By the end of June, most Gannett newspapers had joined the campaign. Other newspapers in 25 states and the District of Columbia had expressed interest in the idea. Rochester reported voter registrations up substantially, but *The Bulletin* properly pointed out that success would be determined by voter turnout on Election Day.

Gannett was well enough to travel with his wife to Chicago in July for the Republican National Convention. There he happily witnessed the rout of the forces of Thomas E. Dewey. He returned pleased with the nomination of Dwight Eisenhower for president and only slightly apprehensive about the Democratic candidacy of Adlai Stevenson. He remembered painfully that Harry Truman in 1948 had surprised everyone who was sure he would lose.

*The Bulletin* warned, "Feeling will run much deeper this year than in 1948 and it will be harder than ever to be objective. . . .

"Read-Think-Vote campaigns in various cities are beginning to pay off in terms of an informed and keenly interested readership. These people will be satisfied with nothing less than the best." [16]

## Truth About Consequences

Presidential politics and the campaign to inform voters competed for attention with daily editorial problems at the fall conference. Paul Martin, chief of GNS's Washington bureau, painted a rosy picture of Republican prospects for an Eisenhower victory. Jones suggested that member newspapers compete for highest voter turnout on Election Day.

Most of the program, however, emphasized methods for strengthening local news coverage, improving editorial pages and creating more attractive products.

From the circulation department came the reminder that they could do a lot more with a 90-percent newspaper on time than a 100-percent newspaper late.

Tripp strongly endorsed those sentiments. He earned a permanent place in the minutes of the conference, however, with a formal speech. He called it "The Pot of Gold." Several editors who were there still spoke of it with awe nearly 40 years later.

It was a heartfelt rejection of federal paternalism and what the speaker called the disruption it caused by playing management and labor against each other. His reason for mentioning it?

"Newspapers are at a dangerous crossroads," he said. "Some of them with big names and long successful records are headed toward a dead end. Disaster, bankruptcy, suspension threaten some you would least suspect."

He urged them to make clear to their subordinates the substance of his warning. "We have access to no inexhaustible magic pot of gold," he said. *"We have to earn it as we go."*

They were threatened, he said, by competition, high taxes, government regulation and soaring costs of material and labor.

"It is our obligation," he said, "to keep solvent, as must a bank or an insurance company, to protect the jobs and benefits of those who have entrusted their future and that of their families to The Gannett Newspapers.

"The cash cost which we must earn for this one purpose is $1,088 per year, per average employee, $20.90 a week in addition to the pay of the average worker of five or more years' service. . . . That creates an annual charge against the whole organization of about $2 million. That is the kind of a grasping, selfish company that we work for. . . .

"The reserves which The Gannett Newspapers have been permitted [by federal tax law] to accumulate would meet this single continuous and recurring employee benefit obligation for less than one year.

"That is the extent of the pot of gold."

He challenged them to:

- Impress upon all that an honest day's production not only is due their job, but is a requisite if the job and its attendant perquisites are to survive.
- Eliminate waste at every level.
- Fight for business and volume as never before.

"You are only 15 percent away from the doghouse," he said. "A 15-percent loss in advertising volume would give you worries and problems such as you have never known. . . .

"There is no pot of gold; no endowment; no angel. . . . Even this sturdy ship could be scuttled by greed, waste and indolence. It is the primary function of management to prevent this.

"And you are management." [17]

## 'We Backed a Winner'

Analysis of Eisenhower's victory led *The Bulletin* to balance precariously on the fence protecting local autonomy.

"The Republican Party leaders," it said, "insist upon misreading the election returns, but there is no reason for us to fall into the same error."

"[The Democrats'] defeat will intensify the cry that America has a one-party press, and we will be wise if we take an increasingly independent stand. ... Albany County, in going for Eisenhower, ... cut little off the basic Democratic strength. But the same type of new voters found little to attract them in a weak Republican local slate. Only one assemblyman made it. We hope that party support can be based on merit, even when it involves reaching across the line to support Democrats." [18]

The Read-Think-Vote effort was a genuine success and Miller promptly congratulated everyone involved. "It has been a great thrill," he said, "to all of us in the Central Office to see how you have handled local efforts – many of which have surpassed anything even hoped for when the campaign was conceived."

Rochester won first prize from the American Heritage Foundation for 'the most intensive and most effective nonpartisan register-and-vote effort' among the nine U.S. cities in the 300,000-400,000 population class. The city's record of getting 98.7 percent of its registered voters to the polls topped the performance in Memphis, Oakland, Louisville, Portland (Ore.), Atlanta, San Diego, St. Paul and Toledo.

Chemung County, which includes Elmira, topped every county in the nation in the 80,000-90,000 population range by getting 43,938 of its 49,906 resistered voters out on Election Day. [19]

Soon after the elections, Miller traveled to Harvard to address that year's Nieman Fellows, journalists on one-year fellowships for professional study.

Miller's invitation must have surprised some veteran Gannett executives. In years past, Blanchard occasionally had derided the Nieman Fellows. It reflected Tripp's oft-stated preference for on-the-job training rather than college education for reporters and editors. That mood obviously had changed. This year, one of the Nieman Fellows was Calvin Mayne, a *Times-Union* reporter who would later become Miller's deputy on its editorial page.

Miller explained the principles that Gannett had espoused in establishing the Frank E. Gannett Newspaper Foundation – independence, local autonomy, community service, tolerance, advertising standards, employee benefits and freedom of the press.

"The Gannett Newspapers," he explained, "are distinguished by the fact that each is a local institution in policy and style, yet strengthened and supported in their primary devotion to the welfare of the localities they serve, by the resources and combined know-how of the parent company." [20]

Directors added two seats to the Gannett board at the December meeting and elected Caroline Gannett and Cyril Williams, board secretary and company comptroller, to fill them. [21]

# Chapter 22

# Editorial Clinic

*"One of the greatest values of the newspaper — certainly one of its greatest aims — is to encourage people to think for themselves. When people think for themselves, they must evaluate the good and the bad. They cannot shut out the evil. The newspaper would be doing them a disservice if it were to play the Polyanna."*

*Lafayette R. (Fay) Blanchard*
*1954*

As head of the News and Editorial Office, Vin Jones was paid to review and criticize anything related to news in the Gannett Company. He offered deserved praise in *The Bulletin*. It was only when he saw something amiss that the criticism might take the damning form of faint praise.

Such a case occurred early in 1953, when Paul Martin, GNS's Washington bureau chief, interviewed Marion Folsom, President Eisenhower's new undersecretary of the Treasury. Folsom asked whether he could see the finished story before publication – a not unusual but rarely obliged request.

*The Bulletin* told its readers:

"Paul agreed readily. Folsom's suggestions turned out to be merely that – not 'musts.' Some of them were offered in a general way and Paul translated them into his own language. Others were specific: Folsom's reluctance to have his home described as 'on *fashionable* Dumbarton Avenue in Georgetown' was motivated by his modesty and his desire to avoid any appearance of having gone social or high hat in the capital.

"The net results were good. We got a better story. Its accuracy was verified *in advance* by the subject. We built confidence in the competence and integrity of the Washington bureau.

"Nevertheless, Paul feels that this is the exception and not the rule.

He does not think that public officials should get the idea that our copy is subject to their editing before it goes out on the wire."[1]

Jones's headline on that item was his most direct comment: "THIS TIME IT WORKED."

The spirit of fairness on labor issues, begun a year earlier, was reflected in an object lesson on euphemisms, entitled "Playing It Straight."

Among terms to avoid, and possible substitutes:

"*Settlement* – Smacks too much of courts, claims, disputes. Why not use *agreement*?

"*Demands* – Almost invariably applied to union contract proposals; rarely to company counter-proposals. The term tends to arouse needless antagonism. Why not call them *proposals*?

"*Arbitration Award* – Implies 'reward' or 'gift.' Use arbitration *decision, finding* or *ruling*.

"*Rank and File* – Implies that employees are faceless people of the lowest echelon.

"*Penalty Pay* – Here the implication is that the company is being penalized for some misdeed. Why not call it *premium pay* or *extra pay for special work*?"

Jones took a shot at some employers' favorite euphemisms, as well. He would not agree that *management* was "coldly imperious," that *union shop* should invariably be *compulsory union membership*, or that *dividends* should be sublimated under such a clumsy camouflage as *payments to shareholders for the use of their money*.

"You don't correct an unbalanced situation," he declared, "by falling out of the other side of the boat."[2]

# Who's Reading Less

Doomsayers had been warning editors and publishers since the advent of radio that fewer people were reading newspapers, magazines and books. When TV became popular, they cried à la Paul

Revere, "The illiterates are coming."

Paul Miller responded with a confident, "Yes, but." He didn't deny that people were reading less. Instead, he produced evidence that people could be persuaded to read more.

*U.S. News and World Report,* he pointed out, had increased its circulation from 275,000 to 600,000 in the preceding six years. It took a little more than 10 years, he argued, for the *Wall Street Journal* to grow from a small business paper with a few thousand subscribers into an influential national publication with hundreds of thousands of readers.

There was a lesson there for Gannett, he said.

"[T]hey have done it by being useful – their No. 1 objective – with entertainment scarcely in the picture.

"If we do more and more of the service type of news coverage and news presentation we, too, will make ourselves increasingly valuable to readers and advertisers and build an even stronger base for ourselves.

"The primary essential is top-notch reporting. For that, only top-notch personnel will suffice." [3]

## New Blood

Miller, who represented the new generation, welcomed new opportunities and responsibilities. He was re-elected to The Associated Press board of directors. He and Lynn Bitner were elected directors of the Gannett Foundation. In June 1953, Bitner also was elected to the company's board.

That summer Miller was elected president of the New York State Publishers Association. The same session honored Frank Gannett for his work as NYSPA president in 1920.

Helping Miller sort out his busy schedule was his new secretary, Mary Golding. She had been a secretary for 14 years in the circulation department of the *Democrat and Chronicle.* Joseph Adams, who was publisher, told her the executive vice president needed a secretary. "I did not ask for the job," she said. "He sent me over there."

"The first five years that I worked for Mr. Miller were difficult for me," Golding recalled. "He was like a racehorse at the starting gate. . . . [H]e was ambitious and he wanted everything just so, just perfect. You know, you work for a circulation man who sells newspapers and then you [go to] this man who has a vocabulary that would choke a horse . . . and contacts all over the world and all over the country. It was difficult to catch on to him. But after five or six years we meshed, and the other 20 were great." [4]

Gannett veterans who knew both Miller and Herbert Cruickshank, a 25-year Gannett veteran in 1954, remember that Cruickshank resented Miller as an interloper and an unworthy rival to lead the company.

Louise Miller remembered a book by a local author that "said something about a man [Paul Miller] riding a white horse into Rochester. That was Cruickshank's general impression, that this man was going to take the job no matter what. . . . There was support, but PM was supposed to be very close to this Cruickshank man." [5]

Golding described him as bitter. "[H]e never came near Mr. Miller's office if he could help it, and Mr. Miller never went near his." [6]

"Cruickshank very much resented having Miller come up there," Jones said. In a capsule history he had written, he recalled that "in the '40s sometime, any number of bright young men had shown up in Rochester as assistant to the president. And they all disappeared without trace, probably with the help of some of the existing executives.

"Well, when Miller got there, he had survival quality. He had been in a rough league at 50 Rockefeller Plaza [AP headquarters]. . . . He was really a very amazing fellow." [7]

# The Senator from Wisconsin

The national controversy surrounding Republican Sen. Joseph McCarthy of Wisconsin was beginning to give the press fits. The fears he created with unsubstantiated denunciations of prominent Americans as subversives were heightened by the lack of initiative of print media, radio and television when McCarthy first began to make his charges of Communist infiltration of the government.

As the senator's claims of the number of "known Communists" accelerated like an arithmetic progression, the media routinely reported them without challenge.

Anti-communism was an article of faith for Gannett and Tripp. Most Gannett newspapers shared that philosophy in their editorials. But the group had not been caught up in the near-hysteria that the McCarthy controversy generated elsewhere.

Even so, by March 1954, Jones was writing about McCarthy to his colleagues:

"Joe McCarthy – and how to cover him – continues to be Problem No. 1 for the nation's editors."

He was pleased that some of the press had criticized McCarthy, helping to disprove Democrats' charges of a "one-party press." Knight Newspapers particularly had induced a flood of angry letters, he said, after editorials faulting the senator's methods.

"At the other extreme," Jones said, "are the McCarthy haters who also think the newspapers are unfair.

"Televiewers who saw Ed Murrow's [CBS] dissection of the senator thought that the pictorial approach offered a very effective way to show up the hammy side of McCarthy, something which seems to have eluded writers who are interested in keeping out of libel suits. Even so, this involves using some of the same 'loaded' tactics which bother even the senator's admirers. But it is a decision which has to be faced."[8]

The previous year, a veteran reporter on Albany's *Knickerbocker News* had refused to answer to a congressional committee whether she was or had been a member of the Communist Party. Two subsequent witnesses testified that she had been an active party member. She was promptly fired.

The reporter had been named several years before in another congressional hearing but she had not been called to testify.

*The Bulletin* said of the incident:

"[The reporter's] refusal to clear her name of such serious charges ended her usefulness as a member of the newspaper itself. . . . Reader reaction left no doubt that the newspaper had taken the only possible course." [9]

Jones grew even more concerned when *The New York Times* reported results of its Youth Forum in March 1954. The young people "roundly abused newspapers for being sensational and unobjective in their reporting of Sen. McCarthy," he wrote. "One youth suggested that press irresponsibility be curbed by law.

"This came at a time when Edward R. Murrow's McCarthy program was being hailed as evidence that radio and TV were ready to show both courage and skill in handling sticky subjects." [10]

"At stake in all this is the basic question of journalistic competence," Jones warned. "Do we [newspapers] have the courage and the skill to get the truth and to print it in such a way that people will read and understand?"[11] It was a question with no immediate answer.

"It's our baby now," said the April 29, 1954 *Bulletin*. "The sad spectacle [Army-McCarthy hearings] being unfolded in Washington has been dumped back in our laps since TV took a cold look at the box office and decided that public service was too expensive."

Two Rochester women went to Washington to sit in on a couple of days of hearings. When they returned, one of them wrote of the experience in a letter to the *Democrat and Chronicle*. "It was a very readable piece," *The Bulletin* reported, "and included many shrewd feminine observations. Most notable was their discovery of the way the senator's handpicked supporters were packed into the reserved seats, ready to hail McCarthy's entrance and to applaud everything that went his way.

"Their conclusion: 'Slightly discouraged, but still idealistic, we conclude that women should pay much more attention to their representatives in government, both before and after election.' " [12]

# Golden Oldies

Binghamton pulled out all the stops to celebrate the 50th anniversary of the *Press*. It published "Fifty Years of Progress," 160 pages in nine black-and-white sections, at that time the largest newspaper ever printed in southern New York state.

In his Page 1 greeting, Gannett recalled observing from Ithaca as the *Press* was started in 1904. He restated his pride in acquiring it as a Gannett newspaper in 1943. He did not mention that Gannett had not acquired a paper since.

True, the company had tried but failed late in 1948 to buy the Albany *Times-Union* from Hearst. It had bought advertising representative J.P. McKinney & Son as a subsidiary in April. Eleven years was a long time, particularly given The Gannett Newspapers' economic health, to go without a newspaper acquisition. In 1954, things began to happen.

The Gannett Company had owned a majority interest in the *Newburgh News* and the *Beacon News* since 1925. At their meeting in May, the directors approved purchase of the minority stock interests in both for $250,000. [13]

In October, the directors approved a deal to buy the 100-year-old *Niagara Gazette* in Niagara Falls, N.Y., for $2.5 million. A contingency was the hiring of Alanson E. Deuel, son of the *Gazette's* deceased owner, and newspaper broker Vincent Manno. They were to be retained for 10 years at $20,000 and $10,000 a year respectively, "to prepare and execute such contracts as may be necessary in connection with their employment." [14]

Frank Gannett welcomed the men and women of the *Gazette* to the group. He assured them that their newspaper would not lose its identity. He told all Gannett employees:

"Ours is not a static organization. In a period of increasing costs in the publishing industry, our Group is expanding instead of retrenching, growing instead of shrinking. I hope that it will always be thus, that we will never become stagnant or complacent, never self-satisfied or smug."[15]

# More of the Same

Holiday greetings at 1954's year end included the standard 10-percent profit share for all eligible employees and the 20-percent bonus to designated executives. Both had become so routine that executives occasionally rebuked their subordinates for taking the windfalls and the man who had created them for granted.

Problems facing editors did not change with the New Year. *The Bulletin* of Jan. 6, 1955, reported that editors had voted Sen. McCarthy the big story of 1954. It punctured their balloon with the reminder that letters to the editor of Rochester's *Democrat and Chronicle,* at least, didn't reflect their view.

Local issues were most important to those readers, and local vehicular traffic was tops on their list. Schools, teachers, taxes, buses, the Civic Center and the War Memorial followed in that order. *The Bulletin* rubbed it in by noting that McCarthy, Indochina and German rearmament didn't come close.

Binghamton's *Press* was battling the Broome County Board of Supervisors over its preference for secret meetings. The elected officials were taking bids on equipment and supplies, interviewing bidding salesmen and discussing $35,000 in purchases, all behind closed doors.

Use of Gannett News Service was still a concern. *The Bulletin* polled Gannett editors about what they used and what they passed up on the GNS wires. Most were mainly interested in local or regional copy. Many of them, *The Bulletin* said, were not making full use of the resources offered by the bureaus in Washington and Albany.

Even when items were used well, credit went mainly to Rochester, Binghamton, Hartford, Niagara Falls and Ithaca. "Editors think some of the copy runs too long," it said, "and that we continue to duplicate many items handled adequately by the press associations. But they find the service very valuable, particularly in competitive situations."[16]

## In Fact, if Not in Name

It had been more than four years since Frank Gannett had suffered his stroke. His recovery had been slow but 1954 had seen him restored to considerable activity. Golding recalled that he was still coming to the office for a few hours every day.

"The chauffeur would bring him down and he would sit in his office and maybe dictate to Florence or something."

She said he preferred to visit in Miller's office, and he would do so every day. "He used to go across my office," she said, "and he tripped over the Oriental rug in my office every single day. . . . He shuffled after the stroke so he couldn't [step over] it."[17]

Golding did not mention that in disrespect of Gannett. She was trying to portray the physical restraints his illness had imposed on him.

On April 15, Gannett fell at his home and was injured seriously enough to be hospitalized. He was still in the hospital on May 19, 1955, when the board of directors conducted a particularly important meeting. Cruickshank resigned as general manager and Tripp appointed Bitner to succeed him.

Gannett's confinement in Highland Hospital was noted and the secretary was instructed to write him regretting his absence and wishing him a complete recovery.

Tripp, who had been named chairman of the board and operating head of the company on Dec. 11, 1951, then read a prepared statement. He told the board that he "had asked Paul Miller, in connection with his duties as executive vice president of the corporation, to carry on in the future as operating head in fact."[18]

# Chapter 23

# 'Yielding Place to New'[1]

*"After Mr. Gannett became ill, and we all knew he wasn't coming back, I wanted to leave. My husband was after me to leave for a long time before I did. And Mr. Tripp said, 'No, Florence, you can't go, because then that will indicate to Mr. Gannett that we know he isn't going to get well. You've got to stay here."*

Florence Messman
1990

His long convalescence in Florida after the stroke had demonstrated to Frank Gannett that his newspapers were in capable hands. That was what he had always intended. "Train the man below you," he had said repeatedly. "Be prepared to take over the job of the man ahead of you."

But now Gannett's prolonged absence left somewhat at loose ends a secretary accustomed to constant demands. Florence Messman had worked at the center of power for 30 years. She jumped when Gannett buzzed. It was he who told her what to do. Other people asked.

A year earlier, the *Gannetteer* had summarized Messman's job and her relationship with her boss:

"A recital of Florence's activities as secretary to the Group's founder would make your head spin. Florence can remember working 'round the clock' with her super-charged chief. Her duties are as varied as his activities. They even included traveling with him on speech-making tours. Her strict attention to her job has led Gannett to jestingly call her his 'Simon Legree.' "[2]

She had a number of autographed photographs of Gannett, gifts from him on special occasions. All were signed to "WBS." "That was supposed to be a big joke between us," she said. "That was 'world's best secretary.' After a while, I thought, wouldn't it be kind of fun

235

just to get all the little balls of yarn in my hand. And I did. But then he couldn't move without me."[3]

During the interview in 1990 from which these recollections are drawn, Messman, then 88, talked of her boss with impatience as well as affection. He had foibles; she knew most of them, but she would talk about few of them. "They're very personal," she said of his quirks, "and I think they cast a certain reflection on his character. I don't mean anything vicious, but I don't think he was very generous.

"I said to him one day – saying it facetiously, really – 'I bet you've got the first dollar you ever earned.'

" 'Yes,' he said, 'I have.' " She laughed and said, almost to herself, "Nice man. Nice man. Nice man."[4]

She worked for him for nine years for $50 a week. Herbert Cruickshank, who had a reputation for not being very generous with the company's money, discovered that, she said. He promptly gave her a $12 raise, to $62 a week, but he told her not to tell Gannett.

Her secretarial duties included social correspondence, sometimes for Mrs. Gannett as well. She signed and addressed the Gannetts' Christmas cards, as many as 1,500, by hand. "I wedged those in," she said. She recalled an incident after the Gannetts returned to Rochester from the convention in Philadelphia, where he had hoped to be nominated for president.

"[Mrs. Gannett] went to the hospital. So she called me. She didn't have a secretary then. And she said, 'Florence, can you come to the hospital?'

"So on my lunch hour, naturally, I went to the hospital. She had a suitcase of letters that had come to her while Mr. Gannett was campaigning. And she handed the suitcase over to me and she said, 'Florence, will you answer all these?' "

Florence did, just "whacked them out" any time she had free moments. "I was a very fast typist," she said.

Early in 1948, 25-year-old Sally Gannett was to be married, in a wedding at home, to Charles Vincent McAdam Jr., son of the president of McNaught Syndicate.

"Everything was expected of me," Messman said. "But he

wouldn't let me alone. I'd work through my lunch hour trying to get uninterrupted work. . . . I was supposed to do all the announcements – no invitations, announcements. Four thousand. So I said, 'I can't do it. You don't leave me alone five minutes a day. *Buzz, buzz, buzz.* Every time you get a bright idea, *buzz, buzz.*' . . .

"So they got some social secretary to do it, and she charged them 8 cents a piece. I was tickled to death, because when I was getting $30 and $40 [a week] he said he never heard of girls getting such salaries." [5]

The reader should interpret that as amusement, not resentment. Messman was a realist, albeit a hard-working one. She was not intimidated by Gannett's prominence. She was not overawed by his wealth. Her demeanor with him was candid but correct. She demonstrated her loyalty to him daily for more than 31 years.

# Editors' Exchange

Fay Blanchard returned to the pulpit in the fall of 1955 with a weekly supplement to *The Bulletin*. Called *The Sanctum*, it focused on the problems faced by editorial page editors and their writers. Like *The Bulletin*, it discussed topics of mutual interest, but *The Sanctum* generated more challenges from colleagues and it published the debates that followed.

An early issue carried a question from Fred Stein, editor and publisher in Binghamton. He raised a point of ethics about which journalists still debate – how deeply should an editor get involved in his community's public life?

"It's hard to comment on something of which you are a part, except favorably," he said. "Yet I feel that an ivory-tower attitude on the part of an editor makes his worth to the community less than active participation." [6]

Miller responded to that one personally. "I don't believe it is possible to have a hard and fast rule," he said. Then he concluded:

"Just as I am sure that no newspaper can do the job it should do unless it is in the thick of community affairs, I am convinced that no editor or publisher can do the job he might – for his community and for himself – unless he does get his own feet wet."

To which *The Sanctum* added, "PM knows. His feet are wet clear to the knees."[7]

*The Bulletin* itself reflected the national fascination with President Eisenhower and the medical care that aided his recovery from a serious heart attack. Ben McKelway, editor of the *Washington Star*, had spoken about it at Rochester's City Club. Jones said the speech "pulled together for the first time all the details about the president's illness, how it was handled, and what the crisis showed about our vague laws and the way in which Ike's 'team' met the challenge."

The *Times-Union* published the long speech in five installments. Jones observed that many editors who published the material had blanched at some of the clinical detail. He continued:

"Failure to deal frankly with Woodrow Wilson's ordeal caused tragic confusion after World War I. Oddly enough, many editors goggled over Dr. White's [Eisenhower's doctor] announcement that the president had had a good bowel movement, and removed this from the text and summary. We think the doctor was right in so reporting; that the public understands this sort of homely fact, whereas it usually is vague about electrocardiographs and other angles of modern medicine."[8]

Paul Martin of GNS told Jones that the clinical detail on the president's illness had caused satirical comment at the National Press Club in Washington. "Later it was pointed out that the first crisis for a heart patient comes at the time of the first movement. A satisfactory report on this point would be understood by virtually all doctors and a considerable number of laymen around the country," Martin reported.[9] Jones's rejection of squeamishness was vindicated.

Even schoolchildren won the attention of Gannett editors. Blanchard had repeatedly emphasized in *The Bulletin* the importance of young readers to a newspaper's growth. He was tested as editor of the *Democrat and Chronicle:*

A seventh-grader wrote a letter suggesting that she and her classmates found *Democrat and Chronicle* editorials difficult to read. The editor published a note of appreciation on the editorial page of his paper. He told the seventh-graders his newspaper's policy was that an editorial should not sound like an editorial. He said he and his staff tried to "write as completely and as clearly as we can. After all, you are not going to stay very long at your present age level. What appeals to you today as helpful might very well seem only sappy a year hence. . . .

"[Y]ou have helped us, showing us we need to watch our step. We think it fine that your school considers the newspaper helpful. We hope to make it more so."[10]

## The Gannett Spirit

All editors had a familiar struggle on their hands as 1956 began: managing the newsprint shortage. The *Commercial-News* in Danville, Ill., was scrambling to fit all the news into the newsprint it had available. Standard features were moved from the front of the second section to the editorial page. It cut a 56-page Sunday paper to 40, discarding entire pages on news of residential and commercial construction and restricting its popular farm news to a page.

Martin posted a notice in the Washington Bureau "that no story out of this bureau filed on the GNS wire will exceed *750 words in length.*" The persistent scarcity of newsprint and limited columns available for news made the austerity necessary.

By March, the shortage became a crisis in Rochester. While they awaited new shipments of newsprint, the *Democrat and Chronicle* and the *Times-Union* took drastic measures. Both published twice without display advertising. Twice they included only classified ads and death notices and once excluded all national advertising.

That was done, *The Bulletin* said, to allow full coverage "for local, national and international news, and all regular features."

Miller took to the road in early 1957 to spread the Gannett philosophy to the North Carolina Press Association. At a dinner at Duke University in Durham, he described the journalist's basic job, "no matter how large the newspaper or how small.

"All you have to do is build and sell ever better newspapers despite ever higher production costs, in the face of ever tougher competition, and for a rightly ever-more-demanding readership. That's all. Simple, isn't it?"

Keep your newspaper useful, he advised. Stay close to readers and advertisers. Never forget that people still come first. Make your newspaper stand for something. Keep your newspaper local.

He summarized a working philosophy in words that personified his entire professional life and would become a Gannett credo: "Do the right thing."[11]

That was a simplification of a statement of principles Miller had issued to Gannett executives in 1956. Imprinted on a desktop card, they read:

"Do the right thing.

"Hire on merit. Recruit and employ without regard to sex, race, creed or color.

"Do not abdicate management responsibilities in union departments.

"Be alert to recognize outstanding enterprise and ability.

"Constantly reappraise and reassess. Weed out early.

"Our actions must be determined not by mere compliance with state or federal law, not by public attitudes, but on the basis of doing the right thing.

"Do the right thing."

Back in Rochester, Miller began what would become a Saturday trademark of the *Times-Union*, a signed column in place of editorials. Cal Mayne, who at one period was editor of the editorial page, said, "He would work on this in bits and pieces, usually starting sometime around Thursday."

"It was a conservative column," Mayne said, "sometimes about Rochester and sometimes about national affairs, carefully written, hedged. Paul was much more vigorous in his opinions personally than he was journalistically."

The column also went out on the Gannett News Service wire, Mayne said, "but nobody ran it except *The Ithaca Journal*. That was one aspect of local autonomy." [12]

Frank Tripp's Sunday column in Elmira had been a fixture there for years. It frequently explained newspaper problems to readers, and occasionally talked back to someone.

One angry resident had sent a letter to the editor of the Sunday *Telegram*, with a copy to City Council. It was not published and the writer demanded to know, "Do we have a public press in Elmira?"

Tripp answered him eloquently in an open-letter column:

"We sure do, and it is yours to express your opinions when they are moderately stated, and printable. It is also a responsible press – responsible for what it prints, and responsible to readers.

"In your case it is hard to think that you were very thoughtful of your implications. Else you would not have referred to your neighbors who hold public office as dishonest. . . .

"Discussion of efficiency and economy is one thing; of honesty it is something else. Sometimes we print letters that exhibit poor taste, bad livers, maybe personal spleen; and we dive to the bottom of charges of dishonesty, wherever it exists.

"But the right to accuse any man or men of dishonesty is not a function of letters to the editor. That is something to which we assign our best and most experienced men.

"Sorry. If you must abuse somebody, don't expect to make us a party to your rancor." [13]

# Making It Official

Miller was elected president of the Gannett Company on April 11, 1957. He was 50. At that meeting of the board of directors, the gravity of Gannett's illness was confirmed. He was elected president emeritus. When the board created a disability pension for him equal to his pay, it was acknowledging that the 80-year-old leader would never return to his desk.

In a statement published in the *Gannetteer,* Tripp recounted for Gannett employees the search for the new president. It is included in its entirety because it reveals a great deal about both Franks as well as Miller:

"If Paul Miller will accept the designation, I am proud to call him 'my boy.'

"It was a long and thoughtful search by both Frank Gannett and me to find a man equipped to someday become the president of The Gannett Newspapers.

"We both were of an age to make the choice necessary when Paul came; and there seemed to be an organization-wide realization at once of his destiny.

"I say he is my boy because I found him. Frank Gannett had barely met him.

"The search was for a man of country-wide acquaintance and newspaper knowledge. We found one who qualifies even worldwide. I believe that Paul Miller is today's best-known man in world journalism, and personally knows more of his contemporaries both in and out of the newspaper field.

"In his [active years], I would have said the same of Frank Gannett. It had to be a rare type to succeed Frank.

"But most important it had to be a man who would accept the traditions of Gannett Newspapers, marry them and perpetuate them. Most of all, the human relations that make for the security of Gannett people.

"Paul has met this test in his every action and attitude. All that Gannett Newspapers have meant to all of us is safe and secure under his leadership. He has no pals to bring along, no strange policies to nurture, no weird newspaper notions.

"In my book, what more can we ask of a successor to the man who built it all – a man we love?" [14]

The future of Gannett and its employees was envisioned by Miller in a talk to representatives of Group circulation departments:

"As to where and when opportunities will come, time and events will tell. Things can happen fast, as you have seen. There are bound to be openings from time to time. Also, our company is not necessarily through expanding. We are not going to expand just for the sake of expanding. But we can be interested in good newspapers in good communities that fit our type of operation." [15]

# Death Watch

The Gannett Newspapers did not immediately expand. Instead they contracted by one. On June 25, 1957, the board approved closing down the Olean *Times-Herald* Printing Company. It sold the company's 490 shares – minority interest – of *Times-Herald* stock for an undisclosed price to E. Boyd Fitzpatrick. That included its share both in the *Times-Herald* and in radio station WHDL.

The *Niagara Gazette,* meanwhile, was preparing to launch a Sunday newspaper in the fall.

The *Democrat and Chronicle* moved to a new *Times-Union* building that summer. The $1.6-million project was undertaken to accommodate the paper's growth and increasing needs for modernized quarters. (The old *D&C* building was sold in 1958 for $216,000.)

Caroline Gannett went to Cornell University in Ithaca to speak for her husband at his alma mater two days after his 81st birthday. It was the dedication of the Gannett Medical Clinic on campus, made possible by the largest single donation to any group by the Frank E. Gannett Newspaper Foundation.

She said of her husband, "He had the best day today since he became sick. . . . He is still in spirit the same vivid person he has always been." [16]

Company assets expanded in November, when the board approved the purchase, for $1.1 million, of station KOVR-TV in Stockton, Calif. It also voted to require company executives to retire at age 70, unless specifically asked by the board to remain.

# Closing the Books

Gannett died at home on Dec. 3, 1957. Erwin Davenport, also 81, was living in retirement in Miami Beach. Tripp, at 75, was the only person still active in the Gannett Company who had been there at the beginning in Elmira. In a published tribute to his old friend, Tripp wrote:

"Few men have lived the satisfying lives that Frank Gannett and I spent with each other. We were together since 1906. Of all who knew him, I probably knew his hopes and aims the best.

"We were opposites in many ways, yet akin in many others. From reporter and editor of a little newspaper, through headaches, heartaches and laughter, surrounded by wonderful associates, we saw dogged effort build an enterprise of great stature.

"Through it all, Frank Gannett was honorable, fair, patient, generous and kind. He was a good man, a courageous man, a loyal friend, a newspaper genius and a great American.

"I loved him." [17]

Gannett's will, dated Jan. 5, 1953, restated the ideals of The Gannett Newspapers and the general principles he had established for the Frank E. Gannett Newspaper Foundation. He added:

"The fact that I have given to the foundation, and am entrusting to its directors, control of the Class A common stock of Gannett Co. Inc. should indicate clearly that, in building up this group of newspapers, I have not been interested in personal financial reward, but have sought only the joy that comes from making a contribution to the general welfare."

(Before Gannett Co. Inc. went public in 1967, the foundation had 100 percent control with its 40,000 shares of stock, with a book value of $300 each. Exchange of shares into one class of voting stock reduced the foundation's influence to 34 percent. That represented, in 1968, 1,666,000 shares whose over-the-counter price had ranged from $22 to $36.) [18]

Now that her boss was gone, there was nothing to prevent Messman from leaving. After three decades of acting and working independently, which her boss's power assured her, she did not adjust happily to his successor. She had continued to open Gannett's mail during his illnesses; "Mr. Miller insisted on seeing it all," she said. "He was so afraid I was going to commit Mr. Gannett to something."

She also was not happy that Miller had kept her busy compiling for Blanchard's *Sanctum* weekly reports on the content of group editorial pages.

After Gannett's death, she said, "I had 32 years of files to go through. Four drawers a year. They were stacked to the ceiling in the filing room. It took me from his death until I got out in April to go through the files and throw away [those] that weren't needed. . . .

"When I announced I was going to leave . . . they couldn't believe that Ma Messman was ever going to leave. I had a small party, just the girls. Mrs. Gannett called me that night from Miami Beach. . . . I was tickled to death to get out of there. I could see no reason to feel bad."

She recalled one aspect of her departure with a touch of sarcasm. "I didn't have much stuff when I came home. One thing might amuse you. I left . . . in April. I'd been there all that time. I had written up my little desk calendar pad for that year, with some personal things, my friends' birthdays and some things. So I said, 'I can't leave this for whoever they're going to have in the office. I want to take it home with me.' They sold it to me. For $2." Then she laughed. "After 32 years." [19]

Messman was 56 when she left. Although she was offered several positions as an executive secretary, she turned them down to travel and play golf with her husband.

Mrs. Gannett was left 8,000 shares of Class A common stock in her husband's will. Since control of all Class A common was vested in the foundation, the board of directors voted to buy it. On June 26, 1958, they approved a price of $300 per share for those 8,000 "plus any additional shares of which she may become possessed under said will." Gannett had seen to his wife's security with a bequest of at least $2.4 million.

In its last order of business at that meeting, the board approved a loan of $50,000 at 3 1/2 percent interest to its subsidiary Northern New York Publishing Co. Franklin R. Little, editor and publisher of Northern New York's Ogdensburg and Massena newspapers, also wrote the board that he wanted to buy out Gannett's 51 percent for $350,000.

That request appealed to the board. It voted to sell the 51 percent but that the proper officers negotiate *"with a view to obtaining a price in excess of the $350,000 offered."* [20]

The era of Frank Gannett was over, but his legacy was in the hands of competent stewards.

# Chapter 24

# Gannett à la Miller

*"A youngster could pick up a lot in the old days just by coming in early and hanging around late. I'm not pining for the good old days. . . . Newsmen's salaries were mostly too low. Hours were often long. It could be, though, that we've overdone the catch-up."*

*Paul Miller*
*1958*

Frank Gannett and Frank Tripp had continuity in mind when they had recruited Paul Miller. Casual observers were misled, however, by Gannett's professional durability and long life. Their mistaken impression late in 1957 was that newspapers nurtured for 51 long years by their founder were now in the hands of some Johnny-come-lately.

That misconception overlooked the fact that "young Paul Miller" had spent 10 years working for "old Frank Gannett." His tenure represented virtually 20 percent of the existence of The Gannett Newspapers. Miller had paid his dues. While he was nominally the heir presumptive, he did not arrive as the heir guaranteed.

Vin Jones had recalled a succession of "bright young men" who had been installed as assistants to Gannett and who later vanished. He said of Miller, "He had a few narrow escapes. One time he did something, he told me, and Gannett said, 'Well, boy, you're all through. You did it wrong this time.' But somehow or other Paul wriggled out of it and survived."[1] Jones didn't know the details, only that Miller remembered it as a close call.

The new president, at 51, was 30 years the late Frank Gannett's junior. Tripp, the chairman, was 75. Some younger faces were being seen around the Central Office, but their circle could qualify as a youth movement only by comparison. Thanks to the retirement of Herbert Cruickshank, Lynn Bitner, 53, was general manager. Cy

Williams, comptroller since 1945, was 51. Jones, head of the News and Editorial Office and the only one of the three who could be called Miller's man, was 52.

Other names would begin to appear with more frequency as Miller began to chart his own direction. There were Thomas P. Dolan, 39, general manager in Saratoga Springs; Robert R. Eckert, 37, assistant general manager in Binghamton; John E. (Jack) Heselden, 37, assistant to Bitner for labor and personnel.

The business-side executives, and those just coming along on papers around the group, would be Miller's spear carriers on the numbers front. He would set broad policy, then trust their abilities to implement it in advertising, circulation, and other non-editorial areas.

That would free him to represent The Gannett Newspapers in more frequent public appearances; to fulfill his part-time duties as a director of The Associated Press; to do what he loved most, work through the News and Editorial Office – and Jones – with the men and women in Gannett newsrooms.

His personal secretary, Mary Golding, recalled that news was his prime interest. "He courted the newsroom," she said. "He'd go downstairs and really spend some time at the newsroom and talk with the managing editor and the editorial boards. Every couple of weeks or so, he'd say, 'I'm going to have a stroll today,' and he'd go downstairs and go through the newsroom." [2]

Jones described Miller's dealings with the public:

"He began to take an active role in the city. . . . Paul took over the faltering campaign to build a war memorial, which happened to be right across from the newspaper. He got that back on the road and got the thing built. He was all over the place. He was into everything, everybody knew him, and it was very stimulating.

"Now on the newspaper, he was always trying to get things done and changed. He was trying to build up personalities." [3]

A *Gannetteer* summary of Miller's community activism recalled his belief in an editor or publisher's getting "his own feet wet." He had headed Rochester Red Cross campaigns and been vice chairman of the 1956 Combined Community Chest and Red Cross drive. In addition to heading the Mayor's War Memorial Committee, he was chairman of the Albert D. Kaiser Award Committee, and a trustee of the Chamber of Commerce, of George Eastman House and of the Rochester Institute of Technology.

In May, Miller flew to California to speak at Stanford University about "The Newspaper of the Future." The occasion was the 20th anniversary meeting of the California Editors Conference of the California Newspaper Publishers Association.

"What were you and your newspaper doing 20 years ago?" he began.

"All of us," he said, "were doing a lot of things differently and not as well as editors like to think we are doing them now. Among other things, and just in a quick run-down, we are getting sharper printing, clearer illustrations, better departmentalization, bigger ads with better art work, more horizontal makeup, improved domination of inside pages by single stories or packages of related stories."

Content he found much improved – more attention to school news; specialized coverage of things such as science and religion; greater emphasis on problems of government; color, "with its headaches and its satisfactions.

"To me," he said, "the general assertion of greater responsibility, primarily in local affairs, but more broadly too, represents one of the most significant advances of modern-day journalism."

Looking ahead, he conceded advances in technology but warned of a major deterrent. He reminded his professional audience that presses cost a newspaper more than all other mechanical departments combined.

"Many newspapers have purchased new press equipment only recently," he said, "or are doing so now. Therefore, it seems safe to conclude that most newspapers will for at least most of the next 20 years continue to be produced on web presses which print by means of impressing a continually running high-speed sheet of newsprint between the blanket cylinder and the plate cylinder.

"Some splendid special equipment is available for such presses and is being added widely – but it's still the same method of printing. . . .

"I am convinced that we will continue and improve in the next 20 years along the lines already pretty clearly indicated by developments and improvements of the past. At the same time, I'm glad the experts at Rochester Institute of Technology and elsewhere are working toward the future, and I hope some of the developments they predict are nearer than I think."[4]

It was in that speech that he alluded to the "good old days" when "newsmen's salaries *were* mostly too low . . . hours *were* often too long." He could comfortably mention such negative images of newspapers because he had done something about them on The Gannett Newspapers.

Some retired colleagues gave him high marks for seeking to make Gannett newsroom pay scales more competitive. "Paul raised salaries all along the board," Dolan recalled. "Paul believed in paying people. He believed in them doing their job to get the pay, but he was willing to pay to get a good job."[5]

Jones remembered working as a young man at Utica for $36 a week for "six days, Sundays, holidays, everything else. Then I finally got to be city editor, and I think I got a little more than a printer got for working five days a week.

"I got to be managing editor, I got $65 a week. . . .

"When Miller came to the company and looked at the salaries, he was appalled. . . . It would have been very hard for him to get a big salary where everybody underneath was at peonage wages. But about the first thing he did was to get together with Tripp and see to it that we all began to get some decent money."[6]

# Shared Experiences

Miller's enthusiasm for professional outreach forced a change in attitudes among Gannett executives as well. On July 1, 1958, he became chairman of the American Press Institute, whose seminars for editors, reporters and managers of newspaper business offices he strongly supported.

Participation by Gannett people at the API seminars had increased during the past 10 years, largely because of Miller, according to Jones:

"He really brought us into the 20th century, because Gannett and Tripp had not paid a great deal of attention to newspaper running, nor were they particularly in the mainstream of what was going on in journalism. . . .

"I'd been involved in the API quite early on, and when Paul really [saw] what they were doing he simply issued an order that we would have a candidate for every API seminar there was. That we never had before because nobody else in the company would have given 5 cents for an API seminar, (Lynn) Bitner or anybody else. They thought that was for the birds. . . .

"They thought that's where you send somebody and somebody else hires them away. That's true. If you are not paying the guy the right salary, that happens." [7]

Miller believed just as strongly in intramural training. He would later ask Jack Heselden to establish internal training programs. Those Gannett Management Seminars, established in 1962, are still operating today. Part of their purpose, at that time, was to prepare promising department heads to become publishers. But they had a broader dimension.

"We thought that it was important," Heselden said, "to give the news personnel an appreciation of the business side and to give the advertising, circulation and production people some understanding of news operations – to break down some of the barriers between news and business."

## Spreading the Word

Miller had once asked Jones to spell out his methods of operating in Utica. Jones's reply, dated Aug. 23, 1948, included this: "Every editor gets invitations to speak. I always accept, because it gives me a chance to tell our story and to smoke out many of the absurd misconceptions which flourish."

Such rules of engagement endeared an executive to Miller. He encouraged public appearances both for the individual's benefit and Gannett's. As executive editor of The Gannett Newspapers, Jones got and accepted many such opportunities.

He spoke in July 1958 at the closing session of a two-week "workshop for educators" at Syracuse University. The program was cosponsored by the university and the International Circulation Managers Association. He was direct:

"Whether you like it or not, monopoly is the predominant fact of modern newspaper life. And whether editors and publishers like it or not, the fact is that this condition is converting most newspapers into semi-public utilities. One dividend of monopoly has been a keen sense of reponsibility. It is a brash editor, indeed, who denies access to his columns to even the most dreadful bore or proven crackpot. His newspaper sometimes may seem to strike a deadly median between dullness and wildness, but the chances are that it reflects the true character of the community."

He said newspapers had only themselves to blame for certain built-in liabilities. Among them:

- "Preoccupation with the trivial, the bizarre, the disastrous, the sensational, the notion that it isn't news unless it is bad news, for someone.
- "An increasingly reckless and ruthless invasion of privacy, a section of the law not nearly so well understood as libel.
- "A tendency to ultra-conservatism. This is entirely proper in an important institution, which represents a huge investment, and is a sound position so long as this institution remains hospitable to new and even weird ideas.
- "Careless reporting, and printing.
- "Ignoring vast areas of public interest.

"I wish that I could tell you that all of these liabilities are on the verge of being converted into assets. They aren't, of course."

He was not pessimistic, however. "Instead of 'playing down' to public taste and indifference, some of the best brains in the business are devoting their writing and editorial skills to making [important] news more inviting and, in effect, constantly nudging the reader upward. This is where educators and editors can make common cause."[8]

## Standard Bearer

Awareness of The Gannett Newspapers was assured by public appearances of company executives, editors and managers. The name Gannett also remained familiar because of Caroline Gannett's busy schedule. Accolades that formerly went to her husband were now coming to her.

Mrs. Gannett was identified closely enough with the newspapers her husband had founded that her public was reminded of their contributions as well.

Elmira College awarded her an honorary doctor of humane letters degree at its June 1958 commencement. The college, in the town where Frank Gannett and Erwin Davenport had joined forces 52 years before, honored her as a director of Gannett Co. Inc. and as a member of the New York State Board of Regents.[9]

She had accepted her place on the Board of Regents in 1947 at her husband's urging. "I cannot accept," she first replied when told she had been proposed for membership. "I do not have any degrees. I gained most of my education from extensive traveling in Europe with my family. I went to a German school in Munich." Gannett had persuaded her that her extensive work with children, particularly the disabled, was qualification enough.[10]

Mrs. Gannett challenged graduating seniors of St. John Fisher College in Rochester at their 1958 commencement. In a speech strongly reminiscent of her late husband, she said:

"Is it not possible for you to think and live in terms of peace instead of war? Can you, for instance, clarify in your creative minds the duties of a minister of peace as a member of the president's cabinet? [Gannett had proposed such a cabinet post to Franklin Roosevelt before World War II.]

"Can you not interpret through the media of modern communications – newspapers, radio, television and magazines – the news of your day in words so effective that sordid literature and stage presentations [of all kinds] can be routed into disuse?" [11]

Late that summer, Mrs. Gannett rallied campaign workers as honorary chairman for the Rochester Eye Bank and Research Society, Inc. fund drive. She told them that two young men had received sight that year because of cornea transplants from her late husband's eyes.

Both she and her husband, she said, had pledged their eyes to the Rochester Eye Bank just a year before his death at 81. [12]

At the end of 1958, Cornell University accepted the papers of Frank and Caroline Gannett. They had announced their intention to make the donation a few days before Cornell dedicated the Gannett Health Center on campus in September 1957. [13]

(As part of its 50th anniversary observance in 1985, the Gannett Foundation gave a grant to Cornell to establish the Frank E. Gannett and Caroline Werner Gannett Archives. The money was used to analyze, arrange, index and store the documents and publish the 156-page "Guide to the Frank E. Gannett and Caroline Werner Gannett Papers." The collection was dedicated as part of the Department of Manuscripts and University Archives, Cornell University Libraries, on Oct. 8, 1987.)

# TV or Not TV

The Gannett Company was never reluctant to spend money to expand its properties or improve their potential. Four such projects were under way in 1958, at a total cost of more than $1.5 million:

- $332,000 in Hartford to expand the press room of *The Times*.
- $300,000 in Utica to complete a third floor on the building hous-

ing both the *Observer-Dispatch* and the *Daily Press*.
- $225,000 in Rochester to remodel a building for studios and offices of WHEC (radio) and the start-up of WHEC-TV.
- $750,000 in Binghamton for a transmitter and equipped studios for WINR (radio) and development of WINR-TV.[14]

Those television projects in Rochester and Binghamton were nagging concerns in a company attuned to spending money wisely and effectively on its newspapers.

Board discussion was summarized thus:

"WHEC is at present engaged exclusively in AM radio broadcasting. It has no facilities for television. Unless the station is able to enter the television field, Gannett Co. Inc. faces a substantial loss [on] its investment. It is the considered judgment of all concerned that, to protect this investment, all needed support, financial and otherwise, must be given by Gannett Co. Inc."

The board followed that statement of quiet desperation by voting to lend WHEC no more than $425,000 at 2 1/2 percent.[15]

Binghamton's situation was no more encouraging. Gannett directors learned in January 1957 that the FCC had approved transfer of ownership of WINR to Binghamton Press Company. The newspaper company planned to continue the radio station and begin prompt construction of a UHF television station on Channel 40. It bought the radio station for $165,000. It estimated costs to complete the project at another $405,000.

"Binghamton Press Co.," the board was told, "may not be financially able to pay the total cost in the short period of time set for completion." It therefore asked for and was granted a loan of $250,000, at 2 percent.[16]

Bitner, the group's general manager, had promised the board that the station would open Dec. 1. Eckert, assistant general manager of the Binghamton *Press*, became involved. He recalled in an interview:

"They made some projections and decided that they probably were going to lose $250,000 to $300,000 the first year. Or maybe they'd see a little daylight. But the *Press* could support it because the *Press* was the godfather of the station.

"Well, they lost $200,000 the first two months. Bitner came down and said, 'What the hell is going on here? We've got to do something about this.' ...

"We cut the losses to $10,000 a month, which were livable, but never put the thing in the black. It was a disaster almost from the word go."[17]

At the time of Gannett's struggle with TV in Binghamton in 1958, 657 television stations had been authorized by the Federal Communications Commission and 492 were on the air.[18]

# Chapter 25

# The Prize and A Prize Catch

*"Although the Utica newspapers won the 1959 Pulitzer gold medal for meritorious public service last May, the icing on the cake really came Nov. 3, 1959. On that day, Utica voters spoke in a loud and clear voice — threw out the boss-controlled Democratic machine, and elected their first Republican mayor in 14 years."*

*Editorially Speaking*
*1959 issue* [1]

Apalachin, N.Y., is a small town about 15 miles west of Binghamton, just a stone's throw off Route 434 where it parallels Route 17 along the Susquehanna River. On Nov. 14, 1957, New York State Police crashed a gangland meeting in the area. The register of mobsters and hoods rounded up in that raid made "Apalachin" a permanent footnote to organized crime.

In the criminal coterie were three men from Utica, where:

- Ten days earlier voters had re-elected the city administration, despite newspaper opposition, by record pluralities.

- Nearly two decades before, two editors had sat on inside information for two years while a federal investigation plodded toward indictment of 68 individuals in 1939.

- Flourishing gambling and vice prompted the New York *Journal-American* to label Utica "Sin City of the East."

Mason Taylor, who had become editor of Gannett's Utica *Press* early in 1956, had covered schools, city hall and Utica politics for 13 years. "For years," he later told colleagues, "vice and gambling had been tolerated in Utica perhaps to the same extent as in most any other medium-size city. After World War II there was a period of great industrial growth, accompanied by an influx of new families, and other indices of community progress. . . . Toward the end of that period, there was a revival of boss control of city government. And there were rumors of a possible alliance between Democratic and Republican leaders and of gangster infiltration into gambling."[2]

Apalachin and the *Journal-American's* mockery fired the long-suffering Taylor with new energy. He was determined to expose the corruption staining Utica. But he couldn't do it by himself and no one on his staff had the necessary experience.

The News and Editorial Office sent him a New York GNS reporter named Jack Germond, who had joined Gannett in 1953.

Germond had quit his job on a small paper in Michigan after two years and driven east with his wife, looking for a job. "I'd been getting $92.50 a week at this paper in Michigan," he recalled, "and [managing editor] Vern Croop would only give me $77 a week to go to work for the *Times-Union*. But I took the pay cut and didn't regret it."

After three years in Rochester, Germond was temporarily assigned to GNS's Albany bureau for four months in 1956, then joined the bureau full-time in 1957. He spoke highly of Taylor.

"He was a very tough guy, and very staunch in pursuing this corruption of the government. And there was a reporter, later editorial page editor, named Bill Lohden, who worked with me on this. He had not done much reporting . . . but he had good instincts and he was a good reporter."

What Taylor hoped to accomplish, Germond said, was to dig up enough evidence to force Gov. W. Averell Harriman to appoint a special prosecutor to investigate Utica's government.

"The Utica city government was rotten," Germond said. "I remember some of the stories. They had only like 30 trucks of their own because all the plowing and trash pickup and so forth was contracted out to a business run by Rufie Elefante. . . . Their trucks were just for . . . city parks and things like that.

"I went over and got all the vouchers out of City Hall . . . and I found that in something like three months they'd bought $35,000 worth of tires for 30 trucks. . . .

"They were paying list price for these tires. . . . Tires have serial numbers on them. I went to the DPW garage one night with a flashlight and got into the garage and crawled around on my back looking at all the tires. I could never find any of the tires.

"Well, what was happening was the tires were going to Elefante and the city was paying. There were things like that. In that same period, there were like $30,000 worth of carburetor repairs to these trucks and that kind of stuff." [3]

When all this corruption was reported, Taylor recalled later, Utica's government responded with "a threat of an advertising tax, a request for an anti-trust probe of the papers and personal attacks on [the] executives. Rumors were circulated that editors were at one and the same time anti-Semitic, anti-Italian, anti-Catholic and anti-Protestant. Newsmen were shadowed, sometimes threatened." [4]

But Taylor's determination paid off for Utica and for Gannett. Gov. Harriman did appoint a special prosecutor to purge the city. And the *Press* and the *Observer-Dispatch* won the 1959 Pulitzer Prize for public service, the first public service citation ever won by a Gannett newspaper.

Germond recalled another tribute that might have meant almost as much to Taylor. "Mason had covered the city government himself before he became executive editor," he said. "I can remember one of the people in City Hall telling me that the worst thing Gannett ever did for Utica city government was promote Mason Taylor. Because as long as he was there, there were limits on what they could do. Once he left, they could steal the place brick by brick." [5]

Taylor summarized for his colleagues the results of the prize-winning series and the special prosecutor's work:

"Thus far," he reported, "he has sent three brothel operators to [county] jail and two to [state] prison. Currently, he is investigating alleged irregularities in city purchasing and contracts. He was given additional authority to investigate tax fraud. Other inquiries at the local, state and federal levels are under way.

"The job is not finished, but much has been accomplished. Perhaps the most important thing is that the public has been made aware, as never before, of what can happen in a community when the mass of its citizens become apathetic." [6]

The ultimate satisfaction for Taylor and his colleagues came at the polls, two years after voters had re-elected the city government with record pluralities. A city official had called that result a "people's mandate" for lax enforcement of vice and gambling laws. In 1959, thanks in great part to the perseverance of the *Press* and the *Observer-Dispatch*, voters mandated an end to 14 years of corrupt government by machine politics.

## Saratoga's Daily Double

Tom Dolan joined Gannett at Massena in 1945. He worked for editor and publisher Franklin R. Little there and at Ogdensburg, eventually as advertising manager, before becoming general manager of the Potsdam *Courier and Freeman*, a Gannett weekly.

On New Year's Day, 1957, he became general manager of *The Saratogian*. Thirty miles away in Albany, the *Knickerbocker News* was not prospering, despite its having ceded the morning market to Hearst's *Times-Union* in exchange for unopposed afternoon circulation.

Dolan enjoyed challenges. He gave one to managing editor Fred Eaton in June 1959. As Eaton explained later:

"Suppose that one morning the boss said: 'You've got to get rid of those fellows who are providing 30 percent of your news and pictures and find some way to fill the space from the rest of your staff.'

"Although admittedly exaggerated, that is approximately the task assigned to me. . . . General manager Tom Dolan handed me a copy of the Cape Cod *Standard-Times* and the New Bedford *Standard-Times*, which for more than 20 years had been doing a job somewhat similar."[7] The New Bedford newspaper was inserted into the Cape Cod paper and circulated as a single issue.

Eaton was to turn *The Saratogian* into a strictly local paper without any of the news that would be found in the *Knickerbocker News*. The localized *Saratogian* would then be wrapped around a Saratoga Springs edition of the *Knickerbocker News* and circulated as before.

According to Dolan, the advantage of this was to boost the Albany paper's circulation, which "picked up another 12,000. That made us the largest daily newspaper between New York and Montreal."[8] Dolan became that paper's assistant general manager, in addition to being general manager in Saratoga Springs.

"The majority of [readers] interviewed were pleased with the change. They felt that they were getting a big-city paper," Eaton said. "No longer could they gripe about not enough national, not enough local, not enough state, not enough sports. This was particularly true in the areas of the county where we compete with Troy and Schenectady papers.

"But an astonishing complaint . . . was that we were giving 'too much newspaper.' Said these people, 'The old package was fine; it was convenient and easy to find things. Now we have to search for them.' . . .

"One other objection was raised, this by staunch old Saratogians. They want, they said, their 'own paper,' not a tieup with some out-of-town outfit. . . . We have taken abuse over the years for not being good enough. Now all at once we discovered that we had been revered and admired as a local product."[9]

The Daily Double, as it came to be called, would run for only two years.

# Another Gannett Newspaper

Paul Miller's signed column on Saturday, Sept. 5, 1959, bore the title, "Welcome to Autonomy." It announced that the Camden *Courier-Post* had joined "The Gannett Group of Newspapers" on Sept. 1. The author had spent $4.86 million in June to buy the New Jersey daily.

William Stretch, the son of the seller and the newspaper's general manager, explained in the *Gannetteer* how much the *Courier-Post* valued its independence and public service:

"Back when my family purchased the *Evening Courier* and the *Morning Post,* we had a rough job on our hands just trying to make the public understand that we were politically independent – and that no advertisers could force us to use their 'news.' Perhaps the greatest shock of all was the fact that a job on the *Courier-Post* could no longer be considered a political plum. . . .

"Some politically minded readers, of course, see politics and a desire for power in every move a newspaper makes but most of our readers . . . believe that we are more altruistic than the average newspaper. . . .

"After 13 years of working for the good of the community, we know that South Jersey understands us. And, if there is anything they don't understand, they waste no time wondering; they ask. And we answer."[10]

# The Editor Jones

Trends in journalism were as irresistible to Vin Jones as clues were to Sherlock Holmes. He absorbed them with a mental sponge for wringing out later to illustrate his gospel of better newspapers. Photography, typography, effective writing, news packaging and display, editorial leadership – he collected and catalogued samples of all of them for use as teaching tools.

Late in 1959, Jones was moderator of a seminar in Seattle, sponsored by the Allied Daily Newspapers of Washington. While he was there, he spoke on the evolution of newspapers to the Northwest Chapter of Sigma Delta Chi (now the Society of Professional Journalists). He applauded newspapers for hiring more college graduates with formal training for journalism. He commended cooperation between newspapers and journalism schools, especially "the practice whereby journalism teachers spend part of their summers working on newspapers."

Each newspaper, he said, should have its own training program. "We do have such a program in the Gannett Group," he said, "but our very diversity and our local autonomy makes it difficult to apply."

He found minimum pay scales "adequate," men at the top well paid, but he expressed concern for "the brilliant reporter or copyreader who hasn't the executive talent to run a peanut stand, or the personality to be a columnist.

"Historically," he said, "the big pay has gone to supervisors, on the ground they take responsibility. . . . We should be just as eager to reward the star reporter who is essential to a quality operation.

"Most important of all: We will always be a training ground for other industries unless we develop a news and editorial program so aggressive and so exciting that it will be a continuing challenge to the very best people." [11]

"Much of the thinking and talking about newspapering today," he said, "seems to me to rest upon what I call some 'dangerous assumptions.' " Some of those assumptions:

- "That fewer newspapers automatically will be better newspapers.
- "That television always will be dominated by entertainment.
- "That very fat – or very thin – newspapers represent quality.
- "That readers will always accept monopoly (or non-competitive) situations as a happy consequence of economics.
- "That America is too big a country for a truly national daily.
- "That readers understand that the fight for freedom of information is *their* fight, and not a desperate effort to preserve a private racket.
- "That people are willing to pay more and more for newspapers, without cutting down on the number they buy. The auto industry, in moving out of the low price class, opened a gap which foreign firms have rushed to fill. But at least the Big Three did get out bigger and better cars."

Instead of battling each other, he said, educators and editors should work together in a common cause.

He closed by alluding to the farmer who resisted the blandishments of a Farm Bureau recruiter with, "I ain't farming half as good as I know how today."

Journalism would make much faster progress, he said, "if all of us would start 'farming as good as we know how.' " [12]

## Down in Albany

Even if the *Knickerbocker News* was the biggest paper between New York and Montreal, thanks to the Saratoga Springs sandwich, it wasn't enough. Early in 1960, Henry Stock, advertising director for the group and Albany's general manager, joined Gannett executives in negotiating with William Randolph Hearst for some kind of joint operation. Dolan, then assistant general manager, explained:

"I always said we were a Protestant paper in a Catholic town, a Republican paper in a Democratic town and a conservative paper in a liberal town. . . . We were in a terrible section of town. The building was dilapidated, a bad old building that just wasn't functional as a newspaper building at all. . . .

"I suggested at that time that we go morning and go head-to-head. I still think it would have been a good idea to give them a shot, but Lynn Bitner, who was general manager of the company at the time, did not feel that that would be very prudent."

At their September 1960 meeting, Miller told Gannett directors that serious losses were ahead for the *Knickerbocker News*. Efforts to arrange a joint operating agreement with Hearst had failed and Miller recommended that they sell the newspaper. The directors accepted the president's advice.

Thirty-two years after Gannett bought the *Knickerbocker Press* and the *Evening News* for $2 million, the directors voted to sell the descendant *Knickerbocker News* to Hearst for $3.75 million.[13]

(The marriage made in Saratoga Springs also was on the rocks. While the arrangement continued briefly after Hearst acquired the Albany paper in 1960, the last combined issue of *The Saratogian* and the *Knickerbocker News* was published Sept. 20, 1961.)[14]

By the fall of 1960, Gannett Co. Inc. consisted of 19 newspapers, four radio stations and two television stations. The company's voting common stock was totally held by the Gannett Foundation. Its two classes of preferred stock, not listed on any exchange, were owned almost entirely by directors, officers and employees.

Gannett was both an operating company and a holding company. As an operating company it ran the Rochester *Times-Union* and the *Democrat and Chronicle,* and Gannett News Service bureaus in Washington, Albany and New York City.

As a holding company, it owned fully 12 of the individual corporations that published Gannett newspapers and had controlling interest of three others.

Wholly owned newspaper companies were in Albany, Binghamton, Camden, Danville, Elmira, Ithaca, Newburgh-Beacon, Niagara Falls, Plainfield and Saratoga Springs. Radio stations WDAN in Danville, WENY in Elmira and WINR and WINR-TV in Binghamton were operating divisions of the subsidiaries in those cities. Gannett also owned all the voting stock of WHEC Inc. radio and television in Rochester and Gannett Advertising Sales Corporation.

Hartford, Malone and Utica were the communities in which Gannett owned controlling interest in the operating companies.

At the September 1960 meeting of Gannett executives, Miller quoted Jones: "Editorially, each newspaper acts independently on local issues. . . . On large national issues we would prefer to be consistent throughout the Group. Over the years we have steered a course which seems to us to be progressive, but which might look conservative to some."

(This limitation of editorial autonomy primarily to local issues was new to the author when he read it in this source. While the files of *The Bulletin* were incomplete, most of those confidential newsletters between 1939 and 1960 were available. This expanded definition of autonomy was not found in any of them.)

# Chapter 26

# The Carl Lindstrom Matter

*"Carl Lindstrom reported his reactions to a seminar for managing editors: [He'll] never be ashamed to be called 'provincial.' [He'll] battle all newspaper critics if [he's] permitted to fight from a citadel of accurate local news. . . . Gannett papers lead the nation, Lindstrom thinks, in much of our news handling, in photo [techniques], and in altruistic public service."*

*The Bulletin*
Oct. 30, 1947

The *Fading American Newspaper* by Hartford's Carl E. Lindstrom was published in the fall of 1960. The book's appearance set in motion the final alienation of a journalist whose literacy and professional guidance had once enjoyed the affection and respect of his colleagues in Gannett.

The book was described in a capsule preceding its review in the *Saturday Review*: "Laments the lack of standards in newspaper journalism today."

It got mixed reviews. Said a review in *Editor & Publisher*:

"[H]e probes with the incisive judgment of long and highly practical experience the daily paper's reporting of science, the newspaper as the last bulwark of simple, vivid English, and journalism's 'worn-out tools.'

"*The Fading American Newspaper* is no diatribe. It is the warm, frank appraisal of the shortcomings of the newspaper profession by a man who loves it, who knows a great deal about it, who wants to strengthen it. It is a book long overdue." [1]

Richard L. Tobin, a 24-year veteran of the New York *Herald Tribune*, and communications editor for *Saturday Review*, found the book "curiously uneven and humorless.

"Nothing in the newspaper business seems to please Mr. Lindstrom now," he wrote, "though his professional life must seem pointless in retrospect if, in fact, he detests his trade so bitterly. . . .

"Perhaps this is a clue to the book: in the first 50 pages the words 'irritating,' 'irritation,' 'irritate, 'irritated,' etc., appear a score of times. Since in Oscar Wilde's phrase all criticism is a form of autobiography, one should, perhaps, search Mr. Lindstrom's professional career for events and embroideries journalistic that goadingly 'irritated' him into such bitterness." [2]

Vin Jones sent a memo to Paul Miller on Oct. 13, 1960:

"The Lindstrom book is very rough on the newspaper business in general and the Gannett organization in particular.

"As you know, [American Newspaper Publishers Association] asked whether we would have any official reaction.

"I'm not sure that this is called for, but I wonder if I shouldn't try my hand at a *Bulletin* for the usual private circulation, refuting some of the things he has said about Central Office domination? Carl's book will filter back through the college and intellectual crowd and our editors and publishers ought to have the facts at their disposal."

Miller told Jones to go ahead.

# Happier Days

Lindstrom worked for *The Hartford Times* before Frank Gannett bought it in 1928. He first came to prominence among Gannett editors in 1946, when the managing editor of *The Times* was hospitalized. Lindstrom, who wrote music and theater criticism for *The Times,* filled in as acting managing editor.

Within two years, he had the job. Lindstrom's name began to appear with increasing frequency in *The Bulletin,* credited first by Fay Blanchard and later by Jones with ideas, observations and new approaches that were recommended to other Gannett editors.

He spoke frequently at the twice-yearly Gannett conferences for editors and executives. His talks often were reprinted in *Editorially Speaking*. The Associated Press Managing Editors named him chairman of its writing committee. He was elected a director of the American Society of Newspaper Editors and began the ascent toward the presidency.

The American Press Institute assigned him to work on a writing handbook, described by API as intended to be "to journalism what *Gray's Anatomy* is to medicine."

Jones wrote in *The Bulletin*, "[API] couldn't have picked a better man for the job. Carl's work with The Associated Press report is so outstanding that no other candidate for the job ever was considered." [3]

Frank Murphy, editor and publisher of *The Hartford Times*, retired in 1953. Lindstrom was promoted to a new position of executive editor, in charge of all news operations.

That same year, he was elected president of the New England Associated Press Council. When the New England Society of Newspaper Editors was created in 1955, he was elected vice president.

The frequency of items in *The Bulletin* over 10 years documents an era of mutual admiration among Carl Lindstrom, his colleagues and corporate executives.

As his professional activities broadened, he was invited more frequently to speak. That was encouraged by Jones and Miller, both of whom considered Lindstrom a professional credit to Gannett and *The Hartford Times* as well as to himself.

# Absent and Aloof

Hints of trouble surfaced early in 1956, when Lindstrom's personal calendar distracted him from his responsibilities as executive editor of *The Times*. At ASNE's annual convention, he failed to appear for associated Gannett meetings in which he was expected to participate. That prompted this May 11, 1956, note from Jones:

"It was my understanding that you planned to attend the Women's Press Club dinner, but that you would be on hand for the meetings, which lasted until midnight.

"While I am fully appreciative of your responsibilities to ASNE as a director, committee chairman, and now as an officer, it did not seem to me that it was asking too much to expect you to be on hand for at least part of an important session. As the head of the news department of one of the three largest newspapers in the Group, and one with special problems of convention coverage, we needed your thinking and your knowledge of the decisions which had been made at Hartford. I suspect that others turned down invitations or changed personal plans to be there and we selected Thursday night as the only one which was completely open."

The note closed, as usual, with "Cordially."

Lindstrom apparently decided to put Gannett cordiality to the test. The fall News and Editorial Conference was held in Hartford. That allowed Jones, as corporate executive editor, to get to know *Times* staff members better through some question-and-answer sessions. To the disbelief of David Daniel, his publisher, Lindstrom had arranged to be in Washington during most of the conference.

Jones summarized the Hartford situation in an Oct. 5, 1956, memo to Miller:

"As you know, [Dave Daniel] and Lindstrom do not hit it off at all well. Dave feels that Carl never has lived up to [Daniel's] conception of the job as executive editor. Specifically:

"Carl is not on top of his department; he refuses to delegate anything to [the managing editor] or to get along with [the editorial page editor]; and his handling of the staff is not good. . . .

"He still fails to consult Dave on outside arrangements. Dave learned of [Washington] AFTER Carl had accepted and was horrified at the idea of Carl absenting himself during the conference.

"Dave feels that Carl is terrific on big speaking assignments, where he has months to prepare, but terrible on hometown dates, or as he was at our conference. . . . Because Carl has failed to consult, Dave feels that all outside work, except New England [AP] Council presidency, is absurd. I explained that the Northwestern speech was valuable, because it involved heads and leaders of all J-schools, but Carl never bothered to sell this aspect of the trip. . . .

"The situation is not good and I hope that we can move in there before some disaster strikes."

Among the notes Miller scrawled on the margin of this memo was a suggestion that they wait for Lindstrom's response to a letter from Jones. He added: "If not satisfactory, can move back hard; if is satisfactory, which I do not expect, can then work out with him. Agree completely situation is a mess. – PM."

The Jones letter (also Oct. 5) criticized both *The Hartford Times's* news story on the Gannett conference and Carl Lindstrom's absence:

"I am sure that you realize that coverage of the Gannett conference by *The Times* did not come even close to measuring up to the lofty standards you outlined in your speech.

"The annotated clipping enclosed is inaccurate, incomplete and downright dull. I can't imagine anyone in Hartford being remotely interested . . . unless the story had explained . . . that the conference, a 30-year-old institution, was devoted to the frankest kind of self-criticism and a concerted effort to do a better job for YOUR readers, among others.

"I am sorry that you were not at the staff meeting Tuesday afternoon when I discussed this because the responsibility rests squarely with you. . . .

"I enjoyed every minute of the staff meeting. There was only one shock. Someone asked me whether it was true that 'Rochester' had laid down a policy that 'no story is worth a libel suit.' I said that no newspaper should deliberately expose itself to libel through carelessness, vindictiveness, or inaccuracy, but that I was sure that any good newspaper from time to time would have to risk libel if it expected to be a real newspaper. Also that it *was* our policy to fight every libel suit all the way to the U.S. Supreme Court.

"Naturally, I took full advantage of the opportunity to compliment the editors on the many things which *The Times* does so well."

There are no Miller notations scrawled on the margin of Lindstrom's casual response. It read simply:

"That wasn't much of a story.

"After two more days in Washington, the 23rd and 24th of October, that job will be finished. For the rest, I am immediately shortening sail on outside activities as far as I am able."

## Author and Lecturer

Early in 1957, Lindstrom received an invitation from *The Atlantic Monthly*, proposing his participation in a centennial issue on "A Perspective of Mass Communications." What the magazine editors had in mind was a piece describing "exactly what has happened to reporters, copyreaders and editors in the last few decades."

A second invitation came from the University of Michigan. Wesley H. Maurer, chairman of the Department of Journalism, invited Lindstrom to be a University Lecturer in Journalism. The university was hoping for a lecture "on any subject about the press you choose, and we should like to have the privilege of publishing it."

Lindstrom sent copies of both letters to Jones, who responded on Feb. 15, 1957:

"Those are two very flattering assignments.

"The lectureship should be of some use in attracting [to Gannett] the better type of Michigan graduate and in giving you further insight into the attitude of college people.

"The letter from *The Atlantic* prompted some misgivings. When you and I and other editors talk shop in newspaper circles we are deliberately critical and we pay little attention to the good things on the theory that everyone knows about them. But when we carry the same critical approach to the public – and particularly to an intellectual group which already has judged us and found us wanting – we must realize that there is an obligation not to aid our competitors and an opportunity, even an obligation, to speak up for all that is good in newspapering. . . .

"What I am trying to say is that the press has plenty of unfriendly critics and that I know that you can discuss our problems and our achievements in a way that will reflect credit upon *The Times* and The Gannett Group. If you have any doubt, then I'd say don't do it."

Penned in the margins of a copy of that letter are these comments from Frank Tripp:

"I'd rather say 'don't do it' anyway.

"Someday he's going to make us very sorry."

On Feb. 23, 1957, Lindstrom wrote to Jones:

"I'm off tomorrow to Ann Arbor where my subject will be 'The Approach Through Science.' My theme is that while journalism is not a science yet, we can afford to use the methods of science in our approach to reporting, editing and management." He promised to send a copy of his Michigan text.

Jones responded on Feb. 26:

"Would your Ann Arbor talk evolve into material for *Editorially Speaking*? I hope to get this out somewhat earlier in 1957 than has been customary.

"I still have grave doubts as to *The Atlantic* assignment and your report on their reaction makes me feel certain that they are counting on you to do an inside job of cracking the safe. I am confident that you will avoid falling into that trap."

## What Did He Say?

Even before giving his talk in Michigan, Lindstrom had set off alarm bells with remarks to the New England Weekly Press Association about newspaper color. He did not allow technology or variations in quality to soften his open contempt for color printing in newspapers. He heard from Jones, who had warned Lindstrom before that he risked professional embarrassment over his extreme and unsubstantiated denunciations.

Jones politely told Lindstrom that he did not know what he was talking about.

"In the first place," he wrote, "it is not clear what kind of color printing you are criticizing. One- and two-color advertising has been used, with great effectiveness, for many years. The technical problems are relatively simple and the results are astonishingly good.

"When it comes to full-color reproduction, and especially of news pictures, the results admittedly are uneven and sometimes even horrible. Still, anyone who follows *The Milwaukee Journal*, the *Miami Herald*, the *Chicago Tribune*, and *The Vancouver Sun* knows that newspaper color – even food – can be sensationally good. . . .

"There are other considerations:

"1. I am sure you realize that at least one newspaper in the Group, the *Niagara Gazette*, is equipped for full-color operation; that the Rochester newspapers have ordered color equipment and that *The Hartford Times* has considered doing so. No one will quarrel with your right to express the opinions of an individual, but you should avoid any statement that would appear to represent *Times* or Gannett policy in this field.

"2. When you say 'we have not yet learned how to print adequately in black and white' you are speaking for yourself. You have only to look at Louisville or Binghamton to see that the knowledge is available. We just don't (most of us) use it.

"3. Finally, you strike a sour note when you appear to attack some of the most enterprising of our brethren. They may be attempting the impossible, but they are showing some nerve and backing their judgment with a great deal of hard cash and hard work. Can we show anything comparable?"

The files contain no evidence of a response. Lindstrom's allies later would denounce Jones for "censorship," despite his repeated attempts to distinguish between Lindstrom's unquestioned right to personal opinions and his responsibility to make clear that those opinions were only his.

Jones received a copy of the Michigan speech on March 1. Lindstrom said he was troubled because Chairman Maurer had asked for the right to publish it. "I don't know what his medium is," Lindstrom wrote, "but *Editorially Speaking* circulates so widely that he might feel that his intention to publish it had been short-circuited.

Naturally my first loyalty is to *Editorially Speaking* but I did say yes when Maurer spoke first."

That dilemma was resolved when Jones read the speech, as he told Lindstrom, "with a mixture of admiration and dismay.

"It is full of the perceptive passages," Jones wrote, "that have made you such an eloquent spokesman for the profession. It also is full of snide and sneering passages which need to be challenged and which have no place in a talk to prospective journalists. At times you sound like a tired, disillusioned gambler reminiscing wryly about the futility of trying to buck a crooked roulette wheel.

"The idea of dealing with our handicaps was a sound one, but I would rather have seen a little more about how we as a profession rise to the challenge. Take the matter of time. It is, as you say, a 'deadly enemy,' but it also is the prime excuse for our existence."

Jones embarked on a rebuttal of what he regarded as offhand misrepresentations and careless misstatements. He cited chapter and verse of "the cracks that do you, *The Hartford Times* and the Group serious harm."

He believed some of Lindstrom's observations were misleading to aspiring young journalists, such as, "There is very little connection between administrative savvy and editorial talents."

Probably the most offensive reference as a primer for would-be journalists, Jones said, was "singularly unalluring":

" 'When the managing editor breaks down, you can always make an editorial writer out of him and if he isn't too far advanced in years, he may hope to become editor of the editorial page.' This very definitely should be cut from the text that you submit to Michigan. I am sure that it will be taken as a reflection upon your colleague in Hartford, not to mention others in the Group (including Fay Blanchard, who showed us how an editorial page could be made to sing), and many of your friends in ASNE."

He concluded with, "This piece is not the sort of thing we want for *Editorially Speaking*, and for which you are justly famous, and I am relying on you to see to it that the published text does not spread some of the harm over a wide area."

Lindstrom replied on March 9:

"A careful reading of my Michigan talk would show that I could not possibly have been reflecting upon any of my colleagues here nor on anyone in Rochester. The reference was to Clifton L. Sherman, former editor here, long since dead and buried."

(However, Ward Duffy, for whom Lindstrom filled in as managing editor at *The Times* during an illness, had been permanently replaced by Lindstrom as managing editor and made editor of the editorial page.)

Lindstrom added flatly, "There will be no more speeches."

He said the text would be amended before publication.

"Your Michigan talk," Jones replied, "received a most careful reading up here. . . .

"Abrupt withdrawal from the speaking platform is a drastic remedy for what I regard as an untypical and temporary case of dyspeptic thinking and bilious writing.

"The point is, of course, that the Michigan talk could not possibly do any good to *The Times*, The Gannett Newspapers, newspapering generally, or Carl Lindstrom. Previous Lindstrom speeches have done plenty for all four."

## Promotional Surprise

Earlier in 1957, Lindstrom had been angered when a subordinate, his telegraph editor, had written a letter of endorsement for an unnamed news service. The service used the endorsement in its advertising, to the anger and embarrassment of *Hartford Times* executives.

Imagine everyone's bewilderment, then, when the Feb. 1, 1958, issue of *Editor & Publisher* displayed a full-page ad for International News Service. The ad was called "Letter from an Editor" and was an effusive endorsement of International News Service by Carl E. Lindstrom of *The Hartford Times*.

Its praise included this bouquet: "Whenever a really big story breaks, the INS hits it first and hard and stays with it and does not allow secondary material to stand in the way."

Jones wrote on Feb. 6 to Lindstrom.

After asking whether INS had obtained permission for the publication, he pointed out:

"Such a letter makes it difficult to (a) terminate a contract, or (b) get a reduction in rates. . . .

"You should consider the possible effect of such a letter on The Gannett Group as a whole, since your enthusiasm for the service is not shared elsewhere. Most of our eggs have wound up in the AP basket — by decision of the individual editors and publishers."

The addressee was away when the letter arrived, so Hartford publisher Daniel responded to the copy sent to him:

"I jumped out of my chair about two feet when I saw the full-page ad in *Editor & Publisher* on Feb. 1. . . .

"Carl is away on vacation but I have learned from his secretary that INS had full authority to reproduce the letter. As a matter of fact, there apparently were two letters written based on telephone conversations and the finished product was a composite of the best remarks of the two letters.

"I thought it was understood . . . that whenever endorsements were requested . . . I would have an opportunity to affirm or veto the judgment of our department heads. I did not have the chance to do so in this case because the matter was never referred to me, although I am the one who signed the new two-year contract with International News Service."

When Lindstrom returned from his vacation, he coolly informed Jones:

"The request from INS to publish my letter embarrassed me but I wasn't resourceful enough to duck out of it. . . . [B]ut having written the letter – and it was quite spontaneously done . . . – I didn't see how I could withhold permission."

## Another Letter to the Editor

The New England Society of Newspaper Editors published a quarterly called the *American Editor*. Lindstrom was its editor. Its first issue of 1958 published an editorial that was excerpted by *Editor & Publisher*. The *E&P* version:

"It is one of the heartbreaks of American journalism today that while some of the best metropolitan papers are having a struggle to keep their heads above water, many small city dailies seem to prosper on mis-, mal- and non-feasance in their obligations to the community.

"If the smallest paper is alone in a not-too-large city, with competition reasonably distant, it can operate about as it chooses and still make money for somebody. It can suppress news, slant news, fail to cover news, fill the pages with boilerplate and second-rate features, omit Democratic news and glamorize Republican affairs (though instances of the reverse would be hard to find).

"There are metropolitan dailies of unimpeachable integrity, with brainy news executives, sound editorial policies which are faced with declining revenues and circulation no matter how they struggle. And struggle they do; changing format, introducing new areas of coverage, re-examining possibly dated techniques and inventing new ones.

"Can it be that the climate is healthier for second-rate newspapers than for first-rate ones, depending upon geography?"

The views were not Lindstrom's most outspoken. They were sufficiently volatile, however, to trigger an ill-advised and intemperate response from Tripp. The malice of the rebuttal would embed itself and occasionally be recalled to the undeserved discredit of The Gannett Newspapers.

The May 3, 1958, issue of *Editor & Publisher* published Tripp's letter to the editor: Among its broadsides:

"The *American Editor* is published in Hartford, Conn., by the New England Society of Newspaper Editors. Its editor also is an editor of *The Hartford Times*. I am president of The Hartford Times Company.

"My aim is to disassociate *The Hartford Times*, its publishers and owners from any connection or agreement with the editorial *in toto*, or any single reference to 'small newspapers' contained therein.

"I have never read an article in any publication, purporting to represent any segment of the newspaper press, that showed so little understanding of our Fourth Estate and what makes it click; such complete disregard and hatred for its grass roots, from which it grew; or which could better feed the fires of those who would destroy us. . . .

"From an important section of our craft it is appalling and most regrettable. Here is one 'damn Yankee' – and his newspapers – who deny, abhor and resent its absurd and vicious content."

Although the letter had clearly spelled out the author's role at *The Hartford Times*, it was not signed simply, "Frank Tripp." Also appended was, "Chairman of the Board, Gannett Newspapers, Rochester, N.Y."[4]

Jones recalled in an interview, "[Tripp] hadn't told Miller or anybody about this. Miller was furious. He went to Tripp and said, 'Don't you ever do that again!' "[5]

The letters that *Editor & Publisher* printed in response did not applaud Tripp.

David Brickman, president of the New England Society of Newspaper Editors and publisher and editor of the *Malden* (Mass.) *Evening News*, wrote that he did not deny Tripp's right to disassociate The Gannett Newspapers from anything in the *American Editor*. But he added:

"It seems to me that the core of the issue is the right of everyone, including ourselves as professional newspaper people, to evaluate and criticize the press without being damned as 'traitors' to our profession. . . .

"One of the greatest disservices we do ourselves is to adopt a 'holier-than-thou' attitude toward our critics, while we often reserve to ourselves the privilege to criticize others."

Arthur E. Rowse of Concord, Mass., wrote:

"To any young cub who wants a glimpse of a reason why American newspapers don't improve any faster, I recommend reading Frank Tripp's letter in *E&P*. . . . I submit his letter . . . as a beautiful illustration of one of the things the editorial writer (who was not I) may have had in mind: the practice of some publishers to meet all criticism with angry words."[6]

Even the editor of a weekly newspaper rang in. Robert M. Conrad of the *Southington* (Conn.) *News* wrote:

"[The editorial] was not a wild haymaker in the general direction of 'small newspapers,' as Frank Tripp suggested in putting his arm around 'the very backbone of the American press.' I read and applauded the editorial for citing the irony in solid business despite weak standards. I don't see how this was damaging to the countless, top-notch dailies that happen to be serving small cities. . . .

"I feel strongly that the field needs more and not less criticism. Our special frustration in the weekly business is that the daily newspaper, regardless of what kind of product, is accepted as big brother to us. It is galling to have a poor daily held up as an example."[7]

## Shakeout

Even before Tripp's letter appeared in *Editor & Publisher*, Jones was writing to Lindstrom, with Miller's approval. A draft dated April 29, 1958, expresses shock at the editorial in the *American Editor*. The letter reads in part:

"I am addressing my protest to you both as an editor and as Gannett Group executive editor. My protest is twofold because (1) I disagree completely with what you said, and (2) in saying this you have, perhaps inadvertently, involved The Gannett Newspapers. . . .

"Your word carries a great deal of weight, because you long have been an eloquent spokesman for constructive newspaper movements. . . . The reader has a right to assume that you know what you are talking about. What's more important to us, he may well assume that your most accurate and intimate knowledge is of The Gannett Group, which is composed principally of small newspapers. Most of them operate in non-competitive towns. . . .

"You know, of course, that all of us up here have been disturbed by the tone of some of your recent speeches and writings. After your talk to the Michigan students you offered to stop making speeches. We made it clear that we were not trying to muzzle you or any other editor in the Group, but that we insisted that you not involve us or *The Times* without specific permission."

Lindstrom replied on May 2:

"The editorial about the smaller newspapers was not categorical. There are good and bad small papers as well as good and bad big ones."

He then cited a number of examples, all in New England, that could be ranked among the bad. "These are simply facts of journalism," he wrote, "and the *American Editor* is trying to face facts."

He quoted Henry Beetle Hough of the *Vineyard Gazette* as declaring that the *American Editor* "has become the most distinguished journal in its field."

Rejecting the suggestion that he might be misunderstood, he declared:

"The integrity of The Gannett Newspapers, and the manner in which they serve their communities, is so well known that I don't see how anyone could try to apply that editorial to any of them, large or small. . . .

"I have already written to Paul Miller to say that I did not write the piece in *Editor & Publisher* on this subject; that I had no knowledge of its being written or sent; that I did not think it newsworthy and would have vetoed it if I'd had the chance."

Jones replied:

"You persist in misunderstanding the argument over reprinting the editorial in *Editor & Publisher*. Our first concern was to establish (1) whether you had written, or endorsed, the editorial, and (2) whether it was quoted correctly and in context. Certainly it was newsworthy and probably it would have been picked up whether or not the Hartford correspondent submitted it. . . .

"No one can quarrel with your purpose in printing 'facts.' These may be 'facts,' but they are only part of the 'facts' about a truly fine

American institution which deserves a great deal better from a publication aiming to become 'the most distinguished journal in its field.' "

On May 7, 1958, Jones sent another letter to Lindstrom. It said in part:

"At the time of the Michigan episode you readily agreed to edit the copy of your speech in case it should get into general distribution. You offered to make no more speeches. I urged you to continue the splendid work which has brought you so much deserved applause.

"Now, however, it is time to request that you stop writing the type of speeches, articles, or editorials which constitute damaging, unwarranted attacks upon the industry as a whole, or any substantial portion thereof. If you insist upon continuing, you should retire from your position as one of the editors of *The Hartford Times*.

"Mr. Miller has read this letter and concurs fully. If, after reading this letter, you would like to discuss the matter further, I should be happy to see you."

There were some discussions, Jones said. "Lindstrom came to Rochester for a conference. He conceded that he had been wrong and promised to drop this line of speaking and writing."[8]

Lindstrom officially retired from *The Times* on June 5, 1959, although he went to the University of Michigan's Department of Journalism in January 1959 as a visiting professor. He was appointed to a permanent professorship in April.[9]

His tenure as a journalism professor was brief, although when he was 65 he was recalling both his "50 years in the newspaper business" and "two and a half years" at Michigan.

Jones's files contain a Nov. 30, 1961, letter from Maurer of the University of Michigan. It was the forum he had provided to Lindstrom five years earlier that had begun the debate between Jones and the Hartford executive editor.

Jones had sent Maurer a copy of his detailed answer to Lindstrom's book after they had met on a flight from Dallas. The Maurer note thanked him. Handwritten by Jones in the lower right corner of the stationery is this:

"When I got on the plane, the man in the seat next to me was asleep. It was Wesley Maurer. He woke up, recognized me and said: 'Vin, why didn't you tell me Lindstrom was such an S.O.B.?' 'You didn't ask me,' I replied. He went back to sleep."

# Chapter and Verse

Jones's answer to Lindstrom's *The Fading American Newspaper* was the Oct. 26, 1960, issue of *The Bulletin*. It was a six-page rebuttal addressing specific items in the book, matching Lindstrom versions of events with responses labeled "FACTS." *The Bulletin* also recapitulated the two-year conflict between Lindstrom and Gannett management.

An introductory note said *The Bulletin* was "presented so that executives in the Group will have an opportunity to judge the validity of some of the broad charges made in this book. Despite the 'confidential' tag on our vignette, you may use this material in any way that you choose."

Wider circulation of Jones's six-page rebuttal was generally well received. Joyce A. Swan, executive vice president of the Minneapolis *Star and Tribune*, proposed that each member of the board of the American Newspaper Publishers Association get a copy.

Editors and publishers wrote to thank him for presenting the other side of the story so well.

One copy that was not well received went to Louis M. Lyons, curator of the Nieman Foundation at Harvard University. He had reviewed the book very favorably in *The New York Times Book Review*. Its double-barreled conclusion said:

"When Lindstrom says the press 'has a pathological fear of criticism,' he speaks out of bitter experience. Within the trade, interest will focus on his own account of the circumstances of his leaving the Gannett employ, after 40 years of devoted service, when they undertook to curb and censor his public speaking and professional writing outside the paper – an incredible attempt to institutionalize the private life of a professional man. Had Lindstrom not been too independent to submit, we would not have this seasoned judgment of a veteran editor on the condition of his calling."

When Jones followed that review with a copy of his rebuttal, Lyons replied curtly:

"Yours is the third copy sent me of the Gannett case against Lindstrom. But I saw the correspondence three years ago undertaking to censor Lindstrom's speaking and writing; and everybody in the newspaper business saw the outrageous Tripp letter in *Editor & Publisher*."

"I am quite content," Jones responded, "to stand on the record of the complete correspondence between this office and Carl Lindstrom three years ago.

"It is a surprise to find you describing objections to some of Lindstrom's remarks to University of Michigan students as censorship. Even he agreed that they were subject to misinterpretation. Furthermore, we had the right – not to say the obligation – to insist that he refrain from involving *The Hartford Times* or The Gannett Group in positions which we could not endorse."

A year before his death, Lindstrom wrote to Stuart A. Dunham, editor of *The Hartford Times,* when he was angered by an Edmund Valtman editorial cartoon on the assassination of Robert Kennedy. He told Dunham in his June 12, 1968, letter:

"The murder of Robert Kennedy has nothing to do with 'violence in the city streets' or what's the matter with America.

"There's nothing the matter with America but much the matter with your head. You are responsible – or were asked to be responsible – for the editorial page of *The Hartford Times*.

"The violence has been mainly in the misanthropic mind of Valtman who in his poisonous hatred has done all in his power to destroy Kennedy. Had this dangerous man been in Los Angeles with a gun in his hand he would, of course, have pulled the trigger. It was in your power to restrain this person with his criminal drawing board but you didn't do so, preferring to fan the flames of malice in the soft brain of a man who holds a fraudulent Pulitzer prize. . . .

"If you happen to know who is circulation manager of *The Times* this week, please tell him to cut me off from the rubbish he has been leaving on my doorstep gratuitously. I spent 43 years doing what I could to make *The Times* the respected paper it used to be. I don't want to be reminded daily of the ruin you and your immediate predecessors have made of it.

"P.S. Please explain to Valtman what the word 'misanthropic' means – if you know."

A few days later, Lindstrom sent an undated note to Valtman apologizing for "the intemperate letter about you that I addressed" to Stuart Dunham. He made clear, however, "that my sincere apology extends only to the ill-considered terms of my letter."

He concluded:

"Nothing in this letter is to be interpreted as a change of mind about your vicious caricaturing of Robert F. Kennedy. It is still my belief that Mr. Dunham failed to do his duty by not restraining you. I repeat that there is nothing wrong with America and that we are not all responsible. The cause was the atmosphere of hatred nourished in the highest places and in such malicious cartoons of which you were repeatedly the author."

Lindstrom died in 1969. He was 73. His obituary in *The New York Times* excerpted Lyons' review of *The Fading American Newspaper*. It contained examples of his opinions on his profession. It also reminded anyone who had forgotten of the original public flap in *Editor & Publisher*. It quoted a 1959 piece from *Time* magazine:

"Last spring he wrote an editorial in *The American Editor*, criticizing some publishers in one-newspaper towns for being too much concerned about profits and too little concerned about getting out a good newspaper. In reply, Frank E. Tripp, board chairman of The Gannett Newspapers, who was in effect Lindstrom's top boss, wrote a scathing letter to *Editor & Publisher*, attacking the editorial. A short time later Lindstrom, who defends a newspaper's need to make a profit but has taken note of the press's 'almost psychopathic sensitiveness to criticism,' decided to accept a standing offer from Michigan."

Carl Lindstrom was given the last word.

# Chapter 27

# Line of Succession

*"This is an appeal for the kind of leadership which disregards party lines . . . leadership which makes readers think; the kind of leadership which makes honest men willing to go into politics . . . and which convinces scoundrels that there is no longer sufficient room for any of them behind a party label."*

*Paul Miller*
*1961*

Company executives were participating more actively in the early 1960s in professional organizations, not despite the risk of being recruited away but because of the opportunity to win new respect for The Gannett Newspapers.

Vin Jones's trip to India was a weather vane showing old timers how the winds had changed in the Gannett Company. International travel was no longer limited to the top executive, be he Frank Gannett or Paul Miller.

The first Asian seminar of the International Press Institute was such an opportunity. The IPI was patterned after the American Press Institute, an established success at Columbia University under its director, J. Montgomery Curtis, and later moved to Reston, Va. Jones was already a fixture at API, having conducted nearly 20 seminars for journalists on such topics as readership, readability, content and photography.

Given those credentials, Jones's invitation to be the only American to participate at the New Delhi meeting in November 1960 is understandable. He told his colleagues later that the invitation was intriguing but conditional:

"This would be no junket. The people running this International Press Institute seminar were spending the Rockefeller Foundation's rupees as carefully as though they came out of their own pockets. They made sure that I would earn my airfare and expenses. The editor from Ceylon who was chairman wrote in high glee, assigning me to run six sessions, and noting that 'at last the Backward East is about to exploit the Imperialistic West.' "[1]

Miller, meanwhile, represented the Gannett Company's commitment to public service by serving as national chairman of Brotherhood Week, for which he would be honored in April 1961 by the National Conference of Christians and Jews. That chairmanship also provided Miller with an anecdote that illustrates the sense of humor he brought to public appearances. He told an audience of a memorable breakfast during the week's observance:

"Not so incidentally, at the same breakfast [President John F. Kennedy] referred warmly to the Pilgrims and the Puritans and the Rev. Billy Graham quoted Pope Leo III. . . . I tell you brotherhood is making some progress, certainly, when a Massachusetts Catholic recalls the Protestant settlers and a Carolina Baptist quotes a pope."[2]

Gannett's president continued to expand his corporate reach, to satisfy not only his personal ambitions but also the passage of time. At the July 1961 board meeting, 79-year-old Frank Tripp and 85-year-old Erwin Davenport resigned as vice presidents. Tripp remained chairman of the board, a position almost totally honorary, since Miller had become operating head in fact even before Frank Gannett's death.

Directors elected general manager Lynn Bitner and treasurer Cyril Williams to fill the vice presidential vacancies. At the same time, they elected general auditor John E. Gartland as assistant treasurer. The corporation's new assistant secretary was Jack Heselden, director of personnel and employee relations.[3]

Miller had expanded Heselden's responsibilities just the month before. He was now in charge of pension and other benefits, general Group purchasing, except newsprint and machinery, but was to relinquish union labor affairs, "insofar as practicable."[4]

Tripp and Davenport, the only remaining direct ties to the company's origins, no longer figured in its direction. Davenport returned to retirement. Tripp remained nominally in charge in Elmira, but a stroke that summer made that academic, as well.

Miller made his first trip to the Soviet Union that summer, one of a group from the American Society of Newspaper Editors to be invited by the Union of Soviet Journalists. He used the forum of the Gannett executives' conference in September 1961 to report on that trip and make clear that Paul Miller shared Frank Gannett's visions.

"This summer," he told them, "I saw at firsthand what it means to live and work where freedom of press and of speech are unknown; where the people, for the most part, are permitted to know only what their rulers wish them to know, to see only what their rulers wish them to see, to go only where their rulers wish them to go, to live only where their rulers wish them to live. . . .

"You can understand why I returned with a deeper appreciation of America and all that America stands for – and with a renewed sense of obligation and responsibility to our country and to the work which joins all of us here – communications."

He challenged Gannett executives to provide "independent leadership of a kind which readers may not always anticipate."

His formula:

"First, let's be more assertive in expressing our pride in our work. Second, let's get closer to our readers and listeners. Third, let's improve our public relations practices. And, finally, let's put still more thought and effort into providing conscientious and stimulating editorial leadership for our various communities." [5]

Along with that leadership, Miller reminded them, was another responsibility. "I have placed considerable emphasis on community activities. It is vital in our Group, where local management is watched by local interests – as it should be – for any sign of primary allegiance elsewhere." [6]

Gannett would have been proud.

# The Tripp Touch

Tripp was released from the hospital to recuperate at home. He immediately picked up his pencil to mark for his Elmira readers his 60th anniversary in the newspaper business. He recounted his growing responsibilities during his 56 years with The Gannett Newspapers, then concluded:

"None of this is significant save that it marks an epoch of newspapering that was borned (sic) and grew from Elmira over 60 years ago. And the active years of a crazy kid who would rather fill paste pots than go to school – and now, near the end of the road, would much rather [do] than be Chairman of the Bored.

"That's right, chairman of the bored." [7]

Those were the regrets of an aging man who had worked and played hard. He frequently had acknowledged that he did the drinking for both Gannett and himself, but he hadn't liked to do it alone. Many of his associates in Gannett had found themselves pressed by Tripp for elbow-bending companionship, particularly when he was in Rochester or on the road.

Mary Golding, Miller's long-time secretary, recalled what a Tripp visit to Rochester could do:

"Lynn Bitner came into Mr. Miller's office one day and he said, 'Paul, Frank is coming to town this afternoon.' They used to die when he was [coming in], because he wanted them to stay up till 4 o'clock in the morning. He'd get in about 4 in the afternoon and he drank right straight through. And they had to get up and go to work the next day. They liked him, they enjoyed him, and they liked to hear him talk. He was a wonderful writer.

"Anyway, this day [Bitner] came and said, 'Paul, Frank is going to be down at the [Hotel] Rochester this afternoon. He's coming in about 4 o'clock. You're coming, aren't you?'

"And Mr. Miller said, 'Well, I have to go to a church meeting tonight. . . . I'll pray for you.'" [8]

The Gannett Company announced the creation of the Frank Tripp Awards to recognize achievement and originality of news and advertising staff members of Gannett Newspapers. Today, renamed IDEAS – Innovator Drive for Excellence Awards – they annually honor a broad spectrum of achievement throughout the Gannett Company.

Whether bored or not, Tripp was certainly ailing and bowing to age. There were problems in Elmira for the *Star-Gazette*, the *Advertiser* and the Sunday *Telegram* beyond his fading energies. In December 1961, Robert R. Eckert, business manager of *The Evening Press* in Binghamton, was named general manager in Elmira.

Eckert recalled:

"Frank Tripp had had his stroke, and he was at home in Elmira, in bed. He could get up a little bit but not very much. I was kind of a brash young guy. I went in to see Frank, to get to know him better, and discovered that he and I had a great love of vaudeville. As a little kid, I haunted vaudeville houses, from the age of 7, 8 or 10. I just loved vaudeville. Frank was a nut about vaudeville and we hit it off just beautifully."[9]

The brash young guy who hit it off just beautifully with the sage of Elmira began to look into things and found that its three newspapers were making "a few thousand dollars a year. . . .

"The morning [*Advertiser*] was 12,000, the afternoon [*Star-Gazette*] was 34,000 and Sunday [*Telegram*] maybe 36,000 or 37,000. I was there about four months and it really didn't take a genius to realize that the morning paper was just a drag. You couldn't make any money, you couldn't charge anything for the advertising . . . you couldn't do anything with it. [No advertiser] would buy it even for a couple of cents an inch in addition to the afternoon paper," Eckert said.

"So I went to see Mr. Bitner and said, 'Lynn, we really have to turn this into an all-day paper.'

"And he said, 'How long have you been in Elmira?'

" 'Well, I guess four months.'

" 'You really know everything about everything, don't you?' he said.

"I said, 'Mr. Bitner, I'm just here to tell you what I think. Something has to be done with this property and this is my suggestion.' . . .

"He said, 'You haven't been there long enough to make decisions like this.'

"But come time for the annual meeting, you went to Rochester and presented your budget for the next year. You presented all the proposals you had in mind, and you told them what you'd done for the year, and so forth.

"I couldn't get that out of my mind, so I wrote this report and said, 'I'm going to present this at the board meeting.' But to avoid what I thought was going to happen [with Bitner], I sent copies to all the directors so that they would be aware of this in advance.

"I got two phone calls, one from Cy Williams, who said, 'My god, this should have been done years ago. Do it. You've got my blessing.' . . .

"And Paul called me. He said, 'This sounds like something we ought to be thinking about. I'm very interested.' "

Eckert laughed as he remembered Bitner's displeasure.

"I went to the meeting and he was in a little bit of a bind because [the directors] wanted to do it. . . . And Lynn said, "OK, I'll go along with it, but you're going to put a name to every one of those numbers you have in there. When you say you're going to reduce people, you tell me who those people are.' " [10]

(Vin Jones recalled in a 1990 interview what was known as Bitner's Law of Automation: "No money is saved until someone goes off the payroll.")

So Eckert was authorized to proceed with creating an all-day newspaper in Elmira.

Also that spring of 1962, the Associated Press Managing Editors met in Minneapolis and Jones was one of the Gannett members who attended. While he was there, he looked up Allen H. Neuharth, who was assistant to the executive editor of the *Detroit Free Press*. Jones asked Neuharth whether he would consider joining Gannett. Neuharth said he was willing to listen. Jones told Neuharth he'd be hearing from Miller. [11]

# Keep the Faith

The public also was hearing from Miller, in his signed column in each

Saturday's *Times-Union*. In that space, he frequently explained to his readers the rights and responsibilities of the press. As a veteran newsman, he knew the press had many critics. He was not thin-skinned about complaints, even from friends, but when he found them unjustified he said so.

Two events in the autumn of 1962 spurred him to explain the press anew. The first was the Cuban missile crisis in October, when the United States discovered that the Soviet Union was installing offensive ballistic missiles on the island 90 miles from Florida.

President Kennedy ordered the Navy and the Air Force to blockade the island and prevent delivery of any Soviet military equipment to Cuba. A week of dreadful uncertainty followed before Soviet Premier Nikita Khrushchev agreed to dismantle the bases, ending the crisis without war.

During that week, news of the blockade and other U.S. actions was strictly controlled by the government. Arthur Sylvester, spokesman for the Pentagon, honestly admitted as much and justified the policy as "speaking in one voice to your adversary."

Miller, like most of his colleagues in the press, was appalled. A month later, Miller's friend Richard Nixon, who had lost to John Kennedy in 1960, also lost his campaign to be governor of California and blamed the press. "You won't have Nixon to kick around any more," he told reporters, "because, gentlemen, this is my last press conference."

On Saturday morning, Nov. 10, Miller combined the two events in his column on the *Times-Union* editorial page. Under the headline, "Candidates, government and the press," he began with Nixon's situation:

"The hide of a walrus is standard equipment for most men who make a career of politics. They have it by the grace of Providence, or they acquire it along the way.

"Richard M. Nixon was sensitive to every sling and arrow from the start.

"That is one conclusion to be drawn from his bitter assessment of campaign news coverage, with which he bowed out after his defeat for governor of California. Another is that he was a physical wreck after the California campaign."

Miller conceded that some newspapers opposed Nixon, even that some reporters did not conceal their dislike of him, but he insisted that they were few.

"Indeed," he explained, "few reporters ever let their own feelings show in their work, whatever their assignment. This is true particularly of political reporters. A good one – [which Miller proudly considered himself] – knows the politicians on both sides, treats them all alike and has their respect even when he reports what they do not want reported – which he often must do. . . .

"Nixon had wide newspaper editorial support in 1960, as in 1962. Then as now, he seemed more stung by the attacks of those who opposed him than pleased by the backing of those on his side."

Miller observed that most defeated politicians blame anything but themselves for their losses. He recalled the words of Benjamin M. McKelway, president of the Associated Press:

"When a politician loses, he blames the press. If he wins, it's a personal triumph."

Miller then turned to the government's manipulation of the news during the Cuban missile crisis. He cited with approval an editorial in the *Washington Star*: "The kind of world we live in seems now to be a world in which [the] truth given the American people of what has happened is that part of the truth selected by officialdom to piece together a desirable image. That image may be a distortion, the inevitable result of an attempt to use the press and its news as instruments of national policy."

Miller concluded:

"All governments try from time to time to 'control' the news one way or another – the more totalitarian they become the greater control they exercise. In the present instance, Sylvester's control was not only 'weaponry' against the Soviet Union but also weaponry against the American people's right to know what their government is doing and why.

"This 'control' of news becomes even more questionable when it is coupled with a complete blackout as far as the press is concerned on reporting activities of the blockading ships and military forces. While disclaiming censorship on one hand, the government exercised during the peak of the Cuba crisis a complete censorship by refusing to allow American correspondents to join the blockading ships, visit Guantanamo or the air forces involved even if the correspondents submitted to full military censorship. This went even beyond the most secret wartime operations, all of which were covered by regular war correspondents." [12]

# New Directions

Feb. 1, 1963, was doubly significant for the Gannett Company. In Elmira, the oldest Gannett newspaper, the afternoon *Star-Gazette*, merged with the morning *Advertiser* to become the all-day paper that Eckert had proposed.

On the same day, Neuharth joined the company as a general executive.

Neuharth was hired by Miller to be general manager of both Rochester newspapers, replacing 69-year-old Donald U. Bridge, who was about to retire.

But as Neuharth wrote in his autobiographical *Confessions of an S.O.B.*, he asked for the nonspecific title of general executive to start so he could freely examine everything about the two newspapers as one of the boys rather than the new boss. He had done the same thing in the *Miami Herald* newsroom for three months before his promotion to city editor there was announced.

When Tripp recruited Miller for the Gannett Company, there was an implicit understanding that Miller was Frank Gannett's intended successor. Had Miller done the same with Neuharth?

"There was nothing in writing," Neuharth said in a 1992 interview, "and there was no guarantee, but Paul made it clear that he was looking for his successor and that if I was as good as he thought I was, that I would be that successor. But I didn't consider that a guarantee. I thought it would come together." [13]

Like the self-described brash Bob Eckert, Neuharth rankled Bitner, the company's general manager. "He had sort of designated himself as the number two person in the company," Neuharth said. "Paul had been very careful never to do that."

"I think Lynn probably resented my presence more than others," Neuharth said, "because he saw pretty quickly that I was not too easy to harness, that I was going to try to work directly with Paul on some things that weren't necessarily in line with what Lynn would have preferred." [14]

Neuharth's position as general manager of the Rochester newspapers was announced a month after his arrival.

In Elmira, meanwhile, Eckert's proposed all-day paper was being touted by Cove C. Hoover, its managing editor, as "the most complete and best-balanced newspaper Elmira has had."

The *Star-Gazette* and *Advertiser* ["and Advertiser" in smaller type on the nameplate] was a five-edition newspaper.

All advertising started in a first regional edition, which hit the streets at 1:20 a.m. That was followed by a city edition, available at 2:30 a.m., a regional north edition at noon, a regional south edition at 12:30 p.m., and a final city edition at 2:15 p.m.

The editor later explained to his Gannett colleagues that the change was necessary because the old system was economically unsound. On the morning *Advertiser*, with only 12,000 circulation, "virtually all . . . copy and content on the city desk level, regional desk, copy desk and editorial page was duplicated in some fashion" by the larger *Star-Gazette*.

An all-day paper, Hoover said, gives people the choice of **when** they want to read rather than **what** they want to read. Giving readers the news as it breaks, as the new paper was doing, minimized complaints about the changes.

The general manager's demand had been met. The consolidation eliminated five jobs, and Bitner surely got their names, as he had asked of Eckert. Hoover said the five employees "were placed with other papers in the Group or in jobs elsewhere. Every effort was made to secure employment for them." [15]

# First Again

Miller was the first former AP employee to become a director of the wire service when he was elected in 1950. In 1960, he became the first former director to be returned to the AP board since it had rescinded a three-consecutive-term limitation in 1942. The Gannett Company president established a new precedent in July 1963 when he was elected AP president, again the first former employee to attain that rank.

"He worked very hard to get to be president of the AP," Jones said, "and he didn't make it the first time he ran for the board. Then they discovered that the AP [had] some screwball form of bonds. . . . They [didn't] pay any interest but they [gave] you votes for election, and the Gannett Company wound up holding quite a few of those bonds." [16]

Miller remained in that position, which was redesignated chairman in 1972, until 1977. He retired from the AP a year before his retirement as chairman of the Gannett Company in 1978.

As a working newsman, Miller was both awed by the mounting intensity of civil rights demonstrations and distressed by the violence that accompanied many of them. In the spring of 1963, he asked Jones, the Group's executive editor, to organize and direct a Gannett project to study what was becoming a national racial crisis.

It was probably the biggest cooperative news and editorial project undertaken by The Gannett Newspapers in their 57-year history. Called "The Road to Integration," it was assigned to Jones and participating Gannett editors to determine "just what is going on in key areas, North and South, and what cities in our own Group might do." The president's memo said in part:

"I suggest you organize, direct and write a series of major pieces – [go] wherever you wish to go, getting help wherever you wish to get it (Washington, Albany, Hartford, Rochester or wherever). . . .

"[I]t seems to me you should go at it from this point of view: Every city has the same problem. If it has not, it soon will have. Every city is trying to find answers. Have any cities found answers that might be useful in Rochester, say? If so, what are they?" [17]

As summarized by Jones late in 1963, "The Road to Integration" had two major objectives:

"1. Find out whether anyone, anywhere, was doing anything constructive about the problem – besides uttering pious platitudes.

"2. Draw up a program which most of our cities could propose and support editorially.

"This is not just another newspaper series. It is a continuing program. My guess is that we will be writing about this story, under whatever title, for the rest of our lives. . . .

"We have tried to take a hard-headed, realistic approach. We see no quick solutions to any phase of the greatest domestic crisis since the Depression. We think that true integration may not come for centuries – if ever. But we all know that civil rights and equal opportunity must come, in fact as well as by law. And we see nothing but disaster in continuing to tolerate conditions where one tenth of the population is either on relief or too poor to be taxpayers or good customers for anything – including our newspapers." [18]

The project's breadth can be deduced from Jones's summary for Gannett executives at their fall conference. It is important to remember from this vantage that the premises and assumptions of 1964 represent earnest perceptions at the dawn of the civil rights movement.

Although Miller had given him the authority to go anywhere, Jones decided with Gannett editors to concentrate on the Northeast, which was their territory.

He told the executives:

"We have tried to avoid two pitfalls:

"1. Offering a Pollyanna-ish brand of propaganda, palpably out of line with the facts of life. This has been fairly easy, because the success stories we have managed to find have been presented against a tidal wave of bad news.

"2. Following the Do-Gooder line of emphasizing what *we* should be doing for the Negroes and overlooking what *they* should be doing to help themselves. . . .

"We decided to concentrate on these main areas:
- "Jobs.
- "Education.
- "Housing.
- "Representation.

"Which should come first? The best evidence indicates that most of the adult Negroes who haven't gotten a toehold on the economic beachhead by now never will make it. Therefore, the only long-range solution is to educate, and to train, the younger generation. Most of us oppose hasty, forced integration of schools – especially by transporting children across town. It seems clear that better jobs are the only way in which the Negroes themselves can solve the housing problem and, with it, the school integration mess. . . .

"The NAACP may call it 'tokenism,' but you see Negroes holding jobs for which they would not even have been considered only a year ago. That includes positions on many of our newspapers. . . .

"We have reported isolated instances of integrated housing that seem to work. . . .

"Similarly, school integration that comes about naturally offers some promise. You can argue that children who will live in a bi-racial world should learn the facts of this new life, however unpalatable, at an early age. But you can't rush it without courting disaster. . . .

"It no longer is a shock to see Negroes in good hotels, motels, restaurants, bars, your church, or on a few boards and committees. Much of the problem seems to me to hinge on the simple fact that most of us simply never have known any Negroes on terms remotely approaching equality.

"As I said, our approach has been very down-to-earth. We think that this problem will be solved – if ever it is solved – at the community level, and not by federal decree.

"This has not endeared us either to the starry-eyed zealots who think that the millenium should arrive at 9 o'clock tomorrow morning, or to some Negro leaders who, understandably impatient, want to undo the sins of centuries of oppression and neglect by what Mr. Kennedy, in a candidate's reckless exuberance, once promised to accomplish with the stroke of a pen.

"Generally speaking, Gannett editors have opposed artificial integration of schools, job quotas favoring Negroes, demonstrations (including the remarkably sober March on Washington), and have expressed serious doubts about the wisdom of the public accommodations section of the federal civil rights program. . . .

"All of these things add up to a pallid ray of hope – and a challenge to every community willing to face up to the situation." [19]

By the time Jones gave that report, Gannett News Service had distributed 60 articles or editorials. Special supplements had been produced in Camden, Danville, Elmira, Hartford, Newburgh, Niagara Falls, Plainfield, Rochester and Utica.

Nearly three decades later, it is interesting to consider Miller's motivation in requesting "The Road to Integration." Gannett's president was a political and social conservative, as traditionally were The Gannett Newspapers. The civil rights struggle was intensely controversial. Newspapers that published straightforward accounts of violent racial demonstrations, particularly photographs of blacks being beaten by police officers, drenched by water cannons or clubbed by angry civilians, were denounced by many readers as troublemaking meddlers.

Except for Rochester, N.Y., Hartford, Conn., and Camden, N.J., most Gannett communities had no substantial minority populations. Why, then, would these newspapers undertake such a task? Because Paul Miller's news experience told him that every city that did not yet have the problem eventually would and that its citizens should understand that.

This coordinated study of civil rights would continue into 1964 and help to make that year one of the company's most memorable to date.

# Chapter 28

# Growth and Acclaim

*"The Trustees of Columbia University in the City of New York make known to all men by these presents that The Gannett Newspapers have been awarded a Pulitzer Prize Special Citation for their public service program, 'The Road to Integration.'"*

May 4, 1964

The year 1964 began as one of hopes realized. Paul Miller's was a larger and better group of Gannett newspapers. He added nine in one acquisition alone. The News and Editorial Office, which had yearned for greater respect from the journalistic establishment, won it with the first Pulitzer Prize for public service ever to be awarded to a newspaper group.

In Rochester, meanwhile, Al Neuharth was paving the way for his own ambitions. He recalled in *Confessions of an S.O.B.* that one reason he had been drawn to Gannett was that Miller shared his faith in Florida's economic future and his interest in starting a newspaper there. Rochester's general manager was looking ahead and he knew that such a project would need extensive research and promotion.

Neuharth turned to Vince Spezzano, then chief political writer on the *Times-Union*, where he had worked for nine years.

"At the time Neuharth came [to Rochester]," Spezzano recalled in 1990, "he really had nobody to pal around with and I had the kind of a job that he would like in any community. So I used to invite him to ward meetings and that sort of thing. I got to know him very well. He always needed a backboard to bounce things off and I was that person for a while."[1]

Neuharth created for the Rochester newspapers a Department of Public Service, Research and Development and appointed Spezzano its director.

"He suggested that I might want to consider learning the business side of the newspaper," Spezzano said, "and I asked him if I was doing something wrong. He said, no, he wanted me to set up a promotion and marketing department. . . . I told him that if I were he, the last person I would consider for setting up an ad department was Vince Spezzano. I had no training, no experience whatsoever. . . . He said anybody who's a good reporter can be a good anything on a newspaper.

"Paul Miller was upset. He didn't think anybody ought to leave the newsroom at all. He told me that I could try it out, and I should, but if I had any qualms about it he would see to it that I went back into the newsroom."[2]

# Hail and Farewell

Circulation of The Gannett Newspapers grew by 200,000 and their number jumped to 24 on April 1, 1964, when the company bought the nine dailies and one weekly of Westchester-Rockland Group Newspapers. It did not disclose how much it paid Valentine E. Macy Jr. and J. Noel Macy for their newspapers.

The Macy brothers continued as directors of Westchester County Publishers, Inc., the new subsidiary.

The newest nameplates, in New York's Westchester and Rockland Counties were: White Plains's *The Reporter-Dispatch*, Ossining's *The Citizen-Register*, Tarrytown's *The Daily News*, Yonkers's *The Herald-Statesman*, Nyack's *Journal-News*, New Rochelle's *The Standard Star*, Mount Vernon's *The Daily Argus*, Port Chester's *The Daily Item*, Mamaroneck's *The Daily Times*, and the weekly Bronxville *Review Press and Reporter*.[3]

William L. Fanning, the Macys' executive vice president, was promoted to president of the newly acquired property. It was Miller's personal friendship with Fanning that gave Gannett the advantage on the purchase. That would be the case many times over as the Gannett Company continued to buy newspapers.

Also that spring, Miller traveled to Syracuse University to accept a plaque honoring Frank Tripp. The award saluted his "long and distinguished service to the profession of journalism." Tripp himself was too ill to attend.

Miller told the audience that he had telephoned Tripp the day before to tell him about the honor. "You who know him will know exactly what he said," Miller told them. "Less a word or two, he said, 'That's what I need – a plaque.' " [4]

Tripp died on May 1, 1964. He was 82. The account of his long and active life took four full pages of the *Star-Gazette*. It recounted his long association with Gannett, his friendship with such prominent theater figures as Will Rogers and composer/conductor Victor Herbert, and his direction of successive World War II campaigns that sold billions in war bonds. Throughout the account, however, was the underlying truth that no matter how prominent his friends, or how distant his heavy responsibilities, Tripp's life and loves were embodied in Elmira.

John Quinn, who joined Gannett in 1966, recalled the story told in Rochester "about taking the company plane to Elmira for Frank Tripp's funeral. Of course, Frank Gannett was deceased then, and he had been a teetotaller, but Mrs. Gannett was not. So they went to the funeral.

"[Neuharth] was on the plane and Paul Miller and Mrs. Gannett and a few others. Anyway, as Al tells the story, they went back to the house to visit with the family and then got back on the plane about midday and headed for Rochester. At Mrs. Gannett's suggestion they all mixed themselves martinis. But it's a short flight from Elmira to Rochester and they were scarcely through the first martini when they were ready to land. Mrs. Gannett ordered them to fly over [Lake Ontario] for another 20 minutes so they could have a second martini. She said, 'Frank Tripp would want us to do this.' " [5]

Nine months after Tripp's death, the *Star-Gazette* reported the probated value of his estate. As a young reporter he had temporarily left Frank Gannett and Erwin Davenport because they couldn't afford to meet the $2 dollar raise the opposition promised him. More than 60 years later, Gannett's chairman, and president and publisher of the Elmira newspapers, left an estate valued at $1,290,202.20. [6]

# Our Pulitzer: first of its kind'[7]

"The most coveted Pulitzer Prize each year since their inception in 1917," the *Gannetteer* reported proudly, "has been the journalistic award for meritorious public service. The trustees this year awarded that regular prize to the *St. Petersburg* (Fla.) *Times*, noting that Pulitzer rules dictate it must go to an individual newspaper. Then they voted the special public service citation to the entire Gannett Group of newspapers."[8]

Two months after "The Road to Integration" won for The Gannett Newspapers the first public service Pulitzer awarded to a group, riots erupted in Rochester. The weekend of July 24-26, 1964, stunned the city's established leaders, including those at Gannett.

Miller's reaction can be sensed in a *Times-Union* editorial:

"Rochester can now demonstrate what must be done when hoodlums, under the guise of a racial problem, or civil rights legislation, seek to defy the law and place themselves above authority. . . .

"There were many voices of racial reason in Rochester. They were drowned out by the shattering glass and jeering, looting crowd. They are being heard again, even now, and progress will be resumed when order has been restored."[9]

Down the hall, the *Democrat and Chronicle's* editorial staff observed:

"We must not end any of the excellent interracial projects that have made Rochester famous. . . . But we must blend with it a new kind of intolerance . . . intolerance of phonies, of demagogues, of headline-seekers, of smoke-screen experts, of flouters of the law, of hoodlums."[10]

# Looking for Answers

Just two days after the riots, Vin Jones wrote a postmortem at the AP's request. It clearly conveys the surprise of the Rochester establishment to discontent among the city's blacks. Later that year Jones's commentary won first prize in the annual New York State Associated Press News Enterprise Writing Contest. He wrote:

"Rochester erupted the night after the flames died down in Harlem. Everyone had expected trouble in Harlem. No one, especially city officials, had expected anything really serious in Rochester."

Most of Rochester's black residents, Jones explained, had arrived after 1950. For the most part, they lacked the skills for the city's available, good-paying jobs.

He conceded that there had been discrimination in both jobs and housing, but pointed out that slums had been replaced with public housing and urban renewal. New York State's 20-year-old laws against discrimination had been obeyed, and Monroe County's Human Relations Commission had had few complaints of discrimination.

The school board was trying to recruit better teachers and to establish open enrollment, despite public opposition. Rochester's bi-racial Police Advisory Board was 18 months old, and restaurants and hotels were generally open to all.

"The city's newspapers and broadcasting stations for years have reported the racial problem sympathetically and in depth," he said, which was why the riots had caught city officials and most citizens completely by surprise."[11]

Part of the reporting to which Jones referred was a series in the 1960s called "Winds of Change," which had been published in the *Times-Union*. It correctly forecast growing discontent in the black community. "Subsequent reporting," Jones said, "indicates that little progress has been made in solving the basic problems of housing, employment, and education, despite new programs and intensified efforts by agencies already in the field."[12]

While Miller had instigated the ambitious "Road to Integration," he expected citizens to be law-abiding and compliant. Cal Mayne, who was editor of the *Times-Union* editorial page under Miller, expressed the greatest admiration for his former boss. But in 1990 he remembered Miller as a hard-nosed conservative who opposed anything that went outside the orderly process of change led by the establishment.

In autumn of 1964, Saul Alinsky of Chicago, a sociologist described by champions as a social activist and by opponents as a rabble-rousing radical, arrived in Rochester. He had been invited by the Board for Urban Ministry to organize Rochester blacks. Alinsky helped to create a minority group called F.I.G.H.T. The *Times-Union* thoroughly covered all the group's activities, but its editorials adamantly opposed Alinsky and F.I.G.H.T.'s local leadership.

# The Miller Position

In April 1965, the Syracuse University School of Journalism gave Paul Miller its Distinguished Service Medal. His topic at the school's annual banquet was group operations, particularly Gannett's.

He explained local autonomy, outlined the responsibilities that it placed on editors and publishers, and restated the purposes and the $3.5 million in philanthropies of the Gannett Foundation.

He conceded that most Gannett newspapers labeled themselves "independent" or "independent-Republican," but pointed out that in 1964, 23 of 25 Gannett newspapers endorsed Lyndon Johnson over Barry Goldwater for the presidency.

He mentioned the strengths available to Gannett newspapers through cooperative effort, citing the success of "The Road to Integration," and its winning of the Pulitzer Prize. Then he turned to newspaper coverage of the Alinsky affair. He told of sending three trained journalists – one of them Mayne – to Chicago to study Alinsky's operations.

"The *Times-Union* published a three-part, 10,000-word report by Mayne," Miller said. "[Gannett's] WHEC put on an uninterrupted one-hour telecast twice in prime evening time and also a radio version. From both sides in the controversy came praise for the reports as informative and objective." [13]

Mayne recalled that Chicago assignment:

"I came back and I wrote a draft of the series that I wanted to do, which presented this balanced picture. Well, Paul was furious.

"I came into a Saturday conference with Paul Miller and Al Neuharth and they said, 'Where do you come up with all this crap? What do you mean writing this kind of a piece?'

"I was ready to risk my career at that point. I said, 'Look, you sent me out to do a news job and this is what I've found as a newsman. It's all documented.'

"Now to Paul's credit, he let that piece run. And the greatest compliment I ever got in the newspaper business was when I saw Saul Alinsky [later] and I said, 'Saul, what did you think about the series? Was it fair?' And he said, 'Yes, dammit.' But when it came to the editorial posture of the Rochester *Times-Union*, I lost that battle almost hands down." [14]

Even Jones conceded that *Times-Union* editorials during the Alinsky controversy were "on the wrong side of the argument," no matter how creditable the paper's news coverage. [15]

A month after Miller's honor at Syracuse University, the National Conference of Christians and Jews gave the Rochester newspapers its 1965 Superior Merit Brotherhood Award for outstanding contributions to better human relations.

The black ministerial association of Rochester bitterly protested to the NCCJ.

## A Man of Strong Views

People who worked long and closely with Miller unanimously speak of him with genuine admiration and great respect. Yet most of them also affectionately recall a man whose arbitrariness could be exasperating.

Arrogance would have violated his religious upbringing, but he was supremely confident of his political and social views. That was evident in the political campaign in the autumn of 1964.

"Paul was a good solid newspaperman," Mayne said, "but he was not above using the news pages – and the editorial pages, which was his right – not above using the news pages to promote his friends and attack his enemies."

"I think one of the worst sins I ever saw Paul commit in journalism was when Bobby Kennedy was running against Ken Keating, trying to oust Keating as senator. . . .

"Ken Keating was a Rochester man, a friend of Paul's, and he was coming to Rochester to have a climactic rally in the War Memorial, right near the end of the campaign.

"So Paul Miller ordered that for the week preceding the rally, there would be a news story every day on Page One based on some aspect of Ken Keating's campaign and the fact that Keating was coming to this rally. Of course he jam-packed the War Memorial.

"When Bobby Kennedy was coming into town, if there was too much attention to Bobby, the editors would hear about it. Well, Bobby was anything but a fool, and he knew what was going on," Mayne said.

"After the election, Paul, in what he considered a magnanimous gesture, took a bunch of us one Saturday morning down to New York to see Bobby Kennedy and kind of make peace. I remember Bobby sitting there with those steel gray eyes of his, just looking at Paul Miller and not budging at all. He really didn't forgive Paul, because he knew that Paul had been after him, not just in the editorial pages but in the news pages. It was a very uncomfortable meeting, and I think Paul felt very uncomfortable with it, too." [16]

# Chapter 29

# The Next Step

*"Readers do not have to love a newspaper to welcome and respect it. They can detest the editor, deplore the newspaper's policy, criticize the way it handles the news – and still be avid and devoted readers. If they are . . . just keep on doing what you're doing."*

Paul Miller
Jan. 7, 1966

Al Neuharth became a director of the Gannett Company on July 29, 1964, and tapped Bob Eckert, who had been general manager in Elmira for 2 1/2 years, to be his assistant. Eckert remembered:

"I went up and Al and I talked. We hit it off very well, very easily, very quickly, and Al offered me the job. . . . He said, 'You won't have the title you should have but you'll be a general executive, initially. And then, the first of the year, we'll make you director of operations, but you really will be my assistant.'"[1]

"It took me about two weeks," Eckert said, "to realize why I was in Rochester. . . . [H]e had to have a person like me there before he could make any move at all. He made the Florida move because he had to get out of Rochester. He had to make a move that would distance himself and yet make the name for himself, because Paul simply wasn't ready to make him the heir apparent."[2]

"The Florida move" was Neuharth's plan to start a newspaper near the burgeoning space complex at Cape Canaveral. He wrote in *Confessions of an S.O.B.* that he persuaded Paul Miller to support his plan by promising to continue to oversee operations in Rochester even while creating a new publication in Florida almost from scratch. His ability to rely on someone like Eckert, a proven manager, in Rochester was essential.

Miller's support did not guarantee enthusiasm from all of his executives for the ambitious venture, which Neuharth estimated would cost $8 million to $10 million. That figure included money to buy a suitable newspaper as a base, expand and equip its plant, and absorb $3 million to $5 million in losses over five years to give the new paper time to succeed.

Lynn Bitner, corporate general manager, and Cy Williams, corporate treasurer, both opposed the project as too risky and costly. Nevertheless, Miller sent Bitner to Florida to try to buy the *Cocoa Tribune*, a small paper that Neuharth had persuaded him was appropriate. The general manager returned to Rochester and reported that Mrs. C.H. Holderman said her newspaper was not for sale.

Neuharth then visited Mrs. Holderman himself. He had known her for seven years, and got her to fly to Rochester to talk to Miller. At the end of that visit, he and Miller had won her over. She sold them the *Cocoa Tribune* for $1.8 million.

The July 1965 issue of *The Gannetteer* sported a cover photograph of a smiling trio – Miller, Neuharth and Mrs. Holderman. It also reported that the reorganized board of the *Cocoa Tribune* included Miller as chairman, Neuharth as president, and the unenthusiastic Bitner and Williams.

"The Florida move" was under way.

Tom Dolan, who had joined Gannett 20 years before, was general manager in Newburgh. Neuharth offered him the job of general manager in Cocoa and asked him to fly to Florida. He did and then turned down the job. Dolan explained why in a 1991 interview:

"The main reason was I knew I wouldn't be running it. I knew Al would be running it. . . . I could be general manager but I wasn't going to 'general-manage' the property. . . . I knew that he'd be running it and I'd get my ass chewed for anything that went wrong and everything that went right, nobody'd hear about that." [3]

Instead, Neuharth gave the job to Maurice (Moe) Hickey, then business manager at Elmira, described by Dolan as young and very capable. Hickey called Dolan's belief that Neuharth would really run the show, "a very fair assessment. . . . I was only 32, so I think it made sense for me whereas it may not have made as much sense for Tom." [4]

For Neuharth to realize his dream, he had to know the territory. He turned to pollster Lou Harris, whose job, as Neuharth explained in *Confessions of an S.O.B.*, was not to determine whether Gannett should start a new newspaper – that had been decided – but to tell it what *kind* of newspaper would captivate the space-conscious audience around Cocoa.

Market research was another of Neuharth's precepts that Gannett old-timers scorned. Vince Spezzano described in a 1990 interview their reaction to Neuharth's ideas:

"The publishers of The Gannett Newspapers then were good old boys. They had their own lifestyles, and all of a sudden here was somebody who wanted to come in and have research done on their newspaper to find out what they're doing wrong. . . . They were just defending what they did, saying the research was wrong, instead of taking it as a tool. . . . When Al Neuharth came [to Rochester], the first thing he did was to do research on these papers. . . . This was not the worst paper, the paper that needed research most, but he said, 'I've got to do it with my newspaper first before I take them elsewhere.' " [5]

Hickey described Spezzano's importance to the Florida project:

"Vince was a great help to us. It was a difficult promotion . . . because there was no local television to promote the new product and the radio was really scattered and very poor. We actually wound up buying [space on] every billboard in [Brevard] County. I think there were 70 or 80 of them. That was quite impressive. Wherever you went, any billboard, all you'd see was *Today* newspaper. Vince put all that promotion together." [6]

Hickey was the one who came up with the newspaper's name, *Today*. As he remembered:

"We'd been kicking around names like *Brevard Sun*, *Brevard World*, something to encompass more than just the town of Cocoa where we were publishing. I got up real early one morning and scratched it out on a notepad and that's how we came up with it. I suggested the name *Cocoa Today*. . . . We just started out with the name *Today* and dropped Cocoa so we could serve from Melbourne, all of Cocoa

Beach, all the way up to Titusville" (spanning approximately 40 miles and all of Brevard County).[7]

Bitner, who had opposed the Florida venture from the start, apparently tried to create trouble for it. Neuharth said in *Confessions of an S.O.B.* that Bitner tried to sabotage the project, first by botching his assignment to buy the *Cocoa Tribune* and then by trying to persuade Miller to scuttle the new newspaper and make do with an expanded *Tribune.*

Whatever Bitner's intentions, the Neuharth team was not to be stopped. If Bitner had seen himself as Miller's possible successor, his hopes died.

At their December 1965 meeting, Gannett Company directors promoted Bitner to senior vice president and announced that he had asked to retire at the end of 1966, at the age of 62.

Jack Heselden, who finally had realized his dream of becoming a publisher only two years before, was recalled from Plainfield, N.J. He was named general business manager, assigned to perform special assignments for Miller, and to begin assuming Bitner's duties in the spring of 1966.

Dolan, who had spurned the opportunity to be titular general manager in Cocoa, replaced Heselden at the *Courier-News.*[8]

As busy as he was in Florida, Neuharth had not broken his promise to oversee his Rochester responsibilities as well. He had Eckert as his director of operations, Spezzano as his director of marketing. But his team was not yet complete. The previous Thanksgiving, he had made overtures to the managing editor of the afternoon *Providence* (R.I.) *Journal*, John C. Quinn, who had been on that paper for 23 years.

On Christmas Eve, 1965, Quinn said, his wife, Loie, told him, "I can't believe it. I got this huge poinsettia plant from Al." Then things got more interesting:

"About half an hour later the bell rang again. She said, 'You won't believe this. We just got a case of champagne from Al.' The note read, 'When you're ready to toast your new employer.'"

*The Providence Journal* news staff had a memorable Christmas,

thanks to their managing editor's case of champagne. But the day after Christmas, Quinn said, he got a phone call:
"It was Al's secretary. She said, 'I think I've made a horrible mistake. Mr. Neuharth asked me to send flowers to your wife for Christmas and champagne to you. I think I was supposed to send a bottle and I sent a case. Could you return the rest of it?'

(Neuharth confirmed during an interview in 1992 that the attempt to recall the case of champagne was not a Neuharth practical joke but a genuine misunderstanding on his secretary's part).

"So I sat down with Al," Quinn said, "and we had one of the great job conversations of my lifetime. . . . I asked him whether he wanted a colleague or an executive officer, and we talked through how we would deal with one another. Al has a style of dealing with individuals in a way that suits them. A lot of people have worked very successfully and happily with Al because they love having him intimidate them. His style is to be aggressive and abrasive. He and I understood going in that I wasn't going to be kicked around."

"He was trying to build a personal team," Quinn explained, "that he ultimately stylized on the Rochester newspapers where he had a *troika*, a director of marketing, a director of operations and a director of news. That was his pattern through all our years together. He would get three very different people who could argue and disagree and bring very different points of view." [9]

Quinn became director of news for both Rochester newspapers on Feb. 20, 1966.

# *Today* Is Tomorrow

Early in March in Cocoa, Fla., complete prototype issues of *Today* were written, edited, printed and distributed to circulation drop points in a two-week dry run. The newspapers then were collected and destroyed, to keep the opposition as much in the dark as possible.

Beginning March 21, 1966, every residence in Brevard County got the first of 30 free issues of *Today*, 52,000 a day. The strategy, familiar to most newspapers with new products, was to follow the free distribution with a half-price offer to new subscribers. Lou Harris tested the pricing waters.

Neuharth described the results:

"Harris's survey found readers had become hooked quickly. 'You're crazy if you make any half-price offers,' he advised. We threw the discount coupons away and went for it. . . .

"[W]e found out people will pay for a newspaper what they think it's worth. Our prepublication projection for paid circulation called for 20,000 at the end of the first year. The actual results:

" • 33,000 after 10 weeks.

" • 40,000 after 12 months." [10]

Two months later, *Today* was already so successful that Neuharth found himself explaining the philosophy behind the new newspaper to the annual convention of the National Newspaper Promotion Association in San Francisco. He told them:

"There are two big weaknesses in newspapers today:

"1. The failure to match today's product with today's people. Much of the blame lies with editors and publishers who are still editing for yesterday's audience.

"2. The failure to match the promotion to the product. It is not just a matter of over-promoting or under-promoting – but mis-promoting. We are too often not on target with the product or the people."

He described the market research and planning that preceded *Today's* introduction. He explained the design – "a product easy to read; with features easy to find; with sections packaged for the family division of interests; a paper that was breezy and bright and wrapped in news."

"This is the kind of opportunity," he told his audience, "[that exists] from coast to coast, in big cities or small, for the greatest growth and success newspapers have ever had, IF:

"1. We quit flying by the seat of our pants and quit assuming that what worked yesterday will work today.

"2. We get to know our customers; find out what they want; give it to them, and then tell them about it.

"In short: If we match the product to the people and then make sure the promotion matches the product."[11]

The speech was quintessential Neuharth. It defined himself, his beliefs and the future of the Gannett Company under his leadership.

## The President Is Pleased

The fall 1966 conference of Gannett executives was at Shawnee-on-Delaware, Pa., in October. Miller's topic was, "What Makes a 'Best' Year?" After pointing out to those assembled that a "best year" in Gannett "goes far beyond earnings," he said, "The Gannett Group again is experiencing its best year ever! . . .

"[T]his year is, I believe, your best in product improvement and in public service . . . in recruiting [and] training . . . in national and regional awards . . . and, yes, indeed, in earnings without which none of the rest would be possible. . . .

"Group combined circulation has reached 1,171,008 daily and 510,710 Sunday. This is an increase in five years of 17 percent Sunday and more than 40 percent daily. . . .

"Consider a fact about Westchester-Rockland Newspapers. Total advertising for these nine dailies – which joined us April 1, 1964 – now amounts to more than 50 percent of the total for all our other dailies combined. . . .

"The combined total of our daily and Sunday newspaper advertising linage in the first eight months of 1966 topped that for the like period last year by more than 1.25 million column inches. . . .

"Earnings for those first eight months – including Gannett Florida Corp., where some of the brightest newspaper people in the country are building some of the brightest newspapers – are well ahead of last year's."

He evaluated the Group as "one that makes the most of its opportunities for continuing improvement, continuing growth, a continuing high level of service to all, while operating soundly and therefore profitably."

At the end he turned to Bitner. "As you know," he said, "Lynn Bitner will leave us at the end of this year and move to his beautiful home off the South Carolina coast. He has had such powerful influence on the Group in so many ways that we can never forget him. He is a real fighter for the things he believes in, as almost all of you know from experience.

"Lynn, I want you to know how much I appreciate all that you have done for me. It has been a great deal. You are a wonderfully good friend, personally and professionally." [12]

Vin Jones, who spoke at the testimonial dinner for Bitner, would later describe him this way:

"Lynn Bitner was hated, and loved, but he knew more about the business than anybody before Neuharth. He really knew all about the composing room and all about the pressroom, all about advertising, and quite a bit about the news side, too. . . .

"Bitner was really a star. But . . . everybody was scared stiff of him. He got mean, nasty, but god, he was smart. I did a lot of traveling around with him. We were the ones who had to go into a paper and spend two or three days and ferret out all the things that were wrong, and occasionally replace people.

"We had a lot of bad problems like that. Miller was smart. He came in, passed out the bouquets and compliments. He knew what was wrong but had somebody else do the dirty work on it. Well, that was our job." [13]

Dolan described the differences in style between Miller and Bitner. A complimentary note from PM read, "I can't imagine a report reflecting much more credit on all concerned on all levels, from general manager down, than at the Newburgh Beacon News Inc. for the seven months ended July 31, 1965."

Bitner, on the other hand, didn't mince words: "Auditor's report for the first four months of the current year. I can find nothing to complain about in this report. However, we must remember that you have been in Plainfield only a short time and there probably will be plenty of discussion when you are audited next time." [14]

Jones summed up the Bitner style at the testimonial dinner:

"LNB transacted most of his enormous business either man to man or over the telephone. His correspondence was sparse and written with the economy of verbiage that suggested the author was cabling it from Bangkok at his own expense.

"Lynn always expressed his views with force and precision. The recipient (I almost said the victim) of a Bitner missive never had any doubt as to what was meant.

"In 15 years, I can recall seeing only three Bitner letters that took more than a page. . . .

"But here are some gems of wit and wisdom – just as the Great Man uttered them:

- "Of a TV-radio critic whom he regarded as being triply unqualified for the job – the columnist was (1) a graduate of a college Lynn rated as slightly below the average high school; (2) an Italian, and (3) the unpardonable sin, a woman.
- "On the folly of trying to invade the territory of a well-entrenched local newspaper – 'You can't knock a man off his own dunghill.'
- "On the limitations of accounting – 'If the publisher is stealing $500 a week he'll never be caught. But if he gets greedy and tries to steal $501 a week he'll be caught instantly.'
- "On the notorious autonomy of some sports pages – 'They run it as though it were a leased department.'
- "About life on the Fifth Floor [corporate headquarters] – 'This isn't a toboggan slide; it's a roller coaster.' " [15]

Bitner retired Dec. 31, 1966, 30 days after Miller clearly signaled the Gannett Company's future. On Dec. 1, he had named Neuharth executive vice president, and Heselden vice president/operations.

Neuharth became the company's first executive vice president since 1957, when Miller himself relinquished that title to succeed Frank Gannett as president. Miller said:

"Neuharth continues as general manager and operating head of the Rochester newspapers and as president of the Gannett Florida Corporation. But as executive vice president he will work closely with me on overall company matters and will be active particularly in all expansion and development areas."[16]

Neuharth wrote in *Confessions of an S.O.B.* about Miller's reluctance to make his succession clear. He recalled in 1992 Miller's response whenever Neuharth suggested spelling it out.

"He'd answer, 'Everybody knows that,' " Neuharth said.

"My answer was, 'You know it, I hope, and I think I know it, but not everybody else knows it.' "[17]

Now, at the end of 1966, not quite four years after Neuharth joined Gannett, everybody should have known it. The departing Bitner clearly did.

# Chapter 30

# Spreading the Word

*"You have heard or read much in recent years about the so-called 'fading' or 'failing' American newspapers. That's a lot of nonsense. The real newspaper story today is not that of a fading or failing industry, but rather a flourishing one – from coast to coast."*

*Allen H. Neuharth*
*1968*

The Gannett Newspapers had grown by one in 1966 with the creation of *Today*. Early in 1967, Gannett bought two newspapers in northwest Illinois, a state where it already owned the *Commercial-News* in Danville, acquired in 1934.

Rockford, Ill., then became the Group's third-largest city. Its *Morning Star* and *Register-Republic*, with combined daily circulation near 100,000, were fourth-largest in circulation after the papers in Rochester, Hartford and Camden.

Paul Miller told stock analysts in New York a year later that the purchase price was $13.39 million. The Rockford acquisition brought The Gannett Newspapers to 30, with a combined total circulation of 1.25 million daily and more than half a million on Sunday.[1]

That same year, the company started WDAN-FM in Danville. The station, and its AM sister station, were sold four years later for $250,000.)

While negotiations for the Rockford sale were under way, the company issued a call for redemption of all outstanding Class B Convertible Preferred Stock at $110 a share or equivalent conversion to Class B Common, estimated at $659.25 per share upon conversion.

"GCI may sometime make a public offering of stock," the *Gannetteer* reported. But Miller said that "the board of directors has made no decision in this matter and there is no assurance that it will do so in the foreseeable future."[2]

*The Hartford Times* may have been Gannett's second-largest, but it was not growing as most Gannett newspapers were. The bottom line was written in red. Vin Jones summarized the problem:

"When I went to Rochester [in 1950], *The Hartford Times* had 100,000 circulation and *The Hartford Courant* . . . had about 60,000. But [*The Courant*] had a Sunday paper. . . . Twenty years later the [evening] *Times* had 130,000 circulation . . . and the [morning] *Courant* had gone from 60,000 to 140,000. . . .

"The one year (*The Times*) made $1 million, they had a 100-year anniversary. The local people called it 'the new paper.' It was only 100 years old.

"They had this big party. The day after the party, Heselden, not Miller, went to . . . [the] publisher and fired him, even though it was not his fault. There was nothing you could do. You know what the story is on morning and evening papers."[3]

Before that fateful party, Miller called Neuharth's assistant to his office. Bob Eckert remembered:

"He . . . asked if I would go over [to Hartford] and help.

" 'Do I have a choice?' I said.

" 'Oh, yes,' he said, 'you don't have to take it.'

"I said, 'Well, let me think about it overnight anyway.' I went down and Al came right in, because he knew. Al said, 'I think you'd make a mistake to be publisher there.' . . .

"I thought Al wanted me [to stay] so that I'd become publisher in Rochester, [but] that Paul wouldn't ever agree with it. For instance, Al asked Paul to name me assistant general manager. . . . He wouldn't do that. Not that he didn't want me to be the general manager there, but in my opinion, he wasn't going to let Al move until he was ready. And that went on for some time."[4]

Eckert's appointment as general manager of *The Hartford Times* was announced April 7, 1967, by the publisher whom he would replace two months later.

Neuharth had warned Eckert that Hartford was "the coldest town in the United States. Toughest to break into."

The embittered publisher told him much the same thing, Eckert recalled:

"He said to me, 'You'll never be accepted in this town. You'll never have what I had in this town.' ...

"Well, it was the warmest town I've ever been in."[5]

Soon after Eckert's arrival there, Gannett made what Heselden described as "one of the many mistakes in Hartford." *The Hartford Times* started a Sunday edition on Sept. 15, 1967. But to do so, Heselden said, they "cut out the Saturday edition [and] the community was up in arms over that."

*The Times* was already at a competitive disadvantage against *The Hartford Courant,* a situation at least partially the result of what Heselden described as a foolish Gannett mistake. Matt Sullivan, the company's circulation director, was one of the best in the business, Heselden said. Gannett's accommodating leadership had sent Sullivan to Hartford just after World War II to help its competitors at *The Courant* develop their Sunday paper. Two decades later, Heselden said, Gannett "wished to hell that we'd started a Sunday newspaper in Hartford instead of trying to help them." *The Courant's* Sunday success was one of the obstacles that Eckert encountered when he got there.

*The Times's* fate became clear soon after Gannett went public in 1967. Eckert explained:

"Every time [company executives] had a meeting with the analysts, *The Hartford Times* would be brought up. 'What are you doing there?' 'How's that coming along?'

"I don't want to blame [such pressures] for the failure. I don't think it could have been saved. It's been proved again and again. . . . You can't save an afternoon newspaper. . . .

But we went all out for a couple [of] years and then the decision was, let's ride and keep the line black . . . so that we don't have this red ink thing with the analysts. We stopped spending money, which I think was the right thing to do. If there had been any chance, it was gone."[6]

Eckert stayed in Hartford for five years.

# Missouri Shows a Native Son

On May 5, 1967, Miller was in Columbia, Mo., to receive the University of Missouri's Honor Award for Distinguished Service in Journalism. The citation praised:
"His influence in building The Associated Press into a news-gathering giant serving 8,000 newspapers, radio and television stations in more than 100 countries, thus seeking for Americans a fuller international story;

"His determined direction which has helped shape a high-purposed chain of newspapers in The Gannett Group, and won for it the only special group citation in history for balanced and courageous appraisal of the integration issue;

"His creed as a news executive of high ideals stands as an injunction to others: Substance ahead of form; balance ahead of speed; completeness ahead of color; and accuracy ahead of everything." [7]

Although Miller grew up in Oklahoma, he was born in Missouri in 1906, the year Frank Gannett, Erwin R. Davenport and Frank Tripp joined forces in Elmira. Sixty-one years later the last of the trio, Davvy, died on July 4 in Miami Beach, where he had lived since 1952. He was 91. All living links to the company's origins were gone.

Miller had scheduled a trip to Asia in September with his lifelong friend Walker Stone, editor-in-chief of Scripps Howard Newspapers. At the last minute, for reasons not then explained, he was forced to cancel his plans. Vin Jones went in his place. When he returned, he wrote a series of articles on the trip for the Rochester papers. Jones laughed as he recalled the first:

"The precede that Miller put on it is an absolute masterpiece. . . . It said, 'When Paul Miller was unable to go to Asia with his friend, as he had planned to do, he asked Vincent Jones to pick up his reservations and go, as he had planned to go.'

"The result was I wrote a great long piece and then Miller was congratulated by all sorts of people. They'd say, 'I saw your piece in the paper about going to Asia.' " [8]

It became obvious in October why Miller had been too busy to go to Asia. He was appearing at informational meetings arranged by First Boston Corporation in Los Angeles, San Francisco, Chicago and New York to brief potential investors about Gannett. His topic: "The Gannett Group: Why it grows."

"Much of the steady gain in newspaper readership and revenue," he would say, "is being made in smaller or medium-sized communities – some on the fringes of major metropolitan centers, others in prime markets of their own.

"Now, it is precisely in those growth areas that the Gannett Group does most of its business." He would then review Gannett's history and the awards it had won, describe its work force and the principles on which it operated, and outline its growth.

"A review of our last five years," he'd say, "shows that we have grown almost 50 percent from within and 50 percent from acquisitions."

He'd conclude:

"I look for more publishing and broadcasting companies to go public. Groups such as ours benefit by local participation and local stock interest in the individual areas served. . . . [S]tock ownership also offers an interest and incentive for employees and management. And the availability of marketable stock should help in further acquisitions." [9]

The first public offering of Gannett Co. Inc. common stock was made on Oct. 24, 1967. First Boston Corporation offered 500,000 shares of Gannett common at $29 per share and sold out in one day.

On Dec. 29, Miller distributed a statement to all Gannett officers, directors and principal executives. It said in part:

"There have been inquiries as to whether there is a company policy respecting Gannett common stock ownership and transactions by employees of The Gannett Company and its subsidiaries. The answer is 'Yes.' . . .

"[N]o employee should trade in the company's common stock for the purpose of short-term gain and quick profit. Any purchases and sales, or sales and purchases, within a six-month period would be presumed to violate this policy. . . .

"[A]n employee should not enter into transactions which he expects will result in profit if at the time he is aware of confidential information which has not been made public or generally available to the investing public." [10]

According to Jones, Miller's statement bore an interesting connection to another company event announced at this time: the retirement of secretary-treasurer Cy Williams. The company had been recalling shares that would convert 40 for 1 when the company went public. All of a sudden, Jones said, shares originally held by other stockholders began reappearing in the names of Williams, members of his family and others known to him, for conversion at the new rate. When the board became aware of that, his retirement followed. [11]

Many Gannett hourly employees, from clerks to union printers, prospered as a result of the installment stock purchases that Frank Gannett had made possible. Each share of old Gannett preferred stock became 40 shares of the new common stock on Oct. 24, with a market value of $29 per share.

Any employee who owned, for example, five shares of old Gannett stock got 200 shares of the new stock, with an initial value of $5,800. Twenty-five years later, assuming all dividends had been reinvested in Gannett stock, the value of those 200 original shares at the end of 1992 exceeded $259,000.

# The Next Generation

On Dec. 28, 1967, Jones announced the appointment of John Quinn as managing editor of Gannett News Service. Quinn remained director of news for the two Rochester newspapers.

Quinn's broadened duties included supervision of the daily GNS news report and responsibility for a major GNS expansion in 1968. That included broader coverage of national stories by staff members from GNS bureaus and from Gannett newspapers in New York, New Jersey, Connecticut, Illinois and Florida; extension of the GNS feature service, and expansion of wire transmission facilities.

Quinn chose Jack Needham, assistant managing editor of the *Democrat and Chronicle*, to help him set up a Rochester GNS bureau.[12]

Early in 1968, Quinn and the editors of the *Democrat and Chronicle* decided to make a change on the comics page. They turned to Vince Spezzano, director of public service and research for the Rochester newspapers, for help. Spezzano's department suggested letting the readers decide. The editors agreed. More than 2,400 teachers, students, employees and others responded to questionnaires:

Participants were asked to rank from "excellent" to "terrible" four comic strips that appeared daily: "Gasoline Alley," "Redeye," "Buz Sawyer" and "Pogo," as well as four strips being considered as replacements: "Wizard of Id," "Miss Peach," "Karen" and "The Inkids."

When the ballots were counted, "Wizard of Id" became the new comic strip and "Pogo" was dropped.[13]

Whether because of that resort to the readers, or in spite of it, a month later Spezzano was named the first public service director for Gannett's 30 newspapers, three television stations and six radio stations.

Miller said Spezzano and Richard Hare, Gannett research director, would expand public service programs and develop promotion and research projects.

"We want to find out more," Miller said, "about what our readers, listeners and advertisers want from their newspapers and broadcast stations, and how we can most effectively provide it."[14]

Miller's two presidencies, of the Gannett Company and The Associated Press, meant frequent speaking engagements. Neuharth found himself invited to speak more frequently as well, because of *Today's* success and his recent promotion to an executive vice presidency.

Miller boasted of Gannett's continuing financial success. In February 1968 he told the New York Society of Security Analysts:

"Our headlines for today are as follows.

## 1967 WAS GANNETT'S BEST YEAR EVER
## and
## 1968 WILL BE EVEN BETTER

"Every figure was a record in 1967. Here they are, unaudited and rounded off:

"Revenues totaled $110 million compared to $100.6 million in 1966, up 9.3 percent.

"Net income was $7.4 million against $7 million, up 5.9 percent.

"Earnings per share were $1.71, compared to $1.65 on a smaller average number of shares outstanding during 1966. . . .

"The upward trend is continuing in 1968 – due primarily to rate adjustments during the year but also to growth in both advertising and circulation – despite the fact that our average number of shares outstanding will be higher as a result of our offering of 500,000 new common shares in October of 1967."

Why would 1968 be better? In addition to the increased revenues, Miller predicted, Gannett would realize its first full year of earnings from its Rockford, Ill., papers and "our exciting Cape [Canaveral] area operations – which lost more than $2 million in 1966 but only a bit more than half that in 1967 – will be near a break-even by Christmas this year." [15]

In fact, Miller could report by the fall that *Today* "is operating in the black — and that is almost two full years ahead of earliest projections. . . .

"[I]n that one newspaper, *Today*, national Gannett has proved its competence to perform one of the most difficult feats in 20th-century American journalism – the establishment of a self-sustaining new daily newspaper in competition with vigorous dailies in neighboring areas."

He also reported the start of the Sunday *Hartford Times* on Sept. 15, the successful conversion of *The Saratogian* to offset printing and continued refinement of offset printing already established at *The Ithaca Journal*. Miller also announced agreement in principle to purchase the San Bernardino Sun Co. in California. [16]

That company published three newspapers, *The Sun*, mornings, *The Telegram*, evenings, and the *Sun-Telegram* on Sundays. When that agreement became known, United Press International speculated that the price was "in the neighborhood of $24 million." That must have delighted Miller and his cronies at the competing Associated Press, because when the deal was closed, the price was revealed to be $17.7 million.

The Times Mirror Co. had bought the San Bernardino property in 1964 but was later ordered by the U.S. District Court to sell after it was found in violation of antitrust laws. The court finally approved the sale to Gannett on Dec. 9, 1968, and the property changed hands on Jan. 2, 1969, making Gannett truly a national company, with operations reaching from coast to coast.

Miller's pride in the creation and success of *Today* was not lost on the industry, and Neuharth was eager to talk about it and other new directions the Gannett Company might take.

When the International Newspaper Promotion Association came to town, the convention theme was "Putting the pro in motion."

Neuharth approved. "In a couple of decades," he said, "the image of promotion has changed from that of a rather shady means of tricking people, to that of professional advancement of worthful [sic] causes or products. . . .

"Just as the old image of the promoter has faded, so has the old image of newspapers. . . . On most of today's newspapers, quality reporting, quality editing, quality advertising, and quality promotion have become predominant. . . .

"I think we should quit wasting our time fighting with those who criticize everything they see in newspapers – and many things they don't even see. . . .

"Fight with your management for the necessary tools to do a totally professional and positive job. Fight with your own staff members, so that they will use all their skills for truly professional performance. Fight with your readers, but positively and aggressively for their attention, and respect, and confidence.

"If you and I do that, professional journalism and professional newspaper promotion will need no defense." [17]

# Rx for Restive Youth

Neuharth made two other major speeches that year, in both of which he dealt with civil rights and antiwar protests then growing on streets and campuses across the country.

The first was on May 23 at Michigan State University, where he was asked to give the first in an annual series of lectures to honor Frederick S. Siebert, dean emeritus of the College of Communication Arts. He held out to his campus audience a future more exciting and more rewarding for journalists.

"I urge you to bring your youth, your vitality, your spirit, and your new ideas, no matter how revolutionary they may be, to the profession of journalism. . . .

"The protesters in today's society are always unhappy, but never uncertain. I believe we in communications can help turn the nature of tomorrow's protest in a more productive and positive direction. . . .

"Non-conformity, but with a constructive and positive approach, is both healthy and necessary. But we can have it without the beatnik kid, the hippie, the delinquent, the intellectual odd-ball, the New Left radical, the protest marcher, the sitter [one who participated in 'sit-ins']. . . .

"It will be done by intelligent young leaders who walk fast, who walk with a purpose, and who persuade their colleagues to substitute walking fast and walking purposefully for sitting down or marching in purposeless protest. . . .

"Our newspapers and broadcast stations have devoted too much attention to the destructive protester. . . .

"Together, we must take the national spotlight off those who keep raising their voices and lowering their aim, and put it instead on those whose aim is higher than their voices."[18]

Neuharth was more critical of adults in a speech in Chicago to the Inland Daily Press Association, a group of 565 daily newspapers in 17 states.

Neuharth's topic there was "About collegians: 'Are we listening now?' " He alluded to the current catchphrase "Generation Gap" to describe the alienation between young people and their elders. The problem, he argued, was rather a "Communications Gap," and he placed much of the blame for that on the media. "Do we talk to [young people] as we should in our newspapers?" he asked. "Do we listen? Do we respond?"

Referring to student protests, some violent, at Columbia University in New York and the University of California at Berkeley in 1968, he declared:

"[I]f we had listened to the voices of our young people, and had responded, those young people would not now be letting foul-mouthed, loud-mouthed, red-tinged rebels use them as the fuse to ignite our campuses.

"You in the Midwest for the most part . . . have not yet been flooded with [that] kind of intellectual odd-balls or outright criminal kooks. . . .

"You and I and thousands of associates in our profession have a splendid opportunity to close today's communications gap. We can do it if we listen less to today's yippies, or New Left radical, or delinquent, or any of the great assortment of destructive hell-raisers whose voices are so much higher than their aim.

"And if we listen much more instead to that vast majority of our confused or frustrated but sincere young people whose hopes and aims are much higher than their voices." [19]

The 62-year-old Miller could comfortably leave public discussion of the campus revolt to his executive vice president, whose views mirrored his own but whose age was nearer that of the seething generation coming to maturity in the late 1960s.

## Professional Advancement

Colleagues in Gannett and the profession as a whole congratulated Jones in April of 1968 when he assumed the presidency of the American Society of Newspaper Editors.

Soon after Jones's elevation to the ASNE presidency, Neuharth took the first step on his own climb to the top of a professional organization. He was elected a director of the American Newspaper Publishers Association (now the Newspaper Association of America).

That summer, Paul T. Miller II, 23-year-old son of the president, was named publisher of Gannett's weekly *Newark* (N.Y.) *Courier-Gazette* and *Lake Shore News* at Wolcott, N.Y. The younger Miller began working on the weekly *Brighton-Pittsford Post*, near Rochester, and worked as a reporter in Texas and Kentucky before becoming an advertising salesman for the Rochester newspapers.[20]

The financial vacancy created by Cy Williams's retirement was filled Sept. 1, 1968, by John R. (Jack) Purcell, 36. The former assistant controller of United Aircraft in Hartford, Conn., was named vice president/finance. Gannett's directors elected him a member and secretary to the board in December.[21]

Soon after the new year, the New York Stock Exchange approved the listing of Gannett stock. On March 10, 1969, the big board began running the symbol GCI with a listing of 5,321,800 shares of common stock. It opened at 30 1/8, up 1/8 from the preceding Friday's over-the-counter closing.

Miller bought the first 100 shares when NYSE trading opened. He called it a "proud moment for Gannett's 8,000 employees and another indication of the growth of our company." A GNS story in the *Times-Union* of March 10, 1968, added:

"The company goes on the big board with record revenues for the seventh consecutive year.

"Two weeks ago, Gannett reported 1968 consolidated revenues of $123,738,688, up 11.5 percent. Net earnings were $8,624,451, up 15.9 percent. Earnings per share of $1.82 were up from $1.71.

"Earnings before taxes in 1968 of $19,314,451 were up 31 percent over 1967."

# Chapter 31

# Quickening Pace

*"Reduced competition among daily newspapers has brought increased responsibility – indeed it has made responsibility both possible and profitable."*

Vincent S. Jones
1969

*T*oday's creation defied newspaper traditions and its early profitability confounded the profession's doomsayers. Al Neuharth, whom Moe Hickey dubbed "the chief architect" of that success, enjoyed challenging accepted wisdom, particularly when "tradition" was an alibi for maintaining the status quo.

He did just that in March 1969, when he questioned "The Sex Gap in Communications." His forum was the banquet of the University of Missouri-J.C. Penney Awards, which recognize editors and writers for general excellence of feature-writing in newspapers of all sizes.

"I'm going to be both friendly and unfriendly tonight," he warned listeners.

"This audience understands better than any other could," the friendly Neuharth said, "what I mean when I say that a splendid job is being done by today's newspapers for today's women readers – because you are doing it."

The unfriendly Neuharth asked, "Why do so many of you with so much talent allow the sex gap between yourselves and the top jobs in your profession to continue, or even to grow?

"Why don't more of you prepare yourselves for, and set your sights on, such positions as publisher, editor, managing editor, city editor, broadcast station manager, advertising or public relations executive – or any of the top communications jobs on which the 'for men only' sign should come down?"

His purpose, of course, was not at all unfriendly, although it was untraditional. It was to jolt a business still dominated by men and an audience of obviously qualified women to contemplate the presumably unthinkable – that women belonged at all levels of management.

"Some of you," Neuharth told the audience, "probably are thinking right now, 'Sure, easier said than done.' And you're probably saying the speaker and all those damned men he is associated with have a pact to discriminate against us girls no matter how good we are.

"Well, you are wrong. The psychological climate has never been better than it is today for competent and ambitious women in communications to move to top jobs formerly reserved for men. But, you have to push and shove and maybe even scratch and claw a bit to get there.

"You should do it. And if you do, your readers will benefit most of all, because you will vastly improve those areas of the newspaper product which are now designed primarily *by* men, but primarily *for* women."[1]

The address was a bellwether for the rapidly growing Gannett Company.

Soon after Neuharth challenged women in communications to seize the future, Syracuse University honored Vin Jones with its Medal for Distinguished Service in Journalism. Jones, then 62, had worked with the university's programs for more than a quarter century.

As Neuharth had done at Michigan State, Jones addressed the existing climate of dissent and recounted changes he had seen in public dialogue.

"None of us should quarrel seriously with a healthy spirit of questioning, of ruthless re-examination, and seeking new and better methods.

"What disturbs me is the brutal arrogance of so much of today's dissent; the callous disregard of the rights of others, the refusal to accept personal responsibility, and the absurdity or the sterility of the alternatives offered by these new revolutionaries. I find just plain anarchy appallingly dull.

"So where does journalism fit into the picture of a nation discontented in the midst of unparalleled affluence and productivity? . . .

"I am very proud of the progress which newspapers have made in the last 30 years. You have only to leaf through some back files, or microfilm, to realize the strides made in everything from presentation to clear evidence of a true professionalism."

Jones welcomed what he called signs that editors and publishers were taking criticism seriously and recognizing the importance of feedback. Journalists who once had denounced the idea of a press council – an independent reviewing panel to sustain or reject public complaints filed against newspapers – were now seriously considering it. The conflict between advocates of free press and fair trial had evolved into constructive efforts to accommodate both goals. Public ownership of newspapers was increasing, broadcasters were doing better reporting, and journalism education was abandoning what he called "pointless isolation" to involve other departments of the university.

"[T]here never has been a time," he concluded, "when it was so vital for people to be fully informed. It is a challenge which all of us should accept eagerly and cheerfully, knowing that never have we worked with such splendid tools."[2]

## Back to Florida

The number of Gannett daily newspapers rose to 34 on July 1, 1969, when the company paid Perry Publications, Inc., $15.5 million for its Pensacola, Fla., newspapers – the morning *Pensacola Journal*, the evening *News*, and the Sunday *News-Journal*. The newspapers had combined daily circulation of more than 90,000; Sunday circulation was 69,000.

Gannett paid $2 million in cash and pledged the $13.5-million balance in long-term notes at 6.9 percent interest, which the newly created subsidiary, Pensacola News-Journal Inc., would pay off from earnings.[3]

Braden Ball, long-time publisher at Pensacola, retained that post, as was usual in Gannett acquisitions. It would be apparent before the year was out that he did not share Neuharth's stated convictions on opening all-male domains to women. A full page of pictures in the *Gannetteer* portrayed Ball's 15th annual barbecue, described as the paper's "unique method of recognition for its advertisers and public officials who help create its news." Pensacola staff writer Ira Brock described the 1,500-person event as "the *stag* function of an area far beyond the host's circulation territory." [4]

## Revising the Legacy

Nearly 12 years after the death of Frank Gannett, the 34 daily newspapers that now carried his name reversed a fundamental company policy: They began to accept advertising for alcoholic beverages. On Aug. 11, 1969, editors and publishers were furnished this prepared statement by Paul Miller:

"Previously these newspapers were owned by a closely held private company. Now that the company is publicly owned, we concluded that we could not continue to exclude this advertising."

Some Gannett radio stations had been accepting beer advertising for several years. Jones credited that to Lynn Bitner:

"[Bitner] realized that if we didn't take beer advertising, our listeners might not get a certain amount of baseball. . . . [H]e went to the nice Mrs. Gannett . . . and she said, 'Well, I'm not going to oppose you gentlemen. I know how my husband felt but you're running the business.' So we started taking beer advertising." [5]

On Oct. 23, 1969, Rochester Institute of Technology dedicated its Frank E. Gannett Memorial Building. The building recognized Gannett's lifelong enthusiasm and financial support both for new technology and the institute. Miller spoke at the dedication, escorting 75-year-old Caroline Gannett at the ceremonies.

# Changes in Rochester

Late fall and early winter of 1969 created some retirement vacancies in Rochester. Back from Florida came Moe Hickey. At Rochester, he became advertising director of both newspapers, working for general manager Neuharth.

John Quinn turned a December newsroom vacancy into an opportunity to create a new job, at an elevated salary, and quickly drew fire from Neuharth.

The new job was night suburban editor. The new hire was John J. Curley, a newspaperman from New Jersey who was about to turn 31. He'd been the AP's New Jersey editor for five years, night managing editor in Perth Amboy, and had just left the staff of William T. Cahill, for whom he had been press secretary during Cahill's successful campaign for governor.

Quinn recalled the situation during a 1991 interview:

"In trying to run the Rochester newspapers, Al just couldn't keep track of the hiring and firing, and the payroll numbers. Finally he slapped on one of those arbitrary rules that he didn't like to do, and I hate. It said, 'Nobody can hire anybody without getting a little slip from me that shows whose replacement it is.'

"Well, we had a long-time slot editor retire and he was making the magnificent salary of $9,000 a year. Somebody had tipped me off that John Curley had quit the political scene and was looking to get back into the newspaper business and was a hell of a good editor. I wound up taking that job and creating a night suburban job that I wanted . . . and bringing John Curley in at $15,000.

"Al called me in and said, 'What the hell kind of management is this, replacing a $9,000 job with a $15,000 refugee from the political world? Did you two guys go to school together?'

"I said no, we just had mutual friends, and I said I had the other $6,000.

" 'Well, where do you have it?'

" 'Well, it's there.' . . . I knew that I had $6,000 in the payroll that I hadn't spent, because I hadn't filled a vacancy or some damn thing. So he let that go."[6]

The corporate pace of change quickened later that winter as well. In February 1970, the company announced an agreement in principle to merge with Federated Publications of Battle Creek, Mich., a group of newspapers in seven cities in Michigan, Idaho, Indiana and Washington. Jack Purcell estimated the value of the proposed acquisition at $52.2 million.[7]

A month later, Neuharth took another giant step. The company announced that the executive vice president had been elected Gannett's general manager. He was succeeded as general manager of the Rochester newspapers by Jack Heselden.

Neuharth was the first since Bitner to carry the title "general manager of the company." The move was a grudging acknowledgement by a reluctant Miller that he would eventually surrender leadership of the company to Neuharth.

## The Big Surprise

In *Confessions of an S.O.B.*, published in 1989, Neuharth described his frustration with Miller's apparent resistance to his inevitable replacement. Miller admirers faulted that account as unfair. Neuharth associates responded that they were not unaware of harsh conflicts between the two.

One person whose loyalty to Miller is beyond question recalled those difficult days. Mary Golding, his secretary for nearly a quarter century, said at first she was unaware of the friction described by Neuharth, because "Mr. Miller concealed it beautifully.

"[W]hen it came time to transfer the [president's] title to Mr. Neuharth," she said, "he had a hard time doing it. I could hear them arguing, their voices raised, but the doors were always shut. . . . You couldn't hear in my office.

"One day . . . this was before an annual meeting, he said to me,

'I'm going home. I have some things to do.' He left the office about 1:30 or 2 in the afternoon. And I thought, well, that's unusual.

"He called up the next morning and he said, 'I want you to get a corsage for Mr. Neuharth's wife.' I still didn't know what was up. He had got home, called all the directors, got it all signed and sealed and he surprised Neuharth. I mean the poor guy didn't know what to say, because he had no idea it was going to be that day." [8]

The day was May 26, 1970. Miller said at the annual meeting of shareholders:

"Now for an announcement that will come as a complete surprise to Al Neuharth, as it will be to all of his associates who are not members of your Gannett board.

"Directors will meet at 55 Exchange St. following this gathering.

"At that time, I shall propose that Al be elected president of Gannett Co., Inc., and that your speaker take the title of chairman and chief executive.

"Al would be chief operating officer, which, frankly, is what he is now. . . .

"Somehow, I have a feeling that we can get him the votes at our directors' meeting." [9]

He could – and did.

Golding said:

"[H]e had such a hard time giving up, the only way he could do it was to just dump it on Neuharth. And Mrs. Neuharth was flabbergasted. We had to run down and pin the corsage on her, and she had to stand up and be acknowledged and everything." [10]

Shortly thereafter, Miller announced that Jones would become operating head of the Frank E. Gannett Newspaper Foundation on July 1, 1970.

Twenty years after Jones had succeeded his mentor, Fay Blanchard, as the editorial authority for all of Gannett's newspapers, he stepped aside to make way for the Neuharth team. Quinn, who replaced him as the Group's chief news executive, said, "It was again musical chairs.

"About the time I went there," Quinn said, "he was president of [the American Society of Newspaper Editors] and he was very helpful to me. . . . He recognized the sensitivity of a time of transition and he was terrific."[11]

Jones also had been sensitive to the fact that his misbegotten title, "executive editor," created confusion over Gannett's claim of local editorial autonomy. Miller wrote in a memo soon after Quinn had become chief news executive:

"Speaking of 'executive editorship,' that title was abandoned when Vin Jones moved to the Frank E. Gannett Newspaper Foundation. There is no executive editor of the Gannett Newspapers. Vin protested that the title, which he inherited, was a misnomer — as it was. For there never could be, and the title didn't apply even to the much smaller group we were then, an executive editor of the Gannett Newspapers."[12]

Torches had been passed and Gannett's new generation was free to pursue its visions. The company, thanks still to the close personal ties of Miller to newspaper owners everywhere, was about to erupt with new growth.

# Chapter 32

# Change is Progress

*"I know of no top women in journalism today who got there by sleeping with opportunity. I know of many, many who have failed to get there because they slept through opportunity."*

Al Neuharth
June 25, 1970

Moe Hickey was not completely pleased at what he found in Rochester in the fall of 1969. He had become director of advertising, he said, of what "was probably the last major newspaper combination in the United States that had two separate advertising departments. . . . They were both very big departments and they would sell against each other. . . .

"I hadn't been there very long when this fellow who was selling advertising for the *Times-Union* came in and said, 'Moe, I've got a big new full-page advertiser for the *Times-Union*.' And he told me the name of the account.

"I said, 'That's great. But what was this guy doing before?'

"He said, 'Oh he used to run a full page in the Sunday *Democrat and Chronicle*' [which had larger circulation than the daily *Times-Union* and higher rates].

"So in effect we sold the guy down. I said from that point on we were going to consolidate." The two advertising staffs merged in the spring of 1970.

"In a matter of a year," Hickey said, "we were down 30 or 40 people, mostly through attrition."[1]

Rochester saw other changes as well. Roughly six months after John Curley left New Jersey to join Gannett as the *Times-Union* suburban editor, he was back in New Jersey as editor of the Plainfield *Courier-News*.

That quick move back to New Jersey in June 1970 had not been discussed before John Quinn hired him, Curley said in 1992. "We didn't talk about anything other than the Rochester job. The *Times-Union* was the biggest [daily] paper in the company at the time."

Even so, "the Jersey papers," he said, "were so far ahead of the Rochester newspaper in terms of putting newspapers together on a 24-hour basis and taking advantage of stories that broke off cycle. . . . [They] had developed 24-hour operations and I had run the night side of one of them at Woodbridge. . . . So it was an opportunity to show what you could do."[2]

# Reshaping a Man's World

Al Neuharth, meanwhile, returned to the podium to chide the National Federation of Press Women because both journalism and society were "over-manned at the top." He continued the theme he'd begun at the University of Missouri-J.C. Penney awards ceremony a year earlier.

"I believe," he said, "the fact this is still so much a man's world is mostly your fault. This man's world, our own over-manned profession, is ready for you. Too many of you are not ready for yourselves."

He categorized women in three groups, "moderate feminists – or humanists," "radical extremists of the women's liberation movement," and "women who use their femininity as an excuse for lack of professional success."

The third category he dismissed. "Women's Lib extremists," he said, "are wrong about men. They are wrong in presuming that man is woman's natural enemy. They are wrong in wanting to escape from society, and from womanhood itself. Unless they raise their aims, and lower their voices, these extremists may actually block the very social changes they seek.

"Moderate feminists," among which he hopefully included most of his audience, "are the key to whether women can really be equals to men in this society." As role models, he pointed to professional women both famous and unknown:

Syndicated columnist Ann Landers; then free-lancing Gloria Steinem, soon to co-found *Ms.* magazine; Kay Graham, owner of the *Washington Post;* Mary I. Bunting, president of Radcliffe College; a composing room superintendent in Aiken, S.C., a city editor in Yonkers, N.Y., an assistant city editor in Plainfield, N.J.

Take their combined advice, he urged the NFPW members: work, develop backbone, don't accept things as they are, defy tradition, prepare yourselves, establish your own identity.

"If you do these things," he concluded, "not only will you benefit, but so will our over-*manned* profession and our entire society."[3]

Neuharth did not confine his views on women's participation to female audiences. A week after addressing NFPW, he repeated much of his message in Denver at the convention of the International Circulation Managers Association. He told the predominantly male membership:

"[M]ost of our newspaper products still are designed by men editors, even though they are aimed primarily at women. Most of our circulation sales and service setups are designed and run by men, even though they are aimed primarily at women."

To women, Neuharth had held out the challenge of professional achievement. To circulation managers, he added the challenge of economic reality:

"We need more women in our circulation departments," he said, "including more women at the top. Many of you have made a start toward this. . . . That's good . . . but most of you don't have those women help you set your policies and establish your sense of values, and that is where you are wrong.

"For women do have a better sense of values than men. About most social and human values; certainly about the value of a dollar."

Besides making a wake-up call about women, Neuharth predicted that the 25-cent daily newspaper would be a fact of life in the 1970s. He urged circulation managers to act on that. He promised them:

"You will charge for your newspapers what most of your customers think they are worth. . . .

"Your editors and publishers will then be able to afford to produce even better news and editorial products.

"You and your associates in circulation will be able to afford more modern distribution setups.

"Your improved newspapers will be an even bigger bargain for your readers."[4]

## Add Two, but Not Seven

The company had announced in January 1970 that it had agreed to buy another daily in Florida, the *Melbourne Times*. The purchase was delayed temporarily, then approved by the U.S. Justice Department, and finally was made on April 27. The purchase price was $1.4 million.

Gannett's earlier agreement to acquire the seven newspapers of Federated Publications of Battle Creek, Mich., in a $52.2-million merger was cancelled by mutual consent on May 5, 1970.

At some point during the talks with Federated, however, another opportunity arose in Michigan. On July 31, the Gannett Company bought The Times Herald Co. of Port Huron for $5.88 million. Included in the purchase were 58,000 shares of Federated Publications stock, about 4 percent of the total.

The evening and Sunday *Times Herald* had a circulation of nearly 40,000. Gannett paid $1.47 million in cash and the balance in four-year notes at 7 percent. Those would be paid off from the earnings of the subsidiary Times Herald Co., which had grossed $4.5 million in 1969.[5]

These changes brought the number of Gannett dailies to 36.

Ever since Gannett had gone public in October 1967, its executives had tried to educate the financial world about the economic strength of the newspaper business as a whole. When the Financial Analysts Federation convened in Rochester in autumn 1970, Miller and Neuharth shared the rostrum to explain why Gannett stock would attract investors.

Miller projected new records for revenues, net income and earnings per share for 1970 – and for 1971. Rapid growth, he said, had increased total annual revenues from $56,792,000 in 1960, past $90,834,000 in 1965 to $148,987,000 in 1969.

He pointed out that only two of Gannett's 36 dailies had local newspaper competition. He explained local editorial autonomy and the company's standardized business policies.

He predicted more acquisitions and mergers, better management, and improved "production efficiency by every means available."

Then Neuharth saluted managers for "reducing their costs, improving their products and increasing their revenues." He noted that:

For the first eight periods of 1970, operating expenses were up exactly 5 percent, while labor and most major cost items were up 7 percent or more because of inflation; daily circulation was up one-half of 1 percent; advertising revenue was up 2.5 percent, even though advertising linage for the first six months of 1970 was off 2.1 percent; advertising rate adjustments had gone into effect during the year and would be reviewed annually.

In short, record-level earnings would continue into 1971 and beyond.[6]

## Years of Expansion

Miller had promised the analysts continued growth through acquisitions and mergers. The years 1971 and 1972 would see the company grow as never before. There also would be minor adjustments of holdings.

The day after Christmas 1970, Gannett shut down the Cocoa *Tribune*, the property that provided the launching pad for *Today*. The five-day evening paper had faded to 2,900 circulation.[7]

On Jan. 2, 1971, *Editor & Publisher* reported that Paul Miller II had bought the Gannett subsidiary Courier-Gazette Co. for an undisclosed price. The company, which Gannett had bought in 1963, published two weeklies, the *Newark* (N.Y.) *Courier-Gazette* and the *Lake Shore News* of Wolcott, N.Y. The younger Miller had been the *Courier-Gazette's* publisher since 1968. (Miller went on to become president and publisher of Gannett's newspapers in Ithaca and Bridgewater, N.J., and associate publisher in Honolulu, at the *Star-Bulletin,* then owned by Gannett. Miller later became publisher of *The Daily Journal* in Elizabeth, N.J., before moving into the automotive business as owner of a dealership.)

A week later Gannett announced its first "pooling of interests" transaction, acquiring *The Burlington* (Vt.) *Free Press* and the Chambersburg, Pa., *Public Opinion* by exchanging stock with owner J. Warren McClure, their owner.

The two dailies had 45,000 circulation in Vermont, 18,000 in Pennsylvania. For the year ended Sept. 30, 1970, the two McClure properties and related investments had earned $681,000 on gross revenues of $5,317,000.

Gannett acquired the separate corporations with which McClure had operated the two papers for 400,000 shares of Gannett stock. Its market price closed at $33.50 per share on the day the agreement was announced. McClure would continue to operate both newspapers as president of Gannett's new subsidiary, McClure Newspapers, Inc.[8]

McClure, as majority owner of the original corporations, got 240,000 of the 400,000 shares and became Gannett's largest individual stockholder at that time.

In a personal history that McClure wrote for his family, he related the events leading up to the purchase. He knew both Miller and Jack Heselden, since all three worked actively with the Bureau of Advertising (later the Newspaper Advertising Bureau, which merged with the American Newspaper Publishers Association in 1992). In December of 1969, McClure and an associate had been studying the possibility of merging the two newspapers with a larger group. The associate was told to mention to Miller that he and McClure ought to talk about it sometime.

A week before Christmas 1969, Miller contacted McClure. "He asked if he, Jack Heselden and Al Neuharth could stop by Burlington on their flight from Hartford, Conn., to Rochester that afternoon," McClure said.

McClure agreed to meet them at the airport. He did and drove them to the *Free Press,* for a tour of the plant.

"They could not get over our cleanliness and housekeeping," McClure said, "especially in the press room and specifically the appearance of the press."

The Vermont daily was in a new state-of-the-art production building, with one of the earliest offset presses successfully installed for printing newspapers. According to McClure's resume, "The *Free Press* became known nationally for its intense circulation coverage of its area, leading all morning newspapers in the United States in percentage of homes reached."

Two days after the visit, McClure said, "Al Neuharth wrote me, 'You have an operation there of which you can be justly proud and it was an eye opener for us.' "

McClure flew to Rochester for further talks but on Dec. 30, 1969, Purcell called to end the discussions. He told McClure that Heselden didn't believe that Gannett could operate the newspapers more effectively or productively than McClure had been doing, so acquiring them could dilute Gannett's earnings.

"I told Jack Purcell that I understood perfectly," McClure said, "and that we would keep in touch," because Gannett obviously remained interested.

"I could understand exactly what they meant because of our Chambersburg experience [with] innovations there that produced greater sales and profits, creating the funds that would pay off our loans."

A year later, Purcell called again and suggested that he stop by and look at the financial statements of McClure properties.

"I said that would be fine," McClure wrote, "I would be around, but he could not copy any financial statements and could only make notes if he desired regarding Free Press Association, Inc. and McClure Newspapers, Inc. He said he understood perfectly and assured confidentiality."

Negotiations this time quickly led to an agreement to merge. It was concluded after one more round of talks in Rochester. McClure's recall of that event reveals a great deal about him as a businessman and about his future in Gannett.

According to McClure, Miller proposed that the two of them should meet face-to-face to complete the arrangements, and that it could be either in Burlington or Rochester. McClure proposed a single round-trip flight by Gannett to Burlington rather than two round trips for the Gannett plane to pick him up and later return him to Burlington.

He explained:

"I said that I didn't see any point in doubling the cost of transportation. Paul Miller replied, 'That doesn't matter. Why don't you fellows come over here and that way you can meet more of our people.' "

Circled for emphasis in McClure's manuscript is the following paragraph:

"I immediately knew that we had great opportunities for cost savings in Gannett, and I looked upon this as a 'big plus!'

"What I didn't realize is the fact that the larger the operation, the greater the waste. Quite frankly, we [at McClure] couldn't afford waste and all our people knew it.

"At any rate, I must admit I had no idea of some of the expenses that could be reduced; it was all ahead of me to learn."

After the merger, McClure was elected vice president/marketing and a member of the company's six-man operating committee.

Once McClure was aboard, his relationship with Neuharth during his four years in marketing could fairly be described as "arm's length." In his memoir, McClure recalled that during the first Gannett visit to Burlington, his wife, Lois, remarked on Neuharth's "green polyester suit." Such first-impression responses were not uncommon to the distinctive and evolving Neuharth wardrobe.

McClure found Neuharth's corporate lifestyle extravagant and said so. In his memoir, he wrote:

"I ultimately got to be known as 'The strawberry man' when I stated that I felt each strawberry put on Gannett aircraft must cost at least

$2 to $2.50." [9]

After four years as Gannett's vice president/marketing, the 55-year-old McClure retired to Key Largo, Fla., where he became a consultant to newspapers and other businesses in his newly formed McClure Media Marketing Motivation Company. He was a Gannett director until 1985, then became one of two advisory directors. He left the board in 1990.

About the time the McClure merger was being wrapped up, Gannett was looking for a general counsel to help with the legal work of the expanding company. They were referred in late 1970 to a young Wall Street lawyer named Douglas H. McCorkindale.

As McCorkindale explained in a 1990 interview, they asked if he would be interested in joining Gannett. He said no. There followed occasional drinks with Neuharth in New York and an introduction to Purcell. They kept asking until he agreed to visit Rochester.

McCorkindale and his wife, Gloria, made the trip in April 1971. There was still snow on the ground and Mrs. McCorkindale did not like Rochester. They had dinner at the Oak Hill Country Club with Miller, Neuharth, Heselden, Purcell and Quinn.

At one point during dinner, McCorkindale said, his wife lost patience with Neuharth. "Neuharth [had] sat Gloria next to him and while we were eating, he was picking at her food, trying to be cutesy. He used to do that occasionally. . . . She turned to him about halfway through the meal and said, 'Stop acting like a fifth-grader.' Well, the conversation at the dinner table stopped, and Al made some good response and laughed, as he is very good at doing. Dinner continued.

"We went back to the room that night and I said, 'Well, that was fun. We won't have to worry about these folks anymore.' "

But before their scheduled departure next morning, he said, Neuharth called. Gannett wanted to make him an offer. McCorkindale said he thanked Neuharth but replied that he wasn't interested.

Then New York was hit by a railroad strike. That did it.

"I went in to see my partners," he said, "and told them I was going to take a job in Rochester, that I was sick and tired of the damned trains and commuting nonsense. They asked me to leave the room. When I came back in they said they'd keep the partnership open for two years. I could come back on the exact same terms and conditions.

" 'There's no risk then, [I thought] I might as well try this lark in Rochester.' " [10]

McCorkindale joined Gannett as general counsel June 1, 1971. He immediately became involved in acquisitions at what he called "a very busy time." Only a few weeks later, Gannett grew to 45 daily newspapers, numerically the largest group of dailies in the United States.

# Back to Michigan

A year after Gannett and Federated Publications had called off a proposed merger, the seven Federated newspapers joined Gannett on June 30, 1971. The earlier proposed price of $52.2 million had been sweetened – 1,530,666 shares of Gannett stock worth $70 million were issued to shareholders of Federated Publications, Inc., of Battle Creek, Mich.

The seven dailies in four states had aggregate circulation of nearly 300,000. Robert B. Miller and Louis A. Weil Jr., executive chairman and president, respectively, of Federated, joined the Gannett board. Miller – no relation to Paul – was elected senior vice president, Weil vice president/corporate development.

Gannett's newest communities were Lansing and Battle Creek in Michigan, Lafayette and Marion in Indiana, Olympia and Bellingham in Washington, and Boise, Idaho.

The merger's significance was illustrated by the comparative financial standings of the two organizations for 1970. Federated's earnings were $2.67 million on gross revenues of $30 million; Gannett's earnings were $11.45 million on gross revenues of $159 million. [11]

Exactly a month later, the company announced another acquisition, but conversion of a small daily to twice-weekly kept the total of dailies at 45.

The *Sentinel*, a small Michigan daily acquired with the Port Huron *Times Herald*, became a bi-weekly. But in Binghamton, Gannett's subsidiary Binghamton Press Co., Inc., announced its purchase of the 149-year-old *Sun-Bulletin* for $380,000.

Orb Reeder, Binghamton Press Company president, said the company bought the *Sun-Bulletin* "to assure its economic survival and its editorial independence as the morning newspaper of the [New York] Southern Tier." [12]

That summer's "busy time," as McCorkindale described it, did produce a few management changes.

On July 1, 1971, Quinn was named group vice president for news. That September, he launched a weekly publication that would become a monument to the personal energy and professional commitment of Gannett's chief news executive. The influence that the weekly *Bulletin* of M.V. Atwood, Fay Blanchard and Vin Jones had enjoyed with executives of a smaller Gannett Company would be eclipsed by Quinn's *Wire Watch* among his subordinates in the growing news division.

Autonomy, press freedom, professional standards and common sense all were important to him. But paramount would be editors' responsiveness to their readers. He would write (July 29, 1974):

"Permitting the readers to give their views does not forfeit editing responsibility. Indeed, it strengthens it and every Gannett editor and publisher should look today at whether they are treating their readers as one of 'us' or one of 'them.' And make certain 'they' are invited in."

He would frequently expound on the freedoms and restraints of autonomy.

"Autonomy," he would write (Feb. 19, 1973), "in the editorial columns, please. Indeed we hope that all local editorial boards are working harder than ever to be independent, decisive and local."

But there would be *caveats:*

"The corporate News Division (Nov. 24, 1975) keeps hands off local editorial policy, but does maintain a close concern for the responsiveness and responsibility of the editorial page approach."

"In the autonomous opinion in this corner (Feb. 21, 1977), the best contribution a community journalist can make to community activities is to avoid active leadership in them, but that viewpoint does not extend to the office of the publisher. On the contrary, a publisher should be a major figure on the local business and civic fronts and has an obligation to contribute time and effort to their undertakings. That can be done without risk of conflict with the news staff if the ground rules are clearly defined, understood and followed."

When necessary, he would be a stern lecturer (Feb. 23, 1986):

"A couple of disconcerting conversations erupted via last week's Newspaper Division meeting of regional and corporate executives.

"First: Why, a regional exec asked a local editor, did your newspaper put so much local enterprise into a national story of little local impact? Because, the editor reportedly said, we figured it was a natural for a corporate critique. Good grief! Such stupidity.

"Second: A newcomer publisher asked for strategy tips to get his newspaper positioned to win Best of Gannett '86; answer: try doing a good job for your readers.

"Ego journalism has no place in Gannett newsrooms."

The faithful readers of *Wire Watch* would take its contents seriously, even when they were anonymously but painfully direct, because Quinn obviously did. He would write 782 issues of *Wire Watch*, never missing a week in 15 years.

## Adapting to Change

The size of the Federated Publications merger, and the broader transcontinental reach it gave Gannett, also prompted management to reconsider its consistent policy of no management changes after merger.

They decided, in the words of Moe Hickey, "to swap someone from Federated and someone from Gannett to sort of marry the two companies, to get them to know each other's styles." Hickey was the

Gannett candidate. He went to Lansing in September as publisher of the *State Journal.* Federated's man in the swap was Eugene C. Dorsey. He had been publisher in Boise, Idaho, until January 1971, when he had gone to Lansing.

He now moved to the Rochester newspapers, first as general manager. Miller invited Dorsey to the Miller house on the day after Christmas 1971 and told him to write the news story on his own promotion to publisher. He would be the third man, after Frank Gannett and Paul Miller, to hold that title in Rochester.[13]

Miller and Neuharth were in Honolulu on Nov. 1, 1971, to announce another multimillion-dollar purchase. This time, Gannett had bought the six newspapers owned by Honolulu Star-Bulletin, Inc., with 619,918 shares of GCI stock valued at $34 million.

The six papers, with combined circulation of 227,000 daily and 249,000 Sunday, included:

- The evening *Honolulu Star-Bulletin,* and the *Sunday Star-Bulletin and Advertiser,* published jointly with the separately owned morning *Advertiser.*
- The morning *Herald-Dispatch* and evening *Advertiser* of Huntington, W.Va.
- The morning *Dickinson Press* in North Dakota.
- The morning *Pacific Daily News* and evening *Dateline,* both tabloids, on the island of Guam.[14]

The new total of Gannett daily newspapers stood at 51, but for less than three weeks. On Nov. 18, 1971, the company paid $15.5 million in cash and notes for the Fort Myers, Fla., *News-Press,* a morning and Sunday newspaper with circulation of about 45,000.[15]

Aside from Dorsey's promotion to publisher of the Rochester newspapers in December, the other notable event that month was the hiring of a new vice president/production. He was Ronald A. White, an expert on presses and newspaper technology, who came to Gannett from Scripps Howard Newspapers.

In mid-January, however, Miller and Neuharth went to Nashville, Tenn., to announce jointly Gannett's purchase of the 95-year-old evening *Banner.* The company paid James G. Stahlman, the *Banner's* sole owner, $14.1 million in cash and notes, 30 percent down, and two equal yearly installments at 5 1/2-percent interest.

Included in the package was half of the Newspaper Printing Corporation, the vehicle of a joint operating agreement that published both the *Banner* and the independently owned morning and Sunday *Tennessean*.[16]

Gannett's unprecedented two-year spurt of growth ended in June 1972, when it bought the *El Paso* (Texas) *Times*. It paid Dorrance D. Roderick, president and publisher, $27.3 million in Gannett stock for the newspaper and substantial other assets. Miller said the newspaper, circulating 62,000 daily and 90,000 Sunday, accounted for $20 million of the price.

El Paso represented the third joint operating agency arrangement for Gannett in less than a year, after Honolulu and Nashville. The *Times* and Scripps Howard's *Herald-Post* were both produced by El Paso's Newspaper Printing Corporation, with the proceeds divided 60 percent to Gannett, 40 percent to Scripps Howard.[17]

McCorkindale accompanied Miller on most of those trips. "Paul was still clearly the arm-around-the-shoulder, get-the-deal-done person," he said. "Al was not yet the chief executive.

"I can remember the Honolulu acquisition where Paul and Chinn Ho [Honolulu Star-Bulletin, Inc., chairman] were out on a boat fishing, while Stuart Ho [Chinn Ho's son] and I were negotiating the deal. . . .

"Paul was very instrumental in all of the deals through the mid-'70s. He was instrumental in Federated, he was instrumental in McClure, he was instrumental in Nashville with Jimmy Stahlman at the *Banner*. He was instrumental in El Paso, very much so, with Dorrance Roderick, who was his old friend."[18]

All this growth and the activity surrounding Gannett's chairman was not lost on *Time* magazine, which had published several less-than-complimentary pieces on the company in earlier days.

*Time's* issue of May 22, 1972, had a mostly upbeat report on Gannett and Miller, who was characterized in its headline as "The Rochester Acquirer."

Miller, said the magazine, "promised stockholders last week that he would continue his 'aggressive acquisition policy' and feels that the group can be expanded almost indefinitely without spreading its resources too thin. He no longer has to go looking very hard for profitable new properties." [19]

# Chapter 33

# Mixed Emotions

*"Strongly partisan newspapers have declined in number and in influence. Most of the professionals who manage America's successful groups today avoid personal participation in partisan politics. . . . I suggest that what we have lost in color, in individuality, has been offset by a gain in responsibility and in public confidence."*

*Paul Miller*
Finance *magazine, April 1973*

*T*ime magazine said in 1972 that Paul Miller had "come to know someone, along with the newspaper situation generally, in almost every city and town in this country."

"You could call PM the country boy who knew everybody," Louise Miller said of her husband in 1990.

That "country boy" had much to be proud of. He had rubbed shoulders with world leaders such as Mao Tse-tung and Nikita Khrushchev. He had interviewed or had had private conversations in the Oval Office with every U.S. president since Franklin Roosevelt.

His friend Richard Nixon's loss to John Kennedy was particularly galling to Miller, yet when the young president was assassinated in November 1963, the publisher wrote affectionately in his column of Kennedy's "warmth, great wit, buoyancy, a common touch."

Miller also knew and liked Lyndon Johnson, who was far to his left politically. But as an establishmentarian, Miller vigorously defended Johnson against critics of LBJ's Vietnam War policies.

Long-time associates said Miller was the last person to give up on Nixon, even as the Watergate hearings were unraveling Nixon's presidency.

Miller loved to travel and also eagerly sent subordinates on trips that offered new knowledge and experience. He sent Cal Mayne to Europe twice. "If you're going to be editorial page editor," Miller told

Mayne, "you ought to know something about the world. So why don't you go on over and look around, write some stories?"

Mayne recalled the 1967 May Day parade in Warsaw, where he saw for the first time "the vehemence of the communist opposition to what the United States was doing [in Vietnam]. It's a shock when you see a poster of an American soldier bayonetting a Vietnamese child."

As criticism of the war grew, Mayne said, and after the Viet Cong's successful Tet offensive in 1968 dampened U.S. optimism, he proposed to Miller that the *Times-Union* "start looking more independently at the Vietnam War, and the consequences of it for America and the reasons for the deep dissatisfaction that we're beginning to see."

Miller responded, "Well, let's go see Lyndon."

Within a few days, Mayne said, Miller had arranged for a group of editors, "including some doubting Thomases" [one of them Mayne], to meet with the president in the Oval Office.

"We sat there in the evening for about two and a half hours," Mayne said, "listening to Lyndon Johnson, who was just mesmerizing, as only Lyndon could be. Everything from dirty stories that Sam Rayburn had told him to the great patriotic mission of the United States in Vietnam, how we were going to save Southeast Asia and the whole world from the overrun of communism.

"It shut me up for two years, until I started smelling the tear gas at the student rallies. Even then Paul would not bend. Even when Nixon came in."[1]

Those two years ended in May 1970, after U.S. forces made what the White House called a temporary "incursion" into Cambodia in pursuit of North Vietnamese forces. On May 2, the *Times-Union* editorially supported President Nixon's order to enter Cambodia and expressed the hope that the tactic would work.

Seventy-six *Democrat and Chronicle* and *Times-Union* newsroom employees signed a petition to the papers' editorial writers. It read:

"We, the undersigned, implore the editorial writers of Gannett Newspapers, Inc., to take an explicit stand on the U.S. invasion of Cambodia and the resulting chaos on university campuses.

"Writing 'let's hope Nixon's right,' [Sat., May 2] is an inadequate stand for the largest group of newspapers in the U.S.

"We feel it is paramount that you recognize in print the importance of the student strikes in relationship to the national temper, regardless of whether you advocate or abhor them."

Miller was angry. He met with a delegation of the petitioners, but he would only listen. Mayne said he considered their appeal "all a bunch of nonsense." Miller did concede, however, in a memo to the editorial board that he agreed with the third paragraph of the petition.

The editorial board was caught in the middle. On the board were Mayne, associate editor of the *Times-Union;* Desmond Stone, editorial page editor of the *Democrat and Chronicle;* Clifford Carpenter, editorial page columnist of the *D&C* and that paper's former editor; Stuart A. Dunham, executive editor of the Rochester newspapers; and Vin Jones, chairman.

On May 6, soon after Miller had heard the delegation, Jones circulated the usual memo summarizing the day's editorial conference, which briefly outlined the editorial positions that each newspaper would take the following day.

The *Times-Union* planned to salute Nixon's assurance to Congress that the Cambodian offensive would end within seven weeks. It would concede that some military purpose might have been served but contend that "the cost in terms of American division at home, the alienation of youth, the enmity of rising numbers in Congress, the impairment of Nixon's credentials . . . cast grave doubt on whether such short-term military gains are worth the larger loss."

On the margin of his copy of the memo, Miller angrily wrote, "Who says, besides those from whom it would be expected? [Nixon's policy] deserves our support, not this *[New York] Times*-type pseudo-analysis."

To the *Democrat and Chronicle's* proposed remark that Nixon, like Johnson before him, "simply isn't believed and trusted by enough people," Miller scratched in the margin, "How do you know?"

Later that day, Jones dispatched a "Dear Paul" response to Miller:

"The editorial conference discussion notes on Cambodia represent an honest attempt to review the situation and our position.

"We believe that the president is acting in good faith, and presumably on the advice of the military. We think that he underestimated the effect of his decision on the home front and applaud the time limit he has set.

"None of us honestly can support the decision."

Two days later, the editorial board met with representatives of the petitioners. The conference summary specifically challenged the petition's calling the editorial position "an inadequate stand for the largest group of newspapers in the U.S."

Jones responded:

"The petition infers that editorial policy for The Gannett Group is made in Rochester. Each Gannett newspaper determines its own editorial stand. This board acts only for the *Times-Union* and *Democrat and Chronicle*." [2]

# AP or GNS?

On June 26, 1973, Chairman Miller passed to President Neuharth the title of chief executive officer.

The 66-year-old Miller would remain board chairman, chairman of the Executive Committee and head of Gannett's acquisition program, "which has seen the company grow from 19 newspapers in four states to 53 newspapers in 16 states and Guam." [3] Miller also remained AP chairman. That association colored his view of what Gannett News Service should be, particularly in Washington, where Jack Germond had worked since 1962.

Germond had been made bureau chief in 1970, a job that was given to him reluctantly, he said in 1990.

He and Jones, for whom he worked in the '60s, "had some areas of tension, the principal one, in my case, being that I thought I ought to be running the goddamn Washington bureau.

"I was sort of *de facto* running the bureau, with some title like deputy bureau chief," Germond said. When the bureau chief was replaced in 1966, "they brought Bob Lucas down from *The Hartford Times*," Germond said, "to run the Washington bureau and gave me some gimcracky title again and tried to smooth it over. . . . It was a joke. He didn't know anybody in Washington. . . . He'd been an editorial writer and editorial page editor all his life. . . . So Vin and I had a little trouble about this." [4]

Jones recalled in a 1990 interview:

"When we had all this trouble with [the bureau chief] . . . I put Jack Germond in the Washington bureau [in 1962]. That didn't please Miller because Jack Germond is sort of a fat little guy and he's not a Paul Miller type. In fact, Al Neuharth and I went down to look over the bureau one day and Al asked his Detroit friends what they thought of Jack Germond. This Detroit guy said, 'Well, he's a blue-collar bureau chief. I'm a white-collar bureau chief.'

"Anyway, they put in Bob Lucas, who had been in Hartford and [was] a very classy guy, but who knew nothing about running a Washington bureau. He depended heavily on Jack. But they wouldn't stand for Germond. . . . Jack Germond is one hell of a good reporter, and a very good political reporter. . . .

"[He] was very well liked by all of our editors, which was something that Paul didn't seem to appreciate. He knew how to handle stuff that they wanted. The Washington bureau for a bunch of small papers has got to plow all these damned congressmen and senators and that got to be a pretty big job. Germond was very good at that." [5]

"Paul already had this problem of what the role of the bureau should be," Germond recalled, "and if I was going to become the bureau chief, it would be different than if somebody else were."

Back in Rochester, Germond said, he had known and worked for editor and publisher Miller. "I thought Paul was a very good executive in a lot of ways. Generally he promoted very good people. . . . As an editor, I thought, he was closer to too many people in the establishment than maybe he should have been. But at that age, I guess all reporters think that about anybody. One thing I liked about Paul is that although we didn't always agree about things, he was somebody you could talk to on a direct basis and candidly, and he didn't take offense."

In Washington, however, things began to change.

"[Miller] was very AP-oriented, very," Germond said. "The world was changing. More and more papers were having their own bureaus. There were more and more specials developing. But he really wanted a situation where the AP covered all the [major] news, and you covered the local news."

The bureau, Germond said, was "trying to do sort of a split-level job of covering the local delegations in Congress, but also covering some major stories where we could contribute something as good or better than what you could get from other services.

"That was a source of friction because Paul, in particular, wanted us to do nothing but the local business. And my position was [that] good reporters couldn't be kept just doing third-rate stories. If they didn't get a chance to do a good story once in a while, you weren't going to keep them."

By autumn 1973, the names Nixon and Watergate had become permanently entangled, to Miller's acute distress. Germond was writing one column a week in addition to news stories and news analyses. Even Germond admitted that some of the columns on Nixon and Watergate were "pretty stiff." [6]

John Quinn, Germond's boss at that time, recalled:

"We were having real problems between Paul Miller and Jack Germond. It was at the time of Agnew and Nixon, and Miller was very sympathetic to Nixon. Germond was getting pissed all over and [Neuharth] and I were trying to be buffers. I caught more of it than a lot of people realized because I didn't even want to admit to Jack that it was a problem. You could get paralyzed by it." [7]

"About September of '73," Germond said, "John Quinn called me one day and told me that my column was being discontinued because readers were confused about me writing the column and also writing news stories and analysis, which I found absolutely mind-boggling.

"We kept usage studies, and my column was the most used product on the Gannett wire every week. . . .

"I covered politics for Gannett all of the years, in Albany and New

York and Washington, wrote almost nothing but politics. I did not have any trouble. I was not being held down or steered in any direction by the political biases of the management, except in the case of Nixon and Miller."

Although Quinn hadn't wanted to admit to Germond that there was a problem, the bureau chief couldn't help but be aware of it. In a memo challenging Quinn's explanation of why the column was being discontinued, Germond wrote: "You pay me to figure things out and you expect me to believe this?"

"I was monumentally pissed off about the column," Germond explained in 1990, "and the hypocrisy of that whole business. But I was also really troubled about the whole business of dealing with my people and dealing with the corporation. . . . There was an awful lot of memo-writing, and meetings, and channels to go through, and backs to scratch . . . which I found really a pain in the neck."

So in December 1973, Germond joined the *Washington Star*, which was looking for a political columnist. "They were already in bad financial straits," he said, "and I took a hell of a pay cut. It was about a one-third pay cut to go from the job I had with Gannett, which was always well paid, and had bonuses and cradle-to-grave benefits, which we used to call 'the bricks and mortar of the 25-year-club.' I was just fed up with it."[8]

(When the *Washington Star* folded in August 1981, Germond joined the *Baltimore Evening Sun*, since purchased by the Times Mirror Co., with which he is still associated. He also is a regular panel member of the televised public affairs commentary program, The McLaughlin Group).

The frustrations that prompted Germond to quit were not lost on his bosses at corporate.

"It was clear," Quinn explained, "that there were some things that Miller was looking for and Neuharth knew we were going to need in Washington that should be done by a publisher rather than by a bureau chief. A bureau chief was a reporter and not a guy to do corporate lobbying or set up political meetings.

"We were talking about who would be the kind of person who

could bring to Washington both the understanding of the publisher and the understanding of running the news shop without letting one conflict with the other."

The choice was John Curley, who had been president and publisher of the *Courier-News* in Bridgewater, N.J. – formerly in Plainfield – since August 1971. He became chief of GNS's Washington bureau in February 1974.

"Of course," Quinn recalled in 1991, "there were the smart alecks . . . on the business side who said, 'Well, there's one of Quinn's editor friends who couldn't cut it as a publisher, so he's going to go off to Washington.' "[9]

Curley obviously "cut it" to Neuharth and Quinn's satisfaction. Within a year he was given the additional job of general manager of Gannett News Service.

# Chapter 34

# Production Values

*"Quality is the cheapest thing you can deliver because if you don't do it twice, you save one hell of a lot of money. We had an expression, 'Why is there always time to do it over but never enough time to do it right the first time?' That was the sort of approach we kept preaching."*

Ron White
February 1992

Frank Gannett firmly instilled in his company the conviction that technology is opportunity. He avidly sought more efficient and profitable ways to produce newspapers, and many innovations won his early vocal and financial support.

Reporters and photographers had radio transmitters that kept them in contact with their editors back in the office. Air travel had enabled Gannett to cram even more activity into his busy schedule. He quickly embraced the Teletype machine, the tape-fed linotype machine, and advanced photoengraving techniques.

He was primarily responsible for the creation of the Empire State School of Printing in Ithaca in 1922, which was later moved to Rochester with his moral and financial support. There it eventually became the printing and publishing department of Rochester Institute of Technology, which expanded its research and development of new printing processes.

That tradition continued with a new commitment in 1972.

The word "laser" has become so commonplace that few people recognize it as an anagram for the process that created it – Light Amplification by Stimulated Emission of Radiation. Today lasers enable technicians to perform non-invasive surgery, remove cataracts, speed communications, and enhance entertainment. There appear to be no limits to their versatility.

Eleven years after the first continuously operating laser was produced in the United States in 1961, the Gannett Company announced that it had invested $2,514,000 in laser research with newspaper production applications.

In December 1972, the company confirmed that it was supporting Laser Graphic Systems, Inc., of Sudbury, Mass., in the development of "Laser-Graph." A news release described Laser-Graph as "a new non-polluting, non-chemical system to produce printing press plates by laser beams [Laser-Plates] instead of conventional engraving and hot metal."[1]

Gannett's investment gave the company majority interest and control of the process, should it succeed.

Also participating in the Laser-Graph project was Applied Laser Technology, Inc., of Weston, Mass., a privately held firm. Ronald C. Barker, the 33-year-old inventor of the laser platemaking process, was its president.

Dr. Arthur L. Schawlow, professor of physics at Stanford University, and Dr. Brian J. Thompson, director of the Institute of Optics at the University of Rochester, were consultants to the venture.

Within nine months, Gannett's investment had grown to $4,464,000. Paul Miller and Al Neuharth announced successful field tests of the new system by the Elmira *Star-Gazette*. Their joint statement said, "The tests have confirmed the technical feasibility of the Laser-Graph and Laser-Plate system. Marketing and production studies are continuing to determine the extent of commercial feasibility."

Ron White, Gannett's vice president/production, said a pre-production model of the Laser-Plate process would be installed in Elmira for further testing. First production models, he said, might be ready for field installation in 1974.

The new system used laser beams to transmit pasted-up copy images to a metal and plastic plate. The plate with the image then locked directly to a letterpress, which pressed the image directly onto the newsprint. The process was conducted without photo negatives, engraving chemicals or hot metal.

It was demonstrated for the first time on Jan. 22, 1974, in Elmira, after about three months of testing. Barker told the public that his invention "joins the press hardware of today with the publishing technology of tomorrow. Not only is Laser-Graph designed to accept completed page formats from a computer, but it will perform in a manner compatible with existing presses, inks, newsprints and operating personnel."

Meanwhile, Gannett's investment had climbed another $1.2 million, to $5,664,000.[2]

At the end of August 1974, the *Star-Gazette* converted to full-scale production of its 50,000 daily press run on Laser-Plate. Robert L. Collson, publisher, announced the conversion. He said Laser-Plate had produced the entire 40-page edition of the *Star-Gazette* on Aug. 15, and that subsequent daily and Sunday editions had been essentially all Laser-Plate products.

Laser Graphic Systems, Inc., meanwhile, announced that McClatchy Newspapers' *Fresno Bee* had agreed to purchase two new Laser-Graph systems for delivery in January 1975. It was the system's first sale to a non-Gannett newspaper.

By autumn 1974, Gannett's investment had reached $8.3 million.[3]

# Pulling the Plug

After more than a year of mixed results – unpredictable successes and frustrating failures – Neuharth announced on Nov. 28, 1975, that Gannett had stopped funding Laser Graphic Systems, Inc.

"Following lengthy field testing and marketing analysis," Neuharth said, "we have concluded that profitability from the Laser-Graph system is too uncertain and too far off to warrant additional investment."

He said $6 million of Gannett's total investment of $11.5 million had been written off in the first quarter of 1975. The balance would be written down in the fourth quarter after the value of residual Laser-Graph assets had been determined.[4]

In 1992, White discussed the shortcomings of the laser system:

"There were a lot of reasons for it. I didn't recognize them at the time. We didn't have a manufacturing base and this was a manufacturing tool. It was brand-new technology – great technology. And we were working with an inventor. . . . He was smart, but he wasn't a scientist. There's a difference between an inventor and a scientist. The inventor has his ideas. He has the will, the drive to do it. The scientist makes his moves one controlled step at a time. And he writes it all down and he can go back. The inventor can get from here to there, but he's not disciplined. . . .

"We suffered from that in the laser project. We suffered from my inability or my inexperience or both in terms of managing a technological project. I didn't know what it took. . . . We designed that system and we expected that system to be able to make any kind of a plate – make an offset plate, make a relief plate, make a gravure plate. . . . In retrospect, that was an error. At the time, it seemed like the right thing to do. But it was an error. We needed a focus."[5]

## True to Form

The project's failure made it no less a part of the Gannett tradition of supporting new technology. And White's rueful recall of the laser project's failure contrasts sharply with other memories of his tenure as vice president/production.

"I was there during the most exciting time," he said. "The industry was changing technologically and it took a different breed of manager, a different person."

Gannett's strong support of the Empire State School of Printing, he said, made it "one of the finest things that happened to technology in the printing industry."

Offset printing was still in its infancy, he explained, and Gannett was the leader in offset. In fact, he said, it took a giant step in offset when it bought Warren McClure's *Burlington Free Press* in 1971, which had one of the first offset presses ever installed.

"Gannett was early in the technology of what was called inset," White said, "running rolls of paper and then feeding them back through the presses for multicolored offset. . . . Photocomposition was in pieces in Gannett. . . . The pieces were there so . . . what I really had to do was put it all together."

Doug McCorkindale helped develop purchasing programs and research standards for vendors, both in their factories and on their products after delivery, White said.

"Those things just didn't exist in the industry," he said. "Gannett pioneered those, and the production team."[6]

In 1991, Tom Dolan told of building the new plant for the *Courier-News,* moved from Plainfield to Bridgewater, N.J., and equipping it with a new offset press built by the Hoe Company. Hoe went bankrupt a short time later, so the vendor services wisely required by Gannett were not available.

When Dolan left and John Curley succeeded him as publisher in Bridgewater in 1971, the new Hoe press became his problem.

"The press had to be put together piecemeal," Dolan said, "and John did that. I think that's one of the things that really brought him to [Neuharth's] attention. . . .

"Curley knew about as much about that press as the pressmen did. He'd studied it. They couldn't bullshit John on the press."[7]

The press was a "little monster," White said.

"It was an offset press, but it had a water system that was totally dysfunctional. . . . We decided to try to make that press operable and to produce good papers by running what we call dry offset – run it as an offset press but with a relief plate; therefore you didn't need water."

With help from ink and plate manufacturers, White said, "we actually produced a right-reading, plastic relief plate to run on that offset press. And when we put that plate on and started up the test run . . . the ink that we were using popped. You could hear that ink just spitting as we ran it. I wasn't sure if it was going to keep everything together. It was just like machine guns going off. . . .

"I don't know how many newspapers in the country have ever

[run offset without water]. But Gannett did it and we saved a multi-million-dollar investment."[8]

During his time with Gannett, White said, he and his staff sought to give greater responsibility to production employees at individual newspapers.

"When we were satisfied that they'd done their homework, we supported them, even if I disagreed with them. . . . There were a couple of years in there . . . when the numbers that Gannett put on the bottom line were delivered by the production departments," White said. "They took out the costs and when you do that it goes right straight to the bottom line. And there were a couple of years there when they performed magnificently."[9]

White began his newspaper career as a pressman at the *Detroit Free Press*, then went back to school to earn a degree. "It always grated me," he said, "that the production man was considered a second-class citizen. I set a goal in life to raise that status, and we did it for those guys."[10]

White left Gannett in January 1976 to become president of the Graphics Systems Division of Rockwell International.

## Still Growing

The unsuccessful three-year effort to create a productive laser platemaking system did not distract Miller, Neuharth and Jack Purcell from Gannett's big picture – growth. It turned out on occasion, however, that continued growth would require the sale of non-performing assets or less desirable properties.

On Oct. 10, 1973, the Gannett Company sold *The Hartford Times*, which it had tried and failed to make prosperous. Register Publishing Co. of New Haven, Conn., purchased the paper for $7 million.

Lionel Jackson of Register Publishing Co. said, "We are delighted with this opportunity to link the high traditions and journalistic reputation of *The Hartford Times* with the New Haven newspapers."

The purchase agreement guaranteed the pension and other benefit programs for Gannett's former employees in Hartford.[11]

Within a year, Register Publishing sued Gannett on the grounds that it had misstated circulation figures for *The Times*. Gannett countersued. By May 1977, Register Publishing had closed *The Times* and Gannett arranged for Travelers Insurance Co. to guarantee full pension benefits of the former Hartford employees.

Finally, in April 1980, a federal judge in Hartford ordered both companies to pay damages. On Register's claim of $15 million in damages, the judge ordered Gannett to pay $966,000. On Gannett's claim that Register still owed it $1.3 million, the judge awarded $824,000, leaving a net due from Gannett of $142,000.

Neuharth, by then chairman and president, said Gannett considered the verdict fair.

The number of Gannett daily newspapers remained at 51 for more than six months after *The Hartford Times* was sold. Within two weeks in May 1974, however, it returned to 52 and then jumped quickly to 54.

On May 9, Gannett paid $3.14 million in GCI common stock for a newspaper and two radio stations in southeastern Ohio. The paper was *The Marietta Daily Times*, with afternoon circulation of 15,000. The stations were WBRJ-AM in Marietta and WKFI-AM in Wilmington. Newspaper and radio represented consolidated gross revenues for calendar 1973 of $1.86 million.[12]

Two weeks later, Miller and Neuharth were in Salem, Ore., where they paid $15 million in stock for the Statesman-Journal Company's morning and Sunday *Oregon Statesman* and the afternoon *Capital Journal*.

The papers had combined daily circulation of 70,000 and 46,000 on Sunday. The Statesman-Journal Co. had 1973 gross revenues of $6.7 million. Gannett's 1973 gross revenues had been $300 million.[13]

Gannett also began negotiations with Speidel Newspapers Inc. of Reno, Nev., which published 13 daily newspapers in nine states in the West and Midwest. One of their shareholders was Thomson Newspapers, Inc., of Canada, which owned almost 400,000 shares, nearly 7 percent of Speidel's outstanding common stock.

McCorkindale said that representatives of Speidel told Gannett they did not like Thomson's ownership of that much stock and that publisher Roy Thomson was aware of it.

"Thomson wanted to sell the stock," McCorkindale said, "because [it was] an unwelcome stockholder. We agreed with the Speidel people that we would buy [Thomson's Speidel] stock with the hope that someday they would look favorably on us, but we wouldn't buy any more."[14]

Gannett not only acquired a large block of stock in that transaction but also sold a newspaper. On Dec. 30, 1974, it sold to Thomson for $8 million in cash and notes, *The Evening News* of Newburgh, N.Y.[15] On Jan. 6, 1975, it paid Thomson a premium $14 per share, $5.5 million, for his 6.8 percent of Speidel's outstanding common stock.

Before the end of January 1975, Gannett was again down to 50 daily newspapers. On Jan. 31, the 6,000-circulation *Melbourne Evening Times* and the 5,400-circulation Titusville *Star Advocate,* both in Florida's Brevard County, discontinued daily publication. They would be replaced by new all-local weeklies, Gannett announced, in the county where *Today's* 60,000 daily circulation had made it dominant.[16]

Those two small Florida newspapers were replaced in November by two Ohio newspapers barely twice their size. Gannett paid $3.5 million in stock for the Fremont *News-Messenger* and the Port Clinton *News Herald*, with combined circulation of 23,000.[17]

# Keeping Up with the Times

Technology was not the only area of change to which the Gannett Company was sensitive. One of the Frank E. Gannett Newspaper Foundation's most regular contributions was in the form of college scholarships to the youngsters who delivered Gannett papers. What had begun as a work force almost exclusively male had grown over the years to employ an increasing number of girls.

Gannett directors formally acknowledged that on April 5, 1974, by voting to change the Frank Gannett Newspaperboy Scholarships program to the Frank Gannett Newspapercarrier Scholarships, "to more logically fit with today's carrier organizations."

The journalism schools to which some of those scholarship winners would go were wrestling with problems of their own. Gerald M. Sass, Gannett's personnel director, had made a 12,000-mile tour of 12 journalism schools in 1973. The deans of those schools were troubled by their inability to teach young collegians the new technologies being used by the nation's newspapers. They told Sass that their schools could not afford the equipment needed for adequate instruction. The high equipment costs could not be justified in university budgets, they explained, because new technologies so quickly replaced those only recently adopted by the industry.

So in the spring of 1974, Miller announced "Newspaper Technology . . . on the Move, a totally new idea in collegiate journalism education." It was a $275,000 mobile laboratory underwritten by the Gannett Foundation and equipped with the latest electronic technology then in use for newspaper production.

Transported in its own tractor-trailer, the unit could be expanded to a laboratory 17 by 40 feet in which students could write, edit, assemble and print entire newspaper pages in the new "cold type" methods.

The mobile laboratory's three-year mission was to spend two weeks each on selected university campuses. Faculty members at each location would be taught first to use the laboratory's optical character reader, its video display terminals, darkroom camera for page formatting and small offset press. They, in turn, would teach their students the new production methods before the laboratory moved on to the next campus.

In addition to its high initial cost, the vehicle cost $2.50 a mile to operate. But Vin Jones, who was executive vice president of the foundation in 1974, said that the Tech Van, as he called it, "was one of our great successes." [18]

# Changing Places

On June 30, 1975, Moe Hickey came east from Lansing, Mich., to replace Warren McClure as vice president/marketing. Just before the end of the year, Neuharth formalized his *"troika,"* with the creation of three senior vice presidents – Jack Heselden of staff and services, Purcell of finance and business operations, and John Quinn of news and information.

At the same time, Hickey announced the creation of Gannett Newspaper Advertising Service, to be headquartered in New York City. Hickey later recalled:

"Gannett used to be represented by about half a dozen independent people selling their national advertising. So that was a way to get a little presence in New York City. I suggested that we should form our own national representation."

He and his associates also traveled a lot, Hickey said, working on building circulation and sales. "That was the time," he said, "when the alarm went off across America. The publishers were saying, 'We're losing our circulation.' So we beefed up our telemarketing operations." [19]

# Chapter 35

# Big Deals

*"Jack [Purcell] or I, or Jack and I, would get in and work out the final details. . . . Paul was always the arm-around-the-shoulder, 'You should be under the Gannett umbrella, we'll pay you a fair price' person. . . . Some of the little deals along the way, I would just do alone, like New Kensington [Pa.] or Marietta, Ohio."*

Doug McCorkindale
November 1990

The first week of 1976 found the company announcing one of Doug McCorkindale's "little deals." On Jan. 6, it bought the 44,000-circulation *Valley News Dispatch* of New Kensington, Pa., for $8.9 million.

A few weeks later, on Feb. 27, the company completed a deal based on a Paul Miller friendship. Despite Al Neuharth's grudging acquiescence and over McCorkindale's written objections, Gannett paid stock worth $11.85 million to Robert McKinney for his morning and Sunday *New Mexican* in Santa Fe. Its circulation was 18,000 daily, 21,000 Sunday.

"Doug thought it was a bad investment," Neuharth said in 1992, "and I could have blocked it. But Paul wanted it very badly, so I went along."[1]

"Paul wanted to do the deal," McCorkindale recalled in 1990, "but we paid too much and we gave away too many management rights. . . . There's a memo in the file from me to Paul and Al saying, 'We should never agree to this contract. This gives the man too much. He has all those powers.' "[2]

McKinney, who remained as publisher after the sale, would later exercise those powers.

On June 1, Miller and Neuharth announced the purchase of the *Palladium-Item* of Richmond, Ind., for Gannett stock worth $4.72 million. The *Palladium-Item*, daily and Sunday, had circulation of 30,000 in a city of 44,000 population.

The final purchase of the year was completed Dec. 28, 1976, when Gannett bought the *Tucson Citizen*, an afternoon newspaper of 65,000 circulation, and its first in Arizona. It paid 743,243 shares of stock, valued at $30.2 million. William A. Small Jr. remained as president and publisher of the *Citizen* after the sale.

About a week earlier, a few days before Christmas, Gannett's original investment in Speidel stock paid off. On Dec. 20, Miller and Neuharth revealed that Gannett and Speidel Newspapers Inc. of Reno, Nev., would merge. A $141.4 million stock transfer would acquire Speidel and its 13 newspapers in nine states for Gannett.

McCorkindale later explained that Gannett bought the stock from Thomson in 1974 in hopes of winning Speidel's favor. Gannett sold its Newburgh property to Thomson at the same time, McCorkindale said, in anticipation of a merger. Speidel's Poughkeepsie newspaper was too near Newburgh for Gannett to have both, he said. So Gannett sold *The Evening News* on terms presumably more favorable than would have been likely in a sale ordered by the U.S. Justice Department after a merger.[3]

Stockholders of both companies approved the Speidel merger in May. When Gannett announced approval on May 10, it reported that the board also had voted a new annual dividend of $1.20 per share, 20 percent above the previous rate.

"The new annual dividend," a news release boasted, "is up almost 400 percent in four years and will increase the 1977 dividend pay-out by 45 percent from 1976."

The merger and the closing of pending acquisition agreements would bring Gannett to 73 daily newspapers in 28 states and the island of Guam, numerically the largest and geographically the most widespread newspaper group in the nation.[4]

Rollan D. Melton, Speidel president and chief executive, was elected to the Gannett board and named senior vice president of a new newspaper region, Gannett West, to be based in Reno. Speidel vice president Robert B. Whittington was named president of Gannett's new Speidel division.

Besides Reno, new Gannett communities from Speidel included Salinas, Stockton and Visalia, Calif.; Fort Collins, Colo.; Iowa City, Iowa; Little Falls and St. Cloud, Minn.; Fremont, Neb.; Poughkeepsie, N.Y.; Chillicothe, Ohio; and Sioux Falls, S.D.

Only a week after the Speidel merger, Gannett closed an off-again, on-again sale nearly three years in the making, buying two dailies and a Sunday newspaper in Springfield, Mo., and a morning and Sunday newspaper in Muskogee, Okla.

Springfield Newspapers Inc. and Oklahoma Press Publishing Company had tentatively agreed in August 1973 to sell the newspapers, three radio stations and half interest in a television station to Gannett for $33.4 million but the agreement was called off more than a year later because stock prices were down.

The final agreement in May 1977 brought Gannett Springfield's 30,000 morning *News,* its 47,000 evening *Leader and Press,* and its 81,000 Sunday *News and Leader.* Muskogee's contributions were the morning and Sunday *Phoenix and Times-Democrat,* with 23,000 circulation, plus the broadcasting properties. Total value of the transaction was $42 million.[5]

The other pending acquisition agreement mentioned with the Speidel merger closed as promised on June 16. In that transaction, Gannett paid $61 million in cash for three daily newspapers and two radio stations in Louisiana. In Shreveport, it acquired the morning (90,000) and Sunday *Times* (125,000); in Monroe, the morning (37,000) and Sunday *World* (51,000) and afternoon *News-Star* (13,500).[6]

On Dec. 19, 1977, Neuharth appeared in the newsroom of *The Daily News* in the Virgin Islands. He announced that Ariel Melchior Sr., founder and owner, had agreed to sell the 10,000-circulation daily in St. Thomas to Gannett. The sale was completed Feb. 15, 1978, for $3.5 million.

Adding *The Daily News* gave Gannett 74 daily newspapers with circulation of nearly 3 million and, in the words of the Dec. 19 news release, "a reach from this easternmost U.S. territory in the Atlantic to the westernmost U.S. territory of Guam in the Pacific."

# New Tasks, Familiar Faces

Even before all the pending acquisitions of spring 1977 had been completed, it was clear that the growth that came with the Speidel merger required clearer lines of management responsibility.

Besides the regional division, headed by Speidel's Melton, Gannett created three more regional divisions in May – Gannett East, Gannett South, Gannett Central – to oversee operations and allow for further growth.

Melton was joined by three regional vice presidents:
• Tom Dolan, vice president/Gannett East.
• Phil Gialanella, vice president/Gannett South, also to remain publisher of Honolulu's *Star-Bulletin*.
• Moe Hickey, vice president/Gannett Central, who would retain his vice president/marketing duties.

The four regions embraced all Gannett locations except the two largest, the Rochester Newspapers and Westchester-Rockland Newspapers. Those would continue to report directly to corporate, which had recently moved into new headquarters in Rochester's Lincoln Tower.

Gannett East and Gannett Central comprised 14 newspapers with combined circulation of 612,000 in New Jersey, New York, Pennsylvania and Vermont, under Dolan; and 17 papers with combined circulation of 544,000 in Illinois, Indiana, Michigan, Missouri, Ohio and West Virginia, under Hickey.

Melton's Gannett West was made up of 18 daily newspapers with combined circulation of 559,000 scattered across 11 states – California, Colorado, Idaho, Iowa, Minnesota, Nebraska, Nevada, New Mexico, Oregon, South Dakota and Washington.

Gialanella's region had only 13 newspapers, with combined circulation of 710,000, but its geography gave new meaning to the word "South." It embraced Arizona, Florida, Guam, Hawaii, the Virgin Islands, Louisiana, Oklahoma, Tennessee and Texas. One common denominator for five of the properties, including Honolulu where

Gialanella was publisher, was that they were all the joint agency operations in which Gannett was then involved.

Vince Spezzano was named assistant vice president/Gannett South, to help Gialanella deal with the vast territory. Spezzano also remained publisher of *Today* in Cocoa, Fla.

The regional vice presidents became members of the corporate Operating Committee, headed by Al Neuharth and also including Chairman Paul Miller, Jack Heselden, John Quinn and Doug McCorkindale.

McCorkindale had become chief financial officer in March, when Jack Purcell left Gannett to join the Columbia Broadcasting System. He remembers:

"Neuharth called me in and said Purcell was leaving. I expressed the surprise that I was supposed to express and he said, 'Would you like to be the chief financial officer?'

"And I said, 'Well, I could do some of that, but I'm not an accountant.'

"He said, 'That's okay, I don't want to deal with accountants, I want to deal with you.'

"So that's how I became the chief financial officer." [7]

In *Confessions of an S.O.B.*, Neuharth dubbed McCorkindale "Gannett's top bean counter," calling him "the best in the business" but a man who "busies himself being a pest about peanuts."

During a 1992 interview, Neuharth observed that McCorkindale lacked the background to understand news and news people, but then he added, "He's the best financial guy I know, in our business or outside, smart as hell." [8]

# Celebrations

Neuharth's pioneering calls on women journalists to challenge the establishment for executive positions and profession-wide assignments was honored in October 1977.

At a convention ceremony in Honolulu, he became the first man to receive a Headliner Award, the highest honor Women In Communications, Inc., bestows on its members.

Neuharth was one of the first males among WICI's more than 8,000 members, having joined in 1972. He was honored for "encouraging women to seek high positions in the communications industry" and for promoting "many women into management at Gannett newspapers."[9]

Three days later, Miller and Neuharth issued a joint letter to shareholders boasting a quarterly financial pattern on which Neuharth would insist throughout his tenure as president and then chairman.

They reported that Gannett had completed its first 10 years as a public company by announcing the 40th consecutive quarter of record revenues and earnings.

That financial momentum, fueled by Gannett's continued growth through acquisition, increased net income for the third quarter to $16.1 million, compared with $13.5 million for the same period in 1976. Net income for the first nine months of 1977 was $47.3 million, well ahead of 1976's $40.4 million for the year-earlier period.

In their letter to shareholders, Miller and Neuharth pointed to these signs of progress as a public corporation:

- Growth from a regional company of 28 newspapers in five states to a nationwide company of 73 daily newspapers.
- Annual revenue increases from $160 million to more than $500 million.
- Gains in earnings per share from 55 cents in 1966 to $2.22 in 1976.
- Regular increases in dividends from 22 cents per share in 1966 to $1.20 in 1976.

They closed by reminding shareholders that Gannett newspapers had won more than 2,000 prizes for journalistic excellence, including two Pulitzer Prizes.

"We are confident," they concluded, "that Gannett's future is as bright as its past."[10]

Just before the year's end, the structure that had Rochester and Westchester-Rockland newspapers outside the regional loop was tidied up. On Dec. 22, Neuharth, in a solo statement as president and chief executive officer, announced the creation of Gannett Special Divisions to embrace Rochester's *Democrat and Chronicle* and *Times-Union*, the nine Westchester-Rockland newspapers and the international research activities of Louis Harris and Associates Inc.

The Harris organization, which had played a major role in *Today's* success, had become part of Gannett in April 1975, when the company paid Donaldson, Lufkin and Jenrette Inc. $4.47 million for the subsidiary.

Gene Dorsey, publisher at Rochester, was named the new division's vice president and given a 10th seat on the growing Operating Committee.

Gannett Chairman Miller remained one of the 10 Operating Committee members, but the power structure now clearly bore the stamp of Neuharth.

## Tug of War

As Miller had approached his 67th birthday in 1973, he found a long-standing company policy increasingly unattractive. The Gannett board late in 1957 had approved a plan requiring executives to retire no later than their 70th birthdays.

"Because the success of the organization depends so much upon proper training and succession," it resolved then, "no executive should be permitted to retain his job beyond age 70." The policy set up three categories:

- An executive who should be encouraged to remain beyond 65.
- An executive who, for whatever reason, should not be encouraged to remain beyond 65.
- An executive who, though encouraged, does not desire to defer his retirement beyond 65.

Until an executive retired, of course, he continued to draw full salary. After retirement, however, in whichever of the three categories, he continued as a consultant to age 70, for which he was paid on this schedule:

Full salary to age 66; 87.5 percent to age 67; 75 percent to age 68; 62.5 percent to age 69; and 50 percent to age 70.[11]

Then Gannett president, Miller turned 51 a month after the board adopted the plan in 1957. However good he might have thought the idea then, 16 years later he had found that he didn't like it.

Neuharth wrote in *Confessions of an S.O.B.* that he considered leaving Gannett in 1973 because of Miller's reluctance to turn over the reins as promised. Neuharth declared his intent to James Webb, former head of the National Aeronautics and Space Administration, because Webb, a company director, was chairman of its management succession committee. Webb suggested that Miller remain chairman but relinquish the title of chief executive officer to Neuharth. Neuharth agreed.

According to Neuharth, Webb urged Miller to do so voluntarily or the board would be forced to vote the action. Miller acquiesced, Neuharth wrote, on the understanding that he could remain chairman for another five years.

When the board added chief executive officer to his title of president in June 1973, Neuharth was 48 years old. Chairman Miller was 66.

Cal Mayne recalled that during the time of uncertainty about Miller's retirement, the chairman had remarked, "If you want to get me out of here – become a $300 million company."[12]

Gannett reached gross revenues of $300 million in 1973.

Wes Gallagher, a friend and longtime AP associate of Miller, became a Gannett director in October 1976, after his retirement as general manager of The Associated Press. Gallagher later became chairman of the management continuity committee and got to know all the players. He was one of several admirers of Miller who expressed regret at his reluctance to retire.

"Paul could not bring himself to let go," Gallagher said. "The board all liked Paul, they really loved him. But they felt the time had come, because of the changing circumstances in the business and the fact that Al was sitting there and he could go anywhere and get another job. . . . They had to make the change. They did it reluctantly."[13]

Miller celebrated his 71st birthday in December of 1977. That year had seen the Speidel merger, an omen of the pattern of acquisitions to come. Personal relationships no longer carried the weight in negotiating for newspaper groups that they had done with individual owners who knew and trusted Paul Miller.

Mutual friendships and handshakes between individuals were being replaced by brokerage reports, legal briefs and boardroom presentations.

# Chapter 36

# Years of Change

*"Paul Miller, 71, architect of a newspaper acquisition drive without parallel in U.S. publishing, . . . will retire as chairman of the board of Gannett Co., Inc., and as a Gannett employee on Dec. 31 [but] remain active as a director, as chairman of the Executive Committee — and in mergers and acquisitions."*

*Gannett News Release*
*Sept. 11, 1978*

The year 1978 was one of the most momentous in Gannett Company history, certainly in the 31-year-era of Paul Miller. It began with the company's paying its highest price ever for a single newspaper company. That was quickly eclipsed in midyear by a merger agreement that transformed Gannett into a multi-media colossus. And the year's end marked Miller's surrender to time. He relinquished what remained of his power to control the media giant he had done so much to create.

Gannett paid $60 million to the DuPont Co. for *The Morning News, Evening Journal* and *Sunday News Journal* of Wilmington, Del. They were Delaware's largest statewide newspapers, circulating 49,000 newspapers every morning, 81,000 evenings and 120,000 Sundays. The company had been owned for years by Christiana Securities, a holding company for the du Pont family's interests in the giant chemical company and related assets.

Changing federal laws prompted Christiana Securities and the DuPont Co. to merge, an intention they announced in 1972. The News-Journal Co., as it was known then, and other family assets would become property of the company itself. DuPont Co. executives decided to concentrate on the business they knew and sell the newspapers.

While the affluent family's holding company had owned *The*

*Morning News* and *Evening Journal,* the bottom line was not a major concern. Annual profit margins routinely were under 15 percent and occasionally fell to single-digit levels. The newspaper company was appraised in 1972, soon after merger plans were announced, at $24.3 million.

DuPont Co. executives recognized that profitability would have to be improved if the newspapers were to attract responsible buyers and command a respectable price. They assigned a company executive to oversee the daily management of the newspapers. Inevitably, that oversight intruded on the traditional prerogatives of editors.

In a management-editors confrontation, two editors were fired and two others resigned. The result, unanticipated by the DuPont Co., was a public outcry that threatened the salability of the papers. As *The New York Times* described the situation:

"The two papers have been in turmoil recently over the classic newspaper question of who controls the gathering and presentation of news, editors or a board of directors composed mostly of businessmen."[1]

The company brought in Norman Isaacs, an associate dean of Columbia University's Graduate School of Journalism and veteran editor, as president and publisher in January 1975. John Hughes, editor of the *Christian Science Monitor,* and Andrew Fisher, a retired *New York Times* vice president, were added to the board of The News-Journal Co.

The new management started the *Sunday News Journal* in September 1975, using existing staff. By 1977, the financial numbers were attractive enough to allow the DuPont Co. to proceed. It invited $200,000 no-interest deposits from interested parties. A tour of the plant and the opportunity to bid for the newspapers required an additional deposit of $200,000.

Gannett acquired the Wilmington papers Jan. 30, 1978, by outbidding, in order, Hearst Newspapers, the Washington Post Co., Horvitz newspapers of Mansfield, Ohio, and Associated Newspaper Group Ltd. of London. Both the Hearst and Washington Post bids were within $5 million of Gannett's $60-million price, prompting Neuharth mischievously to give Washington Post Co. owner Kay Graham the impression her bid had won.

Before the successful bidder was announced, sentiment among DuPont executives and newspaper employees had been tilted toward Graham's Washington Post. Brian Donnelly, the first Gannett publisher in Wilmington, explained that Irving Shapiro, DuPont Co. chairman, and Andrew Fisher, the publisher, had both been promised seats on the Washington Post Co.'s board of directors if Graham's bid should win. In the Wilmington newsroom, staffers saw more allure in the post-Watergate prestige and national political influence of the *Post* than in the patchwork of autonomous newspapers that constituted Gannett.

Neuharth recalled his first day at the Wilmington newspapers. "I knew full well," he said, "that there was hostility in that newsroom in Wilmington when we came in. . . . But there wasn't as much hostility as there was from Kay Graham herself." [2]

Among those in that first Gannett party to visit the newspaper on Feb. 3 were Paul Miller, Neuharth, Tom Dolan, head of Gannett East, and Donnelly, publisher of Binghamton's *Press* and *Sun-Bulletin*.

By the time of the sale, Isaacs had left the newspapers to return to Columbia University. Fisher had become president and publisher in July 1976. Fisher declined Gannett's invitation to remain as publisher and retired to Florida.

Donnelly was Fisher's replacement. He would frequently tell later, for a laugh at his own expense, of his introduction in the Wilmington newsroom and what he called "my monumental gaffe.

"They asked me to speak," Donnelly recalled. "I said . . . 'I [am] delighted to be here at this newsroom. I'm sure that the staffs of these two newspapers compete just as vigorously as the two that I just left in Binghamton.' And somebody said, 'Didn't anybody tell you that we have a common news staff?' And I had to say, no, that was one part they hadn't told me." [3]

After winning the bidding contest in Wilmington, Gannett bought *The Coffeyville Journal,* a daily of less than 10,000 circulation in Kansas, for $3.75 million. The deal was closed on March 31, 1978.

Acquiring a small Kansas paper may have seemed insignificant when compared to the deal in Delaware, but both would pale in comparison to the mega-deal about to be made.

## Merger Vows

On May 7, 1978, following special board meetings in Rochester, N.Y., and Phoenix, Ariz., Gannett Company, Inc., and Combined Communications Corporation of Phoenix agreed to merge with an exchange of stock valued at $370 million.

The announcement was made jointly by Miller and Neuharth, and their Combined Communications counterparts, John J. Louis Jr., chairman, and Karl Eller, president and chief executive.

Combined Communications owned two metropolitan newspapers, seven television stations, 12 radio stations, and outdoor advertising companies in eight U.S. states and Canada.

The complexity of the merger left some details to be hammered out by the two parties, and the involvement of broadcasting licenses required governmental approval. The parties promised to be quick about all of that.

Neuharth said he would establish an Office of the Chief Executive after the merger, which Eller would join. "In that capacity," he said, "Karl Eller will share responsibility for the overall top management of the merged companies."

The company announcement of the planned merger compared the financial muscle of the respective partners. Gannett had revenues of $558 million and net earnings of $69.4 million for 1977. Combined Communications' revenues totaled $228 million and its net earnings $20.6 million for the same year.[4]

# End of a Second Era

Miller announced on Sept. 11, 1978, that he would yield his chairmanship of Gannett to Neuharth on Dec. 31. He said, however, that he would retain his chairmanship of the Executive Committee of the board and participate in future mergers and acquisitions.

A year earlier, he had resigned as AP chairman, a post he'd held for 14 years. He remained an AP director *ex officio*.

Miller had joined the company more than 31 years earlier as Frank Gannett's executive assistant and logical successor. Gannett and Frank Tripp chose him for his experience as a writer, editor and executive with the AP, his broad personal contacts in the newspaper business and his zest for work.

He would demonstrate the wisdom of their choice by guiding an acquisition program unmatched in the industry. His personal imprint after 31 years with the company would be as distinctive as it was consistent with the mark left by Gannett over half a century.

In the decade before he succeeded Gannett as company president, Miller became editor, and then editor and publisher of Rochester's *Times-Union*, positions held previously only by Gannett. Miller's consuming interest in writing and editing, combined with his political conservatism, made that a fitting progression.

He shared Gannett's vision of newspapers soundly run, editorially autonomous and dedicated to community service. A magazine profile in 1973 remarked his preference for "our newspapers in Camden and at Pensacola, the two of them, [over] one of three or even two newspapers in a city many times their combined size."

Miller also told that writer, "There are 34 states in which we are *not* now doing business. There is no legal reason why we could not be in any number of states with any number of newspapers."[5]

His reappearance at AP as the first former employee to be elected a director, and later AP president, put him in contact with a host of publishers, by most of whom he quickly became both admired and trusted. Such respectful friendships would remove obstacles to many later acquisitions by Gannett.

When Miller became company president in 1957, there were 20 Gannett newspapers in three states. By the time Gannett went public in 1967, there were 28 newspapers in five states. During the four-year period from 1968 through 1971, he oversaw the acquisition of 21 newspapers, which, Gannett pointed out then, made it "the largest numerically and the most widespread by far of all U.S. newspaper groups." It retained that distinction at his retirement in 1978, with 77 newspapers across the country and beyond to the U.S. Virgin Islands, Hawaii and Guam.

Miller's professional stature, as both head of Gannett and Mr. AP, was forged by a travel schedule that he said kept him "away half the time" but on which he thrived. He tirelessly courted new prospects and explained Gannett to analysts and investors. He happily embarked on exhausting foreign trips, during which he would write scores of articles for the *Times-Union* and other Gannett papers. He eagerly expounded at every opportunity, to students, journalists and the general public, his absolute faith in the importance and future of newspapers.

Although he presided over a prosperous and expanding business, his abiding interest was the news. "A newspaper isn't worth the ink used to print it," he said in 1950, "if it doesn't stand for something." In 1964, he enviously observed, "Among the luckiest men and women in the world of tomorrow will be those qualified to hold down challenging jobs in journalism."

He is affectionately remembered, by friends and associates alike, for the credo he applied to all situations, "Do the right thing."

Vin Jones once said of Miller: "It takes 61 lines of fine print and abbreviations in *Who's Who* to list all of Paul's past and present honors and responsibilities."[6]

Paul and Louise Miller established an endowment fund in 1988 at Oklahoma State University's School of Journalism and Broadcasting. Quinn delivered the first Paul Miller Journalism Lecture on March 18, 1988.

At OSU that March day in 1988, Quinn also alluded to *Who's Who*.

Miller, he told his audience, is identified in that biographical entry "simply and eloquently as 'newspaperman.' "[7]

(Miller suffered a stroke in early 1980, just a year after his retirement, and lost his power of speech. He died in August 1991 in Palm Beach, Fla., at the age of 84.)

## 'Warm, Gracious and Generous'

Miller was 72 when he passed his final symbol of power to Neuharth. Three days later, the finality of the change was accentuated. Caroline Werner Gannett, the last direct family link to the company that Miller had joined 31 years earlier, died at 84, after a lingering illness.

The 54-year-old Neuharth, in one of his first statements as chairman, president and chief executive officer, lauded Mrs. Gannett:

"She was a major force alongside Frank Gannett in the early days of building this company. She served her community, state and nation in so many ways. Her great philanthropy will enrich many lives in the future."

Speaking for the Gannett Foundation, of which he remained chairman, Miller reverted to the nickname by which close friends had known Mrs. Gannett:

"Kyrie Gannett was a warm, gracious, generous woman who helped her husband establish the great philanthropy of the foundation that bears his name. Then, for more than two decades after his death, she was deeply interested in guiding its contributions to Gannett communities and to American journalism education. But her most generous contribution was her humanity and her deep, abiding interest in the many people and institutions that received her dedication and devotion."[8]

Another of the offices Miller relinquished in the transfer of power was that of Gannett News Service president. On Jan. 4, Neuharth announced that Quinn, senior vice president/news, would add the GNS presidency to his portfolio. John Curley succeeded Quinn as vice president of GNS.

Late in February, Gannett's shareholders approved the merger with Combined Communications, a vote required by the New York Stock Exchange because of the merger's size and complexity. On June 7, 1979, the FCC approved transfer of Combined's broadcast licenses to Gannett. That day, Neuharth and Eller issued the first joint statement for the new and more diversified Gannett Co.:

"Today Gannett's World of Different Newspapers becomes a World of Different Voices – each strong, free and independent. . . .

"The merged company will have far greater resources with which to serve the public and greater management talent to develop new opportunities in the entire spectrum of communications."[9]

Gannett's newspaper strength was significantly enhanced with the addition of *The Cincinnati Enquirer,* 190,000 daily and 284,000 Sunday, and the *Oakland* (Calif.) *Tribune,* 177,000 daily and 205,000 Sunday.

It had added VHF television stations in Atlanta, Denver, Little Rock, Oklahoma City and Phoenix; UHF stations in Fort Wayne, Ind., and Louisville, Ky.; and AM and FM radio stations in Chicago, Cleveland, Detroit, Los Angeles and San Diego. (The FCC limit of five VHF television stations to one company led to the sale of WHEC-TV in Rochester. That station was sold June 7 to Broadcast Enterprises Network Inc., a black-controlled corporation, for $27 million.)

Especially noteworthy was the new diversity. In 1979, the company whose founder, as a young editor, had applauded the lack of unsightly billboards in Elmira, N.Y., was now in the outdoor advertising business. Gannett now owned outdoor companies in Arizona, California, Colorado, Illinois, Michigan, Missouri and Texas, and in the Canadian cities of Hamilton, Montreal, Toronto, Ottawa, Quebec and Winnipeg.

Eller continued as president and chief executive of Combined Communications, which was now a Gannett subsidiary whose headquarters would remain in Phoenix.

As he had promised when the merger was announced, Neuharth established a five-member Office of the Chief Executive, which was approved by the Gannett board on June 26, 1979. It comprised:

- Neuharth, chairman, president and CEO of Gannett.
- Eller, president and CEO of Combined Communications.
- Jack Heselden, senior vice president and chief of newspaper operations.
- Doug McCorkindale, senior vice president and chief financial officer.
- Quinn, senior vice president and chief news executive.

Neuharth said, "Eller will have full responsibility for all non-newspaper operations and Heselden for all newspaper operations." He also announced that Eller was to be chairman of a new Gannett Development Committee, which would include Neuharth, McCorkindale and retired chairman Miller.

"This group," Neuharth said, "will explore acquisitions, mergers and new ventures in the entire communications field so that we can continue the aggressive expansion in total media which Karl Eller developed at Combined and retain Paul Miller's unique insight and experience in the newspaper field."

The busy reorganizational meeting also promoted to president the vice presidents of all Gannett regions, which had been redefined.

Gannett corporate headquarters would remain in their expanded offices at Rochester, Neuharth said, as had been recommended by an executive committee in 1976. The company also maintained corporate offices in Washington, where Gannett News Service was based, and in New York City with the central offices of Gannett Newspaper Advertising Sales.

Neuharth announced, however, that a new study committee had been formed "to update the review of possible sites and facilities and to make recommendations for the future."[10]

## Short Honeymoon

By all accounts, Eller quickly became disenchanted with his and Combined Communications' subordinate role. McCorkindale recalled his impressions of Eller during and after the merger negotiations.

Eller was dissatisfied, he explained, because although he became a part of the Office of the Chief Executive, as Neuharth had promised, his title tied him to the Combined Communications subsidiary. He was not a "top" Gannett executive.

McCorkindale recalled the 1978 meetings in Atlanta during which the merger was finally arranged.

"I was in the room and Karl was very up front. . . . He wanted it to be understood that he would become president of the Gannett Company. Al made it clear that that was certainly a possibility, but he never committed himself. . . . You've got to listen to what [Al's] saying. He's absolutely masterful at saying something that leaves an impression but that does not commit him. Eller heard what he wanted to hear, not what Al was telling him." [11]

Gene Dorsey shares McCorkindale's view. "I think Karl somehow felt that he could just parlay this [merger] into his becoming the CEO of the Gannett Company," Dorsey said in 1990. "But then I am sure that Louis Weil and Bob Miller [of Federated] thought the same thing. And Warren McClure thought the same thing. Rollie Melton [of Speidel] thought the same thing.

"They all came in with the expectation that they would have a very prominent role, that perhaps one of them would be president and Al would be chairman.

"I wouldn't be surprised if Al [might have said] some things. He was always very careful, though, about what he said. And if you would go back and say, 'Yes, but you told me this,' he could define it in such a way that it would have been quite clear:

" 'I made no commitment. Sure, I raised the possibility, and there was that possibility.' He was very, very cunning about that kind of thing." [12]

By fall of 1979, Eller's frustrations reached the point that he and John Louis flew to Florida to enlist Miller's help against Neuharth. Their visit was ill-timed.

Miller was suffering from an extremely painful case of the shingles and was trying with little success to rest at their home in Palm Beach,

Louise Miller said. "John Louis called here and asked if PM could be seen. I said, 'Yes, John, he can be seen, but he just isn't very well.'

"So he and Karl came here and said that they just had to get rid of Neuharth, that PM just had to do it, that there was no sense in somebody being with the company who was such a tyrant and acting in his style – that he just wasn't good for the company. . . .

"He was bothered an awful lot by this kind of thing, where he had to be the person to fix it up. But he knew there wasn't anything he could do," she said.[13]

In *Confessions of an S.O.B.*, Neuharth wrote about Eller's open challenge to him. Eller telephoned to say that he was resigning his management positions because of serious differences between them "over philosophy, policy and style." He told Neuharth that he planned to campaign with Gannett directors to be elected as Neuharth's replacement.

Neuharth startled Eller by offering him a Gannett corporate plane to use to visit members of the board. In his book, Neuharth stated that Eller could count on the votes of Louis and Thomas A. Reynolds Jr., who had come to Gannett from the board of Combined Communications; that he might have been supported by Warren McClure, who, Neuharth readily conceded, did not regard him very warmly.

Even Miller's vote on Eller was uncertain. Neuharth said Wes Gallagher, chairman of Gannett's management continuity committee, talked to his old friend Miller. He returned to assure Neuharth that Miller would not vote against him but would abstain, so long as Neuharth didn't do anything else before the vote to make him unhappy.

At the directors' meeting in December, Eller's name was never placed in nomination. Neuharth then playfully wanted to offer a resolution proposing that the board replace him with Eller. Gallagher refused to go along, Neuharth said.

Gallagher elaborated on that in a 1990 interview:

"I said, 'No, [Eller's] told a lot of people, Wall Street and us, he's going to take over the company, and he has to explain his failure to do this. He just goes out of here with nothing.' And that's the way it turned out." [14]

A few months later, Eller resigned as a Gannett Company director.

## Change Partners

Gannett had been publishing the afternoon *Nashville Banner* in Tennessee since January 1972, when it bought the paper for $14.1 million. The competing *Banner* and morning and Sunday *Tennessean* were produced in Nashville under a joint operating agreement.

Antitrust laws prohibited single ownership of both newspapers, but they did not bar exchanging one for the other.

On July 5, 1979, Neuharth announced in Nashville that Gannett had bought *The Tennessean,* with circulation of 130,000 daily and 240,000 Sunday, for $50 million.

To make that possible, it had sold the 85,000-circulation *Banner* to three of its executives for $25 million, $10.9 million above what it paid for the paper in 1972.

Thus Gannett acquired not only the dominant newspaper in the Nashville area but also a nationally known journalist in John Seigenthaler, who was named president, publisher and editor of *The Tennessean*.

Seigenthaler had joined *The Tennessean* in 1949, at the age of 22. He left briefly in 1960 to become administrative assistant to Robert F. Kennedy, U.S. attorney general. In May 1961, after civil rights "Freedom Riders" were beaten by white mobs in Montgomery, Ala., he was sent to Alabama as President John F. Kennedy's personal representative. Gov. John Patterson assured Seigenthaler that the state would "fully protect everyone in Alabama" and promised safe conduct for student demonstrators on their way to Montgomery.

Seigenthaler passed those assurances on to President Kennedy, then went to Montgomery himself. There an armed mob attacked the students. Seigenthaler sought to rescue a young woman and was beaten unconscious in the street. He was hospitalized briefly for treatment of concussion.

He was part of a group that accompanied Robert Kennedy on a month-long world tour in February 1962. He resigned from the Justice Department two months later to rejoin *The Tennessean*, this time as editor.

In announcing the purchase of *The Tennessean*, Neuharth described Seigenthaler as "one of journalism's most able executives and one of its most respected and independent spokesmen. In keeping with Gannett's local autonomy," Neuharth said, "he will have full responsibility for all news and editorial matters."

Seigenthaler responded in his published statement, "I am elated by the assurances from Al Neuharth that the independent news and editorial tradition of this newspaper will continue in the years ahead." [15]

Those assurances were especially important to Seigenthaler. About two years earlier, as a panelist at the Honolulu convention of the American Society of Newspaper Editors, he had opposed group ownership of newspapers. The guest invited to open remarks in the debate was the president and chief executive officer of the menacing Gannett Company.

Neuharth told the audience that he had eagerly accepted the invitation to speak on the subject, "The Growing Concentration of Newspaper Ownership – Good or Bad?" He said he had asked, "Which side of the question do you want me to take?"

Instead, he said, "I shall not try to make a case for either chain ownership or individual ownership of newspapers."

After reciting the statistics of 1977 on group ownership vs. individual ownership, Neuharth said, "Now a bit of opinion. Some of the very worst newspapers published in America today are group-owned. So are many of the very best. Many individually owned newspapers are setting the highest standards in this business. Some of them are a disgrace to the profession of journalism."

He cited examples of group representation in professional awards, training, leadership and participation. He concluded:

"In my opinion, (1) big group ownership of newspapers is not nearly as great a threat to this country as big government meddling with the First Amendment, and (2) monopoly should not be as great a concern to the editors of this country as monotony." The latter was a variation on the philosophy of newspaper publisher Barry Bingham Sr. of Louisville, frequently quoted by Miller: "Monopoly is less a threat to press excellence than monotony."

Seigenthaler explained that he had worked all his professional life for the same family-owned newspaper. "I have strong visceral preferences," he said, "for locally owned and controlled newspapers."

He conceded that Gannett had improved the competing Nashville *Banner*.

"There are those with the *Banner*," he said, "who suggest that the changes in their newspaper have made *The Tennessean* a better paper, and that is a suggestion that I reject. I suspect what they mean is that there is a lessening of the level of competitive tension that always existed when the *Banner* was independently owned by Jimmy Stahlman and that they have given their readers and ours something of a break by lessening that competitive tension. I do have the impression that that intensity of competition has abated some on their side. While overheated competition may at times create journalistic aberrations, I am confident in the long run that the readers benefit most from more, not less, competition in the marketplace of ideas."

It was an honest rebuttal to Neuharth's case for group ownership, but beyond that Seigenthaler inadvertently had served Neuharth a softball that he couldn't resist.

"I might raise this question," Seigenthaler said. "At what point in the future will chain ownership be raised as a question which affects the democracy of this very organization [ASNE] or the democracy of [the American Newspaper Publishers Association]?"

"I was a little bit surprised," Neuharth said later in the discussion, "to hear John express a concern about democracy . . . in organizations like ASNE. I was struck at lunch today with the apparent lack of democracy in this organization. The head table was all male and white. Now, if we lined up Gannett managing editors and city editors and publishers, we would not see an entirely white male establishment.

"I think our newspapers more clearly reflect the readership of our newspapers than do some individually owned newspapers and some organizations."[16]

Two years later in Nashville, Seigenthaler concluded in his introductory statement as a Gannett executive, "It is clear that *The Tennessean*, with local independence and autonomy coupled to the national resources of Gannett, will be free to serve its community of readers, remaining true to its unique past under the ownership of Amon Evans and his family."[17]

If those who remembered his earlier position on group ownership found that unpersuasive, they were no less skeptical than he had been when he learned that he had been, in his words, "sold into chains."

McCorkindale remembered in 1990 Seigenthaler's wariness at the time *The Tennessean* joined Gannett in 1979:

"When we did the deal at *The Tennessean*, and Amon agreed to sell [to] us, Seig had been out there peeing all over groups for ages. He comes in and he wants a contract to protect himself.

"And Al says, 'Okay, you work that out with Doug.'

"Well, [then Seigenthaler thought] 'Oh, shit, look out, McCorkindale's going to get me.'

"So I said, 'Write up your contract.'

"So [Seig] writes it up and he sends it up and I say, 'That's okay.'

"[Then he worried] 'Wait a minute, what did I miss?' . . .

"He was positive that he'd missed something. I remember he wanted control over the editorial budget.

"[I said] 'Fine, there's no problem.'

"I mean [Gannett] didn't intend to be all these things that he thought we were going to be. And he'll laugh with you over a drink nowadays about how he protected himself."[18]

Seigenthaler would grow increasingly prominent in his profession and important to Gannett until his retirement at the end of 1991, after which he would intensify his long-standing efforts on behalf of First Amendment causes.

# The Neuharth Stamp

As the end of Neuharth's first year as the man clearly in charge of Gannett, he demonstrated anew his commitment to ethnic and gender diversity throughout the company. Madelyn Jennings, former vice president/human resources for Standard Brands, Inc., agreed to join Gannett in January 1980 in the same role and became its first woman vice president.

Almost exactly a year earlier, Robert C. Maynard, chairman of the Institute for Journalism Education, had been named a Gannett adviser on equal opportunities.

In February 1979, Neuharth's second wife, Lori Wilson, a former Florida state senator and professional consultant on equal opportunities for women, was named an adviser to Gannett.

She and Maynard would oversee Gannett's two Partners in Progress programs, created to assure equal opportunities for women and minorities.

These three appointments were official manifestations of Neuharth's determination to transform "an all lily-white male organization to a very, very diversified company where . . . you really could earn your way by working . . . no matter what your ethnic background or race or religion or sex." [19]

# Chapter 37

# Innovation and Imitation

*"If the response to the prototypes tested in 1981 is favorable, a 1982 launch of the new newspaper is a possibility. If it is not favorable, we expect to use what we learn from that exercise to deliver information in other ways to consumers."*

*Allen H. Neuharth*
*Dec. 16, 1980*

Gannett entered the '80s with Al Neuharth firmly in charge. The wane of Paul Miller's influence on the organization was further underscored less than a week after the first anniversary of his retirement. Early in January 1980, Miller was hospitalized after suffering a stroke at his home in Palm Beach, Fla.

The company, under Frank Gannett and Miller, had always grown. Its new leadership intended for it to continue to grow. Since the merger with Combined Communications, its holdings had become not only more numerous but also more diversified and widely scattered. At the start of 1980, Gannett boasted 78 daily newspapers, seven television stations, 12 radio stations, "the largest outdoor advertising operation in North America and news, marketing, research and production subsidiaries."[1]

Although newspapers still constituted its major strength, Gannett's other holdings required the same skillful management for which its newspapers were known. The new complexity would prompt Neuharth and his subordinates to remodel the table of organization frequently, to master continuing change and accommodate new opportunities.

In March 1980, Neuharth named a four-man task force to "explore any and all possibilities for new ventures in the entire communications field which might even better serve readers, advertisers, viewers or listeners."

He told his inner circle, however, that the task force would be dubbed Project NN, with the specific objective of researching prospects for a national newspaper. Its members were Larry Sackett, 30, formerly director of operations for the *International Herald Tribune;* Frank Vega, 31, formerly circulation director of Gannett's *Oakland* (Calif.) *Tribune* and its fledgling *Eastbay TODAY,* a morning edition launched in November 1979 to increase single-copy sales in the San Francisco Bay area; Thomas Curley, 31, Gannett director of research; and Paul Kessinger, 29, Gannett marketing assistant. Vince Spezzano, then president of the Southeast Newspaper Group and publisher of *Today* in Cocoa, Fla., was their coordinator.[2]

The team was to hole up for months in a small Florida cottage, where its members would wrangle over data each of them gathered on covert research trips around the country. The mission was to establish the feasibility of Neuharth's dream of a national newspaper or provide incontrovertible evidence to scuttle it as a nightmare.

At the first planning meeting on Feb. 29, 1980, Neuharth had told the team, "Some of us now for some time have had a somewhat bigger idea that maybe this somewhat bigger company might be able to start a national and nationwide daily newspaper."

Spezzano said later, "The five of us were going to see whether or not we could spend about $1 million of Gannett money in the course of a year to produce a concept that eventually became *USA TODAY.*"[3]

## On with the Old

Even as Gannett reached for new possibilities, it continued its pattern of growth. In January, it had bought Gateway Productions, a producer of TV documentaries and business films in New York City. Then on March 13, it paid $57.5 million to the Green Bay (Wis.) Newspaper Company for three daily newspapers.

Included in the purchase were two Wisconsin papers, the *Green Bay Press-Gazette* (58,000 daily, 70,000 Sunday) and the *Wausau Daily*

*Herald* (30,000); a Michigan daily, the *Sturgis Journal* (less than 10,000); and Romo, Inc., a silk-screen printing company in Green Bay.

A week later, it expanded its holdings in California by buying the *San Rafael Independent-Journal*, a 45,600-circulation afternoon newspaper serving Marin County, north of San Francisco. The $40 million California purchase, which included a small weekly, made Gannett the nation's largest newspaper group both in terms of numbers, 82, and total daily circulation, 3.58 million.[4]

That same day, Neuharth put to rest rumors circulated for several weeks that Gannett headquarters would move to Washington, D.C. He had appointed a committee in July 1979 to investigate possible headquarters sites other than Rochester.

Neuharth said on March 20 he would recommend to the company's directors that headquarters remain in Rochester and that its lease on quarters in Lincoln Tower be extended to June 1986.

Several locations had been reviewed, Neuharth said, "but none offered any compelling advantage over Rochester in meeting our present corporate needs. As we have grown into 35 states and Canada, we have developed divisional and subsidiary offices in other cities – Washington, New York City, Denver, Phoenix, St. Louis, Boise, Cincinnati, Cocoa, Fla., Honolulu, Reno and Westchester – and we expect that these will continue to grow.

"Meanwhile, Rochester and New York have been very good to and for Gannett through the years and, in light of this most recent sites study, we believe we can continue to be very effective and successful from this headquarters location."[5]

One area in which the company was less effective and successful was communities where it owned both morning and afternoon newspapers. There were few newspaper markets in the country where a.m. circulation was not prospering or at least remaining stable while p.m. numbers deteriorated.

That was the case in 1980 in two Gannett markets, Salem, Ore., and Monroe, La. In Salem, the morning *Oregon Statesman* sold a strong 50,000 a day. The afternoon *Capital Journal*, however, trailed with a feeble 15,000 daily.

The two papers had been combined on Saturday and Sunday mornings for more than four years, with sustained circulation each day of 62,000. Based on that experience, and market research, publisher John McMillan announced on July 1 that the two papers had been combined into the single, seven-morning *Statesman Journal*, offering "more complete results and more effective service for our readers, our advertisers and our community."[6]

The numbers in Monroe, La., were equally skewed, with the *Morning World* circulating 35,500 a day against 9,850 for its evening counterpart, the *News-Star*. Publisher Ken Andrews told readers, "Instead of choosing between two newspapers trying hard to do many of the same things twice, [you] will now get a single newspaper of consolidated resources and considerably improved content."

The enlarged three-edition *News-Star-World* made its debut on the morning of Aug. 4.[7]

## Another First

John Curley had been with the Washington bureau of Gannett News Service since 1974, when he was made bureau chief. A year later he added the title of general manager, and in December 1979 was named vice president/news of Gannett.

The year 1980 brought new laurels to the company and its news service. The Pulitzer Prize judges awarded the Gold Medal for Public Service to GNS, the first such award to a news service, for GNS's series on financial contributions to the Pauline Fathers, a Roman Catholic order. Sixteen years earlier, Gannett had become the first newspaper group ever to win a Pulitzer for public service with the series Miller initiated on national racial problems, "The Road to Integration."

In autumn 1980, a vacancy arose in Wilmington, Del., when Joseph Lyons, president and publisher of the News-Journal papers, as they were known then, resigned to join Hearst Newspapers. John Quinn, who had championed Curley for the GNS job in 1974, recalled the discussions about a replacement for Lyons:

"Al sent a note to those of us who were on the operating committee [saying], 'Let's meet at 2 o'clock today to talk about two or three things, including the vacancy in Wilmington.'

"I sent a note back; 'I hope we don't waste much time meeting on what to do in Wilmington.'

"And I got a note back from him, something to the effect, 'If you're so smart, and [naming Curley is] such a good idea, let's see you sell it at the meeting,' knowing that somebody had another candidate for that job. I can't remember who it was or what the circumstances were, but it was someone from the business side. There was an argument that Wilmington at that time needed a marketing type."[8]

Quinn did sell the idea and on Oct. 16, 1980, Curley became president and publisher in Wilmington.

On Oct. 30, Neuharth reorganized the Office of the Chief Executive, adding new assignments for four of its executives. Jack Heselden, who had been chief of newspaper operations for a year, was promoted to president of the Newspaper Division. He remained a senior vice president of Gannett.

Doug McCorkindale was named president of Gannett Diversified Media Division, a new role in which he became supervisor of the company's broadcast stations, outdoor advertising units and other non-newspaper operations. He remained a senior vice president and chief financial officer of the company.

Quinn, as president of Gannett News Service, was given the added responsibility to provide broadcast news services. He remained a senior vice president and chief news executive.

Madelyn P. Jennings, formerly vice president/human resources, was named senior vice president/personnel and administration. She would continue, the announcement said, "to supervise all people programs and have responsibility for corporate operations and headquarters administration.

"As a member of the Office of the Chief Executive," it continued, "she joins the highest management level of Gannett and becomes one of the highest-ranking female executives of the nation's top 500 corporations."[9]

Less than three weeks after Curley became president and publisher in Wilmington, he was named president of the new Mid-Atlantic Newspaper Group. His region, carved out of the former East Newspaper Group, comprised seven papers in Delaware, New Jersey and Pennsylvania. The last included *The Reporter* in Lansdale, Pa., a 20,000-circulation daily that Gannett had bought for $8.4 million a week after Curley's move to Wilmington.

## Progress Report

The 1980 year-end meeting brought more than 250 Gannett executives to Washington, D.C., to hear of the company's achievements and its prospects. Neuharth had reason to beam.

In addition to the company's second precedent-setting Pulitzer Prize, the December issue of *Dun's Review* ranked Gannett among the five best-managed companies in the United States for its "deftly mixed acquisitions, internal expansion, central planning and local autonomy."

Gannett common stock had split three-shares-for-two in October, the third stock split since it went public in 1967.

Neuharth's greatest satisfaction, however, had to be bringing Project NN out of the closet.

Everything involved was still exploratory, of course, but what Neuharth described as an encouraging year of research supported the possibility of "a new national general-interest daily newspaper" and the creation of a nationwide Gannett Satellite Information Network.

GANSAT, as the communications network was to be known, would install a transmitting earth station at Springfield, Va., "to transmit news, information, advertising and entertainment to an infinite number of satellite receiving stations around the country," Neuharth said.

Moe Hickey was named president of the new satellite subsidiary, with administrative offices in Washington, D.C.

His fellow executives were:

Ronald D. Martin, 43, executive vice president/news, who most recently had been editor of the Baltimore *News-American*.

Thomas J. Baskind, 33, vice president/marketing communications, most recently vice president/communications for CBS Sports.

Frank Vega, 32, vice president/distribution systems, one of the head-bangers of Project NN.

Lawrence Sackett, 31, vice president/operations, the Project NN colleague with whom Vega had banged heads most frequently.

Linda Peek, 29, vice president/public affairs, who had been director of communications for the Jimmy Carter-Walter Mondale re-election campaign and previously special White House assistant for media liaison.

About the projected national newspaper – tentatively titled U.S.A. TODAY (the periods would come out later) – Neuharth said it would compete neither with existing metropolitan newspapers nor with existing Gannett community or regional newspapers.

"If the response to the prototypes tested in 1981 is favorable," he said, "a 1982 launch of the newspaper is a possibility. If it is not favorable, we expect to use what we learn from that exercise to deliver information in other ways to consumers." [10]

As tentative as Neuharth's phrasing was, his track record suggested this bold step also would be taken. The reaction was immediate trepidation on the financial side of the company and incredulity and curiosity in the media. Both would intensify during the period leading up to *USA TODAY's* introduction nearly two years later.

Media skepticism would be far more durable than that within the company. Newspapers and magazines found the concept both ridiculous and irresistible. They would profile and twit Neuharth and report the progress toward a national newspaper with increasing frequency, in spite of or because of their doubts.

The company worriers would eventually be won over or outflanked by the confident Neuharth.

## First Things First

Gannett's traditional pattern of acquisition continued in 1981. In the first eight months, it acquired four newspapers for a total outlay of nearly $57 million. Included in those purchases were:
- March 1981: All outstanding stock of Southland Publishing Co. of Gainesville, Ga., which included the *Gainesville Times* and the *Poultry and Egg News*. The price was $15.65 million.
- June 1981: All assets of *The Knoxville* (Tenn.) *Journal,* partner in a joint operating agreement with E.W. Scripps Co., owner of *The Knoxville News-Sentinel.* The price was $15.1 million.
- August 1981: El Diario Publishing Co., Inc., publisher of *El Diario-La Prensa*, a Spanish-language newspaper in New York City. The price was $9 million.
- November 1981: All outstanding stock of The Bulletin Co., Norwich, Conn., owner of the *Norwich Bulletin.* The price was $17 million.

As impressive as those cash outlays may seem, they were insignificant to a corporation that had paid out hundreds of millions of dollars in mergers such as Speidel and Combined Communications. The total outlay on those four acquisitions was well short of Gannett Co. Inc. earnings for an average six months.

Functionaries dealt with such operational matters in 1981 while top Gannett executives wrestled with Neuharth's dream of a national newspaper.

Much of the year was spent by Ron Martin, GANSAT's executive vice president/news, challenging a team of Gannett's best, loaned from its newspapers, to produce tightly edited, colorful prototypes of such a newspaper. Those prototypes would be used by market researchers to test the response of potential readers and advertisers.

Meanwhile, Neuharth and his team concentrated on orchestrating the case for what he called "one of the toughest decisions any media company has made."[11]

Neuharth could look back to the creation of *Today* in Florida. He could remember the importance of Paul Miller's steadfast support against fainthearted opponents such as Lynn Bitner and Cy Williams, who sought to derail the project before it could prove itself.

*USA TODAY* was a vastly more ambitious undertaking. Even modest estimates foresaw it losing $80 million in its first 15 months. Neuharth knew *USA TODAY* needed at least five years as a fair test. That not only risked a significant drain on Gannett's treasury but also total jeopardy for the professional reputation he was prepared to stake on it.

The creation of *USA TODAY* has been thoroughly documented by Peter Prichard, now editor of the paper and Gannett's chief news executive, in *The Making of McPaper,* and by Neuharth in *Confessions of an S.O.B.* Both paint Neuharth as a visionary, an accolade certainly supported by *USA TODAY's* innovations, its durability and its influence on the industry.

Both books also portray Neuharth as the victor who overcame underhanded resistance by subordinates whose loyalty had never before been in question. (Even some of Neuharth's staunchest allies still reject that as unfair.)

In *Confessions of an S.O.B.*, Neuharth singled out McCorkindale for rebuke. McCorkindale's reservations about *USA TODAY* were written off by Neuharth as the broadsides of a "bean counter." *The Making of McPaper's* perspective allied McCorkindale with Jimmy Thomas, currently senior vice president/financial services and treasurer, and Larry F. Miller, currently senior vice president/financial analysis and controller, in efforts to sabotage the project.

All three were known then, and are today, for their ability to spot financial vulnerability. They are formidable inquisitors of Gannett executives who submit annual budgets or propose major capital expenditures. Cross-examination by any or all of the three is not for the fainthearted or the unprepared. However, in the case of *USA TODAY*, the company's chief executive saw their financial nitpicking not as their acknowledged responsibility but as unexpected betrayal.

# There *Will* Be a USA TODAY

Neuharth overcame the reservations of most of his top executives about *USA TODAY* by winning the necessary vote of confidence in the project from the Gannett board. His Office of the Chief Executive was divided 3-2 against. Neuharth's position was obvious. Quinn was an enthusiastic supporter.

Jennings and McCorkindale both were opposed. So was Heselden, but he assured Neuharth of full support despite his misgivings if the project went forward.

Neuharth informed the board of the split in the OCE. When he put the issue to a vote, however, all eight outside directors voted for it, even McClure, although he did so reluctantly. The four inside directors – Neuharth, Heselden, McCorkindale and Robert Whittington, who came from Speidel – also voted yes.

It was a unanimous go-ahead signal. Early in 1982, Neuharth announced the first executive appointments for the prospective newspaper.

John Curley, back from Wilmington, editor; Phil Gialanella, detached from Honolulu, president; Spezzano, executive vice president; Ron Martin, executive editor; Gerald A. Bean, general manager; and Moe Hickey, senior consultant.

For eight months, these lieutenants and their army of talented hirelings and "loaners" would be worked over, overworked and outworked by the man who proudly anointed himself The Founder of the nation's newspaper-to-be. He knew, of course, that "founder" is also a verb and he was fiercely determined that it would never be applied to *USA TODAY*.

The predictably heavy financial burden that *USA TODAY* posed would be borne by the family's older members, a circumstance that would help to obscure the true costs of the project for as long as Neuharth considered necessary. Gannett newspapers would "loan" to *USA TODAY* hundreds of their best and brightest indefinitely, but continue to carry them on local payrolls. Those "temporary" absences, therefore, created no staff vacancies, and the parent papers were expected to prosper as before.

Jennings had foreseen problems with the loaner arrangement when Neuharth polled members of the Office of the Chief Executive about *USA TODAY*:

"The last two years," she wrote in an October 1981 memo to Neuharth, "have been a time of tight budgets, freezes on hiring and travel, failure to meet budgets due to circulation and advertising losses. Asking our people to tighten their belts more may elicit ennui and turnoff." [12]

Her clairvoyance can be faulted only for the restraint of "ennui." Resentment lingers among some veteran employees at Gannett newspapers. They do not resent *USA TODAY's* success but cannot overlook the stark contrast between the extravagant provisions made to create it and the resultant sacrifices they were expected to endure.

Neuharth dismissed such in-house criticisms when they first arose as the envy of people who hadn't been invited to participate.

As the certainty of *USA TODAY's* launch grew clear, Neuharth announced a move linking the new venture to all parts of Gannett. On Aug. 23, 1982, he named 10 members to Project S, a new task force to research and develop Gannett opportunities in all communications fields. That included, Neuharth said, spinoff possibilities from *USA TODAY*.

Project S chairman was Louis A. (Chip) Weil III, corporate vice president/development. Serving with him were representatives from the corporate staff, the News Division, both radio and television units of the Broadcasting Group, and Gannett Outdoor.

"With our nationwide satellite information system (GANSAT) now in place," Neuharth said, "and our nationwide newspaper *(USA TODAY)* about to begin publishing, Gannett is in a strong position to develop other nationwide information enterprises." [13]

# Power Launch

*USA TODAY* debuted Wednesday, Sept. 15, 1982, and immediately sold out its first 155,000 copies in the Washington-Baltimore market, the launch market. Novelty alone might have accounted for that inaugural success, and Neuharth was determined that the fledgling "nation's newspaper" neither would be forgotten nor ignored.

That night the proud father celebrated the coming out of his four-color debutant with a red, white and blue Capitol Hill spectacle that could not be ignored, especially by those in the media who dismissed the paper as an upstart not to be taken seriously.

With typical showmanship – and audacity – Neuharth enlisted as endorsers of honor for the festivities President and Mrs. Ronald Reagan, Senate Majority Leader Howard Baker and Speaker of the House of Representatives Thomas (Tip) O'Neill. They highlighted a guest list of hundreds of dignitaries – appointed and elected – corporate executives, showbiz celebrities and media figures.

The throng was elegantly wined and dined at *USA TODAY's* expense while President Reagan hailed the new paper as a typical realization of the American dream. The three most powerful men in the nation, Neuharth proudly recalled, adjusted their busy schedules to salute *USA TODAY*. It was no coincidence that the wire service pictures of that trio transmitted throughout the country contained a fourth powerful figure, the smiling founder of the nation's newspaper, happy with a public relations coup that cost only $100,000.

Similar parties with celebrity emcees accompanied the new paper's successive introductions in such markets as Atlanta, Minneapolis-St. Paul, Pittsburgh, Philadelphia, Chicago. None was grander than the one thrown April 11, 1983, in New York, when *USA TODAY* took on the Big Apple.

It was another red, white and blue affair, this time in Radio City Music Hall, whose Rockettes were appropriately costumed and programmed. Dick Cavett was master of ceremonies. Mayor Ed Koch, a self-professed champion of chutzpah, was there to predict success for any newspaper that could bolt 1,700 blue and white vending machines to New York's sidewalks almost overnight.

Earlier, Koch had spent most of that day denouncing *USA TODAY* and Gannett for bolting those 1,700 vending machines to the sidewalks without "permission."

Pittsburgh and Philadelphia, both organized-labor strongholds, were difficult markets for the non-union *USA TODAY*, but their sales resistance was gradually overcome by the strong appeal of its Sports section to readers in both cities.

New York City was even more difficult for the new paper. The unions' denunciations of it as a "scab newspaper" were compounded by public anger over the vending machines, to which Koch had applied much of the heat. Resentment persisted even after legal challenges by unions and city efforts to enact restrictive laws were felled by the First Amendment.

The city became a battleground. Deliverers were threatened, newspapers were destroyed or stolen. Those distinctive – and expensive – vending machines, which had been objects of vandalism in Philadelphia, became opponents' favorite targets of opportunity on New York's streets. They were hammered into useless hulks, demolished by marauding trucks and blown apart with explosive charges.

Peter Prichard reported in *The Making of McPaper* that more than 1,000 *USA TODAY* vending machines were destroyed in Philadelphia and New York that summer of 1983, costing Gannett more than $225,000.

Nevertheless, the paper appealed to increasing numbers of readers. Less than four months old, it began 1983 with a circulation of 400,000. By that summer, it had topped 1 million, encouraging the company to quicken its introduction that fall to Boston, Cleveland, Dallas, Fort Worth and New Orleans.

When it became a year old in September 1983, *USA TODAY* qualified for the first official surveys by the Audit Bureau of Circulations. At year's end, ABC confirmed that the paper had averaged 1.14 million circulation for the last quarter of 1983, making it the nation's third-biggest daily, after *The Wall Street Journal* and New York's *Daily News*.

Its slowness in winning over paying advertisers, however, and its inability to deliver papers to many willing buyers continued to be nagging frustrations.

## Color Them Gray

The successful launch of USA TODAY on Sept. 15, 1982, was a landmark not only for Gannett but also for the newspaper business. It was the first truly general-interest national paper, rather than a paper circulating regionalized editions. Its creative use of color and graphics jolted a profession that venerated the "good, gray New York Times." The consistently high quality of its printing, a Neuharth mandate, was unprecedented for daily newspapers.

Gannett veterans must have remembered how many of their colleagues 30 years before had shrugged off Frank Gannett's enthusiasm for printing in color. He had predicted its inevitability at many Gannett meetings. He said he was talking about newspapers printed on offset presses, capable of producing color far superior to the crude work then being turned out by some dailies.[14] Had he lived to see USA TODAY, he would not have been surprised to find it scorned – but imitated – by the profession and embraced by readers.

USA TODAY's production quality also was a vindication to Neuharth for the professional derision that had been heaped on him and his dream. Those blue-and-white TV-set-style coin boxes still were ridiculed, but often by people more offended by the sales the boxes generated. So the launch was a success, but the durability of the new paper remained to be proved.

The more the public seemed to like it, the more fellow journalists scoffed. Its fast-read concept was promptly characterized as fast-food journalism, with a comparison to fast-food pioneer McDonald's. Hence the term "McPaper" – a label that was quickly and affectionately embraced by the staff.

If it was lampooned, it was also copied. Newspapers whose executives dismissed *USA TODAY* as a garish social climber unqualified to join the club gradually altered their appearance and content. Neuharth recalled an observation made by J. Taylor Buckley, now *USA TODAY* senior editor:

"[He] said that they criticize us as McPaper but they steal all our McNuggets. . . . I think in the public's mind now, whatever perception they have of Gannett is pegged more to *USA TODAY* than any of the other things we do. In the beginning *USA TODAY* was criticized so damn much but now most people will smile and laugh and say, 'Well, my paper looks just like *USA TODAY*.'"[15]

## Back at the Office

While *USA TODAY* commanded most of the attention in the first half of 1982, Gannett corporate operations and business strategies needed to be maintained and developed.

In late spring, Gannett moved for the first time into Mississippi. It paid $110 million to the Mississippi Publishing Co., owned by four brothers named Hederman, for three daily, two Sunday and six weekly newspapers in central and southern Mississippi.

The new properties were the morning Jackson *Clarion-Ledger*, the afternoon *Jackson Daily News* and the afternoon *Hattiesburg American*, with combined circulations of 132,000 daily and 145,000 Sunday. They brought to 88 the number of Gannett dailies and to 37 the number of states with Gannett newspaper or broadcast properties.[16]

In mid-summer, the company announced it would buy WTCN-TV, a VHF station in Minneapolis-St. Paul, from Metromedia, Inc. The purchase was contingent on approval by the FCC, and would require the sale of KARK-TV in Little Rock, Ark., one of Gannett's five VHF stations, to stay within the federal limits on TV ownership.[17] Net value of the deal, including the sales price of KARK-TV, was $75 million.

(In addition to the Little Rock station, Gannett's VHF properties at the time were KPNX-TV in Phoenix, Ariz.; KBTV (now KUSA-TV) in Denver, Colo.; WXIA-TV in Atlanta, Ga.; and KOCO-TV in Oklahoma City, Okla. Today WCTN-TV is known as KARE-TV.)

A week before the debut of the nation's newspaper, Gannett demonstrated its commitment to equal opportunity. Heselden, president of Gannett Newspaper Division, announced the promotions of four women publishers.

• Jo-Ann Huff Albers, 44, who had been publisher and editor of the *Sturgis* (Mich.) *Journal*, became president, editor and publisher of the 20,000-circulation *Public Opinion* in Chambersburg, Pa.

• E. Roanne Fry, 46, who had been director of advertising for the 9,400-circulation Sturgis paper, replaced Albers there.

• Pamela F. Meals, 36, who had been publisher of *The Coffeyville Journal* in Kansas, became president and publisher of the 23,400-circulation *Palladium-Item* in Richmond, Ind.

• Susanne Shaw, 42, who had been associate dean and associate professor at the William Allen White School of Journalism and Mass Communication at the University of Kansas, replaced Meals at the 9,000-circulation Coffeyville paper.

Neuharth said, "The several years of commitment to recruit and promote qualified women to equality in management roles is making its mark at higher management levels as these women join males in moving up the career ladder."[18]

Already on that career ladder was Sue Clark-Jackson, president and publisher at Niagara Falls. The *Niagara Gazette* was an afternoon newspaper, a medium that was shrinking across the country. In September 1982, when the Buffalo *Courier-Express* ceased publication as the only morning newspaper in Western New York, she recognized an opportunity.

The *Gazette* had been publishing morning editions on holidays since 1977, and had switched its Saturday edition to morning in 1979. After four years of study and that experience, Jackson said, management had decided to give readers the *Gazette* every morning, and began to do so Nov. 1, 1982.

By early autumn, Gannett announced it had agreed to buy KRON-

TV in San Francisco from the Chronicle Broadcasting Co. The price would be $110 million and transfer of its KOCO-TV in Oklahoma City to Chronicle Broadcasting. In the announcement, Gannett noted that federal regulations would require it to sell the *Oakland Tribune* in order to operate KRON-TV in the same market.[19]

Neuharth knew that he would soon be able to announce that 1982 was Gannett's 15th consecutive year and 61st consecutive quarter of earnings gains – despite the enormous startup costs for *USA TODAY*. The Founder – aka chairman – was smiling broadly.

# Chapter 38

# Who's in the Wings?

*"Al made me head of the management continuity committee, and almost immediately he started saying, 'Now we've got to look for people to bring into the company to be my successor.' . . . I never believed Al was serious. . . . But that's the one thing that he never varied on from the day I joined the board until he retired. He told me, 'I'm going to retire at 65.'"*

Wes Gallagher
Oct. 5, 1990

On Jan. 1, 1983, Al Neuharth marked his fourth anniversary as Gannett's chairman, president and chief executive officer. He had an able complement of senior vice presidents in Jack Heselden, Doug McCorkindale, John Quinn and Madelyn Jennings, but no designated successor.

Quinn, at 55, was only four years Neuharth's junior. Heselden was a year older than Neuharth. McCorkindale, 41, and Jennings, 45, were youthful enough for consideration but, like Heselden, lacked a qualification Neuharth had decided was paramount. The person to succeed him had to have a news background, consistent with the experience that Frank Gannett, Paul Miller and he had brought to the company's leadership.

Despite Neuharth's putdown of McCorkindale in *Confessions of an S.O.B.*, he respected the chief financial officer's ability and intelligence. He said in 1992 that he had briefly considered McCorkindale as his successor, having always hoped to pick someone from inside the company:

"I concluded that Doug McCorkindale was not the person because he had no news background, and I didn't think he could develop a feel for the news and news people. He's the best financial guy I know.

"I thought he'd run the company OK from a business standpoint, but my conscience couldn't live with putting the company into the hands of a non-news person." [1]

It was at that point, Neuharth recalled, that he suggested to Wes Gallagher, chairman of the board's management continuity committee, that a search outside the company should be made.

"And we looked," Gallagher said. "There was a meeting in my house in California one time where we offered a guy $1 million to come into the company – in stock options and a lot of other things, a package – and it didn't work out. . . . But when we came down to it . . . it seemed best to go within the company." [2]

Early in 1983, the question of succession came up between Neuharth and Quinn one night after they had put the next day's edition of *USA TODAY* to bed. Both worked routinely and tirelessly into the early morning, to the consternation of the newspaper's staff, rewriting headlines, proposing changes in copy and generally putting what they considered the necessary finishing touches on each and every edition. As Quinn remembered:

"In those days, the deadline was around 1 a.m. and we went up to Anna Maria's, which served booze until 2 a.m. and spaghetti until 4 a.m. The two of us got to talking about what are we going to do now, getting ready for the future."

To Quinn, John Curley was clearly the one. [3]

When the decision to keep the line of succession within the company was made, according to Neuharth, "Curley was still pretty far removed. He hadn't really been tested in major operations," although he had had major responsibilities at GNS and in Wilmington.

But the gestation of *USA TODAY* qualified as a "major operation," certainly in Neuharth's mind, and Curley was a major player. Everyone on the start-up team, including Curley, endured the constant scrutiny of both Neuharth and Quinn. By the time of their discussion at Anna Maria's, Neuharth had firsthand knowledge of *USA TODAY's* first editor.

"I began to push Curley along," Neuharth said, "and the more he was pushed, the better he looked." [4]

"The next bit in Al's scenario," Quinn explained, "was for him to get Curley and me together. Neuharth said to me, 'You get Curley to go to dinner early. . . . I don't want to be talking these things over at 2 o'clock in the morning. Get out of USA TODAY for a couple of hours, 6 o'clock, and meet me over at Nathan's in Georgetown.'

"That's where we went and he made the deal with Curley to become president of the Newspaper Division as the first step. I can remember riding over in the cab with Curley and laying the groundwork that this was the first step in an obvious scenario. . . .

"I'm sure that Neuharth had already programmed Curley the other way: 'We've got to work this so that Quinn's happy about taking over your responsibilities as editor without giving up the VP news.' . . . So I think that was a classic Neuharth deal." [5]

The line of succession may have been clear to Neuharth and Quinn, it may even have been obvious to Curley and McCorkindale, but Neuharth's next move did nothing to end the guessing game among others.

To make room for Curley as senior vice president and president of the Newspaper Division, Neuharth named Jack Heselden deputy chairman, a title he retained until his retirement in 1985. On April 24, 1983, Neuharth announced these and three other executive promotions, eliminated the five-member Office of the Chief Executive and created a seven-member Gannett Management Committee.

"This will both strengthen our present operating team," Neuharth said, "and position us to begin planning toward an orderly long-term management transition."

The news release announcing these changes pointed out that Neuharth, who was 59, had recently signed a six-year extension of his contract with Gannett, which would expire in March 1989. [6]

# Affirmative Action

Gannett proceeded with the sale of the *Oakland Tribune* in order to buy KRON-TV in San Francisco. On April 30, 1983, it sold the paper to a group headed by Robert C. Maynard, its publisher and editor. The price was $17.5 million, with Gannett agreeing to help Maynard finance the purchase.

Maynard had been named editor in 1979 when Gannett acquired the 109-year-old *Oakland Tribune* in the Combined Communications merger. He became publisher as well in 1981. Maynard was the first black to hold both of those top positions at a major general-circulation newspaper.

(Less than five months after the *Oakland Tribune* was sold, Gannett and Chronicle Broadcasting Co. called off the KRON-TV transaction. Peter Benjaminson wrote in *Death in the Afternoon* – a study of failing metropolitan newspapers – that KRON-TV's owners simply decided the station had more potential than they had thought and chose to keep it.)[7]

(Maynard continued to publish the *Oakland Tribune* until Dec. 1, 1992, when Alameda Newspaper Group took over the paper. Gannett had continued to assist Maynard during his ownership by not pressing him for repayment on his debt. In 1991, Neuharth, by then head of The Freedom Forum, had provided loans to the debt-plagued newspaper and guaranteed other loans, including Gannett's. Ultimately, Maynard chose not to continue and sold to Alameda.)

The significance of Gannett's 1983 sale to Maynard and other evidence of minority opportunity in Gannett was not overlooked. In late spring, Neuharth was honored with the first Wells Award, named for pioneer black editor and publisher Ida B. Wells of Memphis. The award included $10,000 in scholarships to be given to minority journalism students in Neuharth's name.

The jurors praised Neuharth "for his vigorous and courageous commitment to providing job opportunities for minorities in the communications industry; for leadership in establishing the 'Partners in Progress' program of affirmative action at Gannett Co., Inc.; for creating management appointments, ownership opportunities and professional development activities involving minorities."

Included in the jury's findings:

"Because of the intensified recruitment, training and advancement activities, Gannett executive managers were, by 1980, 23 percent female and 7 percent minority, including two minority editor-publishers, five minority publishers, 11 women publishers and 19 women editors. In the professional ranks in 1982, Gannett employed 9.5 percent minorities and 35 percent women. Of total employment in 1982, 16 percent were minorities and 36 percent women." [8]

In September 1983, another woman executive entered Gannett's senior ranks when Cathleen Black, publisher of *New York* magazine, succeeded Vince Spezzano as president of *USA TODAY*.

# Loss and Gain

The year had not been one of significant growth by acquisition, but it had been one of change. McCorkindale had reported to the board in February that several expressions of interest by Karl Eller in buying Gannett Outdoor Group had prompted an evaluation of the group's value. The firm commissioned to do that set Gannett Outdoor's worth between $550 million and $650 million. The directors decided the outdoor business – the largest in North America – was not for sale.

Good news came in November from the 10th Circuit of Appeals. Gannett had won reversal of a 1980 federal court order restoring ownership of the Santa Fe *New Mexican* to Robert McKinney.

In 1978, McKinney had sued Gannett to regain the paper, charging fraud and deceit. In 1980, a jury had exonerated Gannett of those charges but found it guilty of violating its employment contract with McKinney. U.S. District Judge Santiago Campos then ordered Gannett to relinquish *The New Mexican* to McKinney, an order Gannett immediately appealed.

While the 1983 Court of Appeals ruling effectively continued Gannett ownership of the newspaper, it would not eliminate difficulties with McKinney.

Even better news came that fall. Shareholders were rewarded with another two-for-one stock split. The end of the year marked Gannett's

16th consecutive year and 65th consecutive quarter of record earnings.

## The New Generation

The successful spread of *USA TODAY* nationwide had made Gannett's challenging geography even more complicated. That had tested both the ingenuity and flexibility of the freshman president of the Newspaper Division and his subordinates.

On the April day in 1983 when he was elected president, Curley had immediately reorganized the regions to spread administrative responsibility of Gannett newspapers more equally.

Two months later, the growing success of *USA TODAY* required even further reorganization. Curley realigned four regions into six in order to improve control of printing and circulation for *USA TODAY*. Each regional executive became responsible not only for the Gannett newspapers in his or her region, but also for *USA TODAY's* production and distribution in relevant markets.

In June 1983, he also had been elected to Gannett's board, so he had come to the attention of his fellow directors as well.

Curley's first year grades obviously were high. On March 27, 1984, Gannett's directors elected him president and chief operating officer of the company. Neuharth retained the titles of chairman and chief executive officer.

At *USA TODAY*, on June 15, they acknowledged Jack Heselden's plan to retire in 1985 by promoting the newspaper's president, Cathie Black, to publisher, a position Heselden had held since August 1983.

On Oct. 31, 1984, the company validated again its commitment to minority opportunity. Jimmy Jones, director of affirmative action, was promoted to vice president. He was the first black executive to hold that title in Gannett.

# A Little Growth

Although promotions, retirements and reassignments were the year's dominant activities, Neuharth had surprised Rochester's city leaders and a lot of long-time Gannett employees that summer. On June 27, 1984, he announced that headquarters offices would move in stages to Arlington, Va. The company's 63-year corporate identification with Rochester would end by the summer of 1986.

Neuharth had said in 1980 that the company would stay in Rochester and extended its leases on the Lincoln Tower to 1986, based on a committee's study of other possible sites.

Things had changed, however, since 1980. The popularity of *USA TODAY* had given Gannett a national focus. From the early planning stages through development of the prototypes to *USA TODAY*'s successful launch, Neuharth and most of his news executives had concentrated their attention, their energies and their presence in Arlington.

While other corporate executives were still based in Rochester, intercity travel on company business increased. Because of *USA TODAY*, Gannett had grown away from Rochester and it was beginning the move away as well.

In another relocation, Gannett Outdoor Group, which had been headquartered in Phoenix since the merger with Combined Communications, was moved to New York City at the end of October 1984. The company said the new offices would put Outdoor closer to most of its major customers.

Gannett also grew slightly during the year. In June, it bought WDAE-AM and Prime Time Syndication Service in Tampa, Fla., from Taft Broadcasting for $6.05 million. (Prime Time was sold two years later for $165,000.) The announcement said linking the new property as sister station to Gannett's WIQI-FM in Tampa, acquired in 1980 for $4 million, would make it "better equipped to serve the listening and public service needs of the Tampa Bay market area."[9]

The Broadcasting Group expanded again in December, when

Gannett bought Houston's two largest radio stations from Harte-Hanks for $35 million. KKBQ-AM and FM brought the number of Gannett's radio stations to 16, equally divided between AM and FM.

# Chapter 39

# Certifiably Bigtime

*"I said [in 1972], 'I work for a bunch of shit-kicker newspapers.' . . . The point was that I didn't have any influence, that none of the papers were big city papers. . . . I wasn't really talking about quality, I was talking about the fact that we represented papers in these smaller cities."*

Jack Germond
Aug. 15, 1990

The relatively modest number of acquisitions in 1984 gave way to a two-year shopping spree beginning in 1985. By the end of 1986, after commitments totaling nearly $1.5 billion, Gannett would include influential statewide newspapers in Iowa and Arkansas, and major metropolitan publications in Detroit and Louisville.

In 1985, Gannett Outdoor Group picked up several outdoor advertising companies in Chicago, Houston and Los Angeles for nearly $14 million.

On Jan. 31, 1985, Gannett disclosed its agreement to pay $200 million to Cowles Media Co. for *The Des Moines Register* and *Tribune* in Iowa and *The Jackson* (Tenn.) *Sun*. Only three weeks later it revealed that it was also buying *Family Weekly*, the 12.8-million-circulation magazine carried in 362 newspapers. The seller, CBS Inc., received $42.5 million for the magazine.

On March 4, 1985, Gannett International was created. Its president, David Mazzarella, had been general manager of the New York market cluster for *USA TODAY*. He would direct not only *USA TODAY's* international edition, formerly overseen by Vince Spezzano, but also other opportunities created abroad.

# Working Holiday

Near the end of March, Gannett's directors met in St. Thomas in the U.S. Virgin Islands to deal with issues in advance of the May shareholders' meeting. St. Thomas, of course, was home to the *Virgin Islands Daily News*. Gannett's philosophy has been for the board of directors to meet six times a year – at least once in New York and once or twice at or near corporate headquarters and cities where the company had properties so local executives could meet with the board and directors could visit the units.

At the St. Thomas meeting, *USA TODAY* publisher Cathie Black was given the additional title of executive vice president/marketing for the company. (In August, she joined the Gannett board.)

Neuharth reported with pleasure that Cowles Media Co., from whom Gannett was buying the papers in Des Moines and Jackson, had invited the company also to buy a block of Cowles stock. Gannett's directors approved spending $85 million more to acquire 20 percent of outstanding Cowles stock.[1]

Even more significant were proposals designed not only to mute Neuharth opponents but also to increase the company's protection against a hostile takeover. Neither name was mentioned publicly, but the Neuharth bogeymen at whom the proposals were aimed were J. Warren McClure and Carl Lindner.

Neuharth described both in *Confessions of an S.O.B.* Of McClure, he said:

"Paul Miller had named McClure vice president of Gannett and put him on the board. Mac spent full time trying to become president.

"I told him there was no way he would ever be promoted by me. He retired as veep soon thereafter. Continuing as a board member ... he basically opposed anything with my stamp on it." That included *USA TODAY*, although McClure had voted reluctantly with the majority to launch the national newspaper.[2]

McClure responded in 1992 that he had known for a long time that "the two top positions were reserved for those who had come up in

Gannett from the news side of the business."

He and Neuharth had lunch, McClure said, in May 14, 1975, as he neared his fourth anniversary with the company. Knowing there were no opportunities for advancement, he said, "I told Al that I felt I didn't need one year's experience 'x' number of times . . . and if there was no objection I would take early retirement."

He recalled, as well, "gratifying memos to me from Miller and Neuharth" indicating that "our teamwork was highly successful and widely regarded, as well as profitable."

Carl Lindner was a wealthy Cincinnati investor who had been Combined Communications' major stockholder. He acquired 4 percent of Gannett's stock as a result of the merger and quickly sought more. According to Neuharth, Lindner was thwarted when he tried to buy the 11 percent of company stock held by the Gannett Foundation. But he continued to buy stock and when he notified the Securities and Exchange Commission that his Gannett holdings had passed 5 percent and would probably go still higher, Gannett sought to devise ways to block a hostile takeover. Lindner then tried to sell back his Gannett stock at well above market – the device known as "greenmail." When that was rebuffed, he threatened a proxy fight.[3]

At the St. Thomas meeting, the board voted to amend its qualifications for directors. That measure said in part: "No persons shall be eligible for election or re-election to the board . . . after reaching age 70; or, in the case of any person who has at any time served as an executive of this corporation, [which McClure had] after reaching 65 or electing early retirement [which McClure had]."[4]

McClure said of that change, later dubbed "the McClure Amendment," "Unfortunately, this ruling affected one other director, Jack Heselden. He was possibly Gannett's most loyal and least self-serving director."

Gannett proxy statements sent out in advance of the May 1985 shareholders' meeting contained two additional takeover safeguards. One called for electing only one third of the board each year, to minimize the prospect of totally new control in any given year. The other required that any tender offer to shareholders offer all the same price

for their stock.
Returned proxies assured Neuharth, *et. al.*, that Lindner was beaten.

# Time to Acquire

On June 10, 1985, Gannett sold its AM and FM radio stations in Cleveland to Lake Erie Radio Co. for $9.5 million. That left the Broadcast Group with 14 radio stations and six TV stations.

At the end of June, the company announced that *Family Weekly* would be expanded, redesigned and renamed *USA WEEKEND,* making it a readily identifiable blood relative of *USA TODAY.*

Many publishers among the 362 newspapers that had carried *Family Weekly* were unhappy with the change. They dropped the supplement because they saw *USA WEEKEND* as a competitive promotion for Gannett's national daily in their markets. Such defections produced hard times for the renamed Sunday supplement's staff while it sought new subscribers to help protect revenues and maintain its predecessor's circulation of 12.8 million.

*The Des Moines Register* and *The Jackson Sun* officially became Gannett newspapers on July 1, 1985. The smaller Tennessee paper's evening circulation exceeded 30,000. *The Register,* with morning circulation of 220,000, Sunday 360,000, was Iowa's dominant newspaper, sold throughout the state.

Gannett then announced it would buy KTKS-FM (now KHKS-FM) in Denton, Tex., for $16 million, assuming that the proposed merger of its parent, Capital Cities Communications, Inc., and American Broadcasting Companies would go through (the Federal Communications Commission approved the merger in November 1985). The purchase would be final early in 1986.

At its June 25 meeting, the board had resolved that "the company is extremely well positioned and that it has no reason to pursue major merger possibilities unless these would clearly enhance the position of the shareholders. Specifically, the directors agreed that in any major merger with companies such as those being discussed, the proven record of performance and earnings of Gannett management must not be subordinated."[5]

If the lack of specifics made that resolution mystifying to the uninformed, any questions it raised were soon to be answered.

Neuharth had left Knight Newspapers' *Detroit Free Press* to join Gannett in 1963. On Aug. 29, 1985, he was back in that city to make an appearance with Peter B. Clark, chairman of The Evening News Association. The two of them announced that the Evening News Association would merge with Gannett in a deal worth $717 million.

Predominant among Gannett's newest pending assets was the *Free Press's* competitor, the 650,000-circulation *Detroit News*, behind which Neuharth and his former Knight bosses had ranked second more than two decades before. Now he was back to buy it.

"We are especially aware," Neuharth said, "of the proud tradition of public service by *The Detroit News* for 112 years and we look forward to continuing and enhancing that."

Also included in the merger were four other daily and six weekly newspapers in two states, five television stations in four states and the District of Columbia, and two Detroit radio stations.

The other dailies included *The Desert Sun* of Palm Springs and *The Daily News* of Indio, both in California, and *The Times Journal* of Vineland and *The Millville Daily*, both in New Jersey.

Of the five TV stations included in the merger, Gannett would keep only WDVM-TV (later WUSA-TV) in Washington, D.C., and KVUE-TV in Austin, Texas.[6] Before completion of the merger in March 1986, the company would recover $160 million of its cost by selling to Knight-Ridder, Inc. the other three – WALA-TV in Mobile, Ala.; KOLD-TV in Tucson, Ariz.; and KTVY-TV in Oklahoma City. The two Detroit radio stations, WWJ-AM and WJOI-FM, were sold to Federal Broadcasting Co. for $39 million.

Gannett's final acquisition of 1985 occurred Nov. 27, the purchase of the *Evening Star* (10,500) and *Sunday Star* (12,500) in Peekskill, N.Y., from Ogden Newspapers Inc. The price was $5.5 million.

The International Edition of *USA TODAY*, which had been ferried to Europe by plane from New York's Westchester County, was becoming genuinely international. In October 1985, it began to be printed via satellite and distributed in Asia from a plant in Singapore. Gannett announced that a printing contract with a plant near Zurich, Switzerland, would take effect in May 1986, producing papers for Europe and the Middle East.

(Printing at the Singapore plant was phased out in 1991. In 1988, printing of USA TODAY International had begun in Hong Kong, where it continues as the printing hub for Asia. Gannett has announced plans to begin printing in London late in 1993.)

In November 1985, the company announced that total circulation of Gannett newspapers, including *USA TODAY*, had gone over 5 million for the first time, to 5,058,960. That record was not only a measure of Gannett's success but also an illustration of its immensity.

## The Chairman's Review

Among the important events that occurred in 1986 were John Curley's election as chief executive officer and the unveiling of the new corporate headquarters in Arlington, Va.

The stage was set at the shareholders' meeting on May 20 in Washington.

Neuharth first praised Cathie Black for being "a primary force in ensuring the ultimate success of The Nation's Newspaper."

He singled out Doug McCorkindale for having "helped us wisely invest over $1.25 billion dollars this past year in an acquisition and merger program that is the envy of our industry."

The company's president, John Curley, he said, helped pull it all together. "His skillful operational guidance of our newspapers, broadcasting and outdoor helped keep Gannett's record overall the envy of our industry."

Neuharth then reminded shareholders how Gannett had been transformed since 1973, when he became CEO: From 51 daily newspapers with 2.2 million circulation to 93 with 6.07 million; from 22 Sunday newspapers (1.57 million) to 62 (5.32 million); from one TV station to eight; from no radio stations to 16; from no outdoor advertising business to the largest in North America.

"Then," he said,"the USA had no national general-interest daily newspaper; now the nation has a very vital one, and it's ours.

"Then, our annual revenues were $288 million; this year they will approach $3 billion.

"Then our annual earnings were $23 million; last year they were $253 million."

He reminded them that per-share value of their stock had more than quadrupled and that their annual dividends had increased tenfold.

The 1973 board of 12 white male directors had been turned, he said, into "the most diverse and most prestigious board of 17 men and women of any media company anywhere. And, now, our leadership at every level truly reflects our readership and viewership – in sex, race, religion, creed and philosophy."

Neuharth then told the shareholders that Curley's election as CEO at the board meeting to follow was assured. He invited "a salute and a big round of applause for Gannett's new boss."

Neuharth reminded them that he would remain their "very active chairman" until the end of his contract in March 1989.

"During the next three years," he said, "I will be devoting more time to long-term policy and planning, especially in the area of acquisitions, mergers, new ventures and other such major Gannett matters."

Beyond 1989, he said, "I will continue to serve Gannett after my executive retirement – as a reporter-at-large and an ambassador-at-large."[7]

With that Neuharth invited the audience to cross the Potomac River with him and inspect the new corporate headquarters in Arlington, Va. Those richly ornate digs and their high-tech capabilities, which frequently floored first-time visitors, filled much of one soaring tower. Its adjacent identical twin had housed *USA TODAY* since shortly before the newspaper's launch. Startup teams had shaped the new newspaper there amidst jackhammering crews racing to complete construction. Their noise and dust were considerable challenges to the creative process.

Now *USA TODAY* was nearly four years old and had experienced some inevitable churn as permanent staffers sent original "loaners" back to their newspapers and founding executives went on to other challenges. Among them was Tom Curley, who had been made executive vice president and general manager of *USA TODAY* in December 1985, and became its president in March 1986.

At Gannett, Cecil Walker, who had been acting president of Gannett Television since November 1985, was named president on April 13, 1986. He had been president and general manager of WXIA-TV in Atlanta. (Walker would become president of Gannett Broadcasting on Feb. 1, 1987.)

In May, Gannett Radio moved its headquarters from St. Louis to Los Angeles.

# Detroit Surprise

Soon after the Evening News merger, Detroit's newspaper competitors held a joint news conference. Alvah H. Chapman Jr., chairman and CEO of Knight-Ridder, Inc., and Neuharth on May 9, 1986, unveiled their proposal for the Detroit Newspaper Agency, under which both *The Detroit News* and *Detroit Free Press* would be published.

They said they would ask the U.S. attorney general to approve the joint operating agency. The federal Newspaper Preservation Act of 1970 authorized such arrangements when at least one newspaper in a market was in danger of failing.

Both newspapers had suffered substantial losses during the 1980s, they said. The *Free Press* would make the application as the failing newspaper.

In a JOA, the two newspapers would publish from the same production plant and sell advertising and circulation jointly. Their news and editorial functions would remain totally separate, independent and competitive, as required by the Act.

Disbelief, anger and cynicism were the responses from fiercely competitive news staffs who had battled each other for years. Union leaders and some local politicians vowed to mount a counteroffensive. Professional journalists, academicians and publishers of suburban newspapers scoffed at the idea that newspapers the size of Detroit's could be in danger of failing.

It would take more than three years before impediments to a joint operating agreement would be removed. The Detroit Newspaper Agency finally went into full operation in November 1989.

Moe Hickey, who was publisher of *The Detroit News* during part of the interim, well remembers the wait for approval of the JOA.

When Gannett bought *The Detroit News*, the paper had a Sunday circulation lead of 100,000, "but the dailies were neck and neck," Hickey said.

The March 1986 ABC report on daily circulation figures put *The News* at 655,000 and the *Free Press* at 650,000. Even when the JOA application by the "failing" *Free Press* was announced, the accustomed competitive spirit between the papers persisted, Hickey said.

"What happened in the next six months turned up in the next ABC [circulation audit]. I think unbeknownst to [Knight-Ridder headquarters] they really went to work on the *Free Press* and spent a bundle of money. They had their best six months of daily circulation in their history. They went from 650,000 to something over 662,000 or 663,000."

Hickey said his circulation people told him they couldn't sell any more papers in southwest Michigan. But elsewhere in the state, Hickey said, "the *Free Press* was beating our brains out, because they were a morning paper. . . . However, someone had had the good sense a number of years before to start a morning edition, so *The News* was basically an all-day newspaper.

"That morning paper gave us the vehicle to go out as early as the *Free Press* did in the state. So we went out and we opened up news bureaus and circulation bureaus all over Michigan. . . . We went from 655,000 to about 672,000 or 673,000. So in November, when the numbers came out for the period ending in September . . . I went to [a] lunch where Bob Hall [*Free Press* head of finance] came over to me.

"He said, 'Moe, you son of a bitch, we thought we had you beat. We had the best six months ever.'

"And I said, 'Well, thank God for the state[wide circulation], Bob. You guys have had that for too long.'"[8]

Hickey would leave Detroit and Gannett before approval of the JOA. He resigned in October 1987 to become publisher and chief executive officer of the *Denver Post*.

That was two months after an administrative law judge had presided at a public hearing on the JOA on the order of U.S. Attorney General Edwin Meese III.

In December 1987, Administrative Law Judge Morton Needelman recommended that Meese reject the JOA. Opponents, therefore, were indignant in August 1988 when Meese ignored Needelman's recommendation and approved the JOA.

Michigan Citizens for an Independent Press promptly blocked implementation of Meese's ruling, but in September a federal court upheld Meese.

A three-judge panel of the U.S. Court of Appeals also upheld Meese, by a vote of 2-1, in January 1989, but in February issued a stay on the JOA while it considered opponents' requests that the full court rehear the case. That was denied but the stay was continued.

In May, the U.S. Supreme Court agreed to review the JOA. In November, the high court split 4-4, with one justice abstaining, thereby upholding the lower court's affirmation of the JOA.

Disappointed opponents considered further appeal, despite the unlikelihood of rehearing by the Supreme Court. When asked how often the high court grants rehearings, the opponents' attorney, David Vladeck, replied, "How often does an asteroid hit a moving Corvette?"[9]

The Detroit Newspaper Agency went into operation Nov. 27, 1989. William J. Keating, former AP chairman and former Gannett publisher, executive vice president and general counsel, was its chief executive.

## Failing Family Act

On May 19, 1986 – just a day before Curley's election as CEO – Gannett announced its third major acquisition in a year, the purchase of *The Courier-Journal* and the *Louisville Times*. At the closing in July, Neuharth told the staffs, "It feels like winning the Triple Crown." Barry Bingham Sr. had sold his two highly respected newspapers to Gannett for $305 million.

Louisville, Des Moines and Detroit, Neuharth said, "were three big newspaper races in the USA this past year. Naturally we're pleased that Gannett won them all. Fittingly, Louisville is a sparkling jewel in that crown."

The elder Bingham acknowledged his distress in giving up newspapers his father had bought in 1918. His reluctant decision to sell followed an acrimonious and brutally public power struggle by one of his daughters, Sallie, with Barry Jr., who had run the papers for 15 years, and with her other siblings over the value of her family holdings.

"Change is an inevitable rule of life," the resigned Bingham said in the announcement of the sale. "I subscribe to the Biblical instruction that there is a time to sow, a time to reap.

"My distress is mitigated by the character of the owners who will now guide the destinies of our newspapers, the Gannett publishing company and its chief executive officer, Allen Neuharth. Here are journalists who are responsible, experienced, capable and backed by ample resources."

The two newspapers brought to 93 the number of Gannett dailies. They had combined daily circulation of about 300,000 – 322,000 on Sunday – and annual revenues above $100 million.[10]

A week earlier, Gannett had bought KHIT-FM in Seattle for $6.5 million from Bingham Broadcasting, no relation to the newspaper family. At the end of July, Gannett acquired two radio stations in Kansas City, Mo. – KCMO-AM and KBKC (now KCMO-FM) for $11.2 million.

## Media Concentration Redux

Even before the transfer of power in Louisville, Gannett's accelerated expansion had not been universally acclaimed. In April 1986, the convention of the American Society of Newpaper Editors in Washington renewed that organization's debate on "merger mania."

The session was a panel entitled "Frenzy in the News Business: Where Will It All End?" Its panelists included John Morton, a newspaper analyst; Douglas Ginsburg, assistant U.S. attorney general in charge of antitrust; Ben Bagdikian, author, educator and critic of group ownership in general and the Gannett Company in particular; John Seigenthaler, president, publisher and editor of *The Tennessean*, editorial page editor of *USA TODAY*, and reformed chain-rattler *circa* 1979.

Seigenthaler's participation was of special interest because many remembered his debate with Neuharth at ASNE's Honolulu convention nine years before, where he had declared his "strong visceral preferences for locally owned and controlled newspapers."

Bagdikian, who led off, recalled that Seigenthaler had testified in 1978 before a Federal Trade Commission symposium on concentration of group ownership. "John's point then," Bagdikian said, "and mine now is that the game is about over, and we are not about to get a bill of divorcement for chain papers."

He again denounced chains for their "unusual pressure to produce maximum profits" and the demands he foresaw for uniformity and regularity. He faulted the federal government for being fainthearted in failing to challenge monopoly ownership.

Ginsburg responded by pointing out that what he called the government's forebearance rather than faintheartedness grew "out of a regard for the values that we have in this country regarding a free press."

Concentration of media ownership, Morton said, was no surprise to him, since "it has been happening to every other line of business in this country in this century. I am only surprised that it has taken so long or that it shocks anybody, if it still does."

"Those newspapers that will continue to prosper in the long run," he concluded, "whether owned by a large company or a small one, are going to be those that make strategic investments in editorial quality."

Seigenthaler was last to the podium. With him he carried not only the burden of his premise nine years before but a preemptive barb planted earlier by Bagdikian, who had said: "The presence of John Seigenthaler, of course, reminds us that the distinguished paper of which he is editor and publisher achieved its distinction under local ownership."

With a wry smile, Seigenthaler acknowledged reviewing that 1977 debate "as I was driving over here in Al's limousine." He recalled trying to needle Neuharth in Honolulu, "saying things like he had paid more for Shreveport than the United States government had paid for the Louisiana Purchase."

But Seigenthaler had not come to entertain. "I went back to those remarks I made that day," he said, "to see how embarrassed I would be to stand before you today and cite them. At that time *The Tennessean* was the independently owned morning newspaper in Nashville, and Gannett owned the *Nashville Banner.*"

In 1979, he had said, "It is a trap, I think, to try to equate local independent ownership with quality or to even hint that chain ownership connotes an absence of quality."

"The issue for me," he told his 1986 listeners, "was not whether Gannett had improved the *Banner,* nor should it be an issue here whether it has improved *The Tennessean.* It has, indeed."

In the nine-year interim, he said, he had come to see from a new vantage point both resources and professional integrity he had not sufficiently appreciated before.

Near the end of his remarks, he said, "Nostalgia for the past is nice, but reality is reality. If I had the choice of looking back and making another decision, I would not choose differently."

## A Challenge from the Floor

During the question period, an ASNE member rose to ask whether disappearance of independent family-owned newspapers was so inevitable that there could be no restrictions on heavily financed attempts to eliminate competition.

His question was prefaced, however, by an allusion that brought a startled gasp from the audience: "Mr. Seigenthaler has said, 'I had the same concern you do, young man, but it is really pretty nice out there.' I guess one could get similar imprecations by walking up and down 14th Street here [where prostitutes frequently solicited business] at a certain time of night."

The questioner was Carrick Patterson of the *Arkansas Gazette* in Little Rock, who described himself as "a third-generation editor of a family newspaper who is beginning to feel like the living dead."

Patterson's frustration grew out of the afternoon *Gazette's* draining battle with the *Arkansas Democrat*. That morning competitor was owned by Walter E. Hussman Jr., head of a prosperous group called WEHCO Media. The *Democrat* had been disastrously undercutting the *Gazette's* advertising rates. Although Patterson's sympathizers believed the case against the *Democrat* was clear, the paper had failed to win federal court relief on its claim of predatory pricing by its competitor.

Seigenthaler, a longtime friend and colleague of *Gazette* publisher Hugh Patterson, Carrick's father, calmly responded:

"I obviously have a great deal more respect and regard for Hugh Patterson and you . . . and the other people at the *Gazette* than you have for me, but that is to one side. I think that the real concern has to be not for this Justice Department or this administration, but for one that will look at the antitrust laws in a different way. . . . There will be another Justice Department that will come in and seek to enforce – vigorously enforce – antitrust laws [limiting competitive abuses]. And I think most chains I know about are aware of that, concerned about that and abide by the laws."[11]

Patterson's pointed disdain quickly became more understandable, if not more defensible. He and Seigenthaler had probably shared in April knowledge not learned by most until October.

On Dec. 1, 1986, Hugh Patterson sold the oldest newspaper west of the Mississippi and a two-time Pulitzer Prize winner for $51 million cash. Gannett bought it.

Seigenthaler was a member of the transition team. When the acquisition was completed in December, the elder Patterson became chairman and Carrick Patterson remained executive vice president and editor.

As president and publisher, Gannett chose William T. Malone, an Arkansas native who had been publisher in Springfield, Mo., and regional vice president of Gannett Central Newspaper Group.[12]

McCorkindale recalled in 1990 that he and Neuharth had regularly pressed Hugh Patterson, over a period of 10 years, to sell to Gannett.

"He was always saying that he would," McCorkindale said. "He would if he ever decided to sell. After the litigation, and the fact that Walter [Hussman] was willing to spend as much money as he was, trying to beat up on him, I think Hugh waited too long. He could have made his paper **the** paper if he had handled Walter differently and better, early on."[13]

The importance of Malone in Gannett's strategy was implicit in Curley's comment about the acquisition. "We're pleased to have someone who grew up reading the *Gazette* return to his home state as publisher."[14]

It was a sensible ploy, because the battle between the *Democrat* and the *Gazette* wasn't over. The terrain remained the same but the strategy would change.

# Chapter 40

# A Stronger Lineup

*"It matters not so much whether newspapers are owned by individuals or families or partners or chains. What really matters is what those owners do with them. It matters little how many newspapers serve a town or city. What really matters is how well they serve."*

*Al Neuharth*
*May 2, 1977*

At the time of Nashville's 1979 across-the-hall switch of newspapers, when sale of the *Nashville Banner* cleared the way for purchase of *The Tennessean*, Gannett owned 79 newspapers with combined circulation of more than 3.5 million. Nevertheless, it remained primarily a group of small and medium-sized newspapers.

Adding *The Tennessean* that August brought to four the number of Gannett newspapers whose circulation placed them among the top 100 nationally – and two of those, *The Cincinnati Enquirer* and the *Oakland Tribune*, had joined the family only two months earlier. The fourth among the top 100 was the venerable *Democrat and Chronicle* of Rochester.

By the end of 1986, after Neuharth's celebrated Triple Crown victories in Detroit, Louisville and Little Rock, and the 1985 addition of *The Des Moines Register*, Gannett dailies totaled 93, with combined circulation of 6 million. *The Detroit News*, *The Courier-Journal*, the *Arkansas Gazette* and *The Register* brought the group's top-100 membership to seven – *The Tribune* having been sold in 1983. *The Detroit News*, moreover, represented a giant step for Gannett, since it and its eventual JOA-bedfellow *Detroit Free Press* both consistently ranked among the nation's top 10 newspapers in circulation.

Those standings, however, are a small measure of what Gannett had achieved. From *The Tennessean* through the *Arkansas Gazette* it had absorbed five newspapers with established influence in their regions and editorial prestige acknowledged by the profession.

The new entry from Detroit, of course, was and would remain a behemoth in Michigan. *The Des Moines Register* blanketed Iowa. Little Rock's *Gazette* was first in Arkansas as *The Courier-Journal* was in Kentucky. And *The Tennessean* ranked second only to *The Commercial Appeal* of Memphis in total circulation.

For Gannett, these were individual acquisitions of unprecedented influence and stature. For the newspapers' longtime employees they were unnerving changes of association from family to corporate ownership. Any such change prompts feelings of apprehension and insecurity. Most of them knew about Gannett only what they had heard on the professional grapevine.

The reliability of such impressions was typified by the example of John Seigenthaler. At Honolulu in 1977, he had stood before his colleagues in the American Society of Newspaper Editors and sincerely denounced what he understood to be the Gannett Company. In spring of 1986 he publicly acknowledged to ASNE colleagues, including the skeptical Carrick Patterson of Little Rock, that the Gannett he had painted as a villain nine years earlier was not the Gannett he had come to know firsthand since 1979.

That was typical of the experiences of many newspaper people who reluctantly became part of a Gannett about which they were misinformed. Gannett found that to be true, for example, in both Nashville and Des Moines, but there were subtle differences.

# In the Enemy Camp

At *The Tennessean*, Gannett's difficulty was compounded because the source of much of the employees' apprehensiveness about the group had been Seigenthaler himself, who was their publisher.

When he heard of *The Tennessean's* impending sale, Seigenthaler explained in 1993, "I thought, I'm through. And the owners, Amon Carter Evans and his mother, thought the same thing I thought: He's through. He's been traveling around the country attacking chains, and Gannett, and now he's out."

In appreciation of Seigenthaler's 30 years of loyal service to their paper and because of their concern for his future, he said, they gave him a generous settlement. To his surprise, he said, "Neuharth called me and said, 'I read that you've been offered a job but we want you to stay there.' And I said, 'Great, but I obviously have some problems.'" [1]

Seigenthaler was concerned about retaining both his financial and editorial independence as a Gannett publisher. That was worked out by lawyers to the mutual satisfaction of the parties. The greater problem he had with the acquisition was *The Tennessean's* employees. "It scared them to death," he said. "Here's what you were looking at – an afternoon newspaper [the *Banner*] across the hall. [For] seven years, I'm going to our news meetings, kicking their ass, saying 'Gannett's over there. The giant's across the hall. Beat 'em! Beat 'em! Beat 'em!' . . .

"My idea was, I'm just going to kick Gannett every way I can. And I'd go into the news meeting, [or] the editorial meeting, I'd always have some bullshit story that was negative about Gannett, negative about Neuharth. . . . But I would kick Al, kick Al . . . then McCorkindale, kick the *Banner*. . . . And we had a laugh a day. . . .

"So by the time I was sold into chains, I had created a culture to hate Gannett. And I told them [at corporate], 'You've got to give me the chance to bring them back. I acknowledge what I've done. We were in a competitive situation and I don't apologize for what I did. But if you guys are going to abide by the agreement we've got, give me the time and I'll bring them back.'" [2]

Seigenthaler conceded that his own credibility with his staff was at stake, particularly for the first year. "If Al had pulled the rug out from under me, it would have been a disaster. . . . I think the turning point for us [was] when the staff realized that everything I was telling them about Gannett, and the contract, and the relationship was true . . . [that] as long as there was a legitimate reason to do what we wanted to do . . . the money was there, and that [Gannett was] willing to commit to quality journalism if you provided quality journalism." [3]

# Iowa Contrasts

Sale of *The Des Moines Register* in 1985 did not come as a surprise to its employees. That had been made inevitable the previous year by two of the newspaper's executives who feared that it was about to lose its independence in a possible merger with its larger sister newspaper in the Cowles Media Co., *The Minneapolis Star and Tribune*. The executives, Michael Gartner, president, and Gary Gerlach, publisher, arranged with some local businessmen and Dow Jones & Co. for an unsolicited offer to buy *The Register*. The principals presented the proposal to David Kruidenier, who was chief executive officer of both papers.

Kruidenier was required by law to inform the board of directors of the offer. When shareholders got the word, pressures to sell *The Register* became irresistible. Cowles Media announced in late autumn of 1984 that *The Register* would be sold and invited bids from interested companies.

Gartner and Gerlach, who had unwittingly forced Kruidenier's hand, were placed on indefinite leave. Charles C. Edwards Jr., a nephew of Kruidenier, had been with *The Register* for 14 years and was its marketing director. He was made acting publisher pending the paper's sale. He shared with Richard Gilbert, who was named acting president, the responsibility for day-to-day management of *The Register*.

The two of them, Edwards explained in 1993, also "dealt with the individual buyers as they came in. We were intimately involved in the first impressions of these different buyers as they came in to kick the tires."[4]

Before the potential buyers started to arrive, Edwards said, sentiment, particularly in the newsroom, was strongly for sale to "The New York Times [Co.], or Knight-Ridder, even the Chicago Tribune [Co.]" That attitude changed, he said, particularly among the people who interviewed the bidders and sensed their intentions.

"All of us had started at the front end," Edwards said, "saying,

'God, I hope that . . . one of the family companies ends up buying the newspaper. And at the end, 'I hope Gannett ends up buying this place.'

"It was the attitude of the people who came to see us, the kinds of questions they asked. It was the respect for what was here."[5]

## Uncertainty Tells

Employees in Des Moines were apprehensive, Edwards said, even before they knew who the buyer would be. Economic necessity had forced *The Register* to cut costs, Edwards said, and one method had been an early retirement offer. The number of employees considering that offer, he said, jumped dramatically after the intent to sell was announced, indicating employees' anxiety about their future.

"First," Edwards said, "we just didn't know whether it would be sold, then we knew it would be sold but we didn't know who it would be sold to, and then we knew it would be sold to Gannett but we didn't know anything about Gannett except for what we heard and what we read and what we feared. So it evolved through a number of different stages but the anxiety level always remained very high."[6]

The anxiety was heightened, Edwards said, "because people had gone from feeling quite secure to feeling totally insecure and hurt. They felt that Mike and Gary, for whom they had formed a lot of loyalty, had jeopardized the company for their own selfish interests. They certainly put it at risk of being sold to the wrong company."[7]

Edwards and Gilbert's own uncertainties were not eased by the timetable of the sale. Gannett was declared the successful bidder in January of 1985, but the sale would not become final until July 1. "[We] had to try to manage the place in our acting capacities," he said. "Not knowing whether we had jobs or whether anybody else in the place had jobs, we were going to have to try to keep things under control for six months.

"So at our request, [Kruidenier] called Neuharth and said something to this effect: . . . 'If there's anything you can do to give the company or the people in this company some sense of who is going to be running [it] when you take over, give them any sense of what the future looks like, the better it's going to be for you.'"[8]

Neuharth's response was to accompany John Curley and Bill Keating, then Newspaper Division president, in a corporate visit to Des Moines. They first sat down with *The Register's* management team. Then they demonstrated Gannett's preference for continuity.

Edwards was named publisher – he has since become president and publisher. "They didn't replace anybody," Edwards said. "They didn't bring a new publisher in. They didn't replace the editor. They came back to town and we had a nice reception. . . . Nobody saw them again. Everyone was sort of looking around corners wondering where these guys were, and they weren't there."[9]

Curley made a special visit to Des Moines, Edwards said, "to tell us personally that Gannett was going to keep Michael [Gartner]. . . . He understood how that was going to play in Des Moines and I think he felt a responsibility to communicate that personally. That meant a lot to us and I think that was communicated throughout the newsroom."[10]

(Gartner carried out a variety of corporate assignments before leaving Gannett in 1988 to become president of the television news division of the National Broadcasting Company.)

There were no arbitrary changes in Des Moines of the sort anxious employees feared. *The Register's* highly regarded Washington bureau continued to operate. Its dominance as a statewide newspaper was never put in jeopardy. Its value as a provider of outstanding reporting on agriculture was appreciated and encouraged.

"To this date," Edwards said in 1993, "there haven't been any sweeping changes. We've cycled through some things, the industry has changed, and so we've changed as a result, but the place just hasn't been 'Gannettized.' That was the buzz word . . . we're going to be Gannettized. They're going to have a bunch of clones or . . . a bunch of Al Neuharth robots running around here."[11]

## So What Changed?

Apprehensive employees who foresaw disruption found stability instead, both in Nashville and Des Moines. At *The Tennessean*, anxiety prompted an unsuccessful attempt to unionize the newsroom, to Seigenthaler's dismay. While that was under way, he said later, the dissidents persuaded their fellow employees to spurn the Gannett pension plan. A year later, Seigenthaler said, employees recognized that the Gannett plan was much better than theirs and pressed for it.

"A year ago you said you didn't want it," he said he told them. "But can you get it?" they asked. The change eventually was arranged, he said, and "when we got the Gannett pension plan, there was monumental support for it."[12]

Beyond such personal gains, employees at Nashville also came to enjoy working in what Seigenthaler in 1993 proudly called the most modern plant in the South. New construction, new presses, new printing systems, all the improvements were the result of Gannett's $70-million capital investment in *The Tennessean*.

"What differences does it make to the paper?" Seigenthaler asked. "It looks better, reads better, the color's better. It was a **big** help."[13]

Edwards tallied similar results in Des Moines.

"One of the things that are not very well understood," he said, "this place was a wreck when Gannett bought it. The condition of this newspaper [plant] was a disgrace when Gannett bought it."[14]

Since then, major capital expenditures modernized the mailroom operation, transformed the pressroom and replaced obsolete equipment. *The Register* eight years later had more employees than it had when Gannett acquired it in 1985, and their benefits had been expanded.

# Shared Experience

The first association of any newspaper with Gannett is shaped by its individual character and prospects. Apprehensiveness also surely existed in Louisville, Little Rock and Detroit. In the case of the last however, its size and the complexity of its established operation ruled out any likelihood of turning the place on its ear, even had Gannett uncharacteristically wished to do so.

The defeats and frustrations that the *Arkansas Gazette* continued to suffer in the injurious competition with the *Arkansas Democrat* eclipsed any immediate plans Gannett might have had to reshape that new member of the family. Major advertisers on which the *Gazette* relied for revenues had withdrawn and could not be persuaded to return.

The *Democrat* was soliciting subscriptions with promises that the money would go to the Salvation Army. Seigenthaler, who was part of a Gannett team in Little Rock for the change of ownership, described that campaign:

"[We] found that what they were really doing was half [to the Salvation Army], and the other half went to them, and the [Audit Bureau of Circulations] recorded it as a subscription."

Seigenthaler said Curley quickly accepted a proposal that the *Gazette* counter with a pledge to share new subscription money with every United Way agency.

"I thought early on we had a fighting chance," Seigenthaler said. "But the only way we could compete was to do everything [the *Democrat*] did, and do it one better. . . . I think that . . . after the first six months, we sort of punished out. We said, 'We'll take half the punishment and give some of it back.'" [15]

"The fatal blow," Curley recalled in 1993, "was when Dillard's [department store] dropped out of the paper. We couldn't get Dillard's back [and] he was a lead dog advertiser. . . . I called on Dillard myself. . . . They were friendly, but we weren't going to get any business." [16]

In Louisville, of course, any fear that employees had of Gannett's reputation was eclipsed by their sadness as they watched the tragic disintegration of the family that had won honor and distinction for *The Courier-Journal*.

A longtime employee in Louisville acknowledged some misgivings in a letter he sent to John Curley in 1992. Donald B. Towles, who was retiring as vice president and director of public affairs after 37 years with *The Courier-Journal*, wrote:

"Many of us had apprehensions when the Binghams decided to sell the newspapers in 1986. Those apprehensions have been erased in the past six years as a result of working for a highly professional and highly competent organization.

"Whatever I may have accomplished here was made possible by a strong commitment to journalism – first by the Binghams and later by Gannett. " [17]

The strongest evidence for or against Gannett lies in each case with the newspaper. Especially significant, as Seigenthaler and Edwards pointed out, is that although both their papers now call Gannett home, to readers *The Tennessean* is still *The Tennessean*, *The Register* remains *The Register*. Today's Gannett Company remains faithful in that regard to the clear intent set down by Frank Gannett as he began acquiring community newspapers early in the century.

# Chapter 41

# It's Show Time

*"It's not the same business [as] when I started. Either you have deep pockets or you have a partner with deep pockets to protect you from the terrible economics of this business."*

Grant Tinker<br>October 1990

The influential newspapers acquired by Gannett in 1986 posed major challenges as 1987 began. Add to that Al Neuharth's avowed interest in new ventures and exorbitant ideas among owners and trustees about the market value of available newspapers. The prospect was a period of diminished acquisitions but lively undertakings.

That year, in fact, transactions were limited to sales. WCZY-AM and FM, the radio stations acquired in the Combined Communications merger, were sold early in January to Sky Radio Broadcasting Corp. for $15.5 million. (This entity has no connection to the Gannett unit, USA TODAY Sky Radio.) Gannett Outdoor Group sold Tencon, an electrical sign company in Centerville, Tenn., in August to Plasti-Line Inc. for $7 million.

Among Neuharth's new ventures in 1987 were Gannett's entry into TV show business, which he had announced just before the new year, and an ambitious Neuharth motor tour of every state in the nation, with heavy emphasis on its promotional value to *USA TODAY* and the company itself.

## West Coast Premiere

Neuharth had told the directors in December 1986 that Gannett would invest in a partnership to produce prime-time television programming and films. The partner was Grant Tinker, most recently chairman of the National Broadcasting Company and earlier the co-founder, with his then-wife, actress Mary Tyler Moore, of MTM Entertainment, Inc., well-known for such TV successes as "The Mary Tyler Moore Show," "The Bob Newhart Show," "Lou Grant" and "Hill Street Blues."

Gannett's investment was estimated to be about $40 million for half interest in what would become GTG Entertainment, $25 million to $30 million to buy studios and an additional $15 million to renovate them. A week after Neuharth's revelation, Gannett successfully bid $24 million at a Los Angeles auction for Laird International Studios, the Culver City lot where "Gone With the Wind" and "Citizen Kane" had been filmed.

After the auction, Curley said, "It's natural for us to expand into entertainment programming and we are delighted to team up with Grant Tinker."

This was a new direction for Gannett, but director Julian Goodman, also a former head of NBC, had assured his fellow board members at the December meeting "that Mr. Tinker's chances of success are high in this relatively unpredictable business." [1]

Neuharth, Curley and McCorkindale appeared Jan. 10, 1987, with Tinker at a Los Angeles news conference to explain their intent. "It is their money," Tinker said of Gannett, "and my effort."

"He's the boss," Neuharth said. "We think we'll have some fun and maybe make a little money. Gannett has been looking for ways to get into the software end of this business for quite some time. This is our first stab at it." [2]

Tinker said new shows were not yet being developed but he hoped to have at least one series ready for a major network – later announced as CBS – in the middle of the 1987-88 season.

"We're open to using the project as a springboard to get into production," Neuharth said, "but where it goes and how far and how quickly is really up to Grant. We'll provide the facilities." [3]

By April, GTG had announced that "Van Dyke," starring Dick Van

Dyke, would be on the fall CBS schedule and that two other series would appear sometime the following season. One show also was tentatively scheduled for that season by ABC.

## USA TODAY on TV

On June 23, 1987, GTG Entertainment announced that it was developing a nightly television news program based on *USA TODAY*. Steve Friedman, former producer of NBC's "Today," had been hired to create the show as his first assignment with GTG East.

"We believe The Nation's Newspaper has as much to offer the USA's television viewers as it offers newspaper readers," Neuharth said. He and Tinker said they would decide early in 1988 whether to debut the show that fall.[4]

By February 1988, *The Wall Street Journal* was predicting, "TV Version of USA Today May Be Financial – if Not Critical – Success." It reported that 86 TV stations already had signed up to air the show – without seeing a pilot.

"USA TODAY: The Television Show" debuted in September on 156 stations. It was promptly carpet-bombed by media TV critics: (makes) " 'Sesame Street' look like a course in western civilization"[5]; "a buckshot spray of brief, lightweight features, snippets of interviews and idle trivia. . . . We hate it"[6]; "Steve Friedman has seen the future, and it's $40 million of *filler* gussied up as a slot machine in the middle of what looks like an airport – Big Brotherly monitors and wanton graphics; distended bars of color and broken bars of music; dominoes, cylinders, whirlpools – through which the yupscale anchorpeople wander as hungry for meaning as nomadic goats."[7]

In October 1988, a month after its launch, the show had added a managing editor. By November, Friedman had left to develop other projects for GTG East. *Electronic Media* reported in December 1988 that the show was being "re-launched." Part of its problem, the trade publication said, was that only 122 of the 156 subscribing stations were showing it in prime time access. On the rest it appeared on late night, which, in TV parlance, means in the wee hours.

A year later, the show had its fourth manager, its original staff of 151 had been cut in half and a media deathwatch was on. In January 1993, Curley recalled that Neuharth had recognized as early as 1988 that GTG wasn't going to work, with or without "USA TODAY ON TV." "Doug [McCorkindale] and I tried to get them interested by saying, 'If you take $40 million more can you make something of it?'

"Grant said, 'Absolutely not, we need $200 million more to start and then we don't know where we're going.'

"'Well, can you live with $40 million more, to see where it takes you?' we said. But Grant insisted that they had to have $200 million. So we decided that basically, it was the wrong horse to back."

Tinker and Curley, by then Gannett chairman, president and CEO, announced in November 1989 that the show would end Jan. 7, 1990.

"While we're obviously disappointed that 'USA TODAY ON TV' didn't attract a wider audience," they said, "we're proud of the program's quality and high journalistic standards." [8]

At the Gannett board's February 1990 meeting, McCorkindale reported that Tinker had sought another partner without success and that Gannett's partnership with him would end March 31.

Three GTG network TV shows, "Baywatch," "Raising Miranda" and "Van Dyke," had suffered the fate of "USA TODAY ON TV." Tinker was talking publicly about calling it quits.

Columbia Pictures Entertainment bought The Culver Studios from Gannett on June 26, 1991. The sale price was $80 million.

## Seeing the USA by Bus

Neuharth had hoped to have some fun and maybe make a little money with GTG Entertainment. If that project eventually turned out to be a disappointment, his other new venture in 1987 proved both pleasurable and, in terms of its public relations value, profitable.

On March 16, 1987, Neuharth and a Gannett news team embarked on a six-month "BusCapade," which began in Potosi, Mo., and ended in Washington, D.C. They interviewed governors and ordinary citizens in each state, chronicling their travels in USA TODAY and via Gannett News Service.

"We'll start at the nation's population center," Neuharth said, "and end at the world's action center."[9]

Given Neuharth's flair for promotion, of course, there would be a book in it. In September, the company published a compendium of the color photographs and written reports of the trip: *BusCapade: Plain Talk Across the USA.*

In June, while Neuharth was with BusCapade in his home state of South Dakota, he received a telegram from Curley with the best promotional news he could have wanted for USA TODAY:

"McPaper has made it. USA TODAY broke into black with profit of $1,093,756 for month of May, six months ahead of schedule. Staff betting you'll forgive us for ruining your prediction that we'd have to wait until end of year. Hope you'll fly back to Washington for champagne celebration tomorrow."[10]

On July 2, 1987, Gannett issued the first comprehensive statement illustrating the cost of creating USA TODAY and confounding its doomsayers.

After-tax operating losses for USA TODAY's nearly five years of existence were approximately $233 million, Neuharth and Curley said in their joint statement. They pointed out that that "total investment" was less than the $305 million paid for the Louisville *Courier-Journal* a year earlier.

Revenues for 1987, the statement said, were about $250 million, which was what Gannett had projected at the start in 1982. For 1987, it said, losses had been projected at $34 million, but were expected to be one-third of that.

In addition to the operating losses expensed by Gannett on a period-by-period basis, there were certain capital expenditures for USA TODAY, including $30.3 million for 134,981 street corner vending machines. Other Gannett expenditures for production and press equipment could not be accurately allocated to USA TODAY because it also was used for printing other Gannett newspapers, the statement said.

There was no reference to the costs borne by other Gannett newspapers for the salaries, living expenses and costs of benefits for the army of "loaners" that had sustained the fledgling national newspaper in its early years.

The statement declared USA TODAY's second quarter "close to break-even" and looked ahead to "a meaningful profit for the fourth quarter of 1987."[11]

# Good News, Bad News

USA TODAY's problems with circulation and advertising persisted, despite the first – and temporary – appearance of black ink on the balance sheet. Advertisers remained elusive, even though pundits had predicted that their reluctance would vanish once the new paper had achieved a magic 1 million paid circulation, which it had surpassed in its first full year of publication. Its inaugural Advertising Partnership Program, which promised six months of free advertising to anyone signing a contract for the first 15 months, generated encouraging but insufficient commitments. For nearly five years, a small army of sales personnel had poured new ideas and boundless energy into the campaign for advertising revenue, with persistently disappointing response.

Circulation growth for USA TODAY was a qualified success in spite of itself. Throughout the paper's development and during its introductory period, Neuharth and company had insisted that the paper would be a second purchase in all markets. They assured critics that it was not intended to supplant other newspapers and pointed to its vast, single-copy distribution network as proof.

The result, as Jack Heselden later described it, was that USA TODAY's soaring popularity with readers caught Gannett "flatfooted," unprepared to satisfy the heavy but unanticipated demand for mail and home delivery. Correcting that meant even greater financial burdens.

"People did want it delivered," Heselden said, "and also we needed those [circulation] numbers, so we spent a lot of money on home delivery. We weren't ready with the billing operation. . . . It upset people that we weren't ready to deliver, that we didn't do the delivery that we should have done. And then the billing was terrible. When you upset people in three areas of your relationship with the customer, when you lose them, it's hard to get them back."[12]

Strong reader acceptance and stubborn advertiser resistance were a paradox that Gannett and *USA TODAY* would have to combat for years to come.

## The CEO Reports

Curley confirmed at the annual management meeting in December 1987 what executives had expected to hear. Gannett would end the year with revenues close to $3.1 billion. And *USA TODAY*, which had had its first profitable month in May, would record its first profitable quarter at the end of the year.

"For *USA TODAY*, that's a $50-million-plus turnaround in a year," Curley said.

Only a few executives at the December meeting were old enough to remember, as Cal Mayne had recalled, when Paul Miller had said, "If you want to get me out of here, become a $300-million company."

Other good news in 1987 included:

• The company would report its 20th year and 81st quarter in its unbroken string of consecutive earnings increases.

• *The Des Moines Register* had brought Gannett its 37th Pulitzer Prize, for feature photography.

• Both *The Detroit News* and the *Arkansas Gazette*, acquired only the year before, and operating in fiercely competitive markets, had pro-

duced gains in circulation and advertising market share.
 • Outdoor Network, USA, a consortium of outdoor advertising firms headed by Gannett Outdoor, had shown a 50 percent increase in new business.

"We're cautiously optimistic," Curley said, "but prepared to scale down as necessary if conditions warrant." [13]

Gannett began 1988 by paying Harte-Hanks Communications Inc. $155 million in February for two television stations – WFMY-TV in Greensboro, N.C., and WTLV-TV in Jacksonville, Fla. – bringing Gannett's share of the U.S. TV market to 11 percent.

Later that month, it picked up $128 million when Cowles Media Co. bought back the stock it had sold to Gannett in 1986.

In July, Gannett spent $44 million to acquire New York Subways Advertising, Inc., a transit shelter advertising operation in a number of major markets around the country.

And before the year was out, Gannett sold the *Coffeyville Journal* in Kansas to Hometown Communications Inc. for $2.4 million.

Most significant of the year's events was the December board meeting at which the directors affirmed that Curley would become the chairman when Neuharth retired in March 1989.

The *Sturgis* (Mich.) *Journal* and the *Fremont* (Neb.) *Tribune* were sold in March 1989. Hometown Communications purchased the *Journal* for $4 million and the *Tribune* for $10 million.

# Flight Plan

The company's highest-paid travel writer had been encouraged by the substantial media coverage of BusCapade to think global. Local and national coverage of Neuharth's 50-state reporting trip had been tremendous.

Whether the reports were straightforward or nitpicking – and there were many of both – the tour had been heavily publicized and *USA TODAY* was invariably featured.

Neuharth had announced at the end of BusCapade that it would be JetCapade in 1988. The intent was similar, albeit considerably more ambitious. Interviews with more than 30 world leaders and hundreds of their fellow citizens appeared regularly in *USA TODAY* and on the GNS wire between February and September 1988.

Several books came out of the trip, most notably *Window on the World: Faces, Places & Plain Talk from 32 Countries*.

Together, BusCapade and JetCapade provided a wall-covering gallery of photographs of the type often irreverently characterized as Famous People Who Have Met Me.

Neuharth's globe-trotting JetCapade won *USA TODAY* and Gannett's chairman worldwide attention. That was a plus in a year that found Curley and his associates wrestling with both the likely failure of "USA TODAY ON TV" and GTG Entertainment and the unwelcome distractions created by the volatile Robert McKinney at *The New Mexican* in Santa Fe.

Neuharth, Curley and McCorkindale had told the board in December 1987 they were confident of a better working relationship in Santa Fe. Events through 1988 thwarted that hope. McKinney would be one of the persistent problems with which Curley would have to deal after he succeeded Neuharth as chairman.

At the Gannett board meeting March 22, 1989, Neuharth's last as chairman, he made the surprise announcement that he would also resign his directorship at the annual shareholders' meeting April 27.

Neuharth's resignation as a director came two years before his term expired. He explained:

"I am convinced that when a retired former CEO remains on the board of directors of a corporation, his/her mere presence is often an inhibiting factor. I do not wish to risk bridling either my successor or the board in any way."[14]

The third distinctive era in the evolution of Gannett was ending – a quarter-century of unprecedented expenditures and earnings; of phenomenal growth by acquisition and, more significantly, by creation of new products; of newly established professional opportunities and stature for minorities and women, and of controversy and acclaim delightedly induced by the studied idiosyncracies of Allen H. Neuharth.

With the blessing of Paul Miller, he had defied all the prophets and made a success in record time of a brand new newspaper, *Today*, in Florida. He had applied the lessons of that regional success to the patently ridiculous idea of creating a totally different national newspaper – and confounded the prophets again.

He smiled as detractors scorned *USA TODAY* as McPaper, satisfied that, like McDonald's after which it was derisively named, he could confidently escalate its promotional boasts – 1 million read, 2 million read, right on up to more than 5 million read.

With the help of Miller and his close friendships with a host of newspaper owners, Neuharth quickened the growth of Gannett that Miller had fostered. Later, when institutional imperatives supplanted personal relationships in the newspaper world, he combined his acquisitive instincts with the legal and financial savvy of Doug McCorkindale in transactions that awed Gannett's competitors.

He had the respect – and wary skepticism – of his peers. Myopic critics concentrated on the flair of his wardrobe and the unpredictable in his social life, apparently or deliberately blind to his immense influence on a profession he had loved from childhood.

His colleagues and subordinates found him single-minded, demanding but fair, consistently working harder himself than he expected them to do.

How did the retired Neuharth see the working Neuharth?

"[Work] was not my only interest," he said, "but it was my strongest and primary interest. I hope I did not and I don't think I ever asked anybody to work any harder or maybe even as hard as I did.

"I liked starting new things," he said. "Every time we turned the press on a new paper – whether it was a new Sunday edition somewhere or whether it was *FLORIDA TODAY*, or *USA TODAY*, or *EastBay Today* or *Westchester Today* – to me that's creating something. I never did get a hell of a lot of kick out of buying [newspapers]. I knew we had to do it to expand and grow."

His biggest single achievement? "I'd be lying or kidding if I didn't say that [it] was *USA TODAY*. . . . if you look at the pull, what it did and is doing to Gannett's image, and what it did and has done in creating hundreds . . . of opportunities for our people to move into a major league operation in these days.

"I would put the financial success of Gannett as number three on the list of whatever contributions I made," he said. "I think the first was the people program. That did more to advance the diversity of people and opportunities for people of all sexes and races over a period of 10 or 20 years than any other company, and my own feeling is that I made a greater contribution to that than I did in anything else.

"I think the second is the product. I did have some influence in hiring good editors and letting them edit and putting more money into news operations.

"And the third, I think we had pretty good financial success but I don't think that was number one. . . . I certainly never devoted as much time and attention to the bottom line as I did to the people and to the product." [15]

Like Miller before him, Neuharth relinquished leadership of Gannett but he remained chairman of the Gannett Foundation, for which he had big plans.

Curley became chairman, president and chief executive officer April 1, 1989.

# Chapter 42

# Change of Command

*"I'd like to see us become known for our products, . . . as good community newspapers, at whatever level, . . . as a company that put a lot of money back into newspapers . . . [and to] continue with the innovation that became a hallmark of Neuharth's tenure, to bring out things that just make sense for the information age."*

John Curley<br>June 16, 1992

All Neuharth watchers had been fascinated by the contrasts between him and John Curley since Curley's promotion to CEO in 1986. They grew even more watchful with Neuharth's retirement.

Immediately obvious was Curley's indifference to a range of expensive perks that were emblematic of Neuharth's rank. Jet airplanes, helicopters and limousines were, to Curley, simply means of transportation. If one of them was necessary to get him where he had to go, he would use it.

"John and I will take the Metro (Washington subway) over to a meeting," Doug McCorkindale said in 1990. "There are still some folks in the Gannett Company who don't understand that that happens to be quicker and easier. They're like Al, he'd jog five miles and then take a limo two blocks. . . .

"[John] takes whatever's the most practical air transportation. Al doesn't understand that. He wants to arrive in a grandiose style . . . and John just wants to get there."[1]

Curley's rejection of those executive perquisites and his emphasis on economy at corporate headquarters prompted a wisecrack among Neuharth needlers that his departure had produced an immediate saving of $14 million.[2]

Such comparisons were as misleading as they were facile.

Neuharth and Curley both had solid experience as reporters, editors and publishers. Curley's commitment both to Gannett and *USA TODAY* was no less than Neuharth's.

As the national newspaper's first editor, Curley endured with The Founder the derisive dismissals: "the New Non-Journalism,"[3] "an appeal to information junkies,"[4] an editorial page that "lowered unpredictability to a new level of uninspired treacle."[5]

Curley also shared Neuharth's pleasure in *USA TODAY's* eventual respectability, as well as its earlier obvious influence on major U.S. newspapers. And he was as pleased as the chairman he would replace when he reported during BusCapade in 1987 that *USA TODAY* had posted its first profit.

When Neuharth chose Curley as his successor, he was not looking for a clone. He had sought someone as committed as he to the news side of newspapers, a spirit as free as he to dare to be different.

Neuharth never pretended he would be another Paul Miller – some of whose strengths Neuharth conceded he lacked. Nor did he expect his successor to be another Neuharth. The Neuharth/Curley watchers showed little perception of that during the transition.

# The Santa Fe Tra(va)il

One of Curley's first impediments as the new Gannett chairman was the persistent problem in Santa Fe. Robert McKinney had been a pain in the family since Gannett had bought *The New Mexican* at Miller's behest in 1976.

McKinney had successfully sued Gannett to recover *The New Mexican* but was thwarted when Gannett won a reversal on appeal. Despite continued attempts by various Gannett executives to mediate the differences, the tumultuous relationship with McKinney had continued to deteriorate.

By June 1989, after what Curley called "severe executive turnover" at *The New Mexican,* McKinney had agreed to allow Gannett to appoint a manager for the paper. Then he changed his mind.

McCorkindale and Gary Watson – at the time president of the Community Group of Gannett papers – had met with McKinney, who had offered $20 million to repurchase *The New Mexican*. Since the executive committee had turned down an offer of $25 million early in the year, McCorkindale again had said no and told McKinney that higher prices had been offered by other interested parties.

McKinney had the right of first refusal, McCorkindale told the board, but was unlikely to exercise it if the price were substantially above $20 million.

In a 1992 interview, Curley recalled the situation he confronted in Santa Fe when he became chairman. He sought an informal meeting with McKinney.

"Rather than prolong this thing," he said, "I wanted to see where he really was and what we could do about working together. Instead of returning the call, he had a lawyer call back and say that the lawyers would meet with us."

They met with the lawyers at least twice, he said, and then decided it wasn't going to work.

"We went out and found a couple of potential buyers," Curley said, "and we told McKinney that if he wanted to make an offer, fine, we'd entertain that. He basically said no. Then, when we found a buyer and told him we had, he sued us again."

After several more talks, McKinney's lawyers made an offer in late 1989. "The price tag was good," Curley said, "but beyond that, it wasn't going to work and we weren't going to spend more time trying to deal with the idiosyncracies of McKinney."[6] The price tag was 800,000 shares of Gannett stock valued at $33.5 million.

Gannett also sold *El Diario*, its Spanish-language newspaper in New York, in August 1989, for $15 million.

Early in 1990, Gannett made its first major acquisition in nearly two years. It paid $41 million to Cowles Media Co. for the *Great Falls Tribune*, Montana's second-largest daily.

# Foundation Ferment

Former chairman Neuharth was gone but not forgotten. He had become chairman of the Gannett Foundation in 1985 and retained the position after he retired from Gannett. He retained his flamboyance, as well, the first signs of which were moving the foundation from Rochester to Arlington in November 1989 and building a lavish headquarters in an office building across the street from Gannett. Barbara Whitney, who had designed the posh interiors of Gannett headquarters, was commissioned to select $1 million worth of art.[7]

Spending at the foundation's Gannett Center for Media Studies at Columbia University more than tripled, from $5.9 million in 1988 to $19.3 million in 1989.

Gene Dorsey, foundation president, quickly differed with the chairman's new directions for Frank Gannett's philanthropies. Dorsey decided in November, just before he was about to move from Rochester, to take early retirement and remain in the Flower City.

"I tried to exercise some fiscal restraint," he said in a 1990 interview. "I felt that there were just too many areas in which his standard of living would be in conflict with the purposes and the mission of the foundation, so I raised these issues with Al. Al then very quickly raised them with the executive committee of the foundation. The executive committee was unwilling to oppose Al.

"Al was very fair with me, very open. He said he didn't want to lose my experience and hoped I would stay. He said I could choose to become vice chairman of the foundation and continue to do a lot of the things that I had been doing."[8] Dorsey said he thought about it and decided to leave anyway.

To replace Dorsey as president, Neuharth chose Charles Overby, who had resigned as Gannett's vice president/news in July 1989 to take the post of executive vice president at the foundation.

The increased spending for the new headquarters, larger staff and perquisites aggravated a problem the foundation had always had. Federal law required it to distribute annually 5 percent of the value of its capital – nearly 16 million shares of Gannett stock worth more than $560 million at prevailing trades then around $36 a share.

Since Gannett dividends provided an annual return of about 3 percent or less, the foundation frequently had to distribute stock or sell assets to meet the federal requirement.

April 1990 saw significant changes in the relationship between the company and the foundation:

- John Quinn, who had started in Rochester 24 years before, retired. Curley chose Peter Prichard to replace him as chief news executive and editor of *USA TODAY*. Quinn became a trustee and member of the executive committee of the Gannett Foundation.

- Neuharth announced that the foundation's Gannett stock was for sale to the highest bidder. That block represented 10 percent of the company's outstanding stock, so the announcement triggered immediate speculation about Gannett's vulnerability to an unwelcome takeover or merger.

Gannett executives, including Curley, had to resign immediately from the foundation board to avoid conflicts of interest over sale of the stock. Curley and McCorkindale talked with Neuharth and Overby in April about buying the stock, but they could not agree on a price. Since Gannett was trading then between $36 and $37 a share, Curley and McCorkindale considered that a reasonable range. Neuharth and Overby, however, remembered that a few years back, before the October 1987 stock market crash, Gannett had been trading at $55 a share. They weren't satisfied with $36 or $37.

Things grew more strained when large blocks of Gannett stock began to be traded in anticipation of a drop in earnings for the second quarter of 1990.

# War of Words

In July, Gannett reported its first quarterly drop in earnings in its 22-year history as a publicly held company. Neuharth had always relished announcing consecutive increases in earnings. When the series stopped at 90, Neuharth observed publicly that there was no reason it could not have gone to 91.

Times had changed, however. The country had entered a recession. The tide of acquisitions that had fueled Gannett's previous earnings gains had slowed to a trickle. Advertising and circulation revenues were soft throughout the industry. And it didn't help relations with the foundation leadership when *The Wall Street Journal* reported that some analysts believed the company under Curley was more efficient and cost-conscious than it had been under Neuharth.

Gannett publishers and editors were stunned in June by an indefinite delay in the foundation's Community Priorities Program, annual grants that were payable in Gannett stock. That program was one of many foundation philanthropies that had demonstrated, as Frank Gannett had intended, the commitment of the Gannett Co. to those communities served by its operating units.

On July 31, Overby wrote to Gannett publishers with the good news that the foundation had approved nearly $1 million in those delayed community grants. The bad news was that it had rejected applications for nearly $2 million. He explained that since the foundation's Gannett stock was on the block, shares were no longer available for the program.

Alarmed executives in the field turned to the corporate parent in desperation. Whether or not those annual grants had been viewed as discretionary dollars, as Overby had suggested in a letter to operating unit heads, they had become persuasive evidence in their towns that Gannett cared.

Curley responded in an Aug. 30 letter to Gannett executives. It mentioned no names but made clear that negotiations on sale of the stock had been snagged on the price issue.

"We do not plan to do a transaction," Curley wrote, "which puts unreasonable pressure on you to provide unrealistic earnings."

He also described as "untrue and unfounded" reports attributed to foundation representatives that Gannett had welcomed a down second quarter in order to lower the stock price, and that the company had been unwilling to negotiate on the stock purchase.

"Whatever the reasons," Curley wrote, "for the foundation's policy changes, the holdback on grants and the lack of specificity as to why grants are not acceptable, it has nothing to do with the Gannett Company nor any lack of desire on our part to acquire the foundation stock."

Curley's letter touched a nerve. On Sept. 7, 1990, a six-page letter, again over Overby's signature, went out to "local Gannett CEOs" with copies to the Gannett Management Committee, Gannett Board of Directors, Gannett Foundation Trustees and Gannett Foundation senior executives.

It expressed concern that the half-century relationship between the foundation and the company was coming apart, but said that was unnecessary and unfortunate.

The letter sought to narrow the focus of the problem. "Can Gannett Company local executives," it asked, "and the Gannett Foundation share a positive, creative partnership in a new, independent relationship that will suit changing times, circumstances and needs?"

"No one at the foundation is mad at anyone," the letter said, but it singled out Curley and McCorkindale by name.

"Criticism of the foundation's grantmaking in John Curley's August 30 letter to you is his right," it said, "but it is hardly his responsibility."

It accused McCorkindale of helping to drive down the market value of the foundation's assets by "leaking to selected analysts word of the expected decline [in Gannett earnings] 10 days in advance of the public announcement."

The letter explained that when Frank Gannett established the foundation, he had made clear he did not wish to run it from the grave – as indeed he had – and that his wishes in any case had become academic when Gannett became a publicly held company in 1967.

The letter reviewed the earlier commitments that the foundation would continue to meet, detailed the programs that were suspended or delayed, and said the company and its operating units would have to choose their local philanthropies.

"We can work constructively together," the letter concluded, or, it warned in an angrily fractured cliche, "a few short-sighted Gannett Company leaders [can] squander future opportunities by kicking a gift-horse in the mouth."

Curley announced on Oct. 24, 1990, that the company would set aside $4 million to $5 million for 1991 to help replace foundation cutbacks in grants to local charities. A Management Contributions Committee would review applications and approve grants to a maximum of $25,000. The program was called the Gannett Communities Fund.

A day later, the foundation announced that it would provide $10 million in 1991 "to foster First Amendment freedoms across the USA and around the world and to support related community activities."

Half that amount was for challenge grants in Gannett communities, to be matched by the corporation, its local subsidiaries or other organizations.

## Transformation

Eventually, the impasse was resolved as business improved and Gannett stock appreciated. On June 19, 1991, the foundation sold its stock to Gannett at fair market, $670 million. By that time it had become the Freedom Forum, with its slogan – classically Neuharthian in its alliteration – "Free Speech, Free Press, Free Spirit."

Neuharth discussed the name change and his views of the relationship between the company and the foundation during a 1992 interview.

The name change, he said, was to eliminate confusion. "Headlines would call it Gannett when it was the Gannett Foundation or call it Gannett Foundation when it was Gannett. It was just total confusion. . . . I felt there should be more of a separation and it should be clearly delineated. There was no reason we couldn't be friends and deal with each other, but that we ought to do it at arm's length. . . .

"The Gannett Company, when I was in it, was a very poor corporate citizen. We didn't do anything for the community. The foundation did. And that's two entirely different things. So I felt that we ought to have that division, where the company assumed some corporate responsibility as a citizen, and where the foundation didn't devote all or nearly 100 percent of its resources to Gannett communities. . . .

"So I said I think we ought to develop a bigger staff and set certain standards. That's when Quinn conducted the study where we defined our mission, where it applies to Gannett communities, but it applies elsewhere now, too. But I knew that wouldn't be very popular." [9]

Curley saw it slightly differently.

"I don't think it was a cop-out that the company used the foundation," he said in 1992, "because the foundation was set up for that very purpose. I think that was the way it was supposed to be. Once [the foundation] took off in a different direction, then we had a responsibility to provide the money. We couldn't provide as much as they provided but we started at about $4 million and change and added a couple hundred thousand this year, and by next year we're going to get back to the matching dollar [gift] program and some other things. So we're going to keep going. If we have a good year or two, then we can throw even more money into the project." [10]

## Wider Focus

Many things competed for Curley's attention in 1991. Further reorganization of the newspapers was in prospect. Paramount was Curley's determination to increase reinvestment in the company's newspapers, to improve both content and customer service, and position them for the future.

One problem that needed resolution was the financially draining battle in Little Rock, between Gannett's *Arkansas Gazette* and WEHCO Media's *Arkansas Democrat*. Curley recalled that the price for the widely respected *Gazette* in 1986 had not been high ($51 million cash) and the purchase had seemed to be a smart one.

"But we saw," he said, "as soon as we got the books and the numbers, that the trend line in circulation had already gone the other way. And that the more you tried to do to raise the prices, the more people deserted you. . . . The only way you could hold them was to cut the prices and every time you cut the prices you lost another few million dollars. . . .

"As we saw, after about the second or third year, that it wasn't going to work, . . . we tried to see if there were buyers, from coast to coast. One person that we approached said he had a deal for us, too. He said he'd sell us the Brooklyn Bridge. . . . Basically we turned to Hussman [owner of the rival *Democrat*] after trying to get a lot of other people involved."[11]

Walter Hussman had adapted to the situation. When the deep-pockets campaign that subsidized his financial drain on the *Gazette* forced Hugh Patterson to sell to Gannett, Hussman made himself the endangered local species. He perversely – and successfully – portrayed himself as an anemic homeboy David against an alien Goliath on steroids.

The last issue of the *Arkansas Gazette* appeared on Oct. 18, 1991, the day Gannett announced the sale. As part of the $68.5-million sales agreement with Hussman, there was no farewell edition of the esteemed newspaper, said to be the oldest west of the Mississippi. It simply disappeared into the maw of the *Arkansas Democrat,* with its epitaph being subordinated hyphenation of *Gazette* in the nameplate of its victorious rival.

In August 1991, Gannett paid 399,137 shares of stock and assumed debts – total value of about $42 million – for the Times Journal Co. This was an arc of small dailies and weeklies serving suburban Maryland and Virginia outside the Washington, D.C., Beltway, plus a printing plant and a data services subsidiary. Their acquisition, Curley said, "was touch and go. Our interest was the printing site, the facilities to print *USA TODAY*, because if we'd had to go out and build that we'd have had to spend like $25 million overnight. . . . We got the opportunity to get the presses at a price that was really no more than the asset itself was worth."

Gannett had tried to find a buyer for the newspapers even before the sale was completed. The newspapers themselves had not been of interest to Gannett and the company had anticipated that the FCC would prohibit Gannett's ownership of the newspapers and WUSA-TV in the same market. It was not interested in getting rid of WUSA-TV.

Curley said the company considered transforming the papers to three times a week to get around the FCC restriction but abandoned the idea as unworkable. It would have been willing, he said, to spend the money necessary to build a circulation network "up to a point where the advertisers might be interested. But the big advertisers in this market were not interested in another 150,000 subscribers because they already had *The Washington Post*, which provided probably 70 percent of the market."

Eventually, Newsco, Inc. relieved Gannett of the Journal newspapers at the end of December 1991 for $8 million. The new owners went immediately into what Curley described as "a cost-cutting mode to see if they could get the cost structure under control." [12]

# A Look to the Hills

Gannett had owned a daily newspaper in Allegheny County, Pa., since 1976, when it bought the *Valley News Dispatch*. That paper and related publications were produced in Tarentum, Pa., just northeast of Pittsburgh.

In the late '80s, the company had become more interested in the affluent Allegheny County area called North Hills, a growing community of hotels, shopping centers and suburban housing about 30 minutes north of Pittsburgh. Gannett published a twice-weekly newspaper there. By spring of 1992, after several years of analysis and planning, it had decided to launch a new daily that fall. "It was always going to be in the fall," Curley said, "when football is hot in western Pennsylvania."

Then a Teamsters strike in May shut down both *The Pittsburgh Press* and *Pittsburgh Post-Gazette.*

"The strike came," Curley recalled, "so we said let's go. We already had a circulation planning team in there and some other people, so we just jumped on it that week, May 18, and took off. That was not a 'Gee whiz, there's a strike, let's go.' That was a well-conceived plan to go."

The *North Hills News Record* began with a first-day paid circulation of nearly 26,000 (as compared with the twice-weekly's circulation of 17,624). In the absence of the Pittsburgh dailies, the fledgling *News Record* caught on quickly. When the Pittsburgh Penguins hockey team won its second successive Stanley Cup, a souvenir edition of the *News Record* virtually sold out, eclipsing its previous 29,500-copy sales mark with a total of 44,420 sold.

By the end of June, the daily's home delivery reached 18,000, surpassing the total circulation of its biweekly predecessor. That figure continued to climb at the rate of 1,000 every 10 days. Soon after *News Record* home delivery reached 30,000 in late October, E. W. Scripps Co. announced that it had agreed to sell the strike-bound *Pittsburgh Press* to Blade Communications, owner of the also-idled *Pittsburgh Post-Gazette.*

When Pittsburgh's surviving daily resumed publication in January 1993, it dampened the *News Record's* immediate prospects. By February, the company announced that net paid circulation for its new daily was about twice the 17,624 of the biweekly from which it had sprung. Yet beyond the strike settlement and the return of Pittsburgh's morning daily, the *News Record's* long-range prospects continued to seem bright.

"The demographics are wonderful," Curley said. "It's stable. Every demo fits a newspaper reader including the fact that the people [are] well-educated, [they] like to stay in the market, like to shop in the shopping centers, and that means advertising for the paper." [13]

# Getting to Know You

Soon after he became chairman, Curley had warned Gannett editors that the days of C+ editors and C+ newspapers were over. The company demonstrated Curley's commitment to newpaper quality in June 1991 with the launch of News 2000, a companywide strategy to improve its newspapers by focusing on the changing needs of readers.

The program was the product of six months of brainstorming by 30 Gannett publishers, editors and other executives, under the leadership of Philip R. Currie, vice president/news in the company's Newspaper Division.

Implementing the program, Curley said, would "catapult our newspapers into the 21st century."

News 2000 created a structure that combined general qualities of newspaper excellence with methods of tailoring each newspaper to the individual interests and needs of its community.

It began with that stress on community interests. With that, it emphasized the special needs for a newspaper to protect the First Amendment; represent women and minorities; offer compelling presentations; provide needed information; evoke emotion; be consistent; be immediate; encourage interaction with readers; and anticipate change.

In explaining the program, Currie said:

"Many of these points aren't new. We've been talking about them for a long time. What is new is the bringing all of the elements of a reader-driven newspaper together in a comprehensive program."

"Reader-driven" newspapering wasn't new, either, but the idea was anathema to many professional and academic journalists, for whom it was taken for granted that they know best what a newspaper should be. The preposterous notion that you should ask readers what they might like in their newspaper was simply *declassé*, the sort of thing typical of non-intellectual papers like that upstart *USA TODAY*. At least this was the way the journalistic establishment saw it.

Unfortunately, the establishment had been building newspapers on its arrogant assumption for generations, but fewer and fewer people were coming to its vending machines.

Simmons Market Research distributed by the Newspaper Association of America in *Facts About Newspapers* told the story. More than three-quarters of U.S. adults surveyed – 78 percent – said they'd read a newspaper the day before when they were polled in 1970. By 1990, that proportion had shrunk to 62.4 percent.

News 2000 was not a once-and-done proposition. Under the directorship of Mark Silverman, who had been executive editor of the *Rockford Register Star* in Illinois, executives and staffs of each Gannett newspaper would create their local blueprint of News 2000 on a strict timetable.

Those plans would be reviewed and approved – or returned for amendment – and then implemented. Every six months, each newspaper's performance would be evaluated and publicly graded.

Supplementing the structural reviews was a mentoring program, designed, Currie explained, particularly for young editors new to their jobs. It was, he said, "a big brother or big sister approach to answer the kinds of questions new editors really don't know the answers to."

A second part of the mentoring plan, Currie said, was to help editors of what Curley had called C+ newspapers "get to the next level of quality with the help of an editor [from one of Gannett's larger papers] who's better at it."

Despite its daunting complexity and pressures to shatter the operational status quo, News 2000 engendered impressive cooperation and response. If not all the participants were enthusiastic, most were zealous in their compliance.

Newspaper staffs that might have felt threatened at the outset, Currie said, were won over when they realized that News 2000 was intended to be locally driven. "If you do this really right," Currie said they were told, "you're actually going to be a more unique newspaper, reflecting your own community. If you figure out what the key topics are for your community, then you're automatically going to be doing a better local job of coverage."

At the introduction of the program, Curley had encouraged newspapers to design their own programs, not as a "mini-*USA TODAY*, but using some of the reader-friendly techniques that had worked for the nation's newspaper.

"Game plans don't have to be fancy to be winners," Curley said. "The Gannett Company is looking for basic high-quality performance. After we get the basics right, we can get fancy."[14]

Acceptance of the challenge and the start on getting the basics right were encouraging. So the company quickly followed with a similar comprehensive program for improving advertising sales and service – ADvance.

ADvance reflected News 2000 in that it would be customer-driven. Carleton Rosenburgh, Newspaper Division senior vice president, explained to Gannett publishers, ad directors and marketing executives that ADvance would start to think about what advertisers needed from Gannett rather than how advertisers could meet Gannett's needs.

The program focused on new advertising and marketing goals, better hiring, training and pay, keener understanding of markets and pricing, and improved communications.

"We must continue," Curley said at the unveiling of ADvance, "to publish newspapers that both readers and retailers trust. . . . We need to listen and learn from our customers, ensuring *our* success and *their* success."[15]

Early in 1993, Curley called News 2000 and ADvance the most important programs the company had going. "If we can get newspapers to be more relevant for people who are interested in news," he said, "and get our advertising people to be more responsive to advertisers – now that they don't have 80 percent of market share – then I think we can see newspapers begin to be a growth industry again."

The new programs' significance was also demonstrated by changes in the company's recruiting on college campuses. That began in the late 1950s, when the personnel department under Heselden interviewed potential employees while they were still in school.

Phil Currie was one of the early recruits, whom Heselden met at Penn State and persuaded to visit Rochester. The program grew to become a major source of potential newsroom talent. Its value later prompted the company to broaden recruiting to other disciplines, particularly those important to ADvance through advertising sales and management.

# Where Are We Now?

Gannett marked 25 years as a publicly held company in October 1992. It was bigger, stronger and more diversified, with 82 daily newspapers, including *USA TODAY*, the weekend newspaper magazine *USA WEEKEND*, 10 television stations, 15 radio stations and the largest outdoor advertising company in North America. Its work force had grown from approximately 7,000 in late 1967 to nearly 37,000.

Even as that anniversary approached, the company had continued its tradition of expanding, contracting and evolving.

The most recent example of expansion, of course, was creation earlier in 1992 of the new daily in North Hills, Pa. But there had been many examples of internal growth, even though not quite as dramatic as the creation of *USA TODAY*.

Gannett's years as a publicly held company included the creation of Sunday editions in 13 communities already served by Gannett dailies. Those introductions – in Marin County and Palm Springs, Calif., Lafayette and Marion, Ind., St. Cloud, Minn., Bridgewater and Camden, N.J., Rockland and Saratoga Springs, N.Y., North Hills and Tarentum, Pa., Burlington, Vt., and Wausau, Wis. – represented by 1993 a combined Sunday circulation increase of more than 580,000.

On Aug. 21, 1992, Gannett announced the sale of Gannett Outdoor Co. of Arizona in Phoenix, one of the outdoor companies acquired with Combined Communications. The buyer was Eller Investment Co., Inc., and the price was $20 million, which included rights to rename the company Eller Outdoor, as it had been known before its acquisition by Gannett. The deal brought about the brief reappearance of Karl Eller, who had come to Gannett as president and chief executive officer of Combined Communications in the 1979 merger and left in frustration less than a year later.

A month later, Gannett surprised industry watchers when it concluded that what had worked in Nashville should also succeed in Honolulu. The company announced that it would buy its morning competitor, *The Honolulu Advertiser,* and sell the afternoon *Honolulu Star-Bulletin,* which it had owned for 21 years. Both the 104,000-circulation daily *Advertiser* and the 88,000 daily *Star-Bulletin* are produced under a joint operating agreement by The Hawaii Newspaper Agency Inc., which continues for 20 years.

In addition to acquiring *The Advertiser,* the company announced that the *Sunday Star-Bulletin and Advertiser* would become the *Sunday Advertiser.*

Gannett paid $100 million in stock to Persis Corporation and assumed liabilities that brought the price of *The Advertiser* to $250 million. Whle the switch may have come as a surprise, it reflected Gannett's demonstrated preference for morning rather than afternoon publication, based on the pattern of stronger circulation growth among a.m. newspapers.

Sale of the *Star-Bulletin,* required by antitrust laws prohibiting ownership of both Honolulu newspapers, took until early 1993. On Jan. 30, 1993, the afternoon paper became the property of Liberty Newspapers Limited Partnership, whose general partner is a corporation owned by Rupert Phillips of Destin, Fla.

# We're No. 1

A month before Gannett's 25th anniversary event, *USA TODAY* became doubly noteworthy. It celebrated its 10th anniversary in September 1992 and finally passed *The Wall Street Journal* in total circulation to become the nation's biggest newspaper.

As the end of 1992 approached, its daily circulation was above 1.9 million, nearly twice the number originally invoked as the magic key to profitable advertising volume. Yet while *USA TODAY* had had some profitable months, even some quarters in the black, none of its 10 years had produced an annual profit.

Early in 1993, publisher Tom Curley was conceding a 1992 loss of $8 million to $10 million for the daily, but pointing out that 1991's loss had been double that. Reduction of annual losses nearly to single-digit figures was no small achievement against a background of losses that exceeded $800 million, most of that in the first half of *USA TODAY's* 10 years.

Although ad revenues had not made the daily profitable, volume was growing slowly but steadily. As 1993 opened, *USA TODAY's* assured ad business was more than double that of a year earlier. In any case, the undiminished popularity of the nation's newspaper with an estimated six million readers and its highly visible association with the name Gannett sent strong signals that *USA TODAY* was in no immediate danger.

*USA WEEKEND*, on the other hand, had worked its way to success despite the initial desertion of many subscribing publishers and a sharp decline in tobacco advertising, which represented a substantial portion of its revenue. Jack Heselden called it a major turnaround, first in regaining the circulation lost with those defecting publishers and then contracting with a new printer at a great reduction in costs.

John Curley pointed both to the business success of publisher Brette Popper, who found new advertising to counteract the decline in tobacco accounts, and the editorial efforts of editor Marcia Bullard.

"We worked with [Bullard] in the early days," Curley said, "to get an agenda and go out for a different market from *Parade* [the competing Sunday supplement]. We all settled on baby boomers and agreed that we wouldn't worry over what people thought about skewing the product to the young; we would just stay with the program. It's become successful."

That success could be measured early in 1993 by *USA WEEKEND's* distribution in 378 Sunday newspapers with a total circulation of 16.3 million.

# Power Shift

Among the significant changes to which Heselden contributed in his career with Gannett was the dramatic increase in the operational authority of management and a decrease in organized labor's ability to shut down a newspaper.

"Labor was all-powerful," Heselden remembered, "in the '30s, '40s and '50s. Now we can publish in a strike situation with the help of the new technology and temporary or permanent replacements."

Among the most powerful unions with which the Gannett Co. had to deal was the International Typographical Union. Even when the Taft-Hartley Act outlawed the closed shop shortly after World War II, ITU locals easily thwarted the law by blocking acceptance of non-union co-workers.

That power eroded as computers and video display terminals moved typesetting from the composing rooms to the newsrooms and business departments of newspapers.

Contributing to that transfer of power was an accompanying change in Gannett management's approach to labor relations. Gary Watson, president of Gannett's Newspaper Division, recalled a 10-week strike in Rockford, Ill., in late 1970 and early 1971, where he was once secretary of the Newspaper Guild.

"I've never lost sight of the fact," Watson said, "that that strike could have been avoided – should have been avoided. All it would've taken was a little more dialogue, a little more willingness on the part of management to recognize problems earlier and to deal straight with the people that they worked with and who worked for them. . . .

"I don't think there's any question Gannett still takes a very tough line. But as I've watched this business over the last 25 years, almost every newspaper strike comes because management either didn't do its job or did something stupid. . . .

"I think our managers are smarter, and clearly the company, in terms of benefit programs and everything else, treats our employees very fairly, so I guess the proof is in what has happened over the last several years."

The differences to which Watson referred included:
- the virtual disappearance of strikes against Gannett.
- in 13 union representation elections since 1980, the company won seven. Of the six in which unions won the vote, none had succeeded in negotiating a contract by 1993 and in three cases the victorious union had since been decertified.
- a startling succession of other elections since 1980 in which company employees decertified more than 20 union locals that claimed to represent their interests.

Such decertifications, Curley said, come because Gannett executives have convinced people that they are better off without having to pay for union representation.

John B. Jaske, senior vice president of labor relations, said the pattern in Gannett "follows a national trend of the decline of unions in the private sector over the last 30 years, [reflecting] more enlightened management, making unions unnecessary."

Paul Miller had pointed out in a speech in February 1968 that Gannett then had 7,000 employees, of whom more than 28 percent (2,000) were represented by unions. Gannett's annual report for 1992 reported that 20 percent of the company's nearly 37,000 employees were represented by 162 local bargaining units affiliated with 18 international unions.

# Where Do We Go from Here?

USA TODAY not only prevailed in spite of the cynical oddsmakers but also spawned prosperous offspring whose kinship was obvious:
- USA TODAY Baseball Weekly tells even baseball fans more than they expected to know about the national pastime. It appears weekly during baseball season and every other week out of season. A month after its introduction in April 1991, USA TODAY Baseball Weekly was selling a quarter-million copies. At the end of its first full year of pub-

lication, that circulation remained firm and it was contributing nearly $10 million in revenue.

- *USA TODAY Sky Radio* delivers live news, financial reports, sports and weather throughout the day to passengers on commercial aircraft.
- *USA TODAY Update* delivers, electronically, 18 executive news summaries worldwide.
- *USA TODAY Books* produces volumes comprising specialized material that has appeared in the newspaper.

Other new products include *USA TODAY* spinoffs for library research, including news-in-review products that use CD-ROM technology, an interactive computer sports information center and classroom curricula with *USA TODAY* as the instructional core.

Wherever new computer and communications technology offer a market for the assets on tap with *USA TODAY,* Gannett is ready to fill it. One such opportunity prompted Gannett to invest $5 million in a project called Interactive Network. Its developers explained it as a television entertainment system that will allow home subscribers "to interact directly with live television sports events, game shows and other television programs."

Curley described it as a venture capital arrangement for Gannett. "We have the right," he said, "to put up an additional $5 million, and possibly more [to] see how interactive television and games develop. There's also the potential to do interactive news – the kids doing homework with the library, and things like that. We figured a stake like this would be worth it to see where the technology goes."

What of the Gannett Co. of tomorrow?

"New media," Curley said in 1992, "[what] we call everything in the new product range, will probably grow faster than lots of other things, simply because we see some opportunities there, in projects like Sky Radio, to add value and to get into businesses that really don't exist. . . .

"If we did anything in television it would have to be at a good price, because I think where we are is fine. . . .

"Radio I don't see as a long-term situation for growth. There is growth potentially out there because of FCC rules changes, but it's such an entrepreneurial business where one family or two partners . . . can do better than a company that tries to square everything off and give everybody the same compensation.

"Outdoor has been a good business over the years, even though certain kinds of national advertising have declined. I don't see us adding to outdoor except if something became available in a market where we already had something else . . . or possibly overseas where the business continues to grow. . . .

"I think newspapers and the other media will be the two areas where the growth will come from." [16]

As Gannett observed its 25th anniversary as a publicly owned company in October 1992, it clearly bore the Curley stamp. Its 82 daily newspapers, 10 television stations, 15 radio stations and the largest outdoor advertising company in North America constituted a prosperous and diversified media giant. Its primary focus remained, however, the newspaper business that grew out of $20,000 gambles by each of two partners in Elmira, N.Y., 86 years before.

Frank Gannett and Erwin Davenport might be amazed at the company's immensity and diversity. They would not be surprised at its success, nor would they be disappointed at the stewardship of Paul Miller, Al Neuharth and John Curley.

Characteristically, they would be impatient to see what surprise the product of their gamble will achieve next.

# Footnotes

# Chapter 1
(1) Samuel T. Williamson, *Imprint of a Publisher*, Robert M. McBride & Co. 1948. Page 11.
(2) *Ibid.*, page 23.
(3) *Ibid.*, page 78.
(4) *Ibid.*, page 88.

# Chapter 2
(1) Russell Chapman and Connie Davenport Chapman, interview, Rochester, N.Y., June 11, 1990, page 1, Gannett Co. Inc. Archives.
(2) Williamson, *op. cit.*, page 89.
(3) *Ibid.*
(4) *Ibid.*, page 91.
(5) *Ibid.*, page 93.

# Chapter 3
(1) Williamson, *op. cit.*, page 105.
(2) *The Bulletin*, confidential publication for executives of The Gannett Newspapers, May 3, 1951, page 1. Gannett Co. Inc. Archives.
(3) Williamson, *op. cit.*, page 111.

# Chapter 4
(1) Henry W. Clune, *The Rochester I Know*. Garden City, N.Y. 1972: Doubleday & Co. Inc., page 77.
(2) Richard Polenberg, *Frank E. Gannett: A Progressive Publisher in Politics*, Rochester, N.Y. The Gannett Foundation, Series Paper No. 1, 1987, page 12. Published to mark the dedication of the Gannett Archives at Cornell University.

## Chapter 5

(1) Frank E. Gannett and Caroline Werner Gannett Papers, Department of Manuscripts and University Archives, Cornell University Libraries, Box 54, Folder 7.

(2) *Editorially Speaking*, Volume 14, 1956, pages 19, 20. Gannett Co. Inc. Archives.

(3) Williamson, *op. cit.*, pages 138-139.

(4) Nancy Tripp Rose, interview, Elmira, N.Y., July 19, 1990, page 10. Gannett Co. Inc. Archives.

(5) Clune, *op. cit.*, page 81.

(6) Williamson, *op. cit.*, pages 143-159.

(7) Henry Adams, *The Education of Henry Adams*, Cambridge, Mass., 1961: The Riverside Press, page 418.

(8) Williamson, *op. cit.*, page 162.

(9) *Ibid.*, page 164.

(10) *Ibid.*, page 161.

## Chapter 6

(1) Williamson, *op. cit.*, page 147.

(2) Frank E. Gannett and Caroline Werner Gannett Papers, Box 54, Folder 24.

(3) Williamson, *op. cit.*, page 176.

(4) Florence Messman, summary memorandum dated Feb. 9, 1973, Rochester, N.Y., and interview, June 13, 1990, Rochester, N.Y., page 2. Gannett Co. Inc. Archives.

(5) Henry Clune, *Main Street Beat*, New York, 1947: W.W. Norton & Co., page 22.

(6) Williamson, *op. cit.*, page 147.

(7) *Ibid.*

(8) Polenberg, *op. cit.*, page 14.

(9) Rose interview, page 1.

(10) Minutes of the board of directors, Gannett Co. Inc., Dec. 31, 1931.

(11) Polenberg, *op. cit.*, page 13.

# Chapter 7

(1) Minutes of the board of directors, Gannett Co. Inc., March 17, 1931.
(2) Williamson, *op. cit.*, pages 134-135.
(3) *Ibid.*, page 145.
(4) *The Gannetteer*, September 1933, page 1.
(5) *The Gannetteer*, July 1933, page 3.
(6) *The Gannetteer*, December 1933, page 1.
(7) Minutes of the board of directors, Gannett Co. Inc., Jan. 23, 1934.
(8) Minutes of the board of directors, Gannett Co. Inc., May 5, 1934.
(9) Frank Gannett, "Our Two Planes Are Indispensable," *Aviation*, March 1937, page 28.
(10) Dixon Gannett, interview, Jupiter, Fla., March 16, 1990, page 1. Gannett Co. Inc. Archives.
(11) Minutes of the board of directors, Gannett Co. Inc., July 7, 1933.

# Chapter 8

(1) *The Gannetteer*, November 1933, page 2.
(2) Jane Donnovan, interview, Arlington, Va., Dec. 15, 1989, page 4. Gannett Co. Inc. Archives.
(3) Messman interview, pages 7-8.
(4) Gannett interview, page 2.
(5) Messman interview, page 8.
(6) *The Gannetteer*, February 1950, page 2.
(7) *The Gannetteer*, December 1973, page 24.
(8) *Ibid.*
(9) *The Gannetteer*, February 1950, page 2.
(10) *Ibid.*
(11) *Ibid.*
(12) Frank E. Gannett and Caroline Werner Gannett Papers, Box 14.
(13) *The Gannetteer*, November 1935, page 3.
(14) *Ibid.*, page 1.
(15) *The Gannetteer*, January 1937, page 1.

(16) *Ibid.*
(17) *Ibid.*
(18) Minutes of the board of directors, Gannett Co. Inc., Dec. 16, 1937.
(19) *The Gannetteer,* January 1937, page 2.

## Chapter 9
(1) Williamson, *op. cit.,* pages 227-228.
(2) *The Gannetteer,* January 1934, page 2.
(3) *The Gannetteer,* March 1934, page 4.
(4) *The Gannetteer,* April 1935, page 1.
(5) Frank Gannett, *Aviation,* March 1937, page 29.
(6) Williamson, *op. cit.,* page 238.
(7) *Ibid.*
(8) *The Gannetteer,* May 1936, page 3.
(9) *Ibid.*
(10) *The Gannetteer,* June 1936, page 1.
(11) Williamson, *op. cit.,* page 154.
(12) Polenberg, *op. cit.,* page 15.
(13) Williamson, *op. cit.,* pages 242-243.
(14) *Ibid.,* page 244.
(15) Polenberg, *op. cit.,* page 17.

## Chapter 10
(1) *The Bulletin,* Dec. 30, 1943, page 7.
(2) *The Gannetteer,* March 1938, page 1.
(3) *The Gannetteer,* April 1938, page 1.
(4) *The Gannetteer,* July 1938, page 5.
(5) *The Gannetteer,* January 1939, page 4.
(6) Williamson, *op. cit.,* pages 263-264.
(7) Frank E. Gannett and Caroline Werner Gannett Papers, Box 9, Folder 43.
(8) Williamson, *op. cit.,* page 265.

(9) *The Bulletin,* June 29, 1939, page 1.
(10) *The Gannetteer,* July 1939, page 5.
(11) Frank E. Gannett and Caroline Werner Gannett Papers, Box 4.
(12) Messman interview, page 12.
(13) Polenberg, *op. cit.,* page 17.
(14) Henry Clune, interview, Aug. 28, 1990, Scottsville, N.Y., page 2. Gannett Co. Inc. Archives.
(15) *The Gannetteer,* December 1939, page 3.
(16) *The Bulletin,* Dec. 30, 1943, page 7.
(17) *Ibid.,* page 7.
(18) *Ibid.,* page 8.
(19) Polenberg, *op. cit.,* page 17.

# Chapter 11
(1) Will Rogers, syndicated newspaper column, June 28, 1931.
(2) Messman memo, *op. cit.*
(3) Messman interview, page 7.
(4) Williamson, *op. cit.,* page vii.
(5) *The Bulletin,* Dec. 30, 1943, page 1.
(6) Polenberg, *op. cit.,* page 19.
(7) *The Bulletin,* May 23, 1940, pages 3, 4.
(8) Frank E. Gannett and Caroline Werner Gannett Papers, Box 10.
(9) *The Bulletin,* June 13, 1940, page 1.
(10) *Ibid.,* pages 1, 2.
(11) Frank E. Gannett and Caroline Werner Gannett Papers, Box 10.
(12) *The Bulletin,* June 13, 1940, page 1.
(13) *The Bulletin,* June 27, 1940, page 1.
(14) Polenberg, *op. cit.,* page 17.
(15) *Ibid.,* page 18.

# Chapter 12
(1) *The Gannetteer,* December 1941, page 5.
(2) *The Bulletin,* April 18, 1940, page 2.

(3) *The Bulletin,* June 6, 1940, page 2.
(4) *The Bulletin,* Feb. 15, 1940, page 2.
(5) *The Bulletin,* May 23, 1940, page 10.
(6) *Ibid.,* page 9.
(7) *Ibid.,* page 10.
(8) *The Bulletin,* July 3, 1940, page 1.
(9) *The Bulletin,* Aug. 15, 1940, page 1.
(10) *The Bulletin,* Dec. 5, 1940, pages 6 and 8.

## Chapter 13
(1) *The Bulletin,* March 13, 1941, page 1.
(2) *The Bulletin,* March 6, 1941, page 1.
(3) *The Bulletin,* April 10, 1941, page 1.
(4) *The Bulletin,* April 17, 1941, page 1.
(5) *The Bulletin,* May 29, 1941, page 7.
(6) *The Bulletin,* Sept. 11, 1941, page 1.
(7) *The Bulletin,* Oct. 9, 1941, page 2.
(8) *The Bulletin,* Nov. 13, 1941, pages 8, 9.
(9) *The Gannetteer,* November 1941, page 2.
(10) *The Gannetteer,* December 1941, page 5.
(11) *The Gannetteer,* January 1942, page 5.
(12) *Ibid.,* page 1.

## Chapter 14
(1) *The Bulletin,* Sept. 30, 1943, page 1.
(2) *The Bulletin,* Dec. 4, 1941, page 1.
(3) *The Gannetteer,* November 1945, page 9.
(4) *The Bulletin,* Dec. 11, 1941, page 2.
(5) *The Bulletin,* Dec. 18, 1941, page 4.
(6) *The Bulletin,* Jan. 1, 1942, page 2.
(7) *The Bulletin,* Jan. 8, 1942, page 1.
(8) *The Bulletin,* Feb. 12, 1942, page 1.
(9) *The Bulletin,* Feb. 19, 1942, pages 1 and 2.

(10) *The Bulletin,* Feb. 26, 1942, page 1.
(11) *The Bulletin,* April 2, 1942, page 1.
(12) *The Bulletin,* May 21, 1942, page 5.
(13) Vincent S. Jones, interview, Rochester, N.Y., June 12, 1990, page 23. Gannett Co. Inc. Archives.
(14) *The Bulletin,* June 4, 1942, pages 1 and 2.
(15) *The Bulletin,* Sept. 17, 1942, page 1.
(16) *The Bulletin,* Oct. 1, 1942, page 2.
(17) *The Bulletin,* Dec. 17, 1942, page 2.
(18) *The Bulletin,* Dec. 23, 1942, page 4.

# Chapter 15
(1) *The Bulletin,* Jan. 14, 1943, page 1.
(2) Clune interview, page 1.
(3) *The Bulletin,* Feb. 4, 1943, page 3.
(4) *The Bulletin,* Jan. 28, 1943, page 1.
(5) *The Bulletin,* April 8, 1943, page 2.
(6) *The Bulletin,* April 15, 1943, page 1.
(7) *The Bulletin,* April 22, 1943, page 1.
(8) Minutes of the board of directors, Gannett Co. Inc., May 27, 1943.
(9) *The Gannetteer,* August 1943, page 1.
(10) *The Bulletin,* July 1, 1943, pages 1 and 2.
(11) *The Bulletin,* July 29, 1943, page l.
(12) *The Bulletin,* Oct. 21, 1943, page 1.

# Chapter 16
(1) *The Bulletin,* April 13, 1944, page 2.
(2) Williamson, *op. cit.,* pages 5 and 6.
(3) *The Bulletin,* June 1, 1944, page 1.
(4) *The Bulletin,* June 8, 1944, page 1.
(5) Williamson, *op. cit.,* page 95.
(6) *The Bulletin,* July 6, 1944, page 2.

(7) *The Bulletin,* July 13, 1944, page 2.
(8) *Star-Gazette* editorial, Elmira, N.Y., Nov. 8, 1944.
(9) *The Gannetteer,* November 1944, page 1.
(10) *The Bulletin,* Nov. 16, 1944, page 1.
(11) Frank E. Gannett and Caroline Werner Gannett Papers, Box 54.
(12) *The Bulletin,* Dec. 21, 1944, page 2.
(13) *The Bulletin,* April 19, 1945, page 1.
(14) Williamson, *op. cit.,* page 230.
(15) *The Bulletin,* April 19, 1945, page 1.
(16) *The Bulletin,* May 31, 1945, pages 1-4.
(17) *The Gannetteer,* April 1945, page 2.
(18) *The Bulletin,* June 21, 1945, page 1.
(19) Minutes of the board of directors, Gannett Co. Inc., Sept. 6, 1945.
(20) *The Bulletin,* Aug. 2, 1945, page 1.
(21) *Ibid.,* page 3.
(22) *Ibid.*
(23) *The Bulletin,* Aug. 16, 1945, Page 1.

# Chapter 17

(1) Williamson, *op. cit.,* page 297.
(2) Jones interview, page 12.
(3) Minutes of the board of directors, Gannett Co. Inc., Dec. 31, 1945.
(4) Minutes of the board of directors, Gannett Co. Inc., Sept. 29, 1959.
(5) *The Bulletin,* Dec. 6, 1945, page 1.
(6) *The Bulletin,* Nov. 8, 1945, page 3.
(7) *The Bulletin,* Dec. 13, 1945, page 4.
(8) *The Bulletin,* Jan. 17, 1946, page 1.
(9) *The Bulletin,* Feb. 7, 1946, page 2.
(10) *Ibid.,* page 3.
(11) *The Gannetteer,* June 1946, page 15.
(12) *The Bulletin,* June 6, 1946, pages 4 and 5.
(13) *The Bulletin,* Sept. 12, 1946, page 3.
(14) *The Bulletin,* Oct. 31, 1946, page 3.

(15) *Facts on File,* 1948.
(16) *The Bulletin,* Oct. 31, 1946, page 2.
(17) *The Gannetteer,* January 1947, page 28.
(18) Gannett interview, page 19.
(19) Minutes of the board of directors, Gannett Co. Inc., Feb. 26, 1947.
(20) *The Bulletin,* May 29, 1947, page 7.
(21) Williamson, *op. cit.,* page 291.

# Chapter 18
(1) *The Bulletin,* Feb. 20, 1947, page 1.
(2) *The Bulletin,* April 3, 1947, page 1.
(3) *The Bulletin,* April 17, 1947, page 1.
(4) *The Bulletin,* May 1, 1947, page 1.
(5) *The Bulletin,* October, 17, 1946, page 3.
(6) *The Bulletin,* May 25, 1944, pages 2 and 3.
(7) Charles Barber, letter, Elmira, N.Y., Nov. 14, 1946.
(8) *The Gannetteer,* August 1947, Page 2.
(9) Louise Miller, interview, Palm Beach, Fla., March 15, 1990, page 1. Gannett Co. Inc. Archives.
(10) Rose interview, page 6.
(11) Miller interview, page 3.
(12) *The Bulletin,* Oct. 30, 1947, pages 2 and 3.
(13) *Ibid.,* page 4.
(14) *The Bulletin,* Nov. 26, 1947, page 1.
(15) Minutes of the board of directors, Gannett Co. Inc., Dec. 10, 1947.

# Chapter 19
(1) *The Gannetteer,* Feb. 5, 1948, page 1.
(2) Messman interview, page 9.
(3) Frank E. Gannett and Caroline Werner Gannett Papers, Box 11, Folder 28.

(4) *The Bulletin*, Sept. 9, 1948, page 2.
(5) *The Gannetteer*, December 1948, page 2.
(6) Minutes of the board of directors, Gannett Co. Inc., Jan. 4, 1949.
(7) *The Gannetteer*, April 1949, page 14.
(8) *The Gannetteer*, June 1949, page 2.

## Chapter 20

(1) Miller interview, pages 5 and 6.
(2) Gannett interview, page 3.
(3) Messman interview, page 5.
(4) Minutes of the board of directors, Gannett Co. Inc., June 8, 1949.
(5) Minutes of the board of directors, Gannett Co. Inc., Sept. 13, 1949.
(6) *The Gannetteer*, September 1949, page 5.
(7) *The Gannetteer*, February 1950, pages 3-7.
(8) Minutes of the board of directors, Gannett Co. Inc., Dec. 12, 1949.
(9) Jones interview, page 6.
(10) *The Bulletin*, Aug. 17, 1950, page 1.
(11) *The Gannetteer*, October 1950, page 1.
(12) *The Bulletin*, Oct. 19, 1950, pages 2 and 3.
(13) *The Bulletin*, Oct. 26, 1950, page 1.
(14) *The Bulletin*, Dec. 21, 1950, page 1.
(15) *The Gannetteer*, November 1950, page 19.
(16) *The Bulletin*, Dec. 28, 1950, page 3.

## Chapter 21

(1) *The Bulletin*, page 1.
(2) *The Bulletin*, March 1, 1951, page 1.
(3) *The Bulletin*, April 12, 1951, page 1.
(4) *The Bulletin*, May 10, 1951, pages 1 and 2.
(5) *The Bulletin*, May 31, 1951, page 2.
(6) *The Bulletin*, July 19, 1951, page 2.
(7) Minutes of the board of directors, Gannett Co. Inc., Aug. 29, 1951.
(8) *The Gannetteer*, December 1951, pages 6-9.

(9) *The Bulletin,* Sept. 27, 1951, page 1.
(10) *The Gannetteer,* January 1952, page 40.
(11) Jones interview, page 13.
(12) *The Bulletin,* Jan. 10, 1952, page 2.
(13) *The Bulletin,* April 24, 1952, pages 3 and 4.
(14) *The Bulletin,* June 19, 1952, page 1.
(15) *The Bulletin,* May 15, 1952, pages 2 and 3.
(16) *The Bulletin,* Sept. 4, 1952, page 1.
(17) *The Bulletin,* Oct. 16, 1952, Attachment.
(18) *The Bulletin,* Nov. 13, 1952, pages 1 and 2.
(19) *The Bulletin,* Feb. 26, 1953, page 1.
(20) *The Gannetteer,* January 1953, Page 3.
(21) Minutes of the board of directors, Gannett Co. Inc., Dec. 18, 1952.

# Chapter 22

(1) *The Bulletin,* March 5, 1953, page 2.
(2) *The Bulletin,* March 12, 1953, pages 1 and 2.
(3) *The Bulletin,* March 5, 1953, page 3.
(4) Mary Golding, interview, Rochester, N.Y., June 13, 1990, pages 1 and 3. Gannett Co. Inc. Archives.
(5) Miller interview, pages 3 and 4.
(6) Golding interview, page 2.
(7) Jones interview, page 8.
(8) *The Bulletin,* March 11, 1954, page 1.
(9) *The Bulletin,* July 23, 1953, page 1.
(10) *The Bulletin,* March 18, 1954, page 1.
(11) *The Bulletin,* March 11, 1954, page 1.
(12) *The Bulletin,* July 1, 1954, pages 1 and 2.
(13) Minutes of the board of directors, Gannett Co. Inc., May 20, 1954.
(14) Minutes of the board of directors, Gannett Co. Inc., Oct. 4, 1954.
(15) *The Gannetteer,* December 1954, page 4.
(16) *The Bulletin,* March 10, 1955, page 1.
(17) Golding interview, page 1.

(18) Minutes of the board of directors, Gannett Co. Inc., May 19, 1955.

## Chapter 23
(1) Alfred, Lord Tennyson, *Morte d'Arthur,* Line 408, 1842.
(2) *The Gannetteer,* May 1954, pages 1 and 2.
(3) Messman interview, page 3.
(4) *Ibid.,* page 12.
(5) *Ibid.,* pages 3 and 4.
(6) *The Sanctum,* supplement to *The Bulletin,* Oct. 13, 1955.
(7) *The Sanctum,* Oct. 27, 1955.
(8) *The Bulletin,* Dec. 1, 1955, page 1.
(9) *The Bulletin,* Dec. 15, 1955, page 3.
(10) *The Bulletin,* June 23, 1955, page 1.
(11) *The Gannetteer,* March 1957, pages 4 and 5.
(12) Calvin Mayne, interview, Rochester, N.Y., Aug. 29, 1990, page 13. Gannett Co. Inc. Archives.
(13) *The Bulletin,* March 7, 1957, pages 1 and 2.
(14) *The Gannetteer,* June 1957, page 5.
(15) *Ibid.,* pages 4 and 5.
(16) *The Gannetteer,* November 1957, page 4.
(17) *The Gannetteer,* January 1958, cover.
(18) Vincent S. Jones, address as secretary, Frank E. Gannett Newspaper Foundation, Inc., Broadmoor Hotel, Colorado Springs, Colo., June 29, 1968.
(19) Messman interview, pages 1, 9 and 10.
(20) Minutes of the board of directors, Gannett Co. Inc., June 26, 1958.

## Chapter 24
(1) Jones interview, page 8.
(2) Golding interview, page 2.
(3) Jones interview, page 15.

(4) *The Gannetteer,* July 1958, pages 2 and 4.
(5) Thomas P. Dolan, interview, Saratoga Springs, N.Y., Sept. 9, 1991, page 4. Gannett Co. Inc. Archives.
(6) Jones interview, page 10.
(7) *Ibid.,* Page 17.
(8) *The Gannetteer,* August 1958, age 2.
(9) *The Gannetteer,* July 1958, page 7.
(10) *The Gannetteer,* June 1964, page 8.
(11) *The Gannetteer,* July 1958, page 3.
(12) *The Gannetteer,* October 1958, page 3.
(13) *The Gannetteer,* December 1958, page 3.
(14) *The Gannetteer,* May 1958, page 3.
(15) Minutes of the board of directors, Gannett Co. Inc., March 20, 1952.
(16) Minutes of the board of directors, Gannett Co. Inc., Jan. 17, 1957.
(17) Robert R. Eckert, interview, Binghamton, N.Y., July 19, 1990, pages 4, 5. Gannett Co. Inc. Archives. WINR-AM was sold Feb. 26, 1971, for $285,000. WINR-TV was sold March 29, 1971, for $780,000.
(18) U.S. Bureau of the Census, Statistical Abstract of the United States, Washington, D.C., 81st edition, 1960.

# Chapter 25

(1) *Editorially Speaking,* Volume 17, 1959, page 46.
(2) *Ibid.,* page 42.
(3) Jack Germond, interview, Washington, D.C., Aug. 15, 1990, pages 1, 5 and 6. Gannett Co. Inc. Archives.
(4) *Editorially Speaking,* Volume 17, 1959, pages 43 and 44.
(5) Germond interview, page 6.
(6) *Editorially Speaking,* Volume 17, 1959, page 44.
(7) *Ibid.,* Page 27.
(8) Dolan interview, page 11.
(9) *Editorially Speaking,* Volume 17, 1959, page 30.
(10) *The Gannetteer,* June 1960, page 13.

(11) *Editorially Speaking,* Volume 17, 1959, pages 17 and 18.
(12) *Ibid.,* pages 18 and 21.
(13) Minutes of the board of directors, Gannett Co. Inc., Sept. 16, 1960.
(14) *The Gannetteer,* November 1961, page 3.

## Chapter 26

(1) *Editor & Publisher,* Oct. 22, 1960, page 50.
(2) Richard L. Tobin, "Old Presses Never Die," *Saturday Review,* Nov. 26, 1960, page 34.
(3) *The Bulletin,* March 27, 1952, page 1.
(4) *Editor & Publisher,* May 3, 1958, page 7.
(5) Jones interview, page 23.
(6) *Editor & Publisher,* May 10, 1958, page 7.
(7) *Editor & Publisher,* May 17, 1958, page 7.
(8) *The Bulletin,* Oct. 26, 1960, page 5.
(9) Carl Lindstrom, *The Fading American Newspaper,* Gloucester, Mass.: Peter Smith, 1964; reprinted 1964 by permission of Doubleday & Co. Inc., page 102.

## Chapter 27

(1) *Editorially Speaking,* Volume 19, 1961, Gannett Co., Inc., page 11.
(2) *The Gannetteer,* April 1961, page 2.
(3) Minutes of the board of directors, Gannett Co. Inc., June 1, 1961.
(4) *The Gannetteer,* June 1961, page 3.
(5) *Editorially Speaking,* Volume 20, 1962, pages 3-5.
(6) *The Gannetteer,* October 1961, page 2.
(7) *Ibid.,* page 11.
(8) Golding interview, page 2.
(9) Eckert interview, pages 5, 6.
(10) *Ibid.,* pages 6, 7.
(11) Al Neuharth, *Confessions of an S.O.B.,* New York: Doubleday, 1989, page 47.

(12) *Times-Union*, Rochester, N.Y., Nov. 10, 1962, editorial page.
(13) Allen H. Neuharth, interview, Arlington, Va., March 17, 1992, page 2. Gannett Co. Inc. Archives.
(14) *Ibid.*
(15) *Editorially Speaking*, Volume 21, 1963, pages 37-39.
(16) Jones interview, page 16.
(17) *The Gannetteer*, June 1964, page 2.
(18) *Editorially Speaking*, Volume 21, 1963, page 19.
(19) *Ibid.*, pages 19-21.

# Chapter 28
(1) Vince Spezzano, interview, Rochester, N.Y., June 14, 1990, page 7. Gannett Co. Inc. Archives.
(2) *Ibid.*, page 1.
(3) *The Gannetteer*, April 1964, page 3.
(4) *The Gannetteer*, March 1964, page 2.
(5) John C. Quinn, interview, Arlington, Va., Nov. 19, 1991, page 8. Gannett Co. Inc. Archives.
(6) *The Star-Gazette and Advertiser*, Elmira, N.Y., Dec. 23, 1965.
(7) *The Gannetteer*, June 1964, page 2.
(8) *Ibid.*
(9) *Editorially Speaking*, Volume 22, 1964, page 28.
(10) *Ibid.*
(11) *Ibid.*, pages 27, 28.
(12) *Ibid.*, page 25.
(13) *The Gannetteer*, June 1965, page 6.
(14) Mayne interview, pages 16, 17.
(15) Jones interview, page 3.
(16) Mayne interview, page 10.

# Chapter 29
(1) Eckert interview, page 7.
(2) *Ibid.*, page 19.

(3) Dolan interview, page 12.
(4) Maurice Hickey, interview, Pittsburgh, Pa., Feb. 19, 1992, page 1. Gannett Co. Inc. Archives.
(5) Spezzano interview, pages 12, 13.
(6) Hickey interview, page 18.
(7) *Ibid.*, page 2.
(8) *The Gannetteer*, January 1966, page 3.
(9) Quinn interview, pages 2, 3.
(10) Neuharth, *op. cit.*, page 65.
(11) *The Gannetteer*, July 1966, pages 5-7.
(12) *The Gannetteer*, November 1966, pages 8-10.
(13) Jones interview, page 13.
(14) Dolan interview, page 10.
(15) Jones interview, pages 13, 14.
(16) *The Gannetteer*, February 1967, page 2.
(17) Neuharth interview, page 3.

# Chapter 30
(1) *The Gannetteer*, May 1967, pages 2, 3.
(2) *The Gannetteer*, April 1967, page 3.
(3) Jones interview, page 19.
(4) Eckert interview, page 10.
(5) *Ibid.*
(6) *Ibid.*, page 21.
(7) *The Gannetteer*, June 1967, page 5.
(8) Jones interview, page 21.
(9) *The Gannetteer*, December 1967, pages 4-7.
(10) *The Gannetteer*, February 1968, page 3.
(11) Jones interview, page 11.
(12) *The Gannetteer*, February 1968, page 3.
(13) *Ibid.*, page 21.
(14) *The Gannetteer*, March 1968, page 3.
(15) Paul Miller, address to the New York Society of Security Analysts, New York, N.Y., Feb. 26, 1928.

(16) *The Gannetteer,* November 1968, pages 6-9.
(17) *The Gannetteer,* June 1968, pages 36, 37.
(18) *The Gannetteer,* July 1968, page 20.
(19) *The Gannetteer,* December 1968, pages 11-13.
(20) *The Gannetteer,* October 1968, page 2.
(21) *The Gannetteer,* December 1968, page 3.

## Chapter 31
(1) *Editorially Speaking,* Volume 27, 1969, pages 19-22.
(2) *The Gannetteer,* May 1969, pages 38-40.
(3) Gannett Co. Inc. news release, July 1, 1969.
(4) *The Gannetteer,* January 1970, page 46.
(5) Jones interview, page 34.
(6) Quinn interview, page 22.
(7) *The Gannetteer,* March 1970, page 3.
(8) Golding interview, page 10.
(9) *The Gannetteer,* July 1970, page 2.
(10) Golding interview, page 10.
(11) Quinn interview, page 5.
(12) Jones interview, page 24.

## Chapter 32
(1) Hickey interview, page 2.
(2) John J. Curley, interview, Arlington, Va., June 16, 1992, pages 1, 2. Gannett Co. Inc. Archives.
(3) Allen H. Neuharth, "The press and our society: both over-manned at the top," New Orleans, La., June 25, 1970. Reprinted in *The Gannetteer,* October 1970, pages 14-15.
(4) Allen H. Neuharth, "Coffee, Tea and We," Denver, Colo., July 1, 1970. Reprinted in *The Gannetteer,* August-September 1970, pages 4, 5.
(5) Gannett Co. Inc. news release, July 31, 1970.
(6) *The Gannetteer,* November 1970, pages 27-30.
(7) Gannett Co. Inc. news release, Dec. 26, 1970.

(8) Gannett Co. Inc. news release, Jan. 7, 1971.
(9) J. Warren McClure, unpublished memoir, Key Largo, Fla., Nov. 23, 1991.
(10) Douglas H. McCorkindale, interview, Arlington, Va., Nov. 29, 1990, pages 1, 2. Gannett Co. Inc. Archives.
(11) Gannett Co. Inc. news release, June 30, 1971.
(12) Gannett Co. Inc. news release, July 30, 1971.
(13) Eugene C. Dorsey, interview, Rochester, N.Y., Aug. 29, 1990, page 1. Gannett Co. Inc. Archives.
(14) Gannett Co. Inc. news release, Nov. 1, 1971.
(15) Gannett Co. Inc. news release, Nov. 18, 1971.
(16) Gannett Co. Inc. news release, Jan. 14, 1972.
(17) Gannett Co. Inc. news release, June 6, 1972.
(18) McCorkindale interview, page 8.
(19) *Time*, May 22, 1972, pages 13, 14.

# Chapter 33

(1) Mayne interview, page 12.
(2) Memoranda, May 4, 6 and 8, 1970, Vincent Jones personal papers, Rochester, N.Y.
(3) Gannett Co. Inc. news release, June 26, 1973.
(4) Germond interview, pages 7, 8.
(5) Jones interview, pages 19, 20.
(6) Germond interview, pages 1-9.
(7) Quinn interview, page 23.
(8) Germond interview, pages 1-10.
(9) Quinn interview, page 23.

# Chapter 34

(1) Gannett Co. Inc. news release, Jan. 22, 1974.
(2) Gannett Co. Inc. news release, Jan. 22, 1974.
(3) Gannett Co. Inc. news release, Aug. 29, 1974.
(4) Gannett Co. Inc. news release, Nov. 28, 1975.

(5) Ronald A. White, interview, Daytona Beach, Fla., Feb. 7, 1992, page 9. Gannett Co. Inc. Archives.
(6) *Ibid.*, pages 3, 7.
(7) Dolan interview, page 20.
(8) White interview, pages 3, 4.
(9) *Ibid.*, page 6.
(10) *Ibid.*, pages 9, 10.
(11) Gannett Co. Inc. news release, Oct. 10, 1973.
(12) Gannett Co. Inc. news release, May 9, 1974.
(13) Gannett Co. Inc. news release, May 23, 1974.
(14) McCorkindale interview, pages 8, 9.
(15) Gannett Co. Inc. news release, Jan. 6, 1975.
(16) Gannett Co. Inc. news release, Jan. 31, 1975.
(17) Gannett Co. Inc. news release, Nov. 8, 1975.
(18) Jones interview, page 26.
(19) Hickey interview, pages 4, 5.

# Chapter 35
(1) Neuharth interview, page 8.
(2) McCorkindale interview, page 13.
(3) *Ibid.*, Page 9.
(4) Gannett Co. Inc. news release, May 10, 1977.
(5) Gannett Co. Inc. news release, May 16, 1977.
(6) Gannett Co. Inc. news release, June 16, 1977.
(7) McCorkindale interview, page 3.
(8) Neuharth interview, page 10.
(9) Gannett Co. Inc. news release, Oct. 9, 1977.
(10) Gannett Co. Inc. news release, Oct. 12, 1977.
(11) Minutes of the board of directors, Gannett Co. Inc., Nov. 11, 1957, page 2 and attachment.
(12) Mayne interview, page 14.
(13) Wes Gallagher, interview, McLean, Va., Oct. 5, 1990, page 8. Gannett Co. Inc. Archives.

## Chapter 36

(1) *The New York Times*, Jan. 21, 1975, page 30.
(2) Neuharth interview, page 12.
(3) Brian Donnelly, interview, Arlington, Va., Oct. 31, 1990, pages 8, 9. Gannett Co. Inc. Archives.
(4) Gannett Co. Inc. news release, May 8, 1978.
(5) *Finance*, April 1973, page 17.
(6) Vincent S. Jones, remarks introducing Paul Miller to Chatterbox Club, Rochester, N.Y., Dec. 1, 1971.
(7) John C. Quinn, Paul Miller Journalism Lecture, School of Journalism and Broadcasting, Oklahoma State University, Stillwater, March 18, 1988, page 1.
(8) Gannett Co. Inc. news release, Jan. 3, 1979.
(9) Gannett Co. Inc. news release, June 7, 1979.
(10) Gannett Co. Inc. news release, June 26, 1979.
(11) McCorkindale interview, pages 5, 6.
(12) Dorsey interview, page 10.
(13) Miller interview, page 14.
(14) Gallagher interview, page 8.
(15) Gannett Co. Inc. news release, July 5, 1979.
(16) *Problems of Journalism*, proceedings of the 1977 Convention of the American Society of Newspaper Editors, Honolulu, Hawaii, May 2, pages 143-157.
(17) Gannett Co. Inc. news release, July 5, 1979.
(18) McCorkindale interview, page 14.
(19) Neuharth interview, page 18.

## Chapter 37

(1) Gannett Co. Inc. news release, March 13, 1980.
(2) Gannett Co. Inc. news release, March 5, 1980.
(3) "*USA TODAY* Fifth Anniversary," Videotape, Sept. 18, 1987. Gannett Co. Inc. Archives.
(4) Gannett Co. Inc. news release, March 20, 1980.

(5) *Ibid.*
(6) Gannett Co. Inc. news release, July 1, 1980.
(7) Gannett Co. Inc. news release, July 10, 1980.
(8) Quinn interview, page 23.
(9) Gannett Co. Inc. news release, Oct. 30, 1980.
(10) Gannett Co. Inc. news release, Dec. 16, 1980.
(11) Peter Prichard, *The Making of McPaper, The Inside Story of USA TODAY.* Kansas City, Mo., 1987: Andrews McMeel & Parker, page 120.
(12) *Ibid.*, page 140.
(13) Gannett Co. Inc. news release, Aug. 23, 1982.
(14) *The Gannetteer,* November 1953, page 2.
(15) Neuharth interview, page 13.
(16) Gannett Co. Inc. news release, April 1, 1982.
(17) Gannett Co. Inc. news release, Aug. 24, 1982.
(18) Gannett Co. Inc. news release, Sept. 8, 1982.
(19) Gannett Co. Inc. news release, Sept. 25, 1982.

# Chapter 38
(1) Neuharth interview, page 10.
(2) Gallagher interview, pages 6, 7.
(3) Quinn interview, page 29.
(4) Neuharth interview, pages 10, 11.
(5) Quinn interview, page 29.
(6) Gannett Co. Inc. news release, April 24, 1983.
(7) Peter Benjaminson, *Death in the Afternoon,* Kansas City, Mo.: 1984, Andrews, McMeel & Parker, page 151.
(8) Gannett Co. Inc. news release, May 31, 1983.
(9) Gannett Co. Inc. news release, June 27, 1984.

# Chapter 39
(1) Gannett Co. Inc. news release, March 26, 1985.
(2) Neuharth, *op. cit.*, page 140.

(3) *Ibid.*, pages 94-100.
(4) Gannett Co. Inc. news release, March 26, 1985.
(5) Gannett Co. Inc. news release, June 25, 1985.
(6) Gannett Co. Inc. news release, Aug. 29, 1985.
(7) Allen H. Neuharth, transcript of remarks to Gannett Annual Shareholders' Meeting, Washington, D.C., May 20, 1986. Gannett Co. Inc. Archives.
(8) Hickey interview, pages 7, 8.
(9) *The Detroit News,* Detroit, Mich., Nov. 14, 1989, page 6A.
(10) Gannett Co. Inc. news release, May 19, 1995.
(11) *ASNE – 1986,* Proceedings of the 1986 Convention of the American Society of Newspaper Editors, Washington, D.C., April 8-11, pages 224-239.
(12) Gannett Co. Inc. news release, Dec. 3, 1986.
(13) McCorkindale interview, page 17.
(14) Gannett Co. Inc. news release, Dec. 3, 1986.

# Chapter 40

(1) John Seigenthaler, interview, Washington, D.C., Feb.1, 1993, page 6. Gannett Co. Inc. Archives.
(2) *Ibid.,* pages 9, 10.
(3) *Ibid.,* page 10.
(4) Charles C. Edwards Jr., interview, Des Moines, Iowa, April 8, 1993, page 6. Gannett Co. Inc. Archives.
(5) *Ibid.,* pages 8, 9.
(6) *Ibid.,* page 8.
(7) *Ibid.,* page 6.
(8) *Ibid.,* page 11.
(9) *Ibid.,* pages 14, 15.
(10) *Ibid.,* page 10.
(11) *Ibid.,* page 11.
(12) Seigenthaler interview, page 13.
(13) *Ibid.,* page 14.
(14) Edwards interview, page 17.

(15) Seigenthaler interview, pages 4, 5.
(16) Curley interview, page 9.
(17) Donald B. Towles, letter to John Curley, Dec. 18, 1992. Gannett Co. Inc. Archives.

## Chapter 41

(1) Minutes of the board of directors, Dec. 9, 1986.
(2) *The Philadelphia Inquirer*, Philadelphia, Pa., Jan. 12, 1987, pages 1E, 8E.
(3) *Detroit Free Press*, Detroit, Mich., Jan. 12, 1987, page 6G.
(4) Gannett Co. Inc. news release, July 23, 1987.
(5) *Daily News*, New York City, Sept. 13, 1988, page C22.
(6) *Time*, Sept. 26, 1988, page 71.
(7) *New York*, New York City, Oct. 3, 1988, page 76.
(8) Gannett Co. Inc. news release, Nov. 22, 1989.
(9) Gannett Co. Inc. news release, March 13, 1987.
(10) Gannett Co. Inc. news release, June 15, 1987.
(11) Gannett Co. Inc. news release, July 2, 1987.
(12) Heselden interview, page 14.
(13) Gannett Co. Inc. news release, Dec. 8, 1987.
(14) Gannett Co. Inc. news release, March 22, 1989.
(15) Neuharth interview, pages 18, 19.

## Chapter 42

(1) McCorkindale interview, page 19.
(2) Quinn interview, page 27.
(3) Mary Alice Kellogg, "The Man and Company Behind USA Today," *Adweek*, April 1982, page NR14.
(4) David Remnick, "Good News is No News," *Esquire*, October 1987, page 156.
(5) K. E. Grubbs Jr., "Inside USA Today," *Inquiry*, April 1983, page 13.
(6) Curley interview, pages 6, 7.
(7) *The Wall Street Journal*, July 30, 1990, page A4.

(8) Dorsey interview, page 13.
(9) Neuharth interview, pages 14, 15.
(10) Curley interview, page 17.
(11) *Ibid*, page 8.
(12) *Ibid.*, pages 9, 10.
(13) *Ibid.*, pages 16, 17.
(14) Gannett Co. Inc. news release, June 11, 1991.
(15) *The Gannetteer*, July-August 1992, pages 4, 5.
(16) Curley interview, pages 10, 11.

# Index

## Glossary of Gannett abbreviations

To save space but provide easy reference, these appear in index sub-entries.

| | |
|---|---|
| AHN | Neuharth, Allen H. |
| DHM | McCorkindale, Douglas H. |
| ERD | Davenport, Erwin R. |
| FEG | Gannett, Frank E. |
| FET | Tripp, Frank E. |
| GCI | Gannett Co., Inc. |
| GNF | Frank E. Gannett Newspaper Foundation, later the Gannett Foundation, then the Freedom Forum |
| JCQ | Quinn, John C. |
| JJC | Curley, John J. |
| LRB | Blanchard, Lafayette (Fay) R. |
| MVA | Atwood, M.V. |
| PM | Miller, Paul |
| TGN | Gannett Newspapers, The |
| VSJ | Jones, Vincent S. |

## Index

ABC. *See* Audit Bureau of Circulations
Acme Photo, price increase by, 210; TGN, wirephoto test for, 168; TGN, wirephoto winner for, 170
Adams, Joseph T., 96, 227
ADvance, launching of, 488-489
*Advance-News*, Ogdensburg, N.Y., 117, 148; FDR, support of, 118-119
*Advertiser*, Elmira, acquisition of, 45; Barber, editor of, 183; FET, start on, 216; *Star-Gazette*, merger with, 297. *See also Elmira Gazette*, early struggle
*Advertiser*, Huntington, W. Va., acquisition of, 358
Advertising managers conferences. *See* Editors conferences
Advertising Partnership Program. *See USA TODAY*, advertising sales
Advertising Research Foundation. *See* Continuing Study of Newspaper Readership
Alameda Newspaper Group. *See Oakland Tribune*, purchase of, 430
Albany (N.Y.) bureau, GNS, use of, 232
Albers, Jo-Ann Huff, Chambersburg, president, editor and publisher in, 424; Sturgis, publisher and editor in, 424
Alcoholic beverages, advertising accepted for, 540
Aldridge, George W., 34; Democrats, defection of, 41; FEG, creditor to, 41; Republican Party, boss of, 41
Alger, Horatio, 3
Alinsky, Saul, Rochester, racial protests in, 309
Allied Daily Newspapers, 264
Allied Newspaper Council, *See* Victory Drive
Allies, 101
America's Town Meeting of the Air, 97
American Broadcasting Companies, 439
American Cooperative Institute, 96
*American Editor*, New England Society of Newspaper Editors, quarterly, 280
American Heritage Foundation, voter turnout, prizes for, 222
American Institute of Motion Pictures, FEG campaign, promotion of, 105-107
American Newspaper Publishers Association, 140; 270, 285, 351; newspaper groups, panel on, 404-405; Neuharth, director of, 335. *See also* Newspaper Association of America
American Press Institute, 289, 291, 344; PM, chairman of, 251-252; seminars, TGN part in, 252
American Society of Newspaper Editors, 127-128, 199, 291, 344; mergers, debate on, 447-449, 453; on VSJ's work, 203
*American*, Rochester. *See* Hearst, William Randolph, competitor
Amherst College. *See* Odegard, Dr. Peter H.
ANPA. *See* American Newspaper Publishers Association
AP Continuing Study Committee, 218
AP. *See* Associated Press
Apalachin, N.Y., 259-260
API. *See* American Press Institute
APME. *See* Associated Press Managing Editors
Applied Laser Technology, Inc. *See* Laser-Graph
Archer, Olin, 214
Arctic League. *See* Tripp, Frank E., on Pearl Harbor
*Arkansas Democrat*, 482; *Arkansas Gazette*, legal battle with, 449-450
*Arkansas Gazette*, 482; acquisition of, 450; advertisers, loss of, 459; *Arkansas Democrat*, legal battle with, 449; circulation, ranking by, 452-453; sale of, 483
Arlington, Va., GCI move to, 433, 441-442
Armstrong, Neil, first step on moon, 1

A History of Gannett 523

Army and Navy Union. *See* Roosevelt, Theodore
ASNE. *See* American Society of Newspaper Editors
Associated Newspaper Group Ltd., 393
Associated Press Managing Editors, 294; LRB on PM, 169; on polling, 218; on VSJ's work, 203
Associated Press, The, 58, 62, 87, 118, 149, 170, 211, 332; on censorship, 135; FEG, director of, 87-88, 102; Gallagher, general manager of, 389; PM, bureau chief of, 169, 193; PM, director of, 202, 227, 249; on PM's hiring by TGN, 184, 186; TGN, wirephoto test for, 168; *Times-Union*, denial to, 59, 62
*Atlanta Journal*, news/ad ratios in, 154
*Atlantic Monthly, The*, Lindstrom, invitation to, 274
Attlee, Prime Minister Clement, 175
Atwood, M.V., 95; death of, 129; on FEG candidacy, 101, 110; on local autonomy, 124; on press, critics of, 114, 119, 124; TGN, associate editor of, 70, 96;
Audit Bureau of Circulations, *USA TODAY*, first survey of, 421
Autonomy, local, 31, 365


Bagdikian, Ben, ASNE debate, panelist on, 447
Baker, Sen. Howard, 420
Balance sheet, new. *See Ithaca Daily News*
Baldwin, Stanley, 87
Ball, Braden, annual barbecue of, 340; Pensacola, publisher in, 339
*Baltimore News-Post*, news/ad ratios in, 154
Bank of Bolivar. *See Elmira Gazette*
Barber, Charles, *Advertiser*, Elmira, editor of, 183; on FET's writing, 183
Barker, Ronald C. *See* Laser-Graph
Barn, The, creation of, 181-182
Baskind, Thomas J., GANSAT, marketing communications, vice president of, 415
Bausch & Lomb, 100
'Baywatch.' *See* GTG Entertainment, history of
*Beacon* (N.Y.) *News*, acquisition of, 52; minority share, purchase of, 231
*Beacon-Journal*, Akron, FEG interest in, 33; news/ad ratios in, 155
Bean, Gerald A., *USA TODAY*, general manager of, 418
Bell Telephone Co., 42
Benjaminson, Peter, on KRON-TV sale, cancellation of, 430

Bingham, Barry Jr., 446
Bingham, Barry Sr., 446
Bingham Broadcasting Co., Seattle, 446
Bingham, Sallie, 446
*Binghamton Press*, acquisition of, 148; anniversary of, 50th, 231; building purchase, 217; on closed meetings, 232; Stein, editor, publisher of, 218; WINR, WINR-TV, 256-257
Binghamton Press Company, 356; acquisition of, 148
Bitner, Lynn N., 340; Elmira, on all-day paper, 293-294; on FET, tippling by, 292; Florida project, role in, 314, 316; GCI, director of, 227; GCI, general business manager of, 217; GCI, general manager of, 233, 248; GCI, senior vice president of, 316; GCI, vice president of, 290; GNF, director of, 227; retirement of, 316, 320-321; WINR-TV, role in, 256-257
'Bitner's Law of Automation,' 294
Black, Cathleen, 441; GCI, director of, 437; GCI marketing, executive vice president of, 437; *USA TODAY*, president of, 431; *USA TODAY*, publisher of, 432
Blade Communications, 485
Blanchard, Lafayette (Fay) R., 138; on censorship, 163-164; on communists, 180; on contest judging, 206; *Democrat and Chronicle*, editor of, 202, 212; on editors' resolutions, 156; France, tour of, 170; on letters to editor, 212-213; MVA, successor to 129; on Nieman Fellows, 223; NYSNE, president of, 169; on PM, 169-170; on post-war challenges, 164; on press unions, 174-175; publishers, criticism of, 170; on readers, young, 238-239; TGN, associate editor of, 129; TGN, general executive editor of, 186, 202; on *Times-Union*, 96; on Voice of America, 212-213; on Wallace, Henry, 181
*Blitz, blitzkrieg. See* Nazis, inflammatory words about
Blum, Leon, 109
Board for Urban Ministry, Rochester. *See* Alinsky, Saul
'Bob Newhart Show, The.' *See* GTG Entertainment, history of
Bolivar Union School and Academy, 5
Borah, Sen. William, 87; as GOP candidate, 88-89; FEG, running mate of, 88-89; on Supreme Court, 92

## 524 A History of Gannett

Boston Traveler, news/ad ratios in, 155
Botany Worsted Mills, 146
Bowen, John, 113
Bradley University. See Gannett, Dixon, on school days
Breeze, Bolivar, N.Y., 7
Bridge, Donald U., Rochester, general manager in, 297; TGN, ad/news feud in, 173
Brighton-Pittsford (N.Y.) Post, 335
Brinkman, David, New England Society of Newspaper Editors, president of, 281. See also Editor & Publisher, Tripp letter, responses to
Broadcast Enterprises Network Inc. See WHEC-TV, sale of
Brock, Ira, 340
Brockaway, Zebulon R. See The Star-Gazette, policy of
Broderick, John. See Monroe County Republican Party, chairman of
Brooklyn Daily Eagle, 63; acquisition of, 53; burden of, 63-64; policy of, 53; Power Trust, effects of, 54-55; sale of, 64-65
Brown, Constantine, 181
Bryan, William Jennings, 28
Buckley, J. Taylor, USA TODAY, senior editor of, 422
Buffalo News, The, 5; news/ad ratios in, 154
Bullard, Marcia, USA WEEKEND, editor of, 491
Bulletin, The, 96, 108, 110, 202, 225, 237
Bulletin Co., The, Norwich, Conn., acquisition of, 416
Bunting, Mary I., 348
Burke, J.A., 96
Burlington (Vt.) Free Press, The, acquisition of, 351; offset presses at, 374
BusCapade, 466, 469-470
BusCapade: Plain Talk Across the USA, 466
Buz Sawyer. See Democrat and Chronicle, comics page, changes on

California, University of, at Berkeley, 334
California Editors Conference. See California Newspaper Publishers Association
California Newspaper Publishers Association, PM, on "Newspaper of the Future," 250
Cambodia, invasion of, 363-364
Campos, U.S. District Judge Santiago. See New Mexican, McKinney suit by
Cape Canaveral, 313
Capital Cities Communications, Inc., 439

Capital Journal, Salem, Ore., acquisition of, 377. See also Statesman-Journal, creation of
Carpenter, Clifford, Democrat and Chronicle, editorial page columnist of, 364
Cavett, Dick, USA TODAY launch, emcee of, 420
CBS, Inc., 436
Censorship, 135, 141, 157
Census, Bureau of the, on newspaper readership, 127
Chamberlain, Rudolph W., See Editorially Speaking, creation of
Chapman, Alvah H. Jr., on Detroit JOA, 443
Chapman, Connie Davenport, 18
Chapman, Russell, 18
Chemical National Bank, 56
Chemung County, N.Y. See American Heritage Foundation, voter turnout, prizes for
Chicago Daily News, 90; news/ad ratios in, 154
Chicago Sun. See Dickson, Cecil B.
Chicago Tribune, 276
Chicago Tribune-New York News Syndicate, 118
Christiana Securities. See DuPont Co.
Chronicle Broadcasting Co., San Francisco, 425, 430
Cincinnati Enquirer, The, 452; acquisition of, 399
Cincinnati Times-Star, news/ad ratios in, 155
Circulation managers conferences, 72, 86, 96
Citizen-Advertiser, The, Albany, N.Y. See Editorially Speaking, creation of
Citizen-Register, The, Ossining, N.Y., 305
Citizenship and Civic Affairs. See Rugg, Prof. Harold B.
City Club, Rochester, on Eisenhower illness, 238
Civic Achievement Award. See Rochester Rotary Club
Civil Works Administration, 68
Clapper, Raymond, 126
Clarion-Ledger, Jackson, Miss., acquisition of, 423
Clark, Peter B. See Evening News Association, merger with
Clark-Jackson, Susan, Niagara Gazette, president and publisher of, 424
Cleveland Press, news/ad ratios in, 155
Clifton, N.Y. See Gannett, Maria, illness of
Clune, Henry, 41, 53; on ERD, 145; on FEG candidacy, 100; on free advertising, 145-146; workweek of, 61
Cobb, Fordyce and Howard, 13, 30, 53
Cocoa (Fla.) Tribune, acquisition of, 314
Coffeyville (Kan.) Journal, The, acquisition of,

A History of Gannett 525

394; sale of, 469
Collson, Robert L., Elmira, on Laser-Graph, use by, 373
Columbia Pictures Entertainment. *See* GTG Entertainment, history of
Columbia University, 114, 124, 128, 289, 334, 393, 477
*Columbus Dispatch*, news/ad ratios in, 155
Combined Communications Corporation, merger with, 395
Combined Community Chest and Red Cross drive. *See* Miller, Paul, community service of
Comic strips, violent content of, 211
Commerce, U.S. Department of, 69
*Commercial Appeal, The*, Memphis, 453
*Commercial-News*, Danville, Ill., acquisition of, 73; Borah, support of, 89; newsprint shortage at, 239
Commercial-News Company, 73
Community Priorities Program. *See* Overby, Charles, GNF stock sale, role in
*Confessions of an S.O.B.*, 297, 322; Florida, PM/AHN plans for, 304, 313-314; on McCorkindale, 386; on PM, succession of, 342; on *Today*, 315
Congress, U.S., 100, 108, 141, 155; on Supreme Court, 91-92
*Congressional Record*, 87
Conrad, Robert M. *See Editor & Publisher*, Tripp letter, responses to
Constitution, U.S., 95
Continuing Study of Newspaper Readership, VSJ, use by, 202
Coolidge, Calvin, 52
Cooper, Kent, 115, 169, 184-186
Copeland, Isaac Seymour, Elmira, partner in, 23, 25
Copeland, Woodford J., Elmira, partner-editor in, 23-26, 28; retirement of, 46-47; severance payment to, 46-47; TGN, vice president of, 36, 38
*Cornell Daily Sun*, 7
Cornell University, 6, 10, 51, 63, 72, 86, 91, 107, 124; Binghamton, role in, 148, 217; Gannett archives, creation of, 255; Gannett Farms, role in, 168; Gannett Health Center at, 255; GNF, donation from, 243
*Courier and Freeman*, Potsdam, N.Y., 262
*Courier-Express*, Buffalo, closing of, 424
*Courier-Journal, The*, Louisville, circulation, ranking by, 452-453; acquisition of, 446; TGN, transition to, 460
*Courier-News*, Plainfield/Bridgewater, N.J., 206; acquisition of, 52; on censorship, 125; circulation gains by, 123;

Dolan, publisher of, 316; Heselden, publisher of, 316; on Ickes, 99; JJC, editor of, 346-347; JJC, president and publisher of, 369; relocation of, 375
*Courier-Post*, Camden, N.J., acquisition of, 263-264
Court of Appeals, U.S. *See* Joint Operating Agreement, Detroit
Court-packing bill. *See* Supreme Court, U.S., reorganization of
Cowles Media Co., 436, 455, 476; stock, GCI acquisition of, 437; stock, repurchase of, 469
Croop, Vern, 260
Cruickshank, Herbert W., 148, 199, 248; on FEG's stroke, 191; GCI, debt of, 63-64; GCI, general business manager of, 186; GCI, general manager of, 217; hiring of, 62; PM, resentment of, 228; resignation of, 233; on RIT, grant to, 200; on Rochester strike, 177; salary of, 69
Cuban missile crisis, PM column on, 295
Culver Studios, The. *See* GTG Entertainment, history of
Curley, John J., AHN, contrasts with, 474-475; Dickinson College, student at, 1
— GCI: chairman, president and CEO of, 465, 469, 472; director of, 432; on future of, 494-495; on GNF, relationship with, 482; GNF stock purchase, role in, 478-481; on GTG Entertainment, 465; News, vice president of, 412; Newspaper Division, president of, 429; senior vice president of, 429; president and CEO of, 441-442; president and COO of, 432
— GNS: bureau chief of, 369; general manager of, 369; vice president of, 398
— TGN: on ADvance, 488; *Courier-News*, editor of, 346-347; *Courier-News*, president and publisher of, 369; on C-plus newspapers, 486-487; on Little Rock impasse, 482-483; on McKinney, intransigence of, 470, 475-476; Mid-Atlantic group, president of, 414; on News 2000, 486, 488; on North Hills market, 485; on Times Journal Co., acquisition and sale of, 483-484; *Times-Union*, hiring by, 341; *Times-Union*, suburban editor of, 341, 346; on *USA WEEKEND*, 491; Wilmington, president and pub-

lisher in, 413
— *USA TODAY:* editor of, 418; on first profits for, 466, 468; regions for, 432
Curley, Thomas, Project NN, member of, 410; TGN, research, director of, 410; *USA TODAY,* executive vice president/general manager of, 443; on *USA TODAY,* financial losses of, 491; *USA TODAY,* president of, 443; *USA TODAY,* publisher of, 491
Currie, Philip R., 489; GCI, vice president/news of, 486; on News 2000, 486-487
Curtis, J. Montgomery, API, director of, 289
Curtiss Commando. *See* Gannett, Frank E., on free advertising
Custer, George A., 2

D-Day in Europe, 156
*Daily Argus, The,* Mount Vernon, N.Y., 305
*Daily Item, The,* Port Chester, N.Y., 305
*Daily News,* New York City, circulation, ranking by, 421
*Daily News, The,* Indio, Calif., acquisition of, 440
*Daily News, The,* St. Thomas, V.I., 437; acquisition of, 384
*Daily News, The,* Tarrytown, N.Y., 305
*Daily Times, The,* Mamaroneck, N.Y., 305
*Dallas Times-Herald,* news/ad ratios in, 155
Daniel, David, *Hartford Times,* publisher of, 271; on Lindstrom, 279
*Dateline,* Guam, acquisition of, 358
Daughters of the American Revolution, Olean chapter of, 114
Davenport, Erwin R., anniversary of, 40th, 171-172; birth of, 17; death of, 327; Elmira, business manager in, 36; debt, share of, 41; FEG, partner of, 13, 18; on free advertising, 145; GCI vice president, resignation as, 290; as innovator, 17; retirements of, 46, 49, 244, 290; Rochester, general manager in, 96; on Rochester expansion, 200; Rochester, secretary-treasurer in, 96; severance payment to, 46-47; as student, 17; war work by, 137
*Dayton News,* news/ad ratios in, 155
*Death in the Afternoon. See* Benjaminson, Peter
*Deborah Sampson Gannett,* Liberty Ship, 155
*Democrat and Chronicle,* Rochester, 4, 34, 118, 452; acquisition of, 53; Adams, editor of, 96; Barn, co-sponsor of, 181;

building expansion for, 200, 243; Clune, employee of, 100, 145; comics page, changes on, 330; editor, letters to, 232; employees, Vietnam petition from, 363-365; farm editor of, 167; FDR death, extra for, 161; LRB, editor of, 202; newsprint shortages at, 137, 239; outreach by, 211; policy of, 197; radio, news link to, 193; on Rochester, riots in, 307; Sanford, editor of, 126, 128, 174, 202; strike, effects of, 177; WWII memorial, role in, 163
Democratic Party, 42, 61
DePauw University. *See Commercial-News*
Depression, The, 63, 71, 83, 106, 147
*Desert Sun, The,* Palm Springs, Calif., acquisition of, 440
*Des Moines Register,* acquisition of, 436, 439, 455; circulation, ranking by, 452-453; GCI, capital spending by, 458; TGN, transition to, 455-457
*Des Moines Tribune,* acquisition of, 436
*Detroit Free Press,* 452; AHN, background with, 440; JOA, partner in, 443
*Detroit News, The,* 452; acquisition of, 440; JOA, partner in, 443; news/ad ratios in, 155
Detroit Newspaper Agency, creation of, 443-445
*Detroit Times,* news/ad ratio in, 154
Deuel, Alanson E. *See Niagara Gazette,* acquisition of
Dewey, Gov. Thomas E., 102, 111, 160, 220
*Dick Tracy. See* Comic strips, violent content of
Dickinson College, 1
*Dickinson* (N.D.) *Press,* acquisition of, 358
Dickson, Cecil B., GNS, chief of, 149; on labor news, 168-169; Washington party, host for, 168-169
Distinguished Public Service Award, U.S. Navy, FEG honored by, 200
Dolan, Thomas P., 249; on Albany market, 266; on *Courier-News,* JJC's work on press, 375; on *Courier-News,* new plant for, 375; *Courier-News,* publisher of, 316; Gannett East, vice president of, 385; *Knickerbocker News,* assistant general manager of, 263; Ogdensburg, ad manager in, 262; on pay scales, PM improvement of, 251; on PM, managerial style of, 320; Potsdam, general manager in, 262; Saratoga Springs, assistant general manager of, 249; *Saratogian,* general manag-

er of, 262; or *Saratogian-Knicker-bocker News* Daily Double, 262-263; on *Today*, 314; TGN, first job in, 262
Donaldson, Lufkin and Jenrette Inc. *See* Louis Harris and Associates Inc., acquisition of
Donnelly, Brian, Binghamton, publisher of, 394; Wilmington, first Gannett publisher in, 394
Dorsey, Eugene C., on Eller, dissatisfaction of, 401; Gannett Special Divisions, vice president of, 388; GNF, president of, 477; retirement of, 477; Rochester, general manager of, 358; Rochester, publisher of, 358
Dow Jones & Co. *See Des Moines Register*, acquisition of
Duffy, J. Frank, 96
Duffy, Ward, *Hartford Times*, 150; editorial page, editor of, 278; managing editor of, 278
Duke University. *See* North Carolina Press Association
*Dun's Review*, GCI, ranking of, 414
Dunham, Stuart A., *Hartford Times*, editor of, 286; Lindstrom, letter from, 286-287; Rochester newspapers, executive editor of, 364
DuPont Co., 392-394

*Eastbay Today*, 471; creation of, 410
Eastman, George, 41, 46
Eaton, Fred, on *Saratogian-Knickerbocker News* Daily Double, 262-263; *Saratogian*, managing editor of, 262
Eckert, Robert R., AHN, assistant to, 313; on AHN, Florida project, 313; Binghamton, business manager in, 293; Binghamton, assistant general manager in, 249; Elmira, on all-day paper, 293-294; Elmira, general manager in, 293; on FET, 293; on *Hartford Times*, decline of, 325-326; *Hartford Times*, general manager of, 325; *Hartford Times*, publisher of, 325-326; on WINR-TV, 256-257
*Editor & Publisher*, 170, 350; on *Editorially Speaking*, 150; on Lindstrom editorial excerpt, 280-282; Lindstrom book, review of, 269; FET, letter from, 280-281; FET letter, responses to, 281-282
*Editorially Speaking*, creation of, 150; response to, 192
Editors conferences, 1933, 71; 1940, 114-115; 1941, 126; 1942, 138; on Barn, 181; on deceptive ads, 126; FEG, return of, 202; FEG, "take a stand" advice of,

219; PM as panelist, 182; on postwar challenges, 156, 162, 166; on radio news, 138; on war news, 115-116; on women readers, 186
Edwards, Charles C. Jr., *Des Moines Register*, president/publisher of, 457; on TGN, transition to, 455-458
Eisenhower, Dwight, election of, 222; GOP, presidential nominee of, 220; heart attack of, 238
*El Diario-La Prensa*, New York City, acquisition of, 416; sale of, 476
*Electronic Media*, 464
Elefante, Rufie. *See* Germond, Jack, on Utica expose
Eller Investment Co., Inc., 489
Eller, Karl, Combined Communications, president and CEO of, 395, 399; dissatisfaction of, 400-403; Gannett Development Committee, chairman of, 400; Phoenix Outdoor, repurchase of, 489; resignation of, 403
Eller Outdoor. *See* Eller, Karl, Phoenix Outdoor, repurchase of
Elmira Civic League. *See The Star-Gazette*, on reform
Elmira College, Caroline Gannett, honors to, 254
Elmira Compact. *See The Star-Gazette*, policy
*Elmira Gazette*, 12-13, 40-41, 172; acquisition of, 13, 15; on billboards, 21; classifieds ads in, 16, 18; on crime, 17; early struggle of, 15-24; equipment of, 20, 23, 50; merger of, 23-26; motto of, 20; policy of, 19; on vice, 16
Elmira Rotary Club, 89
*El Paso* (Texas) *Times*, acquisition of, 359
Empire State Building, 68
Empire State Group, 45, 49, 52, 58
Empire State School of Printing, FEG, support of, 371, 374. *See also* Rochester Institute of Technology
Empire Typographical Conference, PM speaks to, 214-216. *See also* International Typographical Union
Evans, Amon Carter, 406, 453
Evans, Em, 114
*Evening Courier. See* Stretch, William, on *Courier-Post*
*Evening News*, Albany, 266; acquisition of, 53. *See also Knickerbocker News*
*Evening News*, Newark, N.J. *See* Jones, Vincent S., on contest judging
*Evening News, The*, Newburgh, N.Y., 113;

acquisition of, 52; circulation gains by, 123; minority share, purchase of, 231; sale of, 378, 383; staff shortage on, 142;
Evening News Association, The, merger with, 440
*Evening Star*, Elmira, merger of, 23-26, 28
*Evening Star*, Peekskill, N.Y., acquisition of, 440
*Evening Sun, The*, Baltimore, news/ad ratios in, 155, 368
Explorer I, U.S. earth satellite, first of, 2

*Facts About Newspapers. See* Newspaper Association of America, readership, survey on
*Fading American Newspaper, The*, controversy over, 269-287
*Family Weekly*, acquisition of, 436; redesigning of, 439. *See also USA WEEKEND*
Fanning, William L., 305
FDR. *See* Roosevelt, Franklin D.
Federal Broadcasting Co., 440
Federal Communications Commission, 130, 399, 423, 439; TV licensing by, 214, 257
Federal Emergency Relief Administration, 68
Federal Trade Commission, 447; hearing by, 54-55
Federated Publications Inc., Battle Creek, Mich., 342; merger, cancellation of, 349; merger with, 355; stock, purchase of, 349
F.I.G.H.T., Rochester. *See* Alinsky, Saul
Financial Analysts Federation, AHN, PM, speeches to, 349-350
First Amendment, 82. *See also* Freedom Forum, The
First Boston Corporation, 328
Fisher, Andrew, 393-394
Fitzpatrick, E. Boyd. *See Olean Times-Herald*, sale of
*Flammenwerfer. See* Nazis, inflammatory words about
Flesch, Rudolph, 203
Fly, James L., 130
Folsom, Marion, 225
Ford, Lena Guilbert. *See Times-Union*, Rochester, editorials
France, Nazi occupation of, 109
Frank E. Gannett and Caroline Werner Gannett Archives. *See* Cornell University, archives, Gannett
Frank E. Gannett Newspaper Foundation, Inc. *See* Gannett Newspaper Foundation. *See also* Freedom

Forum, The
*Frank Leslie's Illustrated Weekly. See* Gannett, Frank E., editor
Frank Tripp Awards, creation of 292. *See also* Innovator Drive for Excellence Awards
Franklin, Benjamin, 40
Freedom Forum, The, 82; GCI stock, sale of, 478-481; GNF, successor to, 430, 477; Maynard, loans to, 430. *See also* Gannett Newspaper Foundation
'Freedom Riders.' *See* Seigenthaler, John, Robert F. Kennedy, administrative assistant to
Freeman, Charles A.S., 96, 190
Free Press Association Inc., 352
*Fremont* (Neb.) *Tribune*, sale of, 469
*Fresno Bee*, 373
Friedman, Steve. *See* GTG Entertainment, history of
Fry, E. Roanne, Sturgis, publisher in, 424

*Gainesville* (Ga.) *Times*, acquisition of, 416
Gallagher, Wes, on AHN, succession of, 428; AP, general manager of, 389; on Eller challenge to AHN, 402-403; GCI, director of, 389; GCI, management continuity committee, chairman of, 389, 402, 428; on PM, succession of, 389-390
Gannett, Benjamin. *See* Gannett, Deborah Sampson
Gannett, Caroline Werner, 78; on beer, liquor ads, acceptance of, 340; as commencement speaker, 243, 254-255; death of, 398; GCI, director of, 223; doctorate, recipient of, 254; on education, 254; engagement of, 44; eye bank, donation to, 255; FEG, bequest from, 245; FEG, convalescence of, 194-195; FEG, RIT memorial to, 340; FEG, stroke of, 191-192; FET, funeral of, 306; infants, deaths of, 78; letters to, 59, 100, 111, 160; Messman role for, 191, 236-237; motherhood of, 44, 78, 155; philanthropy of, 79; politics, role in, 104; wedding of, 44
Gannett, Charles and Maria, relocations, 3, 4, 5, 8, 10
Gannett, Charles, FEG, father of, 3; as tenant farmer, 3; as hotelkeeper, 4-8
Gannett, Deborah Sampson, Revolutionary War, soldier in, wounded pensioner of, 155-156

Gannett, Dixon, adoption of, 74, 78; on career choice, 198; childhood of, 78; on school days, 198; on Rochester strike, 176

Gannett, Frank E., 1, 68; as author, 184; on aviation, 73-74, 88, 183-184; Ickes, debate with, 97-99; Keuka College, speaker at, 72, 95; Nazi dossier on, 134; paternalism of, 77, 83-84; Philippines, work in, 9-10
— Company, early: debt of, 40-41, 49, 53; as partner, 13; president of, 46, 58; as publisher, 31, 58; radio, interest in, 69
— Company (GCI): Albany, switch in, 93; anniversary of, 40th, 171-172; on *Editorially Speaking*, 150; Gannett Farms, creation of, 167-168; on GCI reorganization, 217; on GNF, hopes for, 80-82; on GNS, bureaus of, 182; on GNS, hopes for, 149; on GNS, praise for, 168; on MVA, death of, 129; on newsprint supply, 135-136, 139; on PM, hiring of, 184; president emeritus of, 241; on Rochester, strike in, 177, 179; salary, cut in, 68; technology, commitment to, 371, 422; on thrift, need for, 139; *Times-Union*, president and editor of, 36; work, return to, 202
— Personal history: as bartender, 32, 61; as business manager, 11; birth of, 3; contrasts in, 2-3, 84, 86; convalescence of, 194-195, 213; Cornell, student at, 6-8; death of, 244; diabetes of, 75; disability, pension for, 241; as editor, 11; engagement of, 44; as entrepreneur, young, 4-5; estate and will of, 79, 244; as father, 44, 78, 155; FET, kinship with, 51-52; financial sacrifice of, 69, 74; hospitalization of, 233; letters from, 44-46, 58, 100, 111, 160; marriage of, 44; mother, devotion to, 44-46, 49; as motivator, 70, 96; naivete of, 167; press, attacks by, 55; as reporter, 5-8; as risk-taker, 53; on sister, death of, 207; stroke of, 191; as student, 5-8; as translator, 9; travel abroad by, 87; typical day of, 50; wedding of, 44
— Philanthropy: 75, 79-82; corneas, donation of, 255; fund drives, role in, 144, 147
— Philosophy: on advertisers, 99, 162; on advertising, free, 145; on agri-culture, 97; on alcohol, 71; on autonomy, local, 61, 66, 90-91, 97, 219; on editorial pages, 107, 151, 167; on free press, 98, 141; on hard work, 78; on profit-sharing, 71, 77, 82, 84, 131; on Prohibition, 32, 51, 61; on radio news, 138; on readers, 72; on "take a stand," 219; on women in newsroom, 157
— Politics: 63, 86, 87-91; on FDR, 73, 86, 89, 95, 100, 101, 159-160; on FDR, death of, 161; on FDR, health of, 161; on FDR, "isolationist press" charge by, 159; GOP, candidacies in, 88-89, 95, 101-102, 144; on New Deal, 86, 97, 107, 109; presidential campaign, motion picture for, 105-107; presidential campaign, travel for, 104; on Willkie, 111
— Titles: AP board, director of, 87-88; as city editor, 10; as editor-in-chief, 45
— World War II: on French occupation, 109; Navy, award from, 200; opposition to, 71, 87, 102, 126-127, 129; on post-war challenges, 162; support of U.S. effort in, 131, 133; war work by, 137, 144

Gannett, Jude. *See* Nazis, FEG, dossier on

Gannett, Maria Brooks, as hotelkeeper, 4-8; FEG, mother of, 3, 40; illness of, 44-45

Gannett, Sally. *See* McAdam, Sally Gannett

Gannett Broadcast Group, stations, numbers of, 434, 439

Gannett Center for Media Studies (Freedom Forum Media Studies Center), 477

Gannett Central, 450; creation of, 385

Gannett Communities Fund. *See* Curley, John J., GNF stock purchase, role in

Gannett Company Inc., 15, 73; as holding company, 267; age rules of, 199; Central Office of, 96; creation of, 46-47, 49; debt of, 62, 63, 82; early growth of, 58; earnings, consecutive gains in, 387, 425, 468, 478; executive bonuses from, 188, 201, 232; executives, retirement policy for, 388-389; FEG, disability pension to, 241; FEG, president emeritus of, 241; FEG, well-wishes to, 233; FEG yacht, purchase of, 74; Gannett Farms, support of, 167-168; headquarters, relocation of, 433; Hearst, purchase from, 93; life insurance plan of, 200-201;

530  A History of Gannett

Hearst, sale to, 266; life insurance rebate by, 218; Little, bid from, 246; Operating Committee of, 386, 388; as operating company, 267; pension plan of, 200-201; pension plan rebate by, 218; profits of, 71; profit-sharing of, 77, 82-84, 187, 232; publicly held company, 25 years as, 489; public ownership of, 82; retirement policy of, 243; RIT, grant to, 200; Rochester building, expansion of, 200; Speidel stock, purchase of, 378; stock sales of, 56, 82; World War II memorial, support of, 163
Gannett Company stock, employee purchases of, 63, 82; FEG, reimbursement to, 69; GNF, block held by, 78, 266; GNF block, purchase of, 478-481; growth of, 244; Lindner, purchases by, 438; preferred, conversion of, 324, 329; preferred, holders of, 266; public offering of, 324, 328-329; sales of, 56, 82; splits of, 414
Gannett Development Committee, creation of, 400
Gannett Diversified Media Division, McCorkindale, president of, 413
Gannett East, creation of, 385
*Gannetteer*, 70, 71, 95, 96
Gannett Farms. *See* Skeffington, L.B., farm editor
Gannett Hill, N.Y., 3
Gannett International, creation of, 436
Gannett Management Committee, creation of, 429
Gannett Management Seminars, 252
Gannett Medical Clinic. *See* Cornell University, GNF donation
Gannett National Service, creation of, 148-150. *See also* Gannett News Service
Gannett News Service, broadcast news, by 413; expansion of, 329; Germond, Washington bureau, work at, 365-368; New York City, bureau in, 182; PM column, use of, 241; Pulitzer Prize, first to news service, 412; Quinn, president of, 398; renaming of, 168; Washington party by, 168-169; use of, 232
Gannett Newspaper Advertising Service, creation of, 380
Gannett Newspaper Foundation, AHN, chairman of, 477-478; board, makeup of, 79; Cornell clinic, support of, 243; creation of, 78-79; FEG's intent for, 79-82, 195, 244; Gannett archives, grant for, 255; GCI stock, negotiations to sell, 478-481; headquarters, spending for, 477-478; relocation of, 477; scholarships from, 378-379; renaming of, 481; Tech Van, support of, 379; voting stock of, 266; VSJ, operating head of, 343. *See also* Freedom Forum
Gannett Newspapers, The, 15, 49, 75, 131, 167, 198-199; associate editor of, 70, 96; circulation gains of, 123, 441; family spirit in, 77; FDR, editorials on, 108; ITU members, 215; Rochester strike, 177; Sunday editions, creation of, 489; U.S., labor strength, changes in, 493; U.S., largest group in, 383, 384, 411; U.S. top 10, papers in, 452; U.S. top 100, papers in, 452; women publishers, 424; WWII, first death in, 144
Gannett Outdoor Co. of Arizona, sale of, 489
Gannett Outdoor Group, 462; creation of, 399; Eller, offer from, 431; estimated value of, 431; expansion of, 436, 469; New York City, relocation to, 433
Gannett Radio (Group), 199; creation of, 193; PM, head of, 193; principles, statement of, 213-214; relocation of, 443
Gannett Satellite Information Network, creation of, 414-415
Gannett South, creation of, 385
Gannett Special Divisions, creation of, 388
Gannett Youth Club. *See* Barn, The
GANSAT. *See* Gannett Satellite Information Network
Gartland, John E., GCI, assistant treasurer of, 290
Gartner, Michael, *Des Moines Register*, president of, 455-456; NBC-TV news division, president of, 457; TGN, assignments for, 457
*Gasoline Alley*. *See Democrat and Chronicle*, comics page, changes on
Gateway Productions, acquisition of, 410
General Features, Tripp syndicated column in, 183
Genesee River, 42
George Eastman House. *See* Miller, Paul, community service of
Gerlach, Gary, *Des Moines Register*, publisher of, 455-456
Gerling, Curt, 40
Germond, Jack, 182, 260; hiring of, 260; GNS, New York bureau, work at, 182; GNS Washington bureau, work at, 365-368; on PM, 366-367; resigna-

A History of Gannett 531

tion of, 368; on Utica expose, 260-261;
Gialanella, Phil, Gannett South, vice president of, 385; *Star-Bulletin*, publisher of, 385; *USA TODAY*, president of, 418
Gilbert, Richard, *Des Moines Register*, acting president of, 455
Gill, 'Bo,' 190
Ginsburg, Douglas, ASNE debate, panelist on, 447
Glennie, A.J., FEG, high school principal, adviser to, 5-6
Golding, Mary, on Cruickshank, bitterness of, 228; *Democrat and Chronicle*, circulation of, 227; on FET, tippling of, 292; on FEG, visits of, 233; on PM, love of newsroom, 249; PM, secretary to, 227; on PM, succession by AHN, 342-343
Goodfellow, Preston. *See Brooklyn Daily Eagle*, sale of
Goodman, Julian, GCI, director of, 463; on GTG Entertainment, 463
GOP (Grand Old Party). *See* Republican Party
Graham, Kay, 348, 394
Graustein, Archibald R., FEG, lender to, 54-55
*Great Falls* (Mont.) *Tribune*, acquisition of, 476
Green Bay (Wis.) Newspaper Company, acquisition of, 410
*Green Bay Press-Gazette*, acquisition of, 410
Grumman Wildcat. *See* Gannett, Frank E., on free advertising
GTG Entertainment, history of, 462-465
Guardians of American Education, Inc. *See* Tripp, Frank E., press, critics of
*Guide to the Frank E.Gannett and Caroline Werner Gannett Papers. See* Cornell University, archives, Gannett

Hagerty, Jim, 160
Hampton Institute. *See* Roosevelt, Theodore
Hancock, Gov. John. *See* Gannett, Deborah Sampson
Hare, Richard, Gannett research, director of, 330
Harriman, Gov. W. Averell, on Utica corruption, 260-261
Harte-Hanks Communications Inc., 469
Hartford Chamber of Commerce, 61
*Hartford Courant, The, Hartford Times*, competition with, 325-326
*Hartford* (Conn.)*Times, The*, acquisition of, 53, 55; anniversary of, 40th, 171; color, use of, 276; *Courant*, competition with, 325-326; expansion of, 255;

FDR death, extra for, 161; FDR, support of, 97, 108; news/ad ratios in, 154; policy of, 61, 90; sale of, 376-377; lawsuit, settlement of, 377; Sunday paper, start of, 331; war gardens, advocacy of, 146; Willkie, support of, 117-118
— Editors: Dunham, 286; Duffy, 150, 278; Hemenway, 169; Lindstrom, 174 (*See also* below); Murphy, 271
— Lindstrom, Carl; arts critic, 270; executive editor, 271; managing editor, acting, 270; managing editor, 278; retirement, 284
— Publishers: Daniel, 272; Eckert, 325; Murphy, 271
Hartford Times Company, The, FET, president of, 280
Harvard University. *See* Nieman Fellows
Hattiesburg (Miss.) *American*, acquisition of, 423
Hearst, William Randolph, Albany, purchase in, 266; Albany, switch in, 93; as competitor, 43, 46, 54, 58-59, 62, 72, 93; on JOA, Albany bid, 266; offers from, 46, 49; as politician, 16, 43, 59; *Times-Union*, GCI bid for 194, 231
Hemenway, C.C., on GNS party, 169
Henderson, Leon, 130
*Herald*, Elmira, short life of, 32-33. *See also Star-Gazette, The*, on reform
*Herald*, Rochester, 60. *See also* Rochester, move to
*Herald-Dispatch*, Huntington, W. Va., acquisition of, 358
*Herald-Dispatch*, Utica, 42
*Herald-Post*, El Paso, 359
*Herald-Statesman, The*, Yonkers, N.Y., 305
*Herald-Tribune*, New York. *See* Tobin, Richard L.
Hersey, John, 172
Heselden, John E. (Jack), 438; retirement of, 432
— GCI: assistant secretary of, 290; Bitner, assistant to, 249; deputy chairman of, 429; on Gannett Management Seminars, 252; general business manager of, 316; on labor relations, 492; Newspaper Division, president of, 413; operations, vice president of, 321; staff and services, senior vice president of, 380
— TGN: *Courier-News*, publisher of, 316; on *Hartford Times*, mistakes on, 326; Rochester, general manager in, 342

— *USA TODAY:* publisher of, 432; on difficulties of, 467-468; on *USA WEEKEND,* success of, 491; on women publishers, 424
Hess, Rudolph, 87
Hickey, Maurice (Moe), *Detroit News,* publisher of, 444-445; *Denver Post,* publisher/CEO of, 444; Elmira, business manager in, 314; on Florida project, 314-316; Gannett Central, vice president of, 385; GANSAT, president of, 415; GCI marketing, vice president of, 380, 385; resignation of, 444; Rochester, ad director in, 341, 346-347; *State-Journal,* publisher of, 357; *USA TODAY,* senior consultant to, 418
Hickson, Lawrence, 69
Hill, David B. *See Elmira Gazette*
'Hill Street Blues.' *See* GTG Entertainment, history of
*Hiroshima. See* Hersey, John
Hitler, Adolf, 87, 110, 116
Ho, Chinn, 359
Ho, Stuart, 359
Hogan, William J. *See Elmira Gazette*
Holderman, Lt. Cmdr. Russell, 73-74
Holderman, Mrs. C.H. *See Cocoa Tribune*
Hometown Communications Inc., 469
Hong Kong, *USA TODAY,* satellite plant for, 441
*Honolulu Advertiser, The,* 358; acquisition of, 490
*Honolulu Star-Bulletin, The,* acquisition of, 358; sale of, 490
Hoover, Cove C., on Elmira all-day paper, 298-299
Hoover, Herbert, 61, 65
Hottelet, Richard, 129
Hough, Henry Beetle, 283
House of Commons, British press probe by, 175
*Houston Chronicle,* news/ad ratios in, 155
Howard, Roy, 62
Hughes, Charles Evans, 35
Hughes, John, 393
Hussman, Walter E. Jr., *Arkansas Democrat,* owner of, 449-450; *Arkansas Gazette,* purchase of, 483

Ickes, Harold, 118-119; FEG, debate with, 97-99
*Imprint of a Publisher,* FEG, biography of, 4; impetus for, 105; later version of, 105
*In-kids, The. See Democrat and Chronicle,* comics page, changes on
Independence League. *See* Hearst, William Randolph, as politician
*Indianapolis News,* news/ad ratios in, 154
Influenza epidemic, 44
Inland Daily Press Association, Neuharth, speech to, 333
Innovator Drive for Excellence Awards, 292
INS. *See* International News Service
Institute for Journalism Education. *See* Partners in Progress
Interactive Network, 494
International Circulation Managers Association, AHN, speech to, 348; VSJ, speech to, 253-254
International News Service, 58-59, 149; wirephoto test for, 168. *See also* Hearst, William Randolph, as competitor
International Newspaper Promotion Association, 332
International Paper and Power Co., 98. *See also* Graustein, Archibald R.
International Paper Co. *See* Graustein, Archibald R.
International Press Institute, VSJ, panelist for, 289
International Typographical Union, 492; profit-sharing, changes in, 187; Rochester, strike at, 175-177; TGN members in, 215
IPI. *See* International Press Institute
Isaacs, Norman, 393-394
*Ithaca Daily News,* 11, 18, 20; FEG, roles on, 10-12, 18; on typhoid fever epidemic, 11; on patronage, political, 11, 41
*Ithaca Journal, The,* 7, 40; blacklist, use of, 31; FEG, co-ownership of, 30; GCI, sale to, 31; policy of, 31, 61;
*Ithaca Journal-News, The,* 211; creation of, 43; flu crisis on, 122; PM column, use of, 241; retention of, 47, 53
ITU. *See* International Typographical Union

*Jackson* (Miss.) *Daily News,* acquisition of, 423
*Jackson* (Tenn.) *Sun,* acquisition of, 436, 439
Jackson, Lionel. *See Hartford Times,* sale of
Jaske, John B., labor relations, senior vice president of, 493
Jennings, Madelyn, GCI, first woman vice president in, 407; GCI human resources, senior vice president of, 413
JOA. *See* Joint Operating Agreements
Johnson, Lyndon, 362-363
Joint Operating Agreements, Albany, bid in,

266; in Detroit, 443-445; in El Paso, 359; in Honolulu, 358; in Knoxville, 416; in Nashville, 359; in Shreveport, 384
Jones, Jimmy, affirmative action, director of, 432; GCI, of, 432; precedent, first black GCI vice president, 432
Jones, Vincent S., 249; on API seminars, 252; on Asia, trip to, 327; ASNE, president of, 334; on contest judging, 205-207; on journalists, training of, 264-265; interests, range of, 264; IPI, panelist for, 289-290; on news coverage, 204; on newspaper monopoly, 253-254; on newspaper outreach, 212; on public speaking, 252-253; Syracuse University, medal from, 338
— FEG: on assistants to, 248; on naivete of, 167; on PM, relationship with, 248; on radio, on views, 138
— GCI: on Bitner, retirement of, 320-321; Neuharth, Gannett overture to, 294
— GNF: on creation of, 79; operating head of, 343; vice president and secretary of, 79; on Tech Van, 379
— Lindstrom: on *Atlantic Monthly*, bid from, 274; book, rebuttal to, 285; on controversy, 270-287; Lyons, reply to, 285; ultimatum to, 284; Maurer, letter from, 284-285
— PM: on achievements of, 397; on AP, PM's election to board, 299; on Cruickshank resentment of, 228; on intentions of, 203; on pay scales, improvement of, 251
— TGN: on Alinsky, coverage of, 310; on autonomy, local, 212, 267, 365; on beer, liquor ads, acceptance of, 340; critiques by, 225; on Eisenhower illness, coverage of, 238; on euphemisms, labor, 226; executive editor of, 79, 138, 202; on Germond, GNS, 366; on *Hartford Times*, 325; on Hiroshima, 172; on libel, 273; on MacArthur hearings, coverage of, 212; on McCarthy, coverage of, 228-230; on prepublication review, 225-226; on reader studies, 202-203; on *Road to Integration*, 300-302; on Rochester newspapers, Vietnam editorials of, 363-365; on Rochester, riots in, 307-309; Utica, editor in, 150; on Utica, move from, 203-204; on wire services, 210; on women readers, 186
*Journal*, Ogdensburg, N.Y., 117
*Journal*, Rochester. *See* Hearst, William Randolph, as competitor
*Journal-American*, New York, on Utica, 259-260
*Journal-News*, Nyack, N.Y., 305
Justice, U.S. Department of, 349, 383

Kaiser, Albert D. Award Committee. *See* Miller, Paul, community service of
Kaltenborn, H.V. *See Brooklyn Daily Eagle*, Power Trust
KARE-TV, 424
*Karen. See Democrat and Chronicle*, comics page, changes on
KARK-TV, Little Rock, Ark., sale of, 423
Kates, Roy, 96
KBKC. *See* KCMO-FM
KBTV. *See* KUSA-TV
KCMO-AM, Kansas City, Mo., acquisition of, 447
KCMO-FM, Kansas City, Mo., acquisition of, 447
Keating, Sen. Kenneth, 311
Keating, William J., AP, chairman of, 445; Detroit JOA, chief executive of, 445; GCI, general counsel of, 445; GCI Newspaper Division, president of, 457
Keefe, Fred, 114
Kennedy, John F., 295
Kennedy, Robert F., 286-287, 311
Kessinger, Paul, Project NN, member of, 410
Keuka College, 72; 50th anniversary of, 95
KHIT-FM, Seattle, acquisition of, 446
KHKS-FM, Denton, Tex., acquisition of, 439
Khrushchev, Nikita, 295, 362
Kilmer, Willis Sharpe. *See Binghamton Press*, acquisition of
King Features, price increases by, 210
Kitty Hawk, first powered flight, site of, 2
KKBQ-AM/FM, Houston, acquisition of, 434
*Knickerbocker News*, Albany, creation of, 53; communism, inquiry on, 229-230; sale of, 266; *Saratogian* Daily Double, role in, 262-263, 266
*Knickerbocker Press*, Albany, 113, 266; acquisition of, 53. *See also Knickerbocker News*, creation of
Knight, Charles Langdon. *See Akron Beacon-Journal*, FEG interest in
Knight, John S., 33
Knight Newspapers, 229
Knight-Ridder, Inc., 33, 440, 443
Knox, Frank, 90; on censorship, 124-126
*Knoxville* (Tenn.) *Journal, The*, acquisition of,

416
*Knoxville News-Sentinel,* JOA, partner in, 416
Koch, Ed, New York mayor, *USA TODAY,* launch of, 420-421
KOCO-TV, Oklahoma City, 424; transfer, plan to, 425
KOLD-TV, Tucson, sale of, 440
Korea, "police action," 212
KOVR-TV, Stockton, Calif., acquisition of, 243
KPNX-TV, Phoenix, Ariz., 424
KRON-TV, San Francisco, decision to buy, 424-425; purchase, cancellation of, 430
Kruidenier, David, *Des Moines Register,* CEO of, 455-456
KTKS-FM. *See* KHKS-FM
KTVY-TV, Oklahoma City, sale of, 440
KUSA-TV, Denver, 424
KVUE-TV, Austin, Texas, acquisition of, 440

Lackawanna Railroad, 19
Laird International Studios. *See* GTG Entertainment, history of
Lake Erie Radio Co., 439
*Lake Shore News,* Wolcott, N.Y., 335; sale of, 351
Landers, Ann, 348
Landon, Alfred E., 90-91
Laser-Graph, 372-374
Laser Graphic Systems, Inc., 372
Laser research, 371-374
Laval, Pierre, 87
LBJ. *See* Johnson, Lyndon
*Leader and Press,* Springfield, Mo., acquisition of, 384
Lee, Gypsy Rose, 145
Lee, Prof. Duncan Campbell. *See Ithaca Daily News*
Liberty Newspapers Limited Partnership, 490
Lincoln Alliance Bank & Trust, Rochester, 82
Lincoln Tower, GCI, Rochester headquarters of, 411, 433
Lindner, Carl, Combined Communications, major stockholder of, 438; GCI stock, purchases of, 438; 'greenmail' incident with, 438
Lindstrom, Carl E., 186, 206; on ad/news feud, 174; AP Council, New England, president of, 271; API, handbook of, 271; APME, committee chairman of, 270; ASNE, director of, 271; colleagues, respect of, 271; on color, newspapers use of, 275; controversy over, 269-287; death of, 287; Dunham, letter to, 286; *Editorially Speaking,* contributor to, 270, 275; on Michigan lecture, 274, 275; Michigan, visiting professor, professor at, 284; NESNE, vice president of, 271; *Time,* obituary of, 287; TGN meetings, nonparticipation in, 272-274; Valtman, letter to, 287; VSJ, replies to, 273-274, 278, 283. *See also Hartford Times, The,* Lindstrom, Carl
Little, Franklin R., 113, 117, 262; offer from, 246; on PM, 169, 186
Little Big Horn. *See* Custer, Col. George A.
Lockheed Lightning. *See* Gannett, Frank E., on free advertising
Lohden, Bill, 260
London, *USA TODAY,* satellite plant for, 441
Longworth, Alice Roosevelt, 16
Longworth, Sen. Nicholas, 16
Los Angeles Times Syndicate, 150
Louis, John J., Combined Communications, chairman of, 395; Eller, dissatisfaction of, 401-402
Louis Harris and Associates Inc., acquisition of, 388; Florida project, polling for, 315, 318
*Louisville Times,* acquisition of, 446
Lucas, Bob, 366
*Luftwaffe. See* Nazis, inflammatory words about
*Lusitania, The,* 32
Lyons, Joseph, resignation of, 412
Lyons, Louis M., on Lindstrom book, 285-286; VSJ, reply to, 285

MacArthur, Gen. Douglas, 184; congressional hearings about, 212
MacDonald, Frank, on pension plan, 201
Macy, J. Noel, 305
Macy, Valentine E. Jr., 305
*Making of McPaper, The. See* Prichard, Peter, on *USA TODAY,* creation of
Malden (Mass.) *Evening News. See* Brinkman, David
Malone, William T., *Arkansas Gazette,* president/publisher of, 450; Gannett Central, vice president of, 450
Management Contributions Committee. *See* Curley, John J., GNF stock purchase, role in
Manno, Vincent. *See Niagara Gazette,* acquisition of
Mao Tse-tung, 362
*Marietta* (Ohio) *Daily Times, The,* acquisition of, 377
Martin, Paul, on Eisenhower illness, 238; on

A History of Gannett 535

Eisenhower prospects, 220; GNS Washington bureau, chief of, 220; on newsprint shortage, 239; on pre-publication review, 225
Martin, Ronald D., GANSAT, news, executive president of, 415, 416; *USA TODAY*, executive editor of, 418
'Mary Tyler Moore Show, The.' *See* GTG Entertainment, history of
Massena (N.Y.) *Observer*, 113
Maurer, Wesley H., VSJ, letter to, 284-285; Lindstrom, lecture for, 274
Mayflower Hotel, 168
Maynard, Robert C., *Oakland Tribune*, publisher and editor of, 430; *Oakland Tribune*, purchase of, 430; *Oakland Tribune*, sale of, 430. *See also* Partners in Progress
Mayne, Calvin, on Alinsky, coverage of, 309-310; as Nieman Fellow, 223; on PM column, 240-241; on PM, conservatism of, 308, 311, 363; on PM, retirement of, 389; *Times-Union*, associate editor of, 364; *Times-Union*, editorial page editor of, 362; *Times-Union*, reporter of, 223; on Vietnam, 363
Mayor's War Memorial Committee. *See* Miller, Paul, community service of
Mazzarella, David, Gannett International, president of, 436
McAdam, Charles Vincent Jr., FEG, son-in-law of, 236
McAdam, Sally Gannett, FEG, daughter of, 44; marriage of, 236-237; Messman, duties of, 236-237; ship christening by, 155
McCann, George, on reporters' pay, FET's feelings about, 187
McCarthy, Sen. Joseph, coverage of, 228-230
McClatchy Newspapers, Laser-Graph, purchase of, 373
McClure, J. Warren, 351, 374, 401; on AHN, relationship with, 353-354, 437-438; GCI, director of, 354; on GCI, merger with, 351-354; GCI marketing, vice presiden of, 353; retirement of, 380; on 'strawberry man,' 353-354
McClure Media Marketing Motivation Company, 354
McClure Newspapers Inc., 351, 352
McCorkindale, Douglas H., 375, 441; on AHN/JJC, contrasts in, 474; on Eller, dissatisfaction of, 400-401; Diversified Media, president of, 413; GCI, chief financial officer of, 386; on GCI, recruitment by, 354-355; GNF stock purchase, role in, 478-481; on GTG Entertainment, 465; on Little Rock, efforts to buy, 450; on Santa Fe purchase, opposition to, 382; on Seigenthaler, apprehensions of, 406, 454; on Speidel, merger with, 383; on Speidel stock, purchase of, 378
McCormick-Patterson-Hearst-Gannett press. *See* Roosevelt, Franklin D., on "isolationist press," 159
McKelvey, Blake, 42
McKelway, Benjamin M., AP, president of, 296; on Eisenhower illness, 238
McKinley, William, 9
McKinney, J.P., 33
McKinney, J.P. & Son, GCI purchase of, 231
McKinney, Raymond H., 116; GCI director, 194
McKinney, Robert, intransigence of, 470, 475-476; *New Mexican*, sale of, 382; *New Mexican*, suit to recover, 431; PM, friendship with, 382;
McLaughlin Group, The, 368
McNaught Syndicate, 236
Meals, Pamela F., Coffeyville, publisher in, 424; Richmond, president and publisher in, 424
Mechanical department conferences, 71
*Media Records*, 154
Meese, Edwin III. *See* Joint Operating Agreement, Detroit
*Melbourne* (Fla.) *Times*, acquisition of, 349; conversion of, 378
Melchior, Ariel Sr., 384
Melton, Rollan D., 401; GCI, director of, 383; Gannett West, senior vice president of, 383; Speidel, president and CEO, 383
Messman, Florence, 60; on Cruickshank, $12 raise from, 236; on desk calendar purchase of, 245; on FEG, candidacy of, 100; on FEG, death of, 245; on FEG, final illness of, 235; on FEG, intent of, 78, 198; on FEG, stroke of, 191; on PM, defiance of, 199; PM, secretary, 104; retirement of, 244-245; *Sanctum*, work on, 245; typical day of, 191, 236-237
Metromedia, Inc., 423
Miami Beach, FEG, recuperation at, 194-195
*Miami Herald*, 1, 276; AHN, city editor of, 297
Michigan, University of, Lindstrom lecture at, 274-275
Michigan Citizens for an Independent Press. *See* Joint Operating Agreement,

536  A History of Gannett

Detroit Michigan State University, Neuharth, speech at, 333
Mid-Atlantic Newspaper Group, creation of, 414
Miles, Mrs. George, GCI insurance, first beneficiary of, 201
Military mobilization, effects on staff, 121, 142
Miller, Larry, GCI, controller of, 417; GCI, financial analysis, vice president of, 417
Miller, Louise (Mrs. Paul), on Eller, dissatisfaction of, 401-402; OSU, endowment to, 397; on PM, 'country boy who knew everybody,' 362; on PM, Cruickshank resentment of, 228; on PM/FEG, 198; on PM, recruitment of, 185-186
Miller, Paul, 1; ASNE, tour for, 199; death of, 398; on FEG, RIT memorial to, 340; on FET, award to, 305-306; on FET, tippling of, 292; legacy of, 396-398; OSU, endowment to, 397; Soviet Union, trip to, 291; stroke of, 398, 409; *Time,* profile by, 359;
— AP: Bureau chief of, 169; director of, 202, 227; president/chairman of, 299; retirement from, 299, 396; TGN, panelist for, 182
— GCI: on AHN presidency, 343; AHN, succession by, 365, 396; on Bitner, retirement of, 320; chairman and CEO of, 343; director of, 194; executive vice president of, 217; FEG, selection by, 198; FEG, executive assistant to, 184; FET, recruitment by, 185-186; on Gannett, growth of, 328; Gannett Radio Group, head of, 193-194; on GCI, future of, 242-243; on GCI stockholding, ethics of, 329; GNF, director of, 227; on GNF, principles of, 223; "operating head in fact" of, 233; president of, 241; retirement from, 299; on retirement policy of, 388-389; vice president of, 194; on pay scales, 251; on racial crisis, 299; on reader research, 330; on readership, 227; on "Read-Think-Vote," 219, 222; to security analysts, 330-331;
— TGN: on Alinsky, coverage of, 309; on autonomy, local, 263; on autonomy, local, variant of, 267; on beer, liquor ads, acceptance of, 340; on *Courier-Post,* 263; on editorial aims, 207-208; on JFK assassination, 362; Messman, defiance by, 199; Lindstrom, controversy about, 270, 273; on "Newspaper of the Future," 250-251; Nixon, column about, 295; on Tech Van, 309; on editorial positions, 379; TGN policies, explanation of, 204-205, 223; on TGN, success of, 319-310; *Times-Union,* columnist for, 240-241; *Times-Union,* editor of, 194; *Times-Union,* editor/publisher of, 202; *Times-Union,* guest editorials in, 214; on *Times-Union,* Vietnam editorials, 363-365; on Vietnam, 362; on VSJ, succession of, 344
— Philosophy: on American freedoms, 291; on brotherhood, 290; on censorship, 297; "Do the Right Thing," motto of, 240; on editors, activism of, 237-238; on journalist's job, 240; on newsroom, love of, 249;
— Public service: 249; Brotherhood Week, national chairman of, 290
Miller, Paul T. II, 335; TGN posts, succession of, 351; TGN weeklies, purchase of, 350
Miller, Robert B., 401; GCI, senior vice president of, 355
*Millville (N.J.) Daily, The,* acquisition of, 440
*Milwaukee Journal,* news/ad ratios in, 155
*Minneapolis Star-Journal,* 276; news/ad ratios in, 155
Minorities' hiring/promotion, progress report on, 430-431
*Mirror, The,* New York City, 125
Mississippi Publishing Co., acquisition of, 423
Missouri, University of, PM, award to, 327. *See also* University of Missouri-J.C. Penney Awards
Miss Peach. *See Democrat and Chronicle,* comics page, changes on
Monroe County Human Relations Commission, 308
Monroe County Republican Party, 89; chairman of, 100
Moore, Mary Tyler. *See* GTG Entertainment, history of
Moran, Gertrude, 207
Morgenthau, Henry J., 147. *See also* Victory Drive
*Morning News, The,* Wilmington, Del., acquisition of, 392
*Morning Post. See* Stretch, William, on *Courier-*

*Post Morning Star*, Rockford, Ill., acquisition of, 324
Morton, John, ASNE debate, panelist on, 447
MTM Entertainment, Inc. *See* GTG Entertainment, history of
Murphy, Frank, *Hartford Times*, editor, publisher of, 271; retirement of, 271
Murrow, Ed(ward R.) *See* Jones, Vincent S., on McCarthy, coverage of
Mussolini, Benito, 87

Nancy. *See* Stutz, Harry, on comic strips
NASA. *See* National Aeronautics and Space Administration
*Nashville Banner*, 448, 452; acquisition of, 358-359; sale of, 403
National Aeronautics and Space Administration, 389
National Airlines, first jet airline service by, 2
National Broadcasting Company, 457, 463
National Committee to Uphold Constitutional Government, 2, 95, 97, 100; creation of, 92; FEG, resignation from, 102. *See also* Supreme Court, U.S., expansion of
National Conference of Christians and Jews, Rochester newspapers, brotherhood award to, 310. *See also* Miller, Paul, public service of
National Federation of Press Women, AHN, speech to, 347
National Guard, 117
National Newspaper Promotion Association. *See* Neuharth, Allen H., on *Today*, success of
National Press Club, on Eisenhower illness, 238
National Recovery Act, 91
National Union of Journalists, on British press probe, 174
Naval Relief Society, New York State Committee, 137; fund drive, FEG head of, 144, 147
Nazis, 109, 110, 116, 156; FEG, dossier on, 134; inflammatory words about, 133
NCUCG. *See* National Committee to Uphold Constitutional Government
Needham, Jack, JCQ, assistant to, 330
Needleman, Morton, administrative law judge. *See* Joint Operating Agreement, Detroit
Neuharth, Allen H., 1; ASNE, newspaper groups, debate on, 447; on BusCapade, 466, 469-470; on JetCapade, 470; legacy of, 471-472; self-assessment by, 471-472

— Awards: Headliner, 387; Wells, 430
— GCI: CEO, 13-year report as, 441; chairman of, 472; chairman and CEO of, 396; on Cowles stock, acquisition of, 437; director of, 313; director, resignation as, 470; on Eller, challenge by, 402; executive vice president of, 321; general manager of, 342; on headquarters, location of, 411, 433; hiring by, 297; on Lindner, 437-438; on McClure, 437-438; on McCorkindale, 386, 417, 427-428; on Office of the Chief Executive, 395, 399-400, 413-414, 418, 429; president of, 343; president and CEO of, 365, 389; Rochester, general executive in, 297; VSJ, Gannett overture from, 294
— GNF: on name, change of, 481-482
— JJC: contrasts with, 474-475; on hiring of, 341; succession by, 427-429
— PM: on being successor of, 297-298, 322, 389, 396
— Speeches: on newspaper promotion, 332; on student protests, 333-334; on women, job opportunities for, 337, 347-349
— TGN: *Cocoa Tribune*, acquisition of, 313-314; on *Hartford Times* suit, settlement of, 377; Rochester newspapers, general manager of, 298; on Santa Fe purchase, opposition to, 382; on women publishers, 424
— *USA TODAY*: on GANSAT, 414; on 'McPaper,' 423; on Project NN, mission of, 410, 414; on Project S, mission of, 419; on start of, 315; on success of, 318-319; on prospects for, 414-415, 417-419
*Newark* (N.Y.) *Courier-Gazette*, 335; sale of, 351
*Newark News*, news/ad ratios in, 155
New Deal, 65, 86, 91, 95, 107, 111; FEG views on, 86, 97, 107, 109; FET views on, 72
New England Associated Press Council, Lindstrom, president of, 271
New England Society of Newspaper Editors, Lindstrom, editorial excerpt from, 280; Lindstrom, vice president of, 271
New England Weekly Press Association, 275
New Jersey Better Newspaper Contest, VSJ, on judging of, 205-206

A History of Gannett 537

*New Mexican,* Santa Fe, acquisition of, 382; McKinney, suit by, 431; sale of, 476
*News,* Pensacola, Fla., acquisition of, 339
*News,* Springfield, Mo., acquisition of, 384
News and Editorial conferences, 99, 101, 126, 138
News and Editorial Office, TGN, 70, 96, 150, 249; on editorial pages, 151; LRB, promotion of, 129; on "Read-Think-Vote," 219-220; VSJ, promotion of, 138, 202
*News and Leader,* Springfield, Mo., acquisition of, 384
Newsco, Inc., 484
*News Herald,* Port Clinton, Ohio, acquisition of, 378
*News-Journal Co., The,* Wilmington, Del., acquisition of, 392-394
*News-Journal,* Sunday, Pensacola, acquisition of, 339
*News-Messenger,* Fremont, Ohio, acquisition of, 378
Newspaper Advertising Bureau, 351
Newspaper Association of America, readership survey by, 487
Newspaper Guild, Rochester strike, nonparticipation in, 175-176
Newspaper Preservation Act. *See* Detroit Newspaper Agency
Newspaper Printing Corp., El Paso, 359
Newspaper Printing Corp., Nashville, 359
News Pictures of the Year. *See* Jones, Vincent S., on contest judging
*News-Press,* Fort Myers, Fla., acquisition of, 358
*News-Star,* Monroe, La., acquisition of, 384. *See also News-Star-World,* creation of
*News-Star-World,* Monroe, La., creation of, 412
News 2000, launching of, 486-487
*New Yorker, The,* 172
New York Newspaper Publishers Association, 170
New York Republican Party, 87
New York Society of Security Analysts, PM, speech to, 330-331
New York State Board of Regents, 6; Caroline Gannett, member of, 254. *See also* Gannett, Frank E., as student
New York State Health Department, birth records, policy on, 157
New York State Insurance Board. *See* Pension and life insurance plan
New York State Mediation Board, on Rochester strike, 175-176
New York State Police, Apalachin, raid at, 259
New York State Publishers Association, FEG honored by, 227; PM, president of, 227
New York State Society of Newspaper Editors, LRB, president of, 169
New York Stock Exchange, 399; GCI stock, listing of, 335
New York Subways Advertising, Inc., acquisition of, 469
*New York Sun,* news/ad ratios in, 154
*New York Times, The,* 88, 104, 125, 393, 422; labor news in, 169; Lindstrom, obituary on, 287; Youth Forum of, 230
*New York Times Book Review, The. See* Lyons, Louis M., on Lindstrom book
*Niagara Gazette,* acquisition of, 231; color, use of, 276; morning publication, switch to, 424; Sunday edition of, 243
Nick the Greek. *See* Gannett, Frank E., as risk-taker
Nieman Fellows, 285; Mayne, member of, 223; PM, speaker to, 223
Nixon, Richard M., 362; Cambodia, invasion of, 363-364; PM, column on, 295
North Carolina Press Association, PM, speaker to, 240
*North Hills* (Pa.) *News Record,* daily, conversion to, 484-485; early growth of, 485; Stanley Cup edition, 485
Northern New York Publishing Company, 117, 119; loan to, 246
*Norwich* (Conn.) *Bulletin, The,* acquisition of, 416
NYSNE. *See* New York State Society of Newspaper Editors

Oak Hill Country Club, 354
*Oakland* (Calif.) *Tribune,* 452; acquisition of, 399; sale, need for, 425; news/ad ratios in, 155; sale of, 429-430
O'Brien, Bernard, WHEC, chief engineer of, 193
*Observer,* Utica, 42
*Observer-Dispatch,* Utica, 150; on censorship, 125; on city, corruption in, 261-262; creation of, 42; expansion of, 255-256; on Hiroshima, 172-173; Pulitzer Prize, first for TGN, 261; struggle of, 44-45
Ochs, Adolph S., 88
Odegard, Dr. Peter H., FEG, criticism of, 128
Office of the Chief Executive. *See* Neuharth, Allen H., on Office of the Chief Executive
Ogden Newspapers Inc., 440

*Ogdensburg* (N.Y.) *Journal,* 113
Ogdensburg (N.Y.) Publishing Co., acquisition of, 56
Ohio, GOP primary in, 89. *See also* Borah, Sen. William, FEG running mate
Ohio Newspaper Woman of the Year. *See* Blanchard, Lafayette (Fay) R., on contest judging
Oklahoma Press Publishing Company, acquisition of, 384
Oklahoma State University, Miller endowment to, 397
*Olean* (N.Y.) *Times-Herald,* 114; sale of, 243; war shortages at, 142
*Omaha Bee. See* Davenport, Erwin R., as innovator
O'Neill, Rep. Thomas (Tip), 420
Operating Committee. *See* Gannett Company Inc., Operating Committee
*Oregon Statesman,* Salem, acquisition of, 377. *See also Statesman-Journal,* creation of
Outdoor Network USA, 469
Overby, Charles, GNF, executive vice president of, 477; GNF stock sale, role in, 478-481; GCI, vice president/news of, 477

*Pacific Daily News,* Guam, acquisition of, 358
*Palladium-Item,* Richmond, Ind., acquisition of, 382
Pan-American World Airways, first globe-circling route by, 183-184
*Panzer. See* Nazis, inflammatory words about
Parker, Alton B. *See Star-Gazette, The,* policy of
Partners in Progress, 407
Patterson, Carrick, 453; *Arkansas Gazette,* executive vice president/editor of, 449-450
Patterson, Gov. John, Alabama. *See* Seigenthaler, John, Robert F. Kennedy, administrative assistant to
Patterson, Hugh, *Arkansas Gazette,* chairman of, 450; *Arkansas Gazette,* owner/publisher of, 449-450
Pauline Fathers. *See* Gannett News Service, Pulitzer Prize, first to news service
Pearl Harbor, 135; Japanese bombing of, 1, 130
Pearson, Frank A. *See* Roosevelt, Franklin D., on gold prices
Peek, Linda, GANSAT, public affairs, vice president of, 415
*Pensacola Journal,* acquisition of, 339
Pensacola News-Journal Inc., creation of, 339

Pension and life insurance plan, introduction of, 200-201; rebate of payments to, 218
Pepsi-Cola Company, 114
Perry Publications Inc. *See* Pensacola News-Journal Inc.
Pershing, Gen. John J., 32
Persis Corporation, 490
*Philadelphia Bulletin,* news/ad ratios in, 155
Philadelphia. *See* Republican National Convention
Phillips, Rupert, 490
Phoebe Snow (train), 64
*Phoenix and Times Democrat,* Muskogee, Okla., acquisition of, 384
Pickering, Louis, 123
Pinchot, Amos, on FEG candidacy, 100. *See also* National Committee to Uphold Constitutional Government, creation of
*Pittsburgh Index. See,* Gannett, Frank E., editor
Pittsburgh Penguins. *See North Hills* (Pa.) *News Record,* Stanley Cup edition of
Pittsburgh Phil. *See* Gannett, Frank E., as risk-taker
*Pittsburgh Post-Gazette,* news/ad ratios in, 154; *Pittsburgh Press,* purchase of, 485; strike, shutdown by, 485
*Pittsburgh Press, The,* sale of, 485; strike, shutdown by, 485
Plasti-Line Inc., 462
Platt, Tom. *See* Republican Party, bosses of
*Pogo. See Democrat and Chronicle,* comics page, changes on
Polenberg, Richard, 63; on FEG candidacy, 100, 107, 111; on gold prices, 72; on court-packing, 91, 92
*Poor Richard's Almanac,* 40
Pope Pius XI, 87
Popper, Brette, *USA WEEKEND,* publisher of, 491
*Post Express,* Rochester. *See* Rochester, move to
'Pot of Gold, The.' *See* Tripp, Frank E., "Pot of Gold"
*Poultry and Egg News,* Gainesville, Ga., acquisition of, 416
Power Trust, 54-55. *See also* Graustein, Archibald R.
Powers Hotel, FEG declaration for presidential nomination, 102
*Press,* Utica, corruption in, 259; Pulitzer Prize, first for TGN, 261
Price Administration, Office of, 130
Price, Byron, censorship, director of, 135, 157
Prichard, Peter, Gannett news, chief execu-

tive of, 417, 478; on *USA TODAY*, creation of, 417; *USA TODAY*, editor of, 417, 478;
Prime Time Syndication Service, Tampa, Fla., acquisition of, 433; sale of, 433
Profit-sharing, method of, 83-84; cost-of-living bonus to, 131; Rochester strike, effects of, 177.
Prohibition, 51, 58, 61, 63
Project NN, creation of, 409-410
Project S, creation of, 419
*Providence Bulletin*, news/ad ratios in, 154
*Providence* (R.I.) *Journal*, 316
*Public Opinion*, Chambersburg, Pa., acquisition of, 351
*Public Responsibility of the Newspaper, The*. See Atwood, M.V., on press, critics of
Public Service, Resarch and Development, Department of, Rochester, 304
Publishers' conferences, 89
Pulitzer Prizes, 261, 304, 307, 387, 450, 468; GNS, first news service winner of, 412
Purcell, John R. (Jack), 342; GCI, finance and business operations, senior vice president of, 380; GCI finance, vice president of, 335; resignation of, 386

Quinn, John, on AHN, hiring by, 316-317; on AHN, succession of, 428-429; on FET funeral, 306; GCI, senior vice president, news and information, 380; GNF, trustee of, 478; on Germond, GNS, 367-369; GNS, managing editor of, 329; GNS, president of, 398; on JJC, AHN's successor, 428-429; on JJC, GNS bureau chief, 369; on JJC, hiring of, 341; on JJC, Wilmington assignment, 413; on PM, achievements of, 398; retirement of, 478; Rochester, director of news, 317; TGN, chief news executive of, 343-344; TGN, vice president for news, 356; on VSJ, succession of, 344; *Wire Watch*, writing of, 356-357

'Raising Miranda.' *See* GTG Entertainment, history of
Rathbone, Gracia Gannett, 46; death of, 207; Elmira charities, efforts for, 158
Rathbone, J. Arnot, FEG, brother-in-law of, 46; GCI, director of, 46; GCI, vice president of, 46

'Read-Think-Vote,' *Times-Union*, voter drive by, 219, 222
Reagan, President and Mrs. Ronald, 420
Red Cross, Rochester fund drive for, 144, 147, 249
*Redeye. See Democrat and Chronicle*, comics page, changes on
Reed, Dr. Virgil D. *See* Census, Bureau of the
Reeder, Orb, 356
Register Publishing Co. *See Hartford Times*, sale of
*Register-Republic*, Rockford, Ill., acquisition of, 324
Reorganization of the Judiciary, defeat of, 91-92
*Reporter, The*, Lansdale, Pa., acquisition of, 414
*Reporter-Dispatch, The*, White Plains, N.Y., 305
Republican National Committee, 144, 185
Republican National Convention, at Chicago, 220; at Philadelphia, 105, 109, 110
Republican Party, 100, 128; bosses of, 41; Eisenhower win for, 222; FEG, candidacies of, 88-89, 95, 101-102, 144; Lincoln Day rally of, 95; N.Y. committee of, 96; presidential candidates of, 88-91
Retirement Plan. *See* Pension and life insurance plan
*Review Press and Reporter*, Bronxville, N.Y., 305
Reynolds, Thomas A., GCI, director of, 402
'Right to work," 179-180
RIT. *See* Rochester Institute of Technology
Rizal, José. *See* Spanish-American War
*Road to Integration, The*, 299; GNS distribution of, 302; PM, impetus for, 299; Pulitzer Prize to, 304, 307; supplements to, 302; VSJ, coordinator for, 299-302
'Roaring '20s,' 68
Rochester, N.Y., FEG/ERD move to, 33-34
Rochester, riots in, 307-309
Rochester, University of, 372
Rochester and Elmira Railroad Co., 20
Rochester Chamber of Commerce. *See* Miller, Paul, community service of
Rochester Eye Bank and Research Society, Inc. *See* Gannett, Frank E., corneas, donation of
Rochester Gas & Electric, 42
Rochester Institute of Technology, FEG, memorial to, 340; GCI grant to, 200; PM, community service of, 250
Rochester Ordnance District. *See* Davenport, Erwin R., war work by
Rochester Police Advisory Board, 308
Rochester Rotary Club, FEG, award to, 95; PM

on TGN, policies of, 204-205
Rochester Telephone Co., 42
Rockefeller Foundation. *See* International Press Institute, VSJ, panelist
Rockwell International. *See* White, Ronald A., resignation of
Roderick, Dorrance D.. 359
Romo, Inc., Green Bay. Wis., acquisition of, 411
Roosevelt, Edith Kermit Carow (Mrs. Theodore), 15
Roosevelt, Ethel, 15
Roosevelt, Franklin D., 68, 72, 111; on censorship, 135, 141; death of, 161; FEG, eulogy by, 161; FEG, war effort pledge by, 131, 133; FEG support of, 2; fourth term of, 159; on France, Italy, 108; on gold prices, 72, 86; as governor, 63, 65; on "isolationist press," 159; on newspapers, 97; third term of, 117
Roosevelt, Quentin, 15
Roosevelt, Theodore, 9, 15-16
Rose, Nancy Tripp, 52, 64; on PM, recruitment of, 185
Rosenburgh, Carleton, on ADvance, 488; GCI, Newspaper Division, senior vice president of, 488
Rough Riders. *See* Roosevelt, Theodore
Rowse, Arthur E. *See Editor & Publisher*, Tripp letter, responses to
Rugg, Prof. Harold B., 114, 124, 128
Rumely, Dr. Edward A., 100. *See also* National Committee to Uphold Constitutional Government, creation of


Sackett, Larry, GANSAT, operations, vice president of, 415; Project NN, member of, 410
St. John Fisher College, Caroline Gannett, speaker at, 254-255
*St. Louis Post-Dispatch*, news/ad ratios in, 155
*St. Petersburg* (Fla.) *Times*, 307
Salary cuts, 68; correction of, 83
San Bernardino (Calif.) Sun Co., acquisition of, 331-332
*Sanctum, The*, on editors' activism, 237-238; LRB, editor of, 237
*San Diego Tribune-Sun*, news/ad ratios in, 155
Sanford, Harold, on censorship, 126; death of, 202; FEG, in defense of, 128
San Rafael (Calif.) *Independent-Journal*, acquisition of, 411
*Saratogian, The*, Saratoga Springs, N.Y., acquisition of, 73; Dolan, general man-

# A History of Gannett 541

ager, 262; *Knickerbocker News Daily Double*, role in, 262-263, 266
Sass, Gerald M., college recruiting by, 379
*Saturday Review. See* Tobin, Richard L.
Schawlow, Dr. Arthur L., 372
Schurman, Dr. Jacob Gould, Cornell University, president of, 7; FEG, adviser to, 7-8; Philippines, presidential adviser on, 9-10
Scripps, E.W., Co. *See* Scripps Howard Newspapers
Scripps Howard Newspapers, 62, 327, 358, 359, 416, 485
*Seattle Times*, news/ad ratios in, 155
Securities and Exchange Commission, 438
Seigenthaler, John, on AHN, negotiations with, 453-454; retirement of, 406; Robert F. Kennedy, administrative assistant to, 403-404; on Little Rock, transition in, 450, 459; *Tennessean*, president, publisher and editor of, 403, 447; on TGN, transition to, 453-454, 458; *USA TODAY*, editorial page editor of, 447
— ASNE; panelist on newspaper groups, against, 404-405, 453; panel on newspaper mergers, member of, 447-449, 453
*Sentinel, The*, Winston-Salem, N.C., acquisition of, 52; sale of, 52, 65
7th Cavalry. *See* Custer, Col. George A.
Shapiro, Irving. *See* DuPont Co.
Shaw, Susanne, Coffeyville, publisher in, 424
Sigma Delta Chi. *See* Society of Professional Journalists
Silverman, Mark, News 2000, director of, 487; Rockford, executive editor in, 487
Simmons Market Research. *See* Newspaper Association of America, readership, survey on
*Sin City of the East. See Journal-American*, New York, on Utica
Singapore, *USA TODAY*, satellite plant for, 441
Skeffington, Janette. *See* Skeffington, L. B.
Skeffington, L. B., GCI, farm editor of, 167
Sky Radio Broadcasting Corp., 462
Small, William A. Jr., Tucson, president and publisher in, 383
Smith, Alfred E., 43, 59, 60, 61
*Smugtown U.S.A. See* Gerling, Curt
Snyder, Leroy E., 60; death of, 184; FEG, aide to, 96; salary of, 69
Society of Professional Journalists, 264
Soper, Royal R. *See Elmira Gazette*, acquisition of

Southeast Newspaper Group, Spezzano, president of, 410
*Southington* (Conn.) *News. See* Conrad, Robert M.
Southland Publishing Co., Gainesville, Ga., acquisition of, 416
Spanish-American War, 9
Spear, Eldridge A., 150
Speidel Division, creation of, 383
Speidel Newspapers Inc., merger with, 383; stock, Thomson ownership of, 377
Spezzano, Vince, on AHN, research for, 304, 315; on *Democrat and Chronicle,* comics changes in, 330; Gannett South, assistant vice president of, 386; Project NN, coordinator of, 410; TGN, public service director of, 330; *Times-Union,* political writer of, 304-305; *Today,* publisher of, 386, 410; *USA TODAY,* executive vice president of, 418
Springfield (Mo.) Newspapers Inc., acquisition of, 384
Stahlman, James G., 358-359
*Standard Star, The,* New Rochelle, N.Y., 305
*Standard-Times,* Cape Cod, 262
*Standard-Times,* New Bedford, Mass., 262
Stanford University. *See* California Newspaper Publishers Association
*Star Advocate,* Titusville, Fla., conversion of, 378
*Star and Tribune,* Minneapolis, 285
*Star-Gazette, The,* Elmira, 38, 42; all-day paper, debut as, 297-299; circulation gains by, 123; debut of, 24, Laser-Graph, use of, 372-373; McCann, editor of, 187; 28; 61; new press for, 26, 28, 30; scrap metal drive by, 141-142; policy of, 25; on Prohibition, 32; on reform, 28-30
State Department, U.S., 170
*State Journal,* Lansing, Mich., 357
*Statesman-Journal,* Salem, Ore., creation of, 411-412
Statesman-Journal Co., 377
Stein, Fred, on editors' activism, 237; on freebies, 218
Steinem, Gloria, 348
*Steve Canyon. See* Comic strips, violent content of
Stevenson, Adlai, Democratic Party, presidential nominee of, 220
Stinson Reliant, 74, 88
Stock market crash, 56, 68
Stone, Desmond, *Democrat and Chronicle,* editorial page editor of, 364

Stone, Walker, 327
Stretch, William, on *Courier-Post,* 263-264
Stromberg-Carlson. *See* Hickson, Lawrence
Sturgis (Mich.) *Journal,* acquisition of, 411; sale of 469
Stutz, Harry, on comic strips, 211. *See also Ithaca Journal, The,* flu crisis at
Sullivan, Matthew G., 96, 174; on circulation gains, 123; *Hartford Courant,* loan to, 326; on newsprint supply, 136, 151; war work of, 142
*Sun, The,* San Bernardino, Calif., acquisition of, 331
*Sun-Bulletin,* Binghamton, N.Y., acquisition of, 356
*Sunday Advertiser,* Honolulu, redesignation of, 490
*Sunday News Journal,* Wilmington, Del., acquisition of, 392
*Sunday Star,* Peekskill, N.Y., acquisition of, 440
*Sunday Star-Bulletin and Advertiser,* Honolulu, acquisition of. 358. *See also Sunday Advertiser*
*Sun-Telegram, The,* San Bernardino, Calif., acquisition of, 331
Supreme Court, U.S., 95; expansion of, 91-92
Swan, Joyce A. *See Star and Tribune,* Minneapolis
Sylvester, Arthur, 295
*Syracuse Herald, The,* 8-9
Syracuse University, FET, award to, 305; PM, Distinguished Service Medal to, 309; VSJ, Distinguished Service Medal to, 338; VSJ, speaker at, 253

Taft Broadcasting, 433
Taft, Sen. Robert A., 102, 111
Taft, William Howard, 10, 31, 61
Taft-Hartley Act, 179, 492
Taylor, Mason, on Utica, corruption in, 259-262
Tech Van, 379
*Telegram,* Elmira, acquisition of, 45; on local autonomy, 124
*Telegram, The,* San Bernardino, Calif., acquisition of, 331
Tencon, Centerville, Tenn., sale of, 462
*Tennessean, The,* Nashville, 359, 448; acquisition of, 403; circulation, ranking by, 452-453; GCI, capital spending by, 458; TGN, transition to, 453-454
*Terry and the Pirates. See* Comic strips, violent content of
*The Fuse Sputters. See* Gannett, Frank E., as

author
Thomas, Jimmy, GCI, financial services, vice president of, 417; GCI, treasurer of, 417
Thompson, Dr. Brian I. *See* Laser-Graph
Thomson Newspapers Inc., Newburgh *Evening News*, purchase of, 378, 383; Speidel stock, sale of, 377-378
Thomson, Roy, 378
*Tide*, on TGN editorials, 151
*Time*, on Lindstrom obituary, 287; on PM, 359-360, 362; on radio news, 138
*Times Herald*, Port Huron, Mich., acquisition of, 349, 356
Times Herald Co., The, Port Huron, 349
*Times Journal, The*, Vineland, N.J., acquisition of, 440
Times Journal Co., acquisition of, 483; sale of, 484
Times Mirror Co., The, 332, 368
*Times*, Rochester, purchase of, 34
*Times*, Shreveport, La., acquisition of, 384
*Times-Union*, Albany, 262; GCI attempt to buy, 194, 231; on switch to a.m., 93. *See also Knickerbocker News*
*Times-Union*, Rochester, 128, 199; Alinsky, coverage of, 309-310; AP, member of, 58-59, 93; Barn, co-sponsor of, 181; Blanchard, 96; building expansion for, 200, 243; content of, 37; creation of, 36-37, 40, 42; debt of, 41; editorials of, 38, 42, 58, 60-61; on Eisenhower illness, 238; FEG, voice of, 197; on FDR, 108, 159-160; first issue of, 37; Germond hiring of, 260; guest editorials in, 214; Hickey, ad director of, 346; news/ad ratios in, 154; newsprint shortages at, 137, 239; offers for, 49; outreach by, 211, 214; PM, columnist for, 240-241; PM, editor of, 194; PM, editorial aims for, 207-208; PM, publisher of, 202; policy of, 37-38, 58; radio, news link to, 193; on "Read-Think-Vote," 219; on Rochester, riots in, 307; strike, effects of, 177; Vietnam, editorials on, 363-365; Vietnam, employees petition about, 363-365; WWII memorial, role in, 163
Tinker, Grant. *See* GTG Entertainment, history of
Tobin, Richard L., Lindstrom book, review of, 269-270
*Today*, Cocoa, Fla., creation of, 313-316, 318, 350; success of, 378
*Toledo Blade*, news/ad ratios in, 154

Torbett, Joseph, 109, 115; on censorship, 124
Towles, Donald B., *Courier-Journal*, vice president of, 460
Townson, Douglas C., GCI, director of, 46; GCI, secretary-treasurer of, 46
Travelers Insurance Co. *See Hartford Times*, sale of
Treasury Department, U.S. *See* Victory Drive, success of
*Tribune*, Cocoa, Fla., closing of, 350
*Tribune, The*, New York City, 125
Tripp, Frank E., *Advertiser*, reporter on, 51; anniversary of, 40th, 130; anniversary of, 50th, 216; anniversary of, 60th, 292; on circulation, 86; as columnist, 182-183, 241; critics, response to, 241; death of, 306; estate, value of, 306; *E&P*, letter to, 280-281, 287; as Elmiran, 52; on FDR, 89; FEG, eulogy to, 244; firing of, 51; FEG, first meeting with, 50; FEG, kinship with, 51-52, 96; *Gazette*, reporter on, 19, 50; *Gazette*, reporter on, 19, 50; GCI, chairman of, 217; GCI, 40th anniversary of, 171-172; GCI vice president, resignation as, 290; on Lindstrom, 275; on local service, 71; McCann's view of, 187; on New Deal, 72; on newsprint supply, 135-136, 151, 163; on Pearl Harbor, 130; on PM as FEG successor, 242; on PM, "operating head in fact," 233; on "Pot of Gold," 220-221; on press, critics of, 119, 128, 130; on Prohibition, 51, 58; salary of, 69; as school dropout, 51; on scrap metal drive, 140-142; *Star*, reporter on, 23, 50; *Star-Gazette*, reporter on, 25; *Star-Gazette*, business manager of, 38; stroke of, 290; Syracuse University, honor from, 305-306; TGN, general manager of, 49, 58, 63, 89; Victory Drive, head of, 147, 171; on VSJ, promotion of, 203; on war replacements, 117, 136; as youth, 51
Truman, Harry, 220. *See also* MacArthur, Gen. Douglas, congressional hearings
*Tucson* (Ariz.) *Citizen*, acquisition of, 383
Tweed, Boss, 41
Typhoid fever. *See Ithaca Daily News*

*Undermining Our Republic. See* Tripp, Frank E., on press, criticism of

Unemployment, U.S., 68
*Union and Advertiser,* Rochester, purchase of, 34
Union League Club, 95
Union of Soviet Journalists, 291
United Press, 62, 170, 332; price increases by, 210
University of Missouri-Encyclopaedia Britannica competition. *See* News Pictures of the Year
University of Missouri-J.C. Penney Awards, AHN, speech by, 337, 347
University of New Brunswick, FEG, honorary LL.D. to, 210
*Unterseebooten. See* Nazis, inflammatory words about
*USA TODAY,* advertising sales, difficulty of, 467; capital expenditures for, 466-467; circulation, ABC's first audit of, 421; circulation, difficulty of, 467; circulation, ranking by, 421, 490; creation of, 416-419; financial losses of, 491; international edition of, 436,440-441; launches of, 420-421; 'McPaper,' nickname of, 422-423; profits, first month of, 466; prototypes for, 416; regions, designation of, 432; U.S., largest in, 490
*USA TODAY Baseball Weekly,* 493
*USA TODAY Books,* 494
*USA TODAY Sky Radio,* 494
'USA TODAY: The Television Show,' 464-465. *See also* GTG Entertainment, history of
*USA TODAY Update,* 494
*USA WEEKEND,* creation of, 439; growth of, 491
*U.S. News and World Report. See* Miller, Paul, on readership
*Utica Press,* 114, 203; expansion of, 256

*Valley News Dispatch,* New Kensington, Pa., acquisition of, 382, 484
Valtman, Edmund, *Hartford Times,* cartoonist for, 286; Lindstrom, letter from, 287
Van Dyke, Dick. *See* GTG Entertainment, history of
Van Voorst, Alvin S., on pension plan, 201
*Vancouver Sun, The,* 276
Vega, Frank, *Eastbay Today,* circulation director of, 410; GANSAT, distribution systems, vice president of, 415; Project NN, member of, 410
Victory Drive, success of, 171; FET, chairman of, 147;
Villa, Pancho. *See* Pershing, Gen. John J.
*Vineyard Gazette,* 283
Virginia, University of, 108
Vladeck, David. *See* Joint Operating Agreement, Detroit
Voice of America, 170, 213

WALA-TV, Mobile, Ala., sale of, 440
Walker, Cecil, Gannett Broadcasting, president of, 443; Gannett Television, president of, 443; WXIA-TV, president/general manager of, 443
Wall, Cpl. Jimmy, on profit-sharing, 163
*Wall Street Journal, The,* 464, 479; circulation, ranking by, 421, 490. *See also* Miller, Paul, on readership
War Bonds. *See* Victory Drive
War Memorial. *See* World War II, Rochester memorial
War Production Board, 140, 142; newsprint cut by, 151
Warnock, William G., WWII, TGN's first death in, 144
Warren, George F. *See* Roosevelt, Franklin D., gold prices
Washington bureau, GNS, Martin, chief of, 220; newsprint shortage at, 239; use of, 232
Washington Post Co., 393
*Washington Star,* 368; news/ad ratios in, 155
*Washington Times-Herald,* news/ad ratios in, 155
*Watkins Glen* (N.Y.) *Express,* FEG, proposed for governor, 96
Watson, Gary, on labor relations, 492; Newspaper Division, president of, 492; Newspaper Guild, secretary of, 492; TGN Community Group, president of, 476
*Wausau* (Wis.) *Daily Herald,* acquisition of, 410
WBRJ-AM, Marietta, Ohio, acquisition of, 377
WCTN-TV, Minneapolis-St. Paul, acquisition of, 423
WCZY-AM/FM, sale of, 462
WDAE-AM, Tampa, Fla., acquisition of, 433
WDAN-AM, Danville, Ill., sale of, 213, 324
WDAN-FM, Danville, Ill., creation of, 324; sale of, 324
WDAN-TV, start of, 214
WDVM-TV. *See* WUSA-TV
Webb, James, GCI, director of, 389; GCI, management succession committee, chairman of, 389; NASA, former head of, 389; on PM succession, 389
WEHCO Media. *See* Hussman, Walter L. Jr.
Weil, Louis A. (Chip) Jr., 401; GCI, corporate development, vice president of,

355; Project S, chairman of, 419
Wells, Ida B. *See* Neuharth, Allen H., awards
WENY, Elmira, 213. *See also* Gannett Radio Group
Werner, Mrs. William E., FEG, mother-in-law of, 44
Westchester County Publishers Inc., 305
Westchester-Rockland Group Newspapers, acquisition of, 305
*Westchester Today,* 471
WFMY-TV, Greensboro, N.C., acquisition of, 469
WHDL, Olean, N.Y., 213; sale of, 243. *See also* Gannett Radio Group
WHEC, Rochester, 213; FEG, investment in, 69; FEG reply to FDR, 108; newspaper link to, 193, remodeling of, 256; Wiig, general manager of, 193. *See also* Gannett Radio Group
WHEC-TV, start of, 214, 256; sale of, 399
White, Dr. (Paul Dudley), on Eisenhower illness, 238
White, Ronald A., on *Courier-News,* JJC's work on press, 375; GCI, production, vice president of, 358; on Laser-Graph, development of, 372-374; resignation of, 376; on technology, GCI commitment to, 374-376
Whittington, Robert B., Speidel Division, president of, 383; Speidel Newspapers, vice president of, 383
WHQ, Rochester. *See* Hickson, Lawrence
*Why Johnny Can't Read. See* Flesch, Rudolph
Widgeon. *See* Gannett Company (Inc.), yacht purchase
Wiig, Gunnar, WHEC, general manager of, 193
Williams, Cyril, 249; GCI board, secretary of, 217; Florida project, role in, 314; GCI, controller of, 217; GCI, director of, 223; GCI, vice president of, 290; retirement of, 329, 335
Williams, Dr. John R., on FEG stroke, 191-192; on FEG convalescence, 194-195
Williamson, Samuel T., FEG biographer, 3; on FEG, naivete of, 167; on FEG sister, 158; on Gannett, Deborah Sampson, 155
Willkie, Wendell, 111, 117-118
Willys, John N., FEG/ERD, financial backer for, 34
Willys-Overland. *See* Willys, John N.
Wilson, Lori, AHN, wife of, 407; equal opportunity, consultant on, 407; Florida, state senator of, 407. *See also* Partners in Progress
Wilson, Woodrow, 30-31, 38, 238; letter to FEG, 32

*Window on the World: Faces, Places & Plain Talk from 32 Countries,* 470
*Winds of Change, Times-Union,* series of, 309
*Winging 'Round the World. See* Gannett, Frank E., as author
WINR, Binghamton, equipment for, 256
WINR-TV, development of, 256
WIQI-FM, Tampa, Fla., 433
*Wire Watch,* introduction of, 356-357
Witch-hunting, political, 108
*Wizard of Id. See* Democrat and Chronicle, comics page, changes on
WJOI-FM, Detroit, sale of, 440
WKFI-AM, Wilmington, Ohio, acquisition of, 377
Women in Communications, Inc., AHN, award to, 387
Women in newsroom, 157-159
Women's Christian Temperance Union, 95
Women's hiring/promotion, progress report on, 430-431
Woodford, James F., FEG, partner of, 23, 25
Woods, William J., 150
*World,* Monroe, La., acquisition of, 384. *See also News-Star-World,* creation of
World War I, 32, 40, 238; Rochester in wartime, 35-38
World War II, 121, 210; D-Day in Europe, 156; German surrender in, 162; Japanese surrender in, 164; Rochester memorial to, 163; TGN, first death in, 144
Wright, Orville. *See* Kitty Hawk
Wright, Wilbur. *See* Kitty Hawk
WTHT, Hartford, Conn., 213. *See also* Gannett Radio Group
WTLV-TV, Jacksonville, Fla., acquisition of, 469
WUSA-TV, Washington, D.C., acquisition of, 440
WWII. *See* World War II
WWJ-AM, Detroit, sale of, 440
WXIA-TV, Atlanta, 424

Zurich, Switzerland, *USA TODAY,* satellite plant for, 441

GANNETT CO., INC.
**Headquarters**
1100 Wilson Blvd.
Arlington, Va. 22234
703/284-6000

DAILY NEWSPAPERS
**Arizona**
Tucson/Tucson Citizen
**California**
Marin County/Marin Independent Journal
Palm Springs/The Desert Sun
Salinas/The Californian
San Bernardino/The San Bernardino County Sun
Stockton/The Stockton Record
Tulare/Tulare Advance-Register
Visalia/Visalia Times-Delta
**Colorado**
Fort Collins/Fort Collins Coloradoan
**Connecticut**
Norwich/Norwich Bulletin
**Delaware**
Wilmington/The News Journal
**Florida**
Brevard County/FLORIDA TODAY
Fort Myers/News-Press
Pensacola/Pensacola News Journal
**Georgia**
Gainesville/The Times
**Guam**
Agana/Pacific Daily News
**Hawaii**
Honolulu/Honolulu Advertiser
**Idaho**
Boise/The Idaho Statesman
**Illinois**
Danville/Commercial-News
Rockford/Rockford Register Star
**Indiana**
Lafayette/Journal and Courier
Marion/Chronicle-Tribune
Richmond/Palladium-Item
**Iowa**
Des Moines/The Des Moines Register
Iowa City/Iowa City Press-Citizen
**Kentucky**
Louisville/The Courier-Journal
**Louisiana**
Monroe/The News-Star
Shreveport/The Times
**Michigan**
Battle Creek/Battle Creek Enquirer
Detroit/The Detroit News
Lansing/Lansing State Journal
Port Huron/Times Herald

**Minnesota**
St. Cloud/St. Cloud Times
**Mississippi**
Hattiesburg/Hattiesburg American
Jackson/The Clarion-Ledger
**Missouri**
Springfield/The News-Leader
**Montana**
Great Falls/Great Falls Tribune
**Nevada**
Reno/Reno Gazette-Journal
**New Jersey**
Bridgewater/The Courier-News
Camden/Courier-Post
Vineland/The Daily Journal
**New York**
Binghamton/Press & Sun-Bulletin
Elmira/Star-Gazette
Ithaca/The Ithaca Journal
Niagara Falls/Niagara Gazette
Poughkeepsie/Poughkeepsie Journal
Rochester/Democrat and Chronicle Times-Union
Saratoga Springs/The Saratogian
Utica/Observer-Dispatch
Gannett Suburban Newspapers
  Mamaroneck/The Daily Times
  Mount Vernon/The Daily Argus
  New Rochelle/The Standard-Star
  Ossining/The Citizen Register
  Peekskill/The Star
  Port Chester/The Daily Item
  Tarrytown/The Daily News
  West Nyack-Rockland/ Rockland Journal-News
  White Plains/The Reporter Dispatch
  Yonkers/The Herald Statesman
**Ohio**
Chillicothe/Chillicothe Gazette
Cincinnati/The Cincinnati Enquirer
Fremont/The News-Messenger
Marietta/The Marietta Times
Port Clinton/News Herald
**Oklahoma**
Muskogee/Muskogee Daily Phoenix and Times-Democrat
**Oregon**
Salem/Statesman Journal
**Pennsylvania**
Chambersburg/Public Opinion
Lansdale/The Reporter
North Hills/North Hills News Record
Tarentum/Valley News Dispatch
**South Dakota**
Sioux Falls/Argus Leader
**Tennessee**
Jackson/The Jackson Sun

Nashville/The Tennessean
**Texas**
El Paso/El Paso Times
**Vermont**
Burlington/The Burlington Free Press
**Virgin Islands**
St. Thomas/Virgin Islands Daily News
**Washington**
Bellingham/The Bellingham Herald
Olympia/The Olympian
**West Virginia**
Huntington/The Herald-Dispatch
**Wisconsin**
Green Bay/Green Bay Press-Gazette
Wausau/Wausau Daily Herald

NON-DAILY PUBLICATIONS
Arizona, Arkansas, California, Colorado, Florida, Georgia, Illinois, Indiana, Iowa, Louisiana, Michigan, Mississippi, Missouri, New Jersey, New York, Ohio, Oklahoma, Oregon, Pennsylvania, Texas, Virginia, Washington and Wisconsin

USA TODAY
**Headquarters**
Arlington, Va.
**Advertising offices**
Boston, Chicago, Dallas, Detroit, Hong Kong, London, Los Angeles, New York

USA TODAY BASEBALL WEEKLY
**Editorial, advertising offices**
Arlington, Va.

USA TODAY SKY RADIO
**Broadcast studios and business/operations offices**
Arlington, Va.
**Advertising offices**
Arlington, Va., Chicago, Los Angeles, New York City

USA WEEKEND
**Advertising offices**
New York City
**Editorial and production offices**
Arlington, Va.

GANNETT BROADCASTING
Television stations
**Arizona**
Phoenix/KPNX-TV
**Colorado**
Denver/KUSA-TV
**District of Columbia**
Washington/WUSA-TV
**Florida**
Jacksonville/WTLV-TV
**Georgia**
Atlanta/WXIA-TV
**Massachusetts**
Boston/WLVI-TV
**Minnesota**
Minneapolis-St. Paul/KARE-TV
**North Carolina**
Greensboro/WFMY-TV
**Oklahoma**
Oklahoma City/KOCO-TV
**Texas**
Austin/KVUE-TV

Radio stations
**California**
Los Angeles/KIIS/KIIS-FM
San Diego/KSDO/KCLX-FM
**Florida**
Tampa-St.Petersburg/WDAE/WUSA-FM
**Illinois**
Chicago/WGCI/WGCI-FM
**Missouri**
Kansas City/KCMO/KCMO-FM
St. Louis/KUSA/KSD-FM
**Texas**
Dallas/KHKS-FM
Houston/KKBQ/KKBQ-FM

GANNETT INTERNATIONAL
**Headquarters**
New York City
**Overseas offices**
London, Zurich, Hong Kong, Singapore
**Product**
USA TODAY International Edition

GANNETT NATIONAL
NEWSPAPER SALES
**Headquarters:** New York City

GANNETT NEW BUSINESS AND
PRODUCT DEVELOPMENT
**Headquarters:** Arlington, Va.

GANNETT/USA TODAY
INFORMATION CENTER
**Headquarters:** Arlington, Va.

GANNETT/USA TODAY
SPORTS AND INFORMATION CENTER
**Headquarters:** Greensboro, N.C.

**GANNETT NEWS SERVICE**
**Headquarters:** Arlington, Va.

**GANNETT OFFSET**
**Headquarters**
Springfield, Va.
**Offset print sites**
Atlanta Offset (Atlanta, Ga.)
Boston Offset (Norwood, Mass.)
Florida Offset (Miramar, Fla.)
Nashville Offset (Nashville, Tenn.)
Phoenix Offset (Chandler, Ariz.)
St. Louis Offset (Olivette, Mo.)
Springfield Offset (Springfield, Va.)

**GANNETT OUTDOOR GROUP**
**Headquarters**
New York City
**Outdoor operations**
**California**
Berkeley, Los Angeles, Sacramento, San Diego, San Francisco
**Colorado**
Denver
**Connecticut**
New Haven
**Illinois**
Chicago
**Michigan**
Detroit, Flint, Grand Rapids
**Missouri**
Kansas City, St. Louis
**New Jersey**
Fairfield, Lakewood
**New York**
New York City
**Texas**
Houston
**Transit operations**
Detroit, Los Angeles, New York City (headquarters), Philadelphia, Rochester, San Diego, San Francisco
**Mediacom**
Headquarters: Toronto, Ontario

GANNETT DIRECT MARKETING SERVICES, INC.
Louisville, Ky.

GANNETT TELEMARKETING, INC.
**Headquarters:** Arlington, Va.

GANNETTWORK
**Headquarters**
New York City
**Other sales offices**
Chicago, Los Angeles, San Francisco

TELEMATCH
Springfield, Va.

LOUIS HARRIS & ASSOCIATES
New York City, London, Paris

7/93

# About the Author

J. Donald Brandt was an active newspaperman for 37 years, 27 of them with the News Journal papers in Wilmington, Del., where he was editor from May 1983 to August 1988. He helped design the prototype editorial and opposite editorial pages for *USA TODAY* and was deputy editorial director for its first six months. He retired from Gannett as a general executive in 1991, remaining a consultant to the company.